THE ESSENTIALS OF MONEY AND BANKING

The ESSENTIALS of MONEY and BANKING

LEONARDO AUERNHEIMER
Texas A&M University and Centro de Estudios
Macroeconómicos de Argentina (CEMA)

ROBERT B. EKELUND, JR.
Auburn University

175 YEARS OF PUBLISHING

1807 1982

JOHN WILEY & SONS New York Chichester Brisbane Toronto Singapore

Library of Congress Cataloging in Publication Data:

Auernheimer, Leonardo, 1936–
   The essentials of money and banking.

   Includes bibliographical references and index.
    1. Money. 2. Banks and banking. I. Ekelund,
Robert B. (Robert Burton), 1940–   II. Title.

HG221.A9143   332.1   81-11466
ISBN 0-471-02103-2   AACR2

Printed in the United States of America

10 9 8 7 6 5 4 3 2 1

for Christa and Martina,
and in Memory of Eva, Dora, and John

PREFACE

Bismarck is said to have once remarked that if he knew he were going to die he would remove himself to Mecklenburg—because everything happened fifty years later in Mecklenburg. The introduction of "received" economic analysis in introductory textbooks often has something in common with events in Mecklenburg. In the case of money and banking textbooks, the lag has been especially acute and, to some extent, this book is designed to fill this gap.

Product differentiation is the backbone of toothpaste, diet drinks, and economy car markets. It is also a characteristic of new books dealing with money, banking, and economic policy. *The Essentials of Money and Banking* is no exception and, like numerous other entries, it is designed as a textbook for use in undergraduate courses in money and banking, monetary theory, and monetary policy. All of the traditional topics of money and banking courses are covered here, but a number of novel and (we hope) useful and innovative features are included as well.

The principal novelty and main feature of this text is the integration of modern concepts of monetary, macroeconomic, and inflation theory with the institutions of money and banking so as to produce an orderly and sound view of contemporary economic policy. This integrative approach is accomplished in five parts. Part I (Chapters 2 and 3) is a general introduction to the study of money and its basic functions. Economic policy and policy-making institutions have no meaning without the organizing force of economic theory. Thus the core of a very contemporary approach to macroeconomic and monetary theory is presented as Part II (Chapters 5 through 8). The cumbersome *IS-LM* construction of total expenditures and macroeconomic equilibrium is not used here. Rather, a more modern and useful variant of the "liquidity preference" approach to total expenditures is developed, with an alternative "loanable funds" structure presented in an Appendix to Chapter 5. Inflation is treated as an integral part of monetary economics in a theoretical presentation rather than an issue that is "tacked on" to the structure as it is in so many other texts. Inflation is identified not with simple increases in the price level in our conception, but with a persistent and continuous process of *rising* prices. (Our approach eliminates the necessity of requiring "outside" readings in order to deal with the matter of inflation.) In spite of these differences, the total theoretical package that we present is no more formidable than the typical fare served up to the average undergraduate reader. In our approach, moreover, students are rewarded with mastery of a useful synthesis of Keynesian and post-Keynesian developments in macro and monetary theory *in which inflation plays a major role*.

Parts III and IV are devoted to the mechanisms, institutions, and instruments of the banking and financial systems. In Chapters 9, 10, and 11, the commercial and central banking systems and their functions in macropolicy-making are examined. A simple money supply model developed in Chapter 9 is used (a) to analyze the instruments of the Federal Reserve System's (the U.S. central bank) control over the money stock in Chapter 11, and (b) to interpret aspects of monetary history and the history of monetary policy in Chapter 16. Other financial institutions and their functions in the U.S. monetary system are the subject of Chapters 12 and 13. The (ultimate) blurring of the functions of banks and other financial institutions fixed in law by the "Depository Institutions and Deregulation Act of March, 1980" is a prominent feature of discussion in Parts III and IV.

Finally, the three chapters (14, 15, and 16) comprising Part V may be read separately but are all applications of the theoretical and institutional structure developed earlier. Chapter 14 is a discussion of recent monetary and macroeconomic policy—a direct application of the theoretical and institutional parts of the book. Chapter 15 is a straight-forward projection of our theoretical model of the "closed economy" to international trade and finance (that is, to the "open economy"), along with a discussion of the institutions related to international markets. Chapter 16, a brief historical account of twentieth century monetary policy up to 1960, concludes the book, but, like the other chapters of Part V, it integrates the theoretical system presented with some of the facts of U.S. economic history.

The material of this book may be presented in sequence, or, if preferences dictate, Parts III and IV may be reversed with Part II; that is, banking and financial institutions may be taken up before theory. In either sequence, Part IV on financial intermediaries and markets may be deleted without disturbing the continuity of the text.

Several other points deserve attention. We take no position on the presently antiquated Keynesian versus Monetarist controversy. Both views are presented and, indeed, integrated. If the Monetarists appear to receive higher marks in our conception of theory and policy, the reason in part lies in the fact that they have had a great deal more to say about inflation—a persistent problem facing advanced nations in modern times.

We have designed this book with students foremost in mind. Wherever possible, concepts in policy and theory are presented in equivalent verbal, graphical, and algebraic forms. This kind of repetition may be called upon to produce a sounder understanding of the more difficult points. Calculus is *not required* for mastery of *any* of the materials in this book, although those students trained in mathematics will recognize the correspondence between formal mathematical expressions and the algebraic forms we use to express monetary and macroeconomic theory. (Economics, we should always remember, is a *social science*, not a branch of applied mathematics.) Footnote references to further reading on some topics covered in the text are provided as an aid to students. Lists of "Key Concepts" and sets of "Questions for Discussion" follow each Chapter. No material is presented which requires previous exposure to economics beyond an ordinary Principles of Economics course taught at virtually all colleges and universities. A review of some basic concepts that are useful in money and banking comprises the second half of the introductory chapter, Chapter 1, as does a list of symbols used in this text.

There are a large number of generous people to thank for having helped with this book. Professors Ray Battalio and Jerry Dwyer (Texas A&M), Ed Price (Oklahoma State), Richard W. Ault (Louisiana State), Richard Rivard (University of South Florida), Bob Hebert and Steve Morrell (Auburn), David Spencer (Washington State), Stephen M. Miller (The University of Connecticut), James T. Lucas, Jr. (Virginia Polytechnic Institute and State University), Herbert M. Kaufman (Arizona State University), James Barth (The George Washington University), John D. Ferguson (Miami University), Walter Johnson (University of Missouri), Dennis R. Murphy (Emory University), Mark L. Ladenson (Michigan State University), David A. Schauer (University of Texas at El Paso), and Claus Wihlborg (New York University) all made valuable suggestions on many earlier drafts. Two very special debts of appreciation in this regard are owed David Saurman (Auburn) and Jack Tatom (St. Louis Federal Reserve). None of these friendly critics should be held responsible for anything contained in the final product. Research assistance was ably provided by Paul Cleveland, Roy Cordato, Katherine Graves, and Charles Thompson. Typists Paula Altieri, Kathy Berry, Sherri Boney, Pat Watson, and Bess Yellen performed, often under the duress of deadlines, with great efficiency. Richard Esposito and the staff of John Wiley (and, earlier, P. J. Wilkinson) were most helpful and supportive. We earnestly hope that the result is useful to students in learning the workings of one of the most important and least understood economic institutions affecting society's well being.

March 1981   *Leonardo Auernheimer*
                                                                       Robert B. Ekelund, Jr.

CONTENTS

Part III. COMMERCIAL AND CENTRAL BANKING: Theory and Institutions   185

Part IV. FINANCIAL INTERMEDIARIES AND MARKETS IN THE ECONOMIC SYSTEM   271

CHAPTER 1

INTRODUCTION
The Essentials of
Money and Banking

The subject of this book is money and, in particular, the reasons why money is important in our economy. Because banks and other financial institutions perform an important role in money creation and in the transmission of economic policy, they are also a major ingredient in the study of money. Money and its role in the economy are a fascinating study and the number of riddles and seeming contradictions to be resolved is a large part of the fascination. If the application of economic analysis to everyday life is an exercise in unraveling fallacies, then economics is at its best in the field of money. But better things are more costly, and in the study of money a higher price is to be paid in the form of material more difficult than in the study of, for example, supply and demand analysis in a single, isolated market such as dog food or diamonds.

The study of anything entails costs and benefits. In the study of money some of the costs arise simply because it is a complex phenomenon. Economists have been concerned with the role of money for hundreds of years and economics certainly has many simple (and correct) insights into its role. Nevertheless, no rigorous, well-structured, single theory concerning what money is and why people hold it is accepted by all economists (not, certainly, to the extent that economists agree about reasons why people are willing to consume eggs or to own machines). Another reason why a study of the role of money in the economy is more difficult than other aspects of economics is that it is a study of a *macroeconomic nature* for which a large number of variables are to be taken into consideration. Thus, the need for simplification and, sometimes, for "unrealistic" assumptions becomes more important. From the viewpoint of the learning process, the main difficulty is that the parts can be understood only as they relate to the whole, but the whole cannot be described without reference to the parts.

So much for the bad news. The good news is that the understanding of some very elementary points in monetary economics may help provide answers to some of the puzzles that cross the mind of anyone who reads the daily newspapers. So many important issues seem impossibly complex, the most basic being the explanation of the workings of the aggregate economy itself. Specific and well-publicized issues are as perplexing. Why, for instance, has the inflation rate during the 1970s and early 1980s approached those commonly found only in less developed countries of the world? Do rising oil prices, foisted upon Western countries by OPEC, cause inflation? If so, why do countries such as Switzerland (a nation that imports *all* of its oil) experience much lower rates of inflation than the United States? If Gross National Product has doubled in less than ten years, why do economists and Presidents continue to issue grave forebodings concerning the future of the US economy? Is there a trade-off between unemployment and inflation as so many news reports indicate? More fundamentally, does a study of the economics of money and banking have anything to offer in understanding and dealing with these vexing questions?

We believe that the answer to the last question is definitely affirmative. Those who conquer the simple principles of money and banking are in a far better position to judge the actions of policymakers and politicians than, say, even very well-educated laymen. The provision of reasoned and sound answers to all of the above questions (and to many more) is the primary purpose of this book. In order to understand policy questions, however, the organizing essentials about the economy must be thoroughly understood. Without these, policy and issues remain imponderable.

Before a summary of the content of the book, some remarks about method are in order. The first concerns the role of theory and models. In the study of economics, as in any scientific discipline, the aim is to discover the truth behind all sorts of complications which are not fundamental to the essence of the problem at hand. An economic model used to discuss a problem is nothing other than a stylized, simplified version of the real world from which nonessential factors or elements have been eliminated. The art of the economist, then, is the ability to detect and separate factors that are not essential from those that are and to make appropriate assumptions conveniently eliminating the former. The reader will find, throughout this book, that many of these simplifying assumptions are used again and again. We all know, for example, that money is not introduced into the economy in the form of gifts (left to individuals at their doorsteps, or dropped from airplanes or helicopters). But, because the essential effects of changes in the quantity of money are the same no matter how money is introduced, such an assumption conveniently disposes of an unnecessary complication. Thus, the reader should not be disturbed by the lack of realism of some of the assumptions. Such lack of realism is a necessary ingredient in theory, and it is the precise element that separates theory from mere description. The real test of theory comes when it must predict and explain, and there is no such a thing as being "correct in theory, but not in practice." Theory is a guide in putting some order into a world of conceptual traps and fallacies, filled with complicating, non-essential details.

Most of economic theory (which might be clear from introductory economics) can be explained either by words, by graphs, or through simple (at our level) arithmetic. We have used all three methods. The very simple arithmetic expressions used in the text are repeated as often as necessary, explained verbally, and, whenever possible, backed up with graphical representation. Arithmetic expressions, as well as graphs, are not intended as an "extra assignment," but as another, alternative but equivalent manner in which to express what has been said in words—an aid to understanding rather than an additional burden.

PLAN OF THE BOOK

After these preliminaries, the different topics comprising the essentials of money and banking, the manner in which they relate to each other, and the reasons for their particular placement are introduced. The book is divided into five parts. Parts I and II discuss the fundamental concepts concerning money and its role and importance in the economy, that is, how and why the quantity of money influences prices, the level of production of goods and services, and other economic variables. These are the bulk of monetary economics, in which the quantity of money is simply taken to be whatever the monetary authority (the government, or more correctly, the Federal Reserve System, an arm of government) decides it to be. A good deal of monetary economics and many important and contemporary real world themes may be understood very well without even mentioning banks. But, because banks are in fact an important ingredient in the process of money creation, this topic is taken up in Part III. Part IV, on financial intermediaries in general and on financial markets in particular, is a necessary digression from the main theme. Finally, Part V includes three concretely applied topics in monetary economics: monetary policy, the case of an open economy, and a brief monetary history of the United States.

Part I establishes the fundamentals. Chapter 2 introduces the basic concepts of money, the problems involved in defining money, and the functions of money. There is a brief historical account of the evolution of monetary systems, as history is very illuminating regarding some of the features of current monetary systems and *current monetary problems*. In addition to a discussion of the difficulties of a conceptual definition of money, several possible working definitions of money are analyzed. After deliberations over definitions, the money stock will be identified as the sum of all currency (dollar bills and coins, produced by government) and all transactions account balances (produced by commercial banks and other financial institutions). Chapter 3 is a treatment of the fundamental concept of the demand for money. The public at all times owns, or "holds," a certain stock of money, and the theory of the demand for money is simply an investigation of the factors that will determine the stock of money the public desires to hold. This is accomplished in much the same way as the theory of demand for ravioli explains how the quantity of ravioli people wish to purchase depends on certain variables such as their income and the price of ravioli.

Part II, which presents basic macroeconomic and monetary theory, consists of an investigation of how the level of the money stock can affect the level of prices, real production of goods and services, and interest rates. Chapter 4 is an introduction to the manner in which the classical economists (those economists writing up to the end of the 1930s) treated the problem. The general features of the attack on the classical position by the British economist John Maynard Keynes and his followers are also briefly discussed, as is the counterattack of the modern synthesis by today's monetarists.

Chapters 5 and 6 present the modern analysis of expenditures, income, and prices. The first of the two is a discussion of how and why the level of the money stock as well as the level of government expenditures is a determinant of total expenditures (that is, the sum of government expenditures and private expenditures on all kinds of goods and services). The second, Chapter 6, considers how changes in the level of total expenditures can affect the level of prices, production of goods and services, and employment.

Chapters 7 and 8 carry the analysis one step further. Instead of simply asking about the influence of the level of the money stock on the level of prices and production, one must analyze the effects of repetitive changes in the level of the money stock (in the form of a continuous rise in this stock, at some constant rate of change, such as 5, 10, or 15 percent per year) on prices and the level of production and employment. Chapters 7 and 8 deal with the causes of inflation, that is, with the widely experienced phenomenon of *permanent, continuous rises* in the level of prices. Chapter 7 considers the long-run consequences of a policy of monetary expansion, and Chapter 8 analyzes the initial, transitional effects of such familiar policies. These two chapters are the corollary of the basic theory discussed in Chapters 4, 5, and 6 and will provide some simple explanations to some of the most important and familiar real-world economic events of today.

Part III recognizes the presence of commercial banks and their crucial role in the process of money creation. As mentioned earlier, one can understand much of monetary economics as well as some important contemporary issues in monetary policy by ignoring the banking system and by assuming that the money stock is made up entirely of currency printed by the *monetary authority or central bank.* (The monetary authority in the United States is the Federal Reserve System, an agency of the federal government charged with control of the money stock and with regulating banks and other financial institutions.) But this approach is possible only in reference to the influence of a given monetary stock (or rate of change in the stock) on prices and production. To assume away all the interesting and important problems raised by the existence of commercial banks is far too simplistic. Banks help to determine the money stock, and their influence in determining the stock is very much a part of monetary economics.

The first chapter in Part III (Chapter 9) discusses the manner in which commercial banks create money. Chapter 10 is a description of the institutional framework in which the US banking system operates under the surveillance of the Federal Reserve System. Chapter 11 discusses concrete channels or *instruments* through which the quantity of money is regulated in the US (and in most countries) and some of the problems encountered in managing the money stock.

Part IV (Chapters 12 and 13) is a digression in the sense that it touches on topics that are both interesting and important, but that are not essential for the global understanding of the manner in which money influences the economy. Chapter 12 concerns the nature and importance of various kinds of financial intermediaries, that is, firms and institutions that act as intermediaries between lenders (buyers of financial instruments) and borrowers (sellers of financial instruments). Chapter 13 considers the particular markets in which financial instruments are exchanged and analyzes in detail a few technical and peculiar aspects of both markets and instruments.

Finally, the three chapters comprising Part V may be read independently of each other, but all of them are concrete applications of much of the theory. In particular, Chapter 14, on monetary policy, is a rather lengthy treatment of some of the practical and complex problems of implementation of monetary policy in the real world, as well as an account of the US policy experience during the last twenty years. Chapter 15 considers the international economy; it accounts for the existence of sales and purchases (of both goods and services and financial instruments) to and from other countries. Chapter 16 is a brief study of some of the main events in US monetary history up to 1960; the account applies and interprets as many of the concepts and theories in this book as possible.

Thus, this book proceeds from the simple to the more complex, from the theory of money and monetary institutions to the realm of monetary policy. In this manner, a logical sequence of concepts is used to present the essentials of money and its importance in influencing economic quantities and events. (Mastery of the basic concepts contained in the remainder of the present chapter, along with the key concepts and discussion questions presented at the end of each chapter, will aid the reader in understanding the more difficult points.) There is an undeniable cost to the study of money and banking, but the payoff is a better understanding of one of the most talked about, but least understood, human contrivances in history.

CONCEPTS FREQUENTLY USED IN MONETARY ECONOMICS

The remainder of Chapter 1 is a mix of some very loosely related topics. Their only connection is that all of them (and there are others which could be added) are particularly relevant to the economics of money. Mastery of these concepts will contribute to the learning of money and banking. (In addition, a list of symbols used in this book is provided for handy reference.)

A QUESTION OF SEMANTICS (OR, A WARNING ON HOW WE CAN DEFINE WORDS AS WE PLEASE, PROVIDED WE STICK TO THE DEFINITIONS)

The reader is undoubtedly aware of how many discussions could have been made easier (or avoided altogether) if the words used by the discussants were well defined. Disciplines other than economics (in particular, the physical and biological sciences) have solved the problem, in most instances by inventing new words. Economics, perhaps because it is a relatively young discipline, still uses many words also used by the layman. Even though those words are precisely defined in technical discussions among economists, they create for the novice a great deal of confusion. Some expressions used in economics have a different meaning from the one assumed in everyday language. Moreover, depending on the context the same expression often has different meanings in everyday life. We say, for example, that Rockefeller "has a lot of money," and also that "Smith had to wash dishes at the restaurant because his date ordered expensive dishes and his funds were insufficient." In the first case, we are clearly saying that Rockefeller possesses a great wealth, not necessarily in the form of money. In the second, we mean exactly what we say: that Smith, though he may be quite wealthy, did not have enough money with him at the time. In this book, as in any textbook in economics, many words used in everyday language—words such as money, wealth, income, and investment— will be used in an economic context. In each case, the reader is strongly encouraged to approach such words cautiously, both in reading and in reasoning. Terms are defined specifically in this book and the reader should make every attempt to interpret and to use expressions consistently.

DIMENSIONS, STOCKS, AND FLOWS

Economics, as everyday life, is full of statements about the level of certain variables. For example, we say that there are ten students in a class, that we have eighteen dollars in our pocket, or that we pay a rent of ninety dollars per month. Each of these statements comprises a pure number (ten, eighteen, ninety) and a variable (students, dollars, dollars per month). Because in economics and in everyday conversations, only variables expressed in the same units (or dimensions) can be compared (and, in particular, added to or subtracted from), it is important to be explicit about the dimensions of the variables in question in order to avoid the mistake of adding "pears and apples."

In particular it is important (in economics in general, and especially in monetary economics) to distinguish carefully between two kinds of variables. These variables differ only because of the presence of a time element in one of them; that is, there is a fundamental difference between stocks and flows. A *stock* (such as number of sudents, number of dollars, or gallons of water) is defined with reference to a *given point in time*; a *flow* (such as students per year, dollars per month, or gallons of water per second) is defined only with reference to some period of time. Compare the water contained in a bathtub at some point in time, with the stream of water flowing from a faucet; the first is a stock, measured, for example, in terms of gallons; the second is a flow, measured in terms of gallons per unit of time (for example, as gallons per second). The rate at which a stock is changing at any point in time has the dimensions of a flow. If the water is flowing from the faucet at the rate of twenty gallons per minute, then the volume of water in the tub (the stock) is changing at the rate of twenty gallons per minute.

Those familiar with business and accounting practices will recognize the distinction between stocks and flows when comparing the balance sheet and the income statement of a firm; the first is a description of stocks measured as a point in time (say, December 31, 1981); the second is a description of flows measured over a time period (say, during 1981): for example, sales amounted to 2.3 million dollars per year during 1981.

LEVELS AND RATES OF CHANGE:
THE PROPORTIONAL RATE OF CHANGE

As we shall often be concerned with the behavior over time of some economic variables such as money, income, and prices, a few things must be clarified at the outset. The graph in Figure 1-1 will prove useful for that purpose: on the horizontal axis t (time) is measured and on the vertical axis, the level of some other magnitude, X (say, the stock of machines in a certain country) is depicted.

Our first concern is to distinguish sharply between the level of the variable in question at some point in time (that is, how low or high the value of the variable is) and the *rate of change* of the variable (that is, whether its value is rising, falling, or stationary). In the case of the situation described by Figure 1-1, for example, the level of the variable (the stock of machines) is lower at time t_3 (August 1, 1981) than at time t_0 (March 1, 1981), but at time t_3 it is rising, while at time t_0 it is stationary. Obviously, a certain magnitude can be high or low, and in each case it can be rising, falling, or stationary. Although

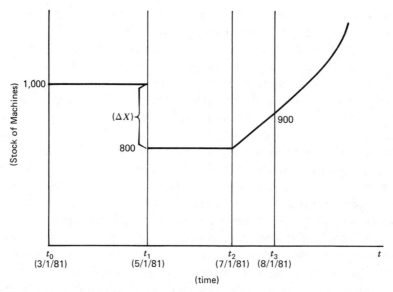

Figure 1-1. Levels and rates of change.

this is so obvious that a warning might seem unnecessary, the reader will find that keeping this distinction in mind is the secret to an easy understanding of the material in, for example, Chapters 7 and 8.

Another important difference is that between a "once-and-for-all" change and a change that occurs smoothly over time. In Figure 1-1, at time t_1 (say, May 1, 1981) there is a once-and-for-all change in the stock of capital, from 1,000 to 800 machines (assume that an earthquake destroyed 200 machines at once). At time t_2 (July 1, 1981), instead, the stock of capital starts to rise (and does so from then on), without any "jump" or once-and-for-all change.

When the change in the level of a certain variable (whether it is a once-and-for-all change, or a change over time) is discussed, the absolute and the proportional change must be distinguished. As a matter of convention, we shall denote the *absolute change* (or "rate of change," if it is happening over time) in the variable X as ΔX, where Δ (delta) means "the change in"; this change can be positive (when the value X increases) or negative (when the value X decreases). In Figure 1-1, at time t_1 (May 1) the stock of capital fell by 200 units over night, thus $\Delta X = -200$.

The *proportional change* of a variable, on the other hand, is the absolute change (ΔX) divided by some *base value* of the variable, usually taken to be the value before the change, or, when the change is occurring over time, at the beginning of the period. In Figure 1-1, the proportional change occurring at time t_1 is $(\Delta X/X) = (-200)/(1,000) = -0.20$. Often this proportional change is measured as a percentage, or $-0.20 = -20\%$, or a 20% decline. Notice, of course, that the change taking place at time t_1 is a once-and-for-all, discrete change.

When the variable in question is changing smoothly over time, we can also apply the idea of a proportional rate of change (over time). In Figure 1–1, the variable X is changing at a proportional rate of zero between t_0 and t_1, and between t_1 and t_2. After time t_2, the variable changes at a constant proportional rate (say, 10% per month).

A convenient notation often used in the literature in discussing the proportional rate at which a variable is changing is to identify $\hat{X}$ as a proportional rate of change over time. When working with proportional rates of change (whether changes are taking place at one point in time, in the form of once-and-for-all, discrete jumps, or taking place over time), we should remember the following equivalences, which are approximate for small changes and exact when the changes are infinitely small:

(a) The proportional rate of the *product* of two magnitudes is equal to the *sum* of the proportional rates of change of the two magnitudes. For example, if total expenditures per month (Z) in the purchase of bananas is the quantity purchased per month (X) times the price of bananas (P), or

$$Z = X \cdot P$$

then

$$\hat{Z} = \hat{X} + \hat{P}$$

That is, the proportional rate of change in expenditures is equal to the proportional rate of change in the quantity plus the proportional rate of change in the price.

(b) The proportional rate of change of the *ratio* of two variables is equal to the proportional rate of change of the numerator minus the proportional rate of change of the denominator. Using the previous example, we can say that, if the quantity of bananas purchased per month (X) is equal to the total amount spent on bananas during the month (Z) divided by the price of bananas (P), or

$$X = Z/P$$

then

$$\hat{X} = \hat{Z} - \hat{P}$$

That is, the proportional change in the quantity purchased is equal to the proportional change in expenditures minus the proportional change in the price.

THE CONCEPT OF ELASTICITY

The reader is already familiar, from a course in Principles of Economics, with the notion of both price and income elasticity as applied to demand and supply. The purpose of this section is to point out that the notion of elasticity is a general concept applying to any relationship in economics (and, for that matter, in other disciplines). The concept of elasticity will be particularly important to material in Chapter 3.

Given any economic relationship between two variables, where one of the variables (for example, the quantity demanded of some commodity) is said to depend on the other (for example, the price of the commodity), the concept of elasticity seeks to be a measurement of the "sensitivity" of the dependent variable with respect to changes in the independent variable. In order to render this measurement independent of the units in which each of the variables is measured, we use *proportional* (rather than *absolute*) changes.

Thus, if x is the independent variable (say, the price of a commodity) and y is the dependent variable (say, the quantity demanded of the commodity), the elasticity is depicted as the ratio $(\Delta y/y)/(\Delta x/x)$, that is, as the ratio of the two proportional changes. Two extreme cases should be noticed: if $\Delta y/y = 0$, then the independent variable does not react at all to changes in the independent variable, and the elasticity is zero. For any given proportional change in the independent variable $\Delta x/x$, a higher and higher proportional change in the dependent variable, $\Delta y/y$ means a larger and larger value of the elasticity measure, up to the limiting point where $\Delta y/y$ tends to infinity and so does elasticity. At some point along the way, the value of the elasticity (in absolute terms) is unity; that is, if the independent variable changes by, say, 10 percent, the dependent variable also changes by 10 percent.

When there is more than one independent variable (for example, in the case of the demand function for a commodity, where the quantity demanded depends upon both the price of the commodity and the demander's income), there are as many elasticities to be measured as independent variables. In the particular case of demand theory, with which the reader is probably familiar, if x^d is the quantity demanded, P is the price of the commodity, and I is the money income, then $(\Delta x^d/x^d)/(\Delta P/P)$ is the *price elasticity of demand*, and $(\Delta x^d/x^d)/(\Delta I/I)$ is the *income elasticity of demand*. The income or interest elasticity of the demand for money is a concept frequently encountered in money and banking.

THE PRICE OF THINGS AND THE PRICE OF MONEY:
THE DISTINCTION BETWEEN NOMINAL AND
REAL MAGNITUDES

From a formal viewpoint, prices are the ratios at which two things are exchanged in a market. In this sense, all prices are relative (denoting the price of one thing in terms of another), as they are the *terms of trade* between two things. If one can exchange two shirts for one hat, then the price of hats in terms of shirts is two (shirts per hat), and the price of shirts in terms of hats is one half (hats per shirt), its inverse.

In a monetary economy it is a matter of convenience to express all prices in terms of the monetary unit, such as a dollar. (Later on we shall refer to this function of money as a "unit of account"), but it would be only tedious computation to express all prices, say, in terms of beer bottles. If all prices are expressed in terms of one "thing," some commodity in a barter economy, or money in a monetary economy, we say that such a thing is being used as the *numéraire*. Because the price of the numeraire itself will be identical to one (the price of one shirt in terms of shirts is one; the price of a dollar in terms of dollars is one, and so on), it follows that in an economy with "*n*" things (including money) there are only "*n* - 1" prices, the price of the *n*th thing (the numeraire) being one.

In monetary economics, as in macroeconomics in general, we are interested in the price of things (commodities, services, and so on) in terms of money, rather than in the price of some things in terms of others. We generally call this price of things in terms of money the *general price level* and denote it by *P*. There are two (equivalent) ways in which one can focus attention on *P* rather than on the price of some things in terms of others. One is to assume that there is only one kind of commodity in the economy; the other is to accept the fact that there are many commodities, so that *P* is an average of the monetary prices of all things, but to assume that the relative prices among those things do not change. Then, and so long as those relative prices among things do not change, we can consider the whole group as a single commodity.

The general price level, *P*, will be defined as

$$P = p_1 \cdot w_1 + p_2 \cdot w_2 + \cdots + p_n \cdot w_n$$

where $P_1, P_2, \ldots, P_n$ are the money prices of the *n* commodities, and $w_1, w_2, \ldots, w_n$ are the "weights" that represent the importance of each good in the total basket of goods. Notice that the sum of the weights must be equal to one; that is, $w_1 + w_2 + \cdots + w_n = 1$. We can then consider the general price level, *P*, as the price of a typical basket of goods, and we shall refer to it as the "price of goods" in terms of money.

There are, of course, as many price indices as baskets of goods one wishes to define. In the United States there are, among others, the wholesale price index, the GNP implicit price deflator, and the consumer price index (the famous CPI often in the headlines). The last one is the (weighted) average of retail prices of goods included in the expenditures of a typical family. The inverse of *P*, the price of commodities in terms of money, is then $1/P$, or the price of money in terms of commodities. In a one-commodity economy producing and selling only pizzas, *P* would be the price of pizzas in terms of money, expressed as "dollars per pizza," and $1/P$ the price of money in terms of pizzas, expressed as "pizzas per dollar."

A *nominal* magnitude is one that is measured in terms of money: the number of dollars received as salary per unit of time, or the value of a house in terms of dollars, or the value in terms of dollars of the stock of money in our pocket, or in the whole economy. A *real* magnitude is one that is measured in terms of goods and services. Specifically, the latter is measured in terms of units of the particular basket of goods and services implicit in the index of the general price level. A real magnitude might be the amount of goods and services that can be bought with the dollars received per unit of time as salary or the amount of goods and services that can be bought with the dollar value of a house, or with the number of dollars in our pocket or in the whole economy. In general, and as a matter of convenience, capital letters will be used in referring to nominal magnitudes, and small letters in expressing real magnitudes. Thus, if Y is the number of dollars per unit of time received as income (that is, nominal income), real income (the amount of goods and services that can be bought with Y) is defined as

$$y = Y/P$$

The definition of real income given by this expression is only one example of the idea of real as opposed to nominal; almost any flow may be expressed in both nominal and real terms (consumption, savings, and so on).

The distinction between nominal and real magnitudes carries over to the case of stocks, and a particularly important case will be the one referring to the stock of money. In this case

$$m = M/P$$

is defined as the real money stock, where M is the nominal stock. The nominal stock (M) is expressed in terms of dollars; the real stock (m), in terms of goods and services.

SYMBOLS USED IN THE BOOK

This brief preview ends with a list of symbols used in this book together with their definitions. They are listed in the approximate order in which they appear in the text. The reader may wish to refer back to them as he or she progresses through the text.

m	= real money stock
M	= nominal money stock
P	= the price level
r	= the real rate of interest
m^d	= desired real stock of money
i	= nominal interest rate
y	= real income (or output)

V	=	velocity of money
k	=	reciprocal of velocity
c	=	consumption expenditures of households
ℓ	=	lending by households
h	=	hoarding by households
I	=	investment goods purchases by businesses
ℓ	=	borrowing by businesses
g	=	government expenditures on goods and services
gb	=	borrowing by government
$\bar{c}$	=	autonomous component of consumption spending
c_y	=	marginal propensity to consume
$\bar{I}$	=	autonomous component of consumption spending
I_r	=	"sensitivity" (coefficient) of investment to the interest rate
L_y	=	"sensitivity" (coefficient) of desired money stock to real income
L_r	=	"sensitivity" (coefficient) of desired money stock to real interest rate
α	=	ratio of I_r to L_r or (I_r/L_r)
b	=	fixed coefficient of difference between desired and actual stocks of money
ℓ_y	=	"sensitivity" (coefficient) of lending to real income
ℓ_m	=	"sensitivity" (coefficient) of lending to real money stock
ℓ_r	=	"sensitivity" (coefficient) of lending to real interest rate
β	=	unit change in investment (or borrowing) per unit shift of the net lending schedule
te	=	total expenditures
y^f	=	full employment level of income
$\dot{y}$	=	rate of change in real income
$\hat{M}$	=	rate of monetary expansion
E	=	expected inflation rate
$\hat{P}$	=	actual inflation rate
u	=	unemployment rate
u^f	=	"natural" rate of unemployment (that is, full employment)
C	=	stock of currency
D	=	demand deposits
R	=	cash reserves
H	=	stock of high-powered money

c = currency/deposit ratio, that is, C/D

r = reserve/deposit ratio, that is, R/D

k = the money multiplier

γ = a symbol (coefficient) representing the "speed of adjustment" between actual income and full employment income, i.e., between $(y - y^f)$.

δ = a symbol (or coefficient) representing the "speed of adjustment" between actual unemployment and the natural rate of unemployment, that is, between $(u^f - u)$.

g = ratio of government deposits to private demand deposits

t = ratio of time deposits (private) to demand deposits (private)

$g\ell$ = government lending through the Federal Reserve

s = savings

t = the balance of trade (exports minus imports)

nco = net capital outflows

P^* = world price level

i^* = world nominal interest rate

r^* = world real interest rate

E = foreign exchange rate

$\hat{E}$ = rate of devaluation

PART I

MONEY
Its Role and Function in the Economic System

CHAPTER 2

A GENERAL CHARACTERIZATION OF MONEY

Chapter 1 established, in general terms, a definition of monetary economics and sought to explain why an understanding of monetary structure and the functions of money is crucial to any student of economics. Understanding the essentials of money and banking must imply, among other things, knowing what money is, where it comes from, and what it does.

As members of a modern society we already know the answers to some of these questions, though we probably have not subjected our knowledge to serious scrutiny. The purpose of the present chapter is to take a close look at *money*, its functions, definition, and forms.

First we shall investigate the functions of money, that is, the various tasks that it performs for us. If we view money as a medium of exchange, its definition as a means of payment for goods and services is "general acceptibility." As a *unit of account*, money serves to reduce significantly the costs of recording prices as they would pertain to a barter system. Money, along with many other commodities and financial instruments, can be used to store wealth, although inflation makes money a poor *store of value*; that is, money may depreciate in value. We will see that only the first function—the medium of exchange function—is *exclusive* to money.

Next, we shall seek a useful definition of money. There is not total agreement on the definition of money or of other important concepts. A framework is provided that is both theoretically simple and easily identifiable for real-world investigations. In other words, many things may look like money, but our concept will permit the observer to examine critically any of these "things" and determine whether they are indeed money.

A final issue considered in the present chapter relates to the evolution of the forms or kinds of money commodity to fiat money. In order to understand this evolution, we must delve into *conceptual history*, or the history of the concept of money. Civilization did not develop smoothly or unidirectionally from primitive man to a modern, technologically oriented society. Over the time span from primitive to modern times, man has progressed (witness Roman and Greek civilization), but not linearly (consider the "Dark Ages" before the

Renaissance). Man likewise has used different forms of transacting from primitive barter to more organized barter to the use of commodity and fiat monies. (Fiat money is government-issued paper currency that is made money by law.) As with the qualities of civilization, these developments did not occur smoothly. In still another analogy with the history of civilization, various forms of money may exist simultaneously. Thus we shall consider the evolution of the concept rather than chronological history itself.

THE FUNCTIONS OF MONEY

Man has put money to a number of uses throughout history. Although money probably served as a unit of account and as a store of wealth in antiquity, its first role was a functional means of exchange.

MONEY AS A MEANS OF EXCHANGE

Most highly cultured civilizations, from antiquity to modern times, have used money. Indeed, the use of money almost seems prerequisite to such development. Self-sufficiency for the individual or family unit simply means that money is not necessary. It also means that specialization and trade—and hence output—are not carried very far. Barter, the trading of goods (services) for other goods (services), characterizes these rather primitive arrangements. Although it is advantageous in the sense that it permits some exchange, barter is costly and places an outer limit on the volume of trade.

Why is barter disadvantageous, or what are the *costs* of barter as a means of transacting? Equivalently, what are the benefits of adopting money as a medium of exchange? There are costs relating to a failure of barter to perform or adequately perform each of the functions of money. A basic problem that comes from the lack of a medium of exchange is that barter requires a double *coincidence of wants.* Suppose that specialization takes place and an individual produces shoes and wants to trade shoes for wine. The individual must be able to find individuals willing to trade the commodities he or she wants (in exact quantities) for the exact quantities of the commodities the person has to trade. Thus, while an individual may find someone willing to trade wine, the other individual may want bread. Even if the second party wants shoes, the two may not be able to come to an agreement if the commodities are indivisible.

An even more significant cost of barter is that it inhibits specialization. The high costs of transacting in a barter system place a definite limit on specialization and the division of labor among tasks. Thus the overall productivity and output potential of a barter society are severely constrained, a fact that may help explain the low economic condition of many primitive societies.

Yet barter takes place even today. Indeed, every individual may be able to recount instances in which he or she has bartered commodities or services. A noted columnist who writes on economic subjects recently reported the story of a housewife's experience at the dentist's office. While waiting her turn, she was told of the dentist's difficulty in securing the services of a bookkeeper. The housewife, having had bookkeeping experience, had the idea of bartering her services in return for dental services. The dentist agreed, and a transaction took place without the use of money. This practice is all well and good on a limited basis, and undoubtedly barter still characterizes some minor aspects of trade. But a modern and productive economic organization the size of the United States would not be possible if free trade were to take place exclusively on these grounds.

Large-scale barter as a replacement for a medium of exchange in, say, the US economy would be unworkable for a number of reasons. The tremendous costs in terms of output reductions due to limits to specialization are an obvious reason, but there is another. The bookkeeper–housewife was lucky in that by chance she found a dentist (whose services she needed) who, in turn, required a worker with her talents. Production and *exchange* on any scale based upon this mode of transacting would entail high costs. The existence of double coincidences of wants is purely random. Thus, barter is very costly in terms of the time and the quantity of trade that can reasonably take place. It is little wonder why trade does not flourish in economies that practice barter exclusively. It should surprise no one that society is in need of some "thing," acceptable to all, which serves as a medium of exchange. This is called *money*.

The medium of exchange function of money, which in various times and places has consisted of gold, gems, elephants, cattle, huge stone wheels, paper, and many other items, is the essential *function* of money. We may say also that the medium of exchange property of money is an exclusive function of money. Only money, in other words, may serve as a medium of exchange. Stated still another way, if it is a medium of exchange, it *must* be money. Things other than money may serve as units of account or as stores of value, but only money is acceptable in the exchange of goods and services.

Immediately, the question arises "Why is money acceptable as a medium of exchange?" Money is acceptable, by and large, because it is acceptable. An individual would be perfectly willing to accept money in exchange for shoes if he or she knew that others would be willing to accept that money in exchange for wine and other goods. The exchange of money for goods requires fewer organized markets than for barter, and huge "marketing" costs are avoided.

What serves as money? Precious metals, for example, have had wide acceptability as a money for thousands of years. (The quality of commodities serving as money varies widely, as we shall see later in this chapter.) When money evolved so that paper representations of commodities, rather than commodities themselves, served as money, a new plateau of acceptability was required. A government, for instance, can issue *fiat* money with no convertibility whatsoever into commodities. The paper will then circulate as a medium of exchange. The government may promote the acceptability of such money by labeling it *legal tender*; that is, it is acceptable in the payment of taxes. Frequently governments have furthered the acceptability of fiat money by a decree that a creditor must forfeit claims on a debtor if the creditor refuses to accept the legal tender in payment of the debt. Thus, *whatever is acceptable as a medium of exchange is money*. Commodities of all types, paper representations of commodities, or just simply paper may perform this function.

MONEY AS A UNIT OF ACCOUNT

Barter imposes on society still other costs of transaction. In addition to the solution of the problem of "double coincidence," use of money as a unit of accounting may eliminate another big problem associated with barter. Consider a small economy segmented by small-scale production units (an individual or the family). Four goods, say, peanuts, bread, wine, and shoes, are traded. Suppose that an individual produces wine and trades for bread. In the first place, he must know the price of all other goods in terms of wine so that he will be able to make a rational choice in his purchases. That is, he must know the price of shoes in terms of wine, the price of peanuts in terms of wine, and so forth, so that he may decide how much of each good he wishes to purchase. A little arithmetic reveals that, as a number of commodities traded increases, the number of real price combinations that must be known increases exponentially!

The existence of money permits fewer and more organized markets. In a simple four-commodity barter world, three markets for peanuts would exist: the peanut–bread market; the peanut–shoe market; and the peanut–wine market. Separate prices would have to be established for *each* market. When money is introduced as a medium of exchange, the number of markets is reduced to *one*, the peanut market. Because all commodities are expressed in terms of the medium of exchange, if one knows the money price of peanuts and all other goods, a simple calculation will yield the "trade ratio" of any two goods. If peanuts are 1 dollar per pound and wine is 2 dollars per bottle, one may easily determine that a bottle of wine is worth two pounds of peanuts. Thus the purely transacting and accounting costs of barter will, when exchange is free, lead to the use of some form of money.

Thus a principal function of money is as a unit of account. The French economist Leon Walras (1834–1910) identified this function as a *numéraire*, a commodity in terms of which all others are stated. When money serves as the numéraire, all prices are quoted in terms of the monetary unit (a dollar in the United States). Money, however, does not necessarily serve as a unit of account. In Latin America, for instance, where much uncertainty surrounds rates of inflation, future prices (promises to buy or sell in the future) may be stated in terms of foreign currencies. Foreign currency, given the above definition of money, is *not* money in these countries. *Pesos* may circulate as a medium of exchange (money), while other items (foreign currencies) are used as a unit of account for future transactions.

Conceptually, there is no reason why any other good—say, potatoes—cannot serve as a unit of account or *numéraire*; that is, all prices could be expressed in terms of potatoes with money circulating as the medium of exchange. An *additional* set of calculations would be required to make potatoes the unit of account, however. In order to conduct business one would have to know both the money price and the "potato price" of all goods and services. The requirement would impose extra costs on society, costs that are avoided when money serves as the *numéraire*.

MONEY AS A STORE OF VALUE

Money may also serve as a store of value; here again, this function is *not* exclusive to money. In fact, it is the least exclusive of the functions of money which we have considered. Chairs, elephants, books, tables, houses, and many other things are also "storehouses of value." All are *temporary* storehouses of wealth, however. Some are "used up" quickly and others, like land and diamonds, may tend to change in value very slowly.[1] Commodities are stores of value under barter conditions, but the non-existence of money—the most liquid of all assets—means that the commodities are not instantly saleable. As asset's or commodity's *liquidity* simply implies the ease or difficulty with which it may be converted into cash when cash is needed. Some commodities have wider markets than others; they are more easily converted into money when money is used. There is a built-in disadvantage to holding any commodity as a store of value in that it must be sold in order to obtain liquidity (money), whereas the holding of money itself requires no separate transaction.

Money, in common with other things, is a temporary storehouse of value. Sometimes it is not a good store of value: its value, or purchasing power, may be eroded by inflation. How many times, for example, have we heard that the "Truman dollar" was worth 25 cents in the Johnson era? Or an even more dramatic example is that of inflation in Germany in 1923. At the height of the inflation, billions of marks were not enough to buy a bowl of soup. The German government enlisted one hundred private printing presses in addition to thirty official ones to supply the demands for paper money. On October 25, 1923, the Reichsbank announced that *daily* production of paper money had been 120,000 billions in paper marks (a German billion equals 1,000,000 *squared*). Demand for the day, however, had reached a trillion (1,000,000 *cubed*). The Reichsbank promised to rectify this situation by raising daily production to a half a trillion.[2]

Ordinarily, and for most twentieth century US monetary experience, the value of money degenerates slowly. In the 1970s, especially the late 1970s, the value of money declined markedly after rates of inflation reached double-digit proportions. A store of value function is necessary to the holding of money (it is not sufficient, as we have seen, to make something money), as people would be unwilling to hold money if it did not perform the function to some extent. But moneyholders are always on the horns of a dilemma with respect to the several functions of money. An individual demands money to use as a medium of exchange. It is the most liquid of all assets—being freely exchangeable for a pack of cigarettes in Bangor, Maine, or in Needles, California, at 1:00 A.M. But its ability to serve as a store of value varies from time to time with changes in the price level. Sometimes other nonmoney, less liquid commodities are better stores of value.

Individuals, in short, must keep two balls in the air simultaneously. Money is the only asset that can serve as "exchange" in present and anticipated transactions, but its value may degenerate more quickly than alternative assets that the individual may hold. Holding the latter types, however, means that the individual *sacrifices liquidity*. (How long would it take to convert land into cash with which to buy cigarettes?) A full answer to these questions awaits us in Chapter 3, but the desired holdings of money for an individual must relate in some way to the costs (opportunities foregone) of holding it. One of those "costs," as we shall see, is the rate at which its "value store" degenerates.

FROM BARTER TO MONEY: THE PRISONER OF WAR CAMP

Before turning to a definition of money, it is instructive to look at a relatively modern real-world case of evolution to money from barter—one that illustrates the advantages pertaining to the use of money which we have discussed. In 1945 R. A. Radford, a former prisoner of war (POW), reported his observations on the economics of POW camp organization in Germany.[3]

Within the German POW camp, prisoners were "endowed" once a week with identical Red Cross rations. Exchange—given that it was not prohibited—would naturally begin to take place, as individuals do not have identical tastes. At first, exchanges were casual and simple (cigarettes for chocolate), but as the volume of trade grew so did the complexities of trading. Rough scales of exchange value developed among the prisoners (1 tin of jam for $\frac{1}{2}$ pound of margarine), but barter became so cumbersome that cigarettes (indeed a commodity in common use) became a standard of value and a medium of exchange. That is, cigarettes became money.

How did cigarettes become money? They became currency when nonsmokers were willing to accept them in exchange for goods, knowing that others would trade goods (that nonsmokers desired) for cigarettes. Radford reports that markets came into spontaneous operation when supply and demand fixed prices. These prices were listed on an Exchange and Mart board (for example, cheese for 7 cigarettes) and were erased when exchanges were consumated.

Many other economic activities that affected price level were undertaken in this "model economy." Arbitrage—buying at low prices and selling later at higher and more profitable prices—helped perfect markets. Some individuals engaged in "time arbitrage" by saving and accumulating capital in cigarettes. On ration issue days (typically Mondays) they bought foodstuffs, toothpaste, etc., when prices for these commodities were low. Prices rose as supplies of these commodities were used up through the week, and on Sundays they would be sold for profit at higher prices. (Time arbitrage would also tend to reduce the spread between Monday and Sunday prices.) Periodic alterations in the supply of cigarettes and food had stark effects upon the price level. The POW economy, like all others, experienced deflation and inflation with changes in the supply of the medium of exchange! The effects on prices of heavy air raids, of good or bad war news, and of waves of optimism and pessimism were all discernible because they affected the nonmonetary demand for cigarettes. With the arrival of the US Infantry at the end of the war, the economic organization of the camp, including its monetary system, collapsed. Chaos replaced order, and, as Radford concluded, "the ushering in of an age of plenty demonstrated the hypothesis that with infinite means economic organization and activity would be redundant, as every want could be satisfied without effort."

The experience of the POW camp illustrates the "naturalness" of the emergence of money as a means of exchange as economies become more sophisticated. The transacting costs of barter inhibit desired exchanges, and the use of money is a normal outcome of the recognition by traders (prisoners) of these costs. Although there were rather obvious costs to using the commodity money as well—in the nature of cigarettes foregone—cigarettes were still able to perform the essential function required of any money.

THE DEFINITION OF MONEY

We might view the three *important* functions of money both abstractly and practically at this point. These functions, discussed in order of "exclusivity," might take the following order:

(A) MEDIUM OF EXCHANGE
(most exclusive function)

↓

(B) UNIT OF ACCOUNT
(typical function, but not exclusive)

↓

(C) STORE OF VALUE
(*least* exclusive function; shared by many other commodities)

We can take an overview of the important properties of money, so arrayed. The medium of exchange function is money's most exclusive function. There are some very restrictive circumstances in contemporary society under which some things serve as a medium of exchange—such as when one corporation buys another corporation with its own *stocks*; however, only money is generally acceptable. In the cases of functions (B) and (C), other things can be used. Although many writers have used both functions (A) and (B) as part of the definition, function (B) is not exclusive to money. It just so happens that money is most often used as a unit of account, but it is not necessary that it perform this function. As we have seen, potatoes can be used as a unit of accounting. Likewise, some writers include function (C) as part of the definition of money, but hosts of nonmoney commodities are regularly held by individuals as stores of value.

THE CONCEPT OF MONEY

What is the definition of money? The answer is that there are a number of definitions. Some of these definitions are based on enumerations of the *items* that are money while others utilize the functions described above as definitional categories. Where does all this leave us? More importantly, what concept or definition of money shall be adopt in the present text on the essentials of money and banking?

Precision is of utmost importance in the definition of any important concept. Consider the term "animal." One might define animal as elephants, zebras, and wildebeests. This definition of the class "animal" is an enumeration of things that mean "animal." All is well until the lion comes along. Given the definition, and if we had never seen a lion, we are not sure whether lions are animals or not. In contrast we may define "animal" as a set of essential characteristics—type of reproductive system, chromosomal structure, blood temperature, etc. Now, if one encounters a walking catfish, a turkey, or a platypus, these essential characteristics may be applied to find out whether we have an "animal" or not.

We adopt the latter approach in our definition of money. For convenience we can present a conceptualized or theoretical definition and then examine the working items (items that we can *examine*) that are money:

Money (*concept*)—anything that is generally acceptable as a medium of exchange

$$\downarrow$$

Money (*working definition* or content of the concept)—currency, coins, and demand and other checkable deposits (checkbook money) at banks and other financial institutions

Thus, the definition of money is *anything that is generally acceptable as a medium of exchange.* By generally acceptable, we eliminate the minor class of items such as "stock of corporations." The items of our working definition—currency, coin, demand and checkable time deposits—are money because they fulfill the essential characteristics of the concept.

JUSTIFICATION OF OUR DEFINITION

The definition of money presented here is the one most accepted and used by economists. But not everyone agrees. Specifically our definition leaves out some things that others include as money or quasi-money. Most important of the excluded items are noncheckable *time deposits* or savings accounts. Let us reflect on why such time deposits are excluded from our definition of money.

Currency, as we all know, is generally acceptable as a medium of exchange. So is checkbook money—demand and other checkable deposits at banks and other financial institutions. If we wish to transfer funds to someone else (or perhaps to pay a bill), we simply use currency or "write a check" in another's favor. After it is "cleared," a check shifts deposits on demand. Time deposits or saving-account money, on the other hand, is not directly transferable. It is not "generally acceptable as a medium of exchange." The fact that time deposits have traditionally paid interest and demand deposits (except in a few states) historically have not, has nothing to do with our *conceptual* definition of money. [Indeed, after the addition of the NOW (Negotiable Order of Withdrawal) accounts in the 1980s most demand deposit accounts pay interest.] If all demand deposits pay interest and noncheckable savings accounts do not, it would not alter whatsoever their character as a medium of exchange.

The advent of electronic banking has blurred and altered the character of some types of time deposits to the extent that they have become *freely transferable* and acceptable between parties *on demand.* They become checkable and thus, according to our definition, money. These "switch hitting" savings or time deposits offered by a variety of financial institutions earn interest but may also be transferred and used on demand to clear debts. They include negotiable orders of withdrawal (NOWs), automatic transfer services (ATS), credit union share draft accounts, and demand deposits at mutual savings banks. All of these devices reflect a growing similarity between deposits in commercial banks and thrift institutions.[4] Our definition of money—the concept—is *not* altered when new items emerge that are freely transferable and acceptable to transacting parties on demand. Items without this characteristic, including many types of saving and time deposits, are not money within our conception.

Another good reason for defining money as a medium of exchange is that the introduction of other assets (such as nontransferable time deposits) opens the floodgates, so to speak. If such time deposits, which are less liquid than money, are introduced, why not include treasury bills as money? After all, are not short-term (often 90-day), highly saleable securities issued by the Treasury (called Treasury bills, or simply "T-bills") also highly liquid, that is, easily convertible into cash? If Treasury bills, why not high-quality issues of municipal or private corporations?

MONEY, AMERICAN STYLE

These complexities are revealed in the Federal Reserve Board's four definitions of the money stock designated M-1A through M-3, and their broad measure of liquid assets, *L*. In Feburary 1980 the Federal Reserve Board reduced the number of money stock and liquidity definitions from seven to five, as listed below:

> M-1A = Averages of daily figures for (1) demand deposits at all commercial banks other than those due to domestic banks, the US government, and foreign banks and official institutions less cash items in the process of collection and Federal Reserve float (to be discussed in Chapter 11); and (2) currency outside the Treasury, Federal Reserve banks, and the vaults of commercial banks.

> M-1B = M-1A plus NOW and ATS accounts at banks and thrift institutions, credit union share draft accounts, and demand deposits at mutual savings banks.

> M-2 = M-1B plus savings and small-denomination time deposits at all depositary institutions, overnight RPs at commercial banks, overnight Eurodollars held by US residents other than banks at Caribbean branches of member banks, and money market mutual fund shares.

> M-3 = M-2 plus large-denomination time deposits at all depository institutions and term RPs at commercial banks and savings and loan associations.

> L = M-3 plus other liquid assets such as term Eurodollars held by US residents other than banks, commercial paper, Treasury bills and other liquid Treasury securities, and US savings bonds.

These definitions are called "money stock measures" or the "monetary aggregates" and they replace seven *old* definitions of money developed by the Federal Reserve Board.[5] Some comparison with the "old" measures and a look at the actual calculation of the new measures will support an understanding of "money." Consider Table 2-1, which reproduces an *actual* calculation of the money aggregates for November 1979.

Note that M-1A is composed to currency plus demand deposits, but that the demand deposit amount is *net* of those due to foreign commercial banks and institutions. Old Ṁ-1 was new M-1A with those foreign commercial bank deposits included. They have been eliminated from the new M-1A for statistical reasons, basically because they do not share the same medium of exchange characteristics of other demand deposits of M-1A. (These deposits amounted to only slightly over 10 billion dollars in November 1979, so that M-1A and old M-1 are very similar measures of money.)

Table 2-1   New Measures of Money and Liquid Assets (November 1979, billions of dollars)

Aggregate and Component	Amount
M-1A	372.2
Currency	106.6
Demand deposits[a]	265.6
M-1B	387.9
M-1A	372.2
Other checkable deposits[b]	15.7
M-2	1,510.0
M-1B	387.9
Overnight RPs issued by commercial banks	20.3
Overnight Eurodollar deposits held by U.S. nonbank residents at	
Caribbean branches of U.S. banks	3.2
Money market mutual fund shares	40.4
Savings deposits at all depositary institutions	420.0
Small time deposits at all depositary institutions[c]	640.8
M-2 consolidation component[d]	-2.7
M-3	1.759.1
M-2	1.510.0
Large time deposits at all depositary institutions[e]	219.5
Term RPs issued by commercial banks	21.5
Term RPs issued by savings and loan associations	8.2
L	2,123.8
M-3	1.759.1
Other Eurodollar deposits of U.S. residents other than banks	34.5
Bankers acceptances	27.6
Commercial paper	97.1
Savings bonds	80.0
Liquid Treasury obligations	125.4

[a]Net of demand deposits due to foreign commercial banks and official institutions.
[b]Includes NOW, ATS, and credit union share draft balances and demand deposits with thrift institutions.
[c]Time deposits issued in denominations of less than $100,000.
[d]In order to avoid double counting of some deposits in M-2, those demand deposits owned by thrift institutions (a component of M-1B), which are estimated to be used for servicing their savings and small time deposit liabilities in M-2, are removed.
[e]Time deposits issued in denominations of $100,000 or more.
Source: Federal Reserve Bulletin.

More interesting is the money aggregate M-1B, which includes "other checkable deposits" along with the components of M-1A. These deposits are the NOW accounts, automatic transfer shares, credit union share draft balances, and demand deposits at "thrift" institutions. (Nonbank institutions such as savings and loan associations or mutual savings banks are considered in detail in Chapter 12.) The amount of these accounts was 15.7 billion dollars in November 1979 so that M-1B is *larger* than the old M-1 measure. But why was a new measure M-1B devised by the Federal Reserve? Basically for two reasons:

(1) the development, in recent years, of *new monetary assets* (NOW accounts, ATS, etc.), and (2) alterations in the basic character of standard monetary assets, that is, the growing similarity of (and substitutions between) deposits of thrift institutions and those of commercial banks.

Definitions of money are not static but evolve with new developments such as checkable deposits at nonbank financial institutions. Items are lumped together because they are more alike in characteristics than other possible groupings. In the Federal Reserve's view, for example, time deposits issued in $100,000 denominations or more (a component of M-3) are more alike in characteristics to the other items listed under M3 in Table 2-1 than to those listed in M-1B or L.

Where does it end? The reader should get the idea. There is a *scale of asset liquidities* with currency and demand deposits at the pinnacle.[6] Many writers on monetary economics (both "Keynesians" and "monetarists") slide down the scale of liquidity to choose a group of these assets and define them as money. Although the inclusion of assets other than demand deposits, currency, and other checkable accounts as money may be useful in analyzing specific problems, we do not believe that there are overwhelming conceptual advantages to their inclusion as a general approach to money. In addition to the matter of simplicity—which is a great advantage of our definition, the definition of money as demand deposits, currency, and transferable savings and time deposits avoids the problems of indeterminacy and arbitrariness which are inherent in broader definitions of the concept.

Every time M (for money) is mentioned in this book (unless otherwise indicated), the reader should think in terms of currency (C) plus demand and checkable time deposites (D) or M-1B in the Federal Reserve listing (occasionally M-1A or old M1 will be used). Currency consists of Federal Reserve Notes (99% of currency) and other residual currencies (which are being phased out) plus coins of all denominations. Demand and checkable time deposits are simply the net balance of individuals' checking account deposits in commercial banks and other financial institutions. Though the relationships between these two components of money will not be fully understood until Chapter 9, the reader is perfectly free until then to conceptualize money simply as currency. A technical understanding of how the two components of money interact is not necessary for a solid appreciation of how M (money) affects important functions and variables in the economic system.

KINDS OF MONEY

We have looked briefly at the major functions of money, at what it is that we wish it to do for us. Further, money has been defined in relation to its function as a medium of exchange. Next we shall investigate the physical things that have been used as money and evaluate the monetary system. This discussion will not be a chronological history, but rather be a conceptual–historical account of how money evolved. Money is not a magical invention that suddenly emerged like Alexander Graham Bell's telephone. Rather money *evolves* as a natural response to particular needs and sociopolitical structures. Historically the transition is not a smooth, unidirectional development from barter (no money) to money. Rather, trial-and-error responses in means of payment to changing conditions took place. It so happens that today practically all societies are money-using (the vast majority using some form of fiat money). However, barter has characterized certain relatively minor forms of economic organization or certain types of transacting in contemporary society. Barter has also been a feature of certain great societies of the past. The following discussion of ancient Egyptian society is an interesting case study of the relationship between type of economic organization and method of transaction before commodities were adopted as money (in the sense used in this chapter).

Ordinarily barter is associated with very primitive forms of economic society. Indeed, it has been suggested that the absence of money is strongly interrelated with self-sufficient economic organization, that is, with every economic unit producing and consuming for itself. (Here the family may be regarded as an economic unit that has—probably from the dawn of civilization —been based upon the division of labor.) In simple societies, the absence of widespread specialization and division of labor does not allow economies of scale in the production of goods and high rates of output. Thus, the high costs of exchange without money limits specialization and division of labor. Pushing this concept a step further, it can be argued that the invention and the use of money are inevitable results of increasing specialization in an economic society. This view is correct conceptually, but restrictions on economic activity, specifically on the freedom to produce and exchange, must also be a factor.

From many points of view ancient Egypt could hardly be termed a primitive society. Certainly in terms of the development of art, architecture, language, and science, Egypt was one of the greatest civilizations of the ancient world. Yet, as late as the 26th Dynasty (663–525 B.C.) money was not "generally accepted" as a medium of exchange, although it was used as a unit of account. Gold, silver, and copper were commonly used in business transactions of all kinds, though far less as a medium of exchange than as a *unit of accounting*.[7] Prices, wages, and allotments to slaves were mainly fixed by law in terms of silver or copper. How then can one explain a society exhibiting a significant degree of specialization without extensive use of money as a medium of exchange?

Economic organization holds the key. Whatever else might be said of Egyptian culture, it was a society based upon power and upon a concept of god as a human being. Pharaoh was the dictatorial personification of a god, and he was accepted as such by the people. Production, though fairly specialized, was carried on by mandate or command and, in many cases, consumption was based upon a socialistic demonstration of "need." In addition to command, the economic organization of Egyptian society was further reinforced by tradition.

The opulence of the Pharoah, and particularly provisions for his comfort in the afterlife, required massive redirections of resources. These redistributions were accomplished by taxation. Practically everything in Egypt was taxed. The farmer, fisherman, herdsman, and hunter each paid taxes on his output. The means of payment, however, was in kind—in either produce or labor. But taxation requires records to record payments and receipts. Records require record-keepers, and maintaining the exceedingly complex system was the job of armies of scribes. Some of our most important historical records of Egyptian civilization consist in these accounts.

An important point is that the Egyptian system that utilized objects—chiefly as a unit of account—approximated a computerized system of accounting and prices not unlike that of the contemporary American Express or Diners Club companies. (In the Egyptian system, however, production, exchange, and consumption were not free. *Society* was the important unit and freedom and individuality were buried under the commands of Pharaoh.) The interesting feature of this payments system is that it is a primitive precursor of modern payments systems where *no* money is used. But, even more important, the Egyptian system demonstrates that societies can specialize in the functions they assign to commodities and that the "unit of account" function of commodities can precede their use as money. For over 2,000 years the Egyptians were on the brink of using commodities as a medium of exchange, but economic organization, to a large extent, made this development unnecessary.

COMMODITY MONEY

Our discussion of the kinds of money has, thus far, focused upon the disadvantages of barter, prime of which are the high costs of transaction. Direct exchange (goods for goods) is far more costly in time and trouble than indirect exchange (goods for money for goods). Thus, a decentralized economic society (unlike Egypt) has especially strong incentives for the introduction of money. This evolution suggests another important question: what thing or things can serve as commodity money?

Theoretically anything can serve as money. In his interesting book on primitive money Paul Einzig identifies almost two hundred items that have been used as money.[8] Often early commodity money was a "common good," that is, a staple consumer good or a good used commonly in export trade. Rice was used in ancient Japan and other Oriental countries, tobacco in the Southern colonies of the United States, beaver and other animal pelts in Canada, and goats in British Africa. Early commodity monies were of great variety. Human skulls, woodpecker scalps, elephants, whale's teeth, women (wives were bought and sold), buffaloes, slaves, wine, cattle, great stone wheels, gold, silver, and assorted metals and minerals were all used as money at one time or another. Many primitive peoples, particularly those with access to the sea, had a long romance with Cowrie shells (oblong, often spotted shells with "teeth") as money.

All these items, at various times and places, correspond to the basic criterion of money; *they were all generally accepted as a medium of exchange.* Obviously, certain things make better monies than others. In fact, some writers attempt to identify money by a list of characteristics: scarcity, transferability, durability, portability, divisibility, ease of recognition, homogeneity, usefulness, and stability of value. All commodities, of course, possess these characteristics in varying degrees, and as long as they are acceptable as a medium of exchange they are money!

Fundamental problems pertain to the use of some commodities as money, however. One problem relates to durability. Milk, orange juice, or pizzas would not make good money on this account. Another more basic one relates to standardization. Chickens make poor monies because chickens are never exactly comparable—one may be skinnier than another. Chicken-moneyusers might standardize the exchange medium by weight, but chickens are not the same in tenderness as anyone knows who has eaten a rooster or an old hen. Besides, the trouble and work involved in standardizing the commodity for use as money represents special costs to the use of chickens as money. In every transaction in which chickens are used, bargaining would have to take place over the relative *quality* and *value* of the chicken in addition to haggling over the price of the commodity.

COSTS OF USING COMMODITY MONEY

The use of commodity money, as in all other things, involves costs and benefits. The clear benefit from the use of some commodity as money is that the transacting costs of barter are reduced. But there are costs to the use of commodity money as well. The price of money, when commodity money is used, is regulated by the costs of producing the commodity. Furthermore the price *level* of all goods and services is equivalent to the inverse of the price of money.

What is the opportunity cost to society of using some commodity as money? That is, what does society forego in terms of its next best alternative use of the commodity? Suppose that gold is used as money and that it takes five units of capital and five of labor to produce one ounce of gold. (Assume that gold is produced at constant average costs). Moreover, assume that one ounce of gold will buy only five units of capital and five units of labor in the market place. In this instance, then, no one will produce gold; that is, money production will cease. In this nonproduction of money situation, what is the cost of using commodity money? Clearly, it is the foregone cost or *opportunity cost* of the money stock in terms of goods and services (or resources) given up. As the gold money stock wears out, resources may be devoted to replenishing the stock, which represents some additional costs. But these additional costs are miniscule compared with the opportunity cost of holding a stock of commodity money. The opportunity cost of using gold as money is the foregone opportunity of utilizing it in jewelry, industry, and so forth, which is gold's next best alternative. Of course, while gold is being used as money it is being used only as money. The value of gold as money, moreover, (say 500 dollars an ounce) must be exactly equivalent to its value in alternative uses, or arbitrage (buying low and selling high) takes place to make them equal.

The significant point is that there are some foregone or opportunity costs to society in using any commodity as a medium of exchange. Pizzas, wine, and chickens have obvious opportunity costs. The cost to society of using any of these commodities is that while being used as money, they cannot be used for other things. Although society may find it acceptable to adopt paper representations of commodities (that is, put all gold in a warehouse) as the medium of exchange, it is easy to see that society has avoided no costs if every single piece of paper is backed by the commodity (for example, gold) up to 100% of its face value. The latter is as pure a system of commodity money as if the commodity itself were used!

The essence of a pure commodity system is that the commodity used has a positive opportunity cost, whereas with fiat money there is a zero alternative use to the holding of money. A fiat money system is one in which the government issues paper currency and makes it legal tender by "fiat" or law. Such paper currency does not represent any commodity (gold, for example), and there is no promise of redemption.

MIXED SYSTEMS OF COMMODITY–FIAT MONEY: A STORY OF PRINCES AND BANKERS

How do commodity money systems evolve into fiat money systems? As we have noted, systems of barter, commodity money, and fiat money often co-exist within the same society. Several historical developments, mostly occurring in the Renaissance, fostered the evolution to fiat money.[9]

In regard to the evolution of money, the history of words and word meanings is interesting. The term "fiat" is often connected with fiduciary, meaning "faith" or public confidence. Although there is not exact equivalence, the expression "fiduciary money" is sometimes used interchangeably with fiat money. We would expect that the concept has something to do with faith, and indeed it does. People are willing to accept noncommodity money on the faith that others are willing to accept it also. But how did these paper representations in which individuals have "faith" come about?

The "Great Transformation" to market societies began in the fifteenth and sixteenth centuries, primarily, but not exclusively, in Southern Europe. During this time precious metals, principally gold, circulated as a commodity medium of exchange. As trade expanded into more distant markets, early traveling entrepreneurs found it convenient to store the medium of exchange in what we might term a warehouse. The trader was issued a "warehouse receipt" for the gold by the "watchman." The receipt could then be carried by the trader in safety, and after a time these "receipts" became as fully acceptable as the money commodity itself. The risk of being knocked on the head for the gold one carried was reduced or eliminated.

Such warehousing arrangements were the beginnings of modern banking. At first the banker (watchman) simply provided a storage service in return for a small fee (the cost of storage and risk). This system is equivalent to the maintenance of 100% reserves in the pieces of paper (the receipts) issued. Any time the holders of receipts wished to exercise an instant repurchase of the commodity, the conversion could be made by the banker to the total extent of the obligation. This system is equivalent to a pure commodity money system.

An important aspect of the situation related to note holders. As confidence grew among note holders that redemption could be made at any time, notes began to circulate. Through experience the banker–warehouser made the important discovery that all his clients did not present their receipts for payment at the same time. Thus, early bankers began to experiment with lending gold or certificates (receipts) at interest. If he found that periodic demand for the commodity required him to hold 50% of his stored gold at all times, he was free to lend and earn income on one-half of his commodity holdings. This development represented the beginning of fractional reserve banking. Further, it was the origin of fiat money, as some of the zero-cost paper representations of money which circulated as a medium of exchange were backed by nothing more than "faith." "Faith" here was a confidence in convertibility rather than a faith in acceptability for payments, although the former faith strongly encouraged the acceptability of these notes in exchange. Hence, fiduciary money became a feature of economic organization.

Another development that took place along with the emergence of banking featured the role of the state in commodity money "certification." (This development relates to the standardization of the commodity money discussed earlier, and it clearly predated the Renaissance.) Because precious metals were capable of being debased—for example, gold could be alloyed with baser metals—an apparent ounce of gold may not equal an ounce of gold at all. The prince or monarch got into the business of stamping metals, for instance, gold, silver, and copper. The charge for minting was often realized by the prince by returning coins with serrated edges (a practice that antedates the form of the modern US dime or quarter). In all cases the difference between the value of the bullion presented to be stamped and the circulating value of the coin was called *seigniorage* (in general, the term means something claimed or taken by the "seignior" or lord by virtue of the prerogative of the sovereign).

In both of these developments (banking and seigniorage) there existed an opportunity to cheat. When circulating certificates issued by the bankers fell in value relative to the specie they (sometimes supposedly) represented, there would be a "run on the bank," a frontier demand for depositor's specie. If the banker misjudged the level of specie reserves required to meet such contingencies or if he greedily lent out too much, he would be driven out of business. The last people to arrive at the bank would be losers. In the case of seigniorage, a clever prince with a monopoly on coin minting would soon discover that he could pinch or clip more than the cost of minting from the bullion presented to him. A profligate monarch, in an attempt to provide funds in support of his own luxury, often had recourse to this alternative. Here everyone loses a little, but the system will not collapse as in the banking case. Why? Because the prince, as a monopolist, could simply eliminate all competition in the stamping and minting of coins, by forbidding all but the coin of the realm to circulate under penalty of law.

Note that these developments were crucial ones in the evolution of our monetary system. Early bankers proved that a fiat money system, although not without some problems, could function, while the behavior of medieval monarchs in this role as "certifiers" of money demonstrated the valuable lesson that monopoly power in money certification may be and often is abused.[10]

GAINS FROM FIAT MONEY: THE CASE OF PANAMA

Fiat money is made possible by the willingness of the public to hold and exchange paper representations of money. However, paper money is not necessarily fiat money.[11] In the early banker case, for example, only part of the circulating medium of exchange was not backed by gold (the money commodity). Let us investigate the nature of the gains by the change from a commodity money to a fiat money system. A good example of the possibilities of these gains relates to the monetary situation that currently exists in Panama.

In Panama (which we may assume to be a closed system, that is, without international trade) US dollars circulate as a medium of exchange. Because Panamanians cannot produce US dollars at zero cost—the only way to obtain these dollars is to trade for the products of real Panamanian resources—US dollars in Panama may be regarded as commodity money. There is a real opportunity cost to holding dollars in Panama. This cost applies to *individual* holders of dollars in Panama as well as to *individual* holders of dollars in the

United States where dollars are a fiat money. Clearly the dollars held by individuals in either country can be used to purchase goods and services.

There is a "social cost" to the aggregate holdings of dollars (commodity money) in Panama which does not exist—in the aggregate—in the United States where dollars are fiat money. The gains in Panama from going to fiat money from this form of commodity may be easily explained. Suppose that the Panamanian government decides to shift to the Balboa standard and to exchange fiat Balboas one-to-one with US dollars. The relative prices of all things exchanged remain the same. Where then are the gains from the introduction of fiat money? The Panamanian government could buy, with the US dollars collected, any of a variety of goods in the United States. It could purchase Cadillacs for its bureaucrats or chocolates for the Panamanian people, or deposit the dollars in New York banks and earn interest on the funds. Balboas (the fiat money) would have a zero alternative cost to society, but the use of US dollars (a commodity money) would not have zero social costs.

CONCLUSION

Most modern nations, in order to avoid the costs of using commodity money, have elected fiat money systems. The evolution to these systems has occurred largely for reasons of economic efficiency and for the motivations of self-interest. An interesting by-product of this evolution to fiat money may be the demand for political independence. Because the production of fiat money is, in general, only possible with political independence, the potential gains from its adoption may have been one of several reasons certain underdeveloped nations in Africa and elsewhere have lobbied for independence.

Money, therefore, is a important institution with respect to economic and political structure. What we call money today is the simple result of the very complex forces of pragmatic institutional change resulting from trial and error over the long and sometimes torturous history of our civilization.

FOOTNOTES

[1] Value, of course, is not "intrinsic" to any commodity but depends on the supply (cost of producing) and the demand for it. Thus, the relative abilities of various commodities to serve as stores of value are determined by future supplies and demands for the items along with their perishability and a host of other things. Precious metals and gems are relatively good stores of value, but sudden, random discoveries of large quantities of them would make them less so.

[2] Constantino Bresciani-Turroni, *The Economics of Inflation, A Study of Currency Depreciation in Post-War Germany*, translated by Millicent E. Sayers (London: George Allen & Unwin, Ltd., 1937), p. 82. The end of such a runaway inflation is in sight when money becomes more valuable as pulp paper than as money.

[3] See R. A. Radford, "The Economic Organization of a P.O.W. Camp," *Economica*, N. S. (November 1945).

[4] Actually such checkable deposits at thrift institutions have been a feature of some New England mutual savings banks for a long while. Currently in many cities, Automatic Teller Machines (AMTs) are located in apartment buildings and airports and outside banks. Among other services, AMTs may be used to transfer funds from your savings account to your checking account. In Minneapolis and elsewhere you can use a special telephone device attached to a computer in your savings bank in order to switch funds from your account to those of department and grocery stores and utility companies. This apparatus is equivalent to the concept of money discussed in the text.

[5] For further details on the new monetary aggregates see "The Redefined Monetary Aggregates," *Federal Reserve Bulletin* (February, 1980), pp. 97–114.

[6] Note that the liquidity of overnight Eurodollars held by nonbank US residents in Caribbean branches of US banks is higher on the scale (M-2) than Eurodollar deposits held elsewhere (L). (Eurodollars are simply deposits in banks located abroad, mostly in Europe, denominated in US dollars.) The M-2 deposits are more variable and transferrable and hence receive a higher ranking on the liquidity scale. Repurchase agreements, or RPs, are *immediately available* funds that are businesses' demand deposits *sold* to banks overnight or for longer terms. The overnight RPs are listed under M-2, whereas the "term" instruments are of less liquidity (M-3).

[7] An interesting example of using precious metals as a unit of account, but not as a medium of exchange, is revealed in a recorded transaction at the time of Ramses II (13th Century B.C.). An ancient document shows that a Syrian girl slave was traded by a merchant to a townswoman for 4 *deben* and 1 *kite* of silver (11 kite = 1 deben) but in objects of all kinds. These objects are described in the following manner: 1 shroud of Upper-Egyptian cloth, makes 5 kite of silver; 1 blanket of Upper-Egyptian cloth, makes $3\frac{1}{3}$ kite of silver; 1 djayt-garment of Upper-Egyptian cloth, makes 4 kite of silver; 3 sdy-garments of fine Upper-Egyptian cloth, makes 5 kite of silver; 1 dress of fine Upper-Egyptian cloth, makes 5 kite of silver. This was not enough, and the woman had to borrow from neighbors and friends various objects such as bronze vessels, a pot of honey, more cloth, and broken copper to make up the difference. Although money itself was not used in the transaction, the trade was made easier by the fact that the value of the traded commodities was expressed in terms of silver.

[8] Paul Einzig, *Primitive Money in its Ethnological, Historical, and Economic Aspects*, 2nd edition (Oxford: Pergamon Press, 1966).

[9] The reader is warned that this is the kind of "concept-history" we talked about earlier in the chapter. Chronologically, fiat money was probably used far in advance of the Middle Ages.

[10] See the section of Chapter 8 in this text dealing with "government revenues from inflation" for a discussion of how modern governments may use their power to "certify" and regulate money as a means of taming society.

[11] There is another obvious sense in which a paper money system is not necessarily a fiat money system. In fact, a paper system can be regarded as a 100% commodity money system. Remember that paper itself has a value! This is correct in the most literal sense, of course, but paper is often so small in value as to be regarded as valueless.

KEY CONCEPTS

functions of money
   medium of exchange
   unit of account
   store of value

fiat money (fiduciary)

commodity money

conceptual history

barter

double coincidence of wants

liquidity

exclusivity

scale of asset liabilities

opportunity cost

seigniorage

definition of money

QUESTIONS FOR DISCUSSION

1. Why are we able to exchange dollars for goods and services in the United States?

2. Can you think of any modern instances where a commodity is the medium of exchange?

3. How do you explain the origin of fractional reserve banking?

4. Name specific modern instances when money is used as a medium of exchange, a unit of account, and a store of value.

CHAPTER 3

THE DEMAND FOR MONEY

The concept of a "demand for money" or, more precisely, of a *desired real stock of money*, is at the heart of the analysis of monetary economics. When a disequilibrium situation exists, there is a discrepancy between the *actual* and the *desired* stock of money. The adjustment of changes in the actual stock to the desired stock determines much of the behavior of changes in variables such as prices, real income, and interest rates. The equilibrium actual and desired stocks are equal, and the determinants of the desired stock are of critical importance in determining the equilibrium values of prices, real income, and interest rates.

The concept of a desired stock of money, either by one individual or by the public at large, is related to the distinction between money and wealth. An individual's *wealth* can be expressed in *nominal* terms, as the dollar value of assets minus liabilities, or in *real* terms, as that nominal value divided by a general price index. There are three broad categories of assets in which wealth can be held: real assets, financial assets, and money. The category real assets includes such obvious items as homes, land, machines, and suits or dresses. Others, which at first sight may seem to be very different assets, should be included here. Equities, or common stock, are one of those assets. Equities are simply pieces of paper, but they entitle their owner to participate·in the profits of a corporation. In a fundamental sense, they represent a certain part of the capital (including machinery, good-will value, and so forth) of the corporation. Another real asset, no less important, is *human capital*. Even though human capital is not traded as an *asset* in a nonslave society, the services of human capital can be traded, and the present value of the flow of income derived from the sale of these services is used to approximate the value of such an asset at any point in time.[1] Financial assets (bonds) are the second broad category of assets in which wealth can be held. Two distinct features of these assets are that they are denominated in terms of dollars (that is, in nominal terms), and they guarantee the reception of a certain stream of nominal payments, that is, *interest*. The third asset in which wealth can be held is money. Money, like bonds, is denominated in nominal terms (a dollar is a dollar is a dollar), but unlike bonds it does not ordinarily pay interest.[2]

Money, then, is but one of many possible items of wealth. At any point in time wealth is held in many alternative assets (physical assets, financial assets, and money), and individuals are interested in maximizing the amount of income generated from wealth. In commonsense terms, any individual with a given income will seek to balance his or her consumptions so that the additional net satisfaction derived from each item he consumes is equal. There are costs and benefits associated with the different components of wealth (physical assets, financial assets, and money). Depending upon the costs and benefits of these components, ordinarily different for different individuals, a given "mix" will be held such that the marginal net return on all of them is equal.

The desired stock of money refers to the part of a given wealth which individuals wish to hold in the form of money. By remembering this, we can readily understand why at some point in time an individual (or all individuals together) may be holding "too much money," that is, too high a proportion of total wealth in the form of money. The concept of the public wishing to hold its wealth in a variety of different assets (including money) is a very important one, and the rearrangement that individuals make to those assets when the desired proportions are disturbed is precisely the essential mechanism behind monetary policy.

An understanding of the demand for money is central to the perception of "how the monetary system works." The purpose of this chapter is to develop the elements of a theory of the demand for money. In order for us to arrive at such a theory, the desired money stock must be expressed as a function of some variables on which such a stock will depend. We can express the demand for money in much the same way as a theory of the demand for peanuts is established, that is, by stating the variables upon which the quantity of peanuts demanded depend and also by stating the *form* of this dependence. The form of dependence indicates how the demand for money depends on the variables specified.

The plan of the present chapter is as follows: First, the meaning of "holding a stock of money" will be clarified, both for the case of an individual and for the case of the public at large. Next, a general characterization of the demand for money is elaborated, without reference to particular theories. In the final three sections of the chapter, the two main approaches to the theory of the demand for money—that is, *neoclassical quantity theory* and the *Keynesian* or *liquidity preference* approach—are discussed. We seek an understanding of why money, in common with a myriad of other things in a modern economy, is demanded by individuals and the public.

THE MEANING OF "HOLDING MONEY"

Real money balances, or houses, are a stock, and there is no difficulty in defining and identifying what that stock is at any point in time, either for an individual or for the public at large.

THE INDIVIDUAL

Let us consider the individual first. An individual may hold a stock of two houses and 1,000 dollars in real money balances (remember the distinction between nominal and real magnitudes from Chapter 1) at any given time. There is a distinctive feature or peculiarity when we consider the stock of money being held by an individual. We can better understand this distinctive feature by tracing the typical path of an individual's money holdings over each *payments period.*

For example, a certain individual receives a monthly income of $1,000. In a monetary economy, income will be received in the form of money. If the individual is "in equilibrium," in the sense that he is holding his desired stock of money over the payments period (a month) he will be spending all of his income either on consumption goods or on assets other than money (either physical assets or financial assets). The path of money holdings for such an individual may be *idealized* as in Figure 3-1. At the beginning of each month, he receives 1,000 dollars in the form of money and spends it gradually but at a constant rate during the month.

We should note at least two simplifications contained in the process described by Figure 3-1. First, anyone who has paid monthly bills knows that payments (transactions) are clustered. Rent and utilities plus other bills are usually paid at the beginning of the month. The model in Figure 3-1 abstracts from this real-world fact, though taking account of it would not alter the conclusions a bit. A second simplification is that in Figure 3-1 the case of an individual who ends the payments period with no monetary reserves is described; a more realistic case would be to assume that the individual keeps some amount of money on which he or she will normally not draw (the classic case of keeping some money "under the mattress"). Figure 3-2 depicts such a case when the same individual of Figure 3-1 keeps 400 dollars as "idle" (as opposed to "active" or "circulating") money balances.

The question "How much money are you holding now?" would meet with different answers according to the time of the payment period at which it is formulated. What is meant by the concept called *the stock of money held by an individual?* In particular, how can an individual be in equilibrium, hold-

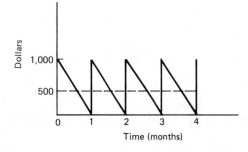

Figure 3-1. Money holdings: typical path for an individual.

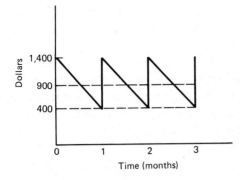

Figure 3-2. Money holdings: path with idle balances.

ing a desired stock, when the actual stock is constantly changing? The answer is that we refer to the *average* of money holdings during the payment period. In the cases shown in Figures 3–1 and 3–2 such an average is very easily calculated given the straight line path of the person's holdings during the period (one month). The simple average between the initial and the final holdings is $(1,000 + 0)/2 = 500$ for the first case (see Figure 3–1), and $(1,400 + 400)/2 = 900$ in the second example (see Figure 3–2). In the second case the average may also be broken down into the average of *active* balances, which is equal to the one of the first case, and the constant amount of *idle* balances, or

$$\frac{(1,000 + 0)}{2} + 400 = 900$$

ALL INDIVIDUALS CONSIDERED TOGETHER

The necessity of referring to some average money holdings does not arise when we are considering the public at large, that is, all money holders together. In this case, some individuals' payments are other individuals' receipts, and at any point in time, there will be a *total money stock* equal to the sum of the holdings of all individuals. If the total money stock is not changing, it will also be equal to the sum of the average holdings of all individuals. For example, if the public at large were composed of only two individuals (say, the one described by Figure 3–2, and another one holding *idle* balances of 500 dollars), the total stock of money in the economy, at any moment during the payment period, would also be the sum of both individuals' total averages, or $900 + 1,000 = 1,900$.

THE DEMAND FOR MONEY: A GENERAL FORMULATION

Money, a nonphysical asset that usually yields no interest, is held by individuals for the same reason that physical assets (machines or houses) are held—because it provides the holder with a stream of services. At this point it is enough to characterize the services of money by recalling its usefulness as a medium of exchange and as the most liquid store of value.

The idea of holding the stock of money for the services it provides allows us to discuss the "demand for money" directly as the "demand for the services of money." The concept is not unique. We are proceeding in the same fashion as we would in discussing the demand for the services of houses, or, for that matter, the demand for any commodity. A final point to be stressed is that, because money is useful only to the extent of its buying power (that is, its real value), the concept "desired stock of money" means, more specifically, the "desired *real* stock of money."

THE COST OF HOLDING MONEY

Any basic study of demand theory will reveal that the quantity demanded of a commodity or a service depends primarily on the price of the commodity or the service and on the level of income or wealth of the demander. When the commodity is the "services of money," the situation is no different. Thus "The price of the services of money,"—or similarly "the costs of holding money"—must, be precisely identified. What is the real cost, per unit of time, of consuming the flow of "services" of a given quantity of real money? Because dollars must be held in order to get the services provided by dollars, the question may be reduced to "What is the real cost, per unit of time, of holding a certain amount of real wealth in the form of money?"

There are two types of costs. The first comes to mind when the concept of opportunity cost is considered. In terms of opportunity cost, the cost of doing something (in this case, holding a certain part of real wealth in the form of money) is measured by what is not obtained as some alternative is given up. If one holds a certain part of wealth in the form of money, part of the wealth is not held in the form of some alternative asset, real or financial, that could have brought a real return. Let m_0 equal the stock of wealth held in the form of money, remembering from Chapter 1 that $m = M/P$, such that m is the individual's command over real goods. The alternative real return that could have been obtained, per unit of time, from holding some other asset (a machine or a bond) at the real rate of return r, (the real rate of interest) would have been (mr) per unit of time. The quantity mr is the real opportunity cost per unit of time of holding a stock m in the form of money.

The second cost of holding wealth in the form of money relates to the fact that money is denominated in nominal terms (again, a dollar is a dollar is a dollar). If prices are rising, it is then necessary continuously to increase the *nominal* number of dollars at a rate equal to the inflation rate in order to keep the *real* stock constant. That is, if the individual decides to hold m_0 worth of real wealth in the form of money, and if prices are rising, say, at a rate of 10%

per year, in order to keep that real stock constant he or she will need to **add** nominal balances to the money holdings at the rate of 10% per year. The second cost may then be expressed arithmetically as follows. If Δ means "a small change in" and $m = M/P$, then

$$\frac{\Delta m}{m} = \frac{\Delta M}{M} - \frac{\Delta P}{P}$$

If m (the part of real wealth held in the form of money) is to be kept constant, $\Delta m/m = 0$, the rate of money stock growth must equal the inflation rate, or $\Delta M/M = \Delta P/P$. (The section on "Levels and Rates of Change" in Chapter 1 may be read or reread at this point.) Thus, expression [3.1] may be obtained,

$$\Delta M = M \frac{\Delta P}{P} \qquad\qquad [3.1]$$

where ΔM is the number of dollars that must be added to nominal money holdings so as to keep the real stock constant when prices are rising at a proportional rate of $\Delta P/P$. The real value of that continuous stream of additions to nominal money holdings is $\Delta M/P$. By dividing the left and right sides of equation [3.1] by P, we find that this real value is

$$\frac{\Delta M}{P} = \frac{M}{P} \frac{\Delta P}{P} = m \frac{\Delta P}{P}$$

An analogy is useful to help understand this concept. A *real* money stock, m, is in this sense like any physical asset that depreciates at some constant rate (a stock of machines or a block of ice that evaporates at a constant rate). *In order to keep the physical stock constant, it is necessary continuously to add to it at a rate equal to the stock multiplied by the depreciation rate.* In the case of money, it is necessary to add to it a real flow equal to m times $\Delta P/P$, or $m(\Delta P/P)$. Of course, if prices are falling instead of rising (that is, if there is some rate of *deflation*), the term $\Delta P/P$ is negative, and the part $m(\Delta P/P)$ of the total cost of holding money will be negative, showing a return rather than a cost.

When the two costs of holding money (the opportunity cost, mr, and the "depreciation" cost, $m(\Delta P/P)$) are added together, the real cost per unit of time of holding a constant real stock of wealth in the form of money is

$$mr + m \frac{\Delta P}{P} = m\left(r + \frac{\Delta P}{P}\right)$$

Because the decision to hold a certain stock of wealth in the form of money is made at the beginning of whatever period is under consideration, such a decision is made on the basis of the *expected* real rate of return, r, and of the *expected* rate of inflation. When the economy is in equilibrium, these *expected* magnitudes will coincide with the *actual* magnitudes. In *disequilibrium* actual and expected magnitudes will not, in general, be the same.

The explanation given above for considering the real cost of holding money as the sum of the return on physical assets (r) plus the rate of inflation ($\Delta P/P$) can be checked against the alternative of holding wealth in another type of assets also denominated in nominal terms, that is, bonds (see Chapter 13). As explained in Chapter 1, the *nominal* rate of return (or the *nominal* interest rate) on these assets is $i = r + (\Delta P/P)$; then, the nominal interest rate, i, may be identified directly as measuring the cost of holding money.

THE LEVEL OF REAL INCOME OF MONEYHOLDERS

The second important variable upon which the demand for money services (or the desired stock of money) will depend is income. Inclusion of the item "income" should present no difficulty, as its inclusion has exactly the same rationale as it has in the demand function for any commodity. The higher the level of real income, the more goods and services individuals will consume, and among those goods and services are the services of money. In other words, the demand for money balances is not an exception to the general rule. Strictly speaking, some measurement of real wealth is probably better than actual real income as an item upon which the demand for money depends, as it is also in the general case of the demand for any commodity. But wealth is a difficult variable to quantify. The wealth measurement problem is not specific to the demand for money, however, and pertains to the demand for any commodity. We shall not elaborate here on the subject, however; we shall simply use *current real income* as a proxy for wealth in the demand for money function.

THE DEMAND FOR MONEY: A GENERAL FORM

From the foregoing considerations we can write as our general form for the demand for money,

$$m^d = L(i, y) \qquad [3.2]$$

where m^d is the real stock of money "desired" (or, alternatively, the flow of services of money demanded), i is the nominal rate of interest, and y is the level real of income. The notation $L(\ )$ means, of course, "a function of" or "is related to."[3] Thus, equation [3.2] tells us that the desired real stock of money, m^d, is a function of, or is related to, the nominal interest rate and current real income.

Just *how* are these variables related to the demand for money? As usual, the use of a graph and a comparison to a more familiar demand curve help provide an understanding of these relations. Figures 3–3a and 3–3b show a demand

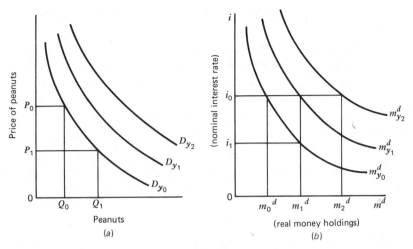

Figure 3-3. The demand for peanuts and the demand for money.

curve for peanuts and the demand curve for money, since the demand for money may be interpreted very much in the same manner as the demand curve for any good. The demand curve for peanuts, D_{y_0}, is drawn up by holding constant all of the determinants of peanut demand, including income (at some level y_0), and then varying the price of peanuts (the cost of consuming peanuts). As the price of peanuts falls, consumers will buy more of them; that is, they will substitute peanuts for other items in their budget. In Figure 3-3a, a price decline from P_0 to P_1 increases the quantity demanded of peanuts from Q_0 to Q_1 along the demand function for the level of income signified by y_0, or more completely, D_{y_0}. But note what happens when the consumer's income rises from y_0 to y_1 to y_2. In this case the demand schedule for peanuts shifts to the right (or increases) to D_{y_1} and D_{y_2} for every possible price of peanuts.

A complete analogy can be drawn from the case of peanuts for the general form of the demand for the services of money. Figure 3-3b depicts the desired stock of money (and therefore the services provided by that real stock measured on the horizontal axis) as a function of the nominal interest rate (measured on the vertical axis), which is the cost of holding the stock or the price of the "services" provided by that stock. This is the same thing as the demand for peanuts as a function of the price of peanuts, except that in this case, "price" is regarded as the cost to the individual of holding money, the nominal interest rate. Assuming all other things equal, income included, what happens when the cost of holding money declines? The answer is the same as in the peanuts case: at a lower cost the individual will wish to consume more services from money, and therefore to increase his or her real money stock. With a fall in this cost (the nominal interest rate) from i_0 to i_1, and with real income being constant at y_0, the desired real stock increases from m_0 to m_1. This is true for any commodity.

When we assume that income *rises* from y_0 to y_1 to y_2, the demand function for money *shifts* to the right from m_{y_0} to m_{y_1} to m_{y_2}. That is, at every nominal interest rate (the cost of holding money), the desired stock of money will be larger. The extent of this shift in the demand for money is given by what is called the *income elasticity of demand*, which is simply the responsiveness of the desired money stock to the change in income, both measured in percentage terms. An identical concept may be applied to peanuts or any other goods or services. With these basic ideas in mind, let us consider some well known and some specific treatments of the demand for money.

THEORIES OF THE DEMAND FOR MONEY

The previous section presented a general sketch of the theory of the demand for money. Here, we discuss in more detail alternative ways in which an equation such as [3.2] has been justified. First, we consider an idea that in general may be called the quantity theory, starting with the classical equation of exchange and ending with the so-called *modern quantity theory* of the demand for money. Second, a brief account is given of the Keynesian demand for money. As a corollary it is interesting that both theories justify a general expression of the form [3.2] above, although the rationale for arriving at this relationship is different in both classical and Keynesian theory.

THE QUANTITY THEORY OF MONEY: OLD AND NEW

The so-called equation of exchange is, in its initial form, an identity rather than an equation; it is, however, at the heart of the quantity theory and is a very useful way of organizing concepts of monetary analysis. It has been at the core of economists' thinking since the philosopher John Locke (1632–1704) wrote about it in the seventeenth century or, more completely, since the writings of Richard Cantillon (1680?–1734). In fact, the central ideas of the quantity theory apparatus can still be learned from Cantillon's posthumously published *Essay on the Nature of Commerce in General* (1754). Cantillon, in discussing the "increase and decrease" of the quantity of money in a State, observed:

> If mines of gold or silver are discovered in a State, & if considerable quantities of material are taken from them, the Proprietor of these Mines, the Entrepreneurs, & all those who work in them will not fail to increase their expenditures in proportion to the riches & the profits which they will make: they will also lend at interest the sums of money which they have over and above what they need for their expenses. All this money, lent as well as spent, will enter into circulation, will not fail to raise the price of commodities & merchandise in all the channels of circulation which it enters.

The increase of money will bring about an increase of expenditure, & this increase of expenditure will bring about an increase of Market prices in the years of most active trade, & by degrees in the least active.

Everybody agrees that the abundance of money, or its increase in trade, raises the price of all things. The quantity of money brought from America to Europe during the last two centuries demonstrates this truth by experience ... [Further] ... an acceleration, or a greater speed, in the circulation of money in trade amounts to the same thing as an increase in standard money, up to a certain degree.

What is so remarkable is that Cantillon, writing almost 50 years *before* Adam Smith's classic defense of market economics in the *Wealth of Nations* (1776), understood these statements about monetary theory to be mere common knowledge! Let us turn to a more formal treatment of these ideas in order that they be even more clearly understood.

THE CLASSICAL EQUATION OF EXCHANGE:
A SIMPLE FORMULATION

Consider a monetary economy under observation during a certain period of time, and suppose that during that period (one week or one month or one year) all "final" transactions are recorded. Final transactions are the sale of *newly* produced commodities to their *final* user, that is, the commodities that enter in the computation of total output or real income.[4] For simplicity, suppose that there is only one commodity in the economy.

Any transaction is the exchange of a certain amount of money (the total payment in the transaction) for a certain number of units of a commodity, with the price per unit relating these two magnitudes. If we call X_i the number of units of the commodity being exchanged in the ith transaction, P_i the price per unit paid in the ith transaction, and D_i the number of dollars exchanged in the ith transaction, for any transaction we can write $X_i P_i \equiv D_i$ so that by adding both sides of the identity across all transactions in the economy during the period, we obtain

$$\sum_{i=1}^{n} (X_i P_i) \equiv \sum_{i=1}^{n} D_i \qquad [3.3]$$

where n is the number of transactions, and $\sum_{i=1}^{n}$ means a summation over all transactions 1 to n. The $\equiv$ means "must equals."

By multiplying and dividing the left hand side of [3.3] by $\sum_{i=1}^{n} X_i$, that is, by the sum of all units of the commodity exchanged during the period, we obtain

$$\frac{\sum (X_i P_i) \; \sum X_i}{\sum X_i} \equiv \sum D_i \qquad [3.4]$$

or

$$\frac{\sum(X_i P_i)}{\sum X_i} \sum X_i \equiv \sum D_i \qquad [3.5]$$

where

$$\frac{\sum(X_i P_i)}{\sum X_i} = P$$

can be recognized as the (weighted) average of prices, or the average price level in the economy for the period under consideration. (Once again, a review of the price level concept outlined in Chapter 1 may be helpful.)

In turn, $\sum (X_i)$, the sum of all the units exchanged and produced during the period, is the *real income* (or output) for that period reckoned as "units of the commodity per unit of time," y. By replacing these two values on the left hand side of [3.5], we obtain

$$Py \equiv \sum D_i \qquad [3.6]$$

where the right-hand side has the dimensions of a flow (dollars per unit of time). A numerical example makes clear that the logic behind the manipulations performed above is simple. Suppose that the single commodity produced and exchanged is pizzas. Take a case in which during the period under consideration (say, one year) only four transactions take place (that is, $n = 4$). The numbers in Table 3–1 are self-explanatory.

Table 3-1   Simple Model of the Equation of Exchange

Transaction Number	Pizzas Exchanged in Each Transaction	Price per Pizza in Each Transaction (P_i) (in Dollars)	Total Value of Sales ($X_i P_i$)	Total Number of Dollars Paid at Each Transaction (D_i)
1	4	1	4	4
2	7	2	14	14
3	2	5	10	10
4	5	4	20	20
	$\sum X_i = 18$		$\sum X_i P_i = 48$	$48 = \sum D_i$

Then

$$\frac{\sum(X_i P_i)}{\sum X_i} \sum X_i = \frac{(48)(18)}{(18)} = 48 = D_i$$

$$\frac{\sum X_i P_i}{\sum X_i} = P \qquad \frac{48}{18} = 2.666$$

$$X_i = y = 18$$

Given the restriction that only final transactions are included in the formulation, each unit of the commodity entering the computation of real income has been exchanged *once and only once*. The same is not the case of the dollars exchanged for those goods in the sense that some dollars that were in the economy during that period may never have been exchanged, while others may have changed hands more than once. Suppose that during the period the stock of nominal dollars in the economy remained constant, at a level M; then the *average* number of times that every dollar in the economy has been exchanged (or "changed hands") can be defined as

$$V \equiv \sum \frac{D_i}{M} \qquad [3.7]$$

where V is called *velocity of circulation.*[5]

From [3.7], $D_i \equiv MV$, which can be replaced in the righthand side of expression [3.6] to obtain the *equation of exchange*

$$MV \equiv Py \qquad [3.8]$$

In our simple numerical example of Table 3–1, $\sum D_i = 48$, that is, the *total* number of dollars exchanged during the period is 48 dollars. If the *stock* of dollars during that period is 48 dollars, then *on the average* each dollar entered once in the transactions process (that is, changed hands only once) so that $V = 1$. But the same transactions could have been performed if the stock of dollars during that period was, say, $M = 24$, provided that on the average each dollar changed hands twice, so that $V = 2$. "Velocity" is not invariant with respect to the length of the period of time under observation, a fact easily verified by noting that the dimensions attached to V are (1/time).

Equation [3.8], the equation of exchange, is nothing but an identity and as such will *always* hold. It can become a theory, however, as soon as something is said about the behavior of V, the velocity of circulation. Suppose we confine ourselves to *equilibrium* situations (the meaning of "equilibrium" in this case will soon become clear). Then the simplest form of a theory about the behavior of V is that

$$V = \overline{V} \qquad [3.9]$$

that is, in equilibrium velocity is a constant. This was, with some qualifications, the initial postulate of the originators of the quantity theory of money (the classics). Velocity was, in the classical view, determined by slowly changing payment institutions and could be assumed constant. By substituting [3.9] into the equation of exchange, [3.8], we obtain

$$M\overline{V} = Py \qquad [3.10]$$

The supporters of the theory would maintain that [3.10] is no longer an identity, but is an equation, that holds in equilibrium.

Expressions [3.10] and [3.8] may look similar, but [3.10] is a **theory** and [3.8] is an identity that *must* hold. The theory expressed by [3.10] places conditions on V (it is assumed constant) as well as on y, real income. Since the classic velocity is assumed to change very slowly and real income to (ordinarily) be at the maximum level obtainable with given resources, the theory of [3.10] exhibits a prediction of a relationship between M and *nominal* income.

Specifically [3.10] predicts that in equilibrium (in the long run after all adjustments have taken place) there is a definite relationship between the stock of money (M) and nominal income ($Y = Py$). This is only one step from saying that there is a direct and proportional relationship between the stock of money and the price level if real income is constant in the long run. The merits and limitations of such a view will become apparent in Chapters 7 and 8, but now we may better understand Cantillon's quotation.

The Cambridge Form of the Quantity Theory of Money. The evolution of the classical "equation of exchange" toward a theory of the demand for money can best be traced by next analyzing the so-called Cambridge Form of the quantity theory. From the equation of exchange [3.8] we can make a small transformation to obtain

$$(M/P) \equiv (1/V)\, y$$

Define $k = (1/V)$, replace (M/P) by m, *real cash balances*, and obtain

$$m \equiv ky \qquad\qquad [3.11]$$

Obviously [3.11] is the same as [3.8], but [3.11] is expressed in a form that allows us to reinterpret velocity. In the new expression [3.11], usually called the *Cambridge equation*, the coefficient k (which is the *inverse* of velocity) is now the ratio of money to income, $k \equiv (m/y)$. The coefficient k is a measurement of money holdings related to income in either real or nominal terms since $(m/y) \equiv (M/P \div Y/P) \equiv (M/Y)$. As in the case of velocity, k, the ratio of a stock (m) to a flow (y), is not invariant with respect to the length of the period being considered.[6]

As in the case of the equation of exchange [3.8], we are, up to this point, dealing only with an identity. But (also as before) the construction becomes a theory when something is asserted about the behavior of the coefficient k. Suppose, again, that the discussion is restricted to *equilibrium* situations—situations where the actual and the desired stock of money are equal and $m = m^d$. Expression [3.11] becomes

$$m^d \equiv ky \qquad\qquad [3.12]$$

Expression [3.12] remains an identity because the coefficient k is still treated as a "residual." In order for [3.12] to become a theory of the demand for money, something must be stated about the behavior of k. The simplest thing to assert is that k is a constant, which is the same as asserting that V is a constant in the equation of exchange.

Consider the following demand for money function

$$m^d = \bar{k}y \qquad\qquad [3.13]$$

which is the classical form of the demand for money as evolved from the equation of exchange taking velocity as a constant. In the light of what we know from previous sections, there is a major shortcoming of a specification like [3.13], namely, that the quantity of real money desired by the public is independent of the cost of holding money. As we shall discover in later chapters, expression [3.13] is not a bad approximation when certain problems are considered, but it can lead to mistaken conclusions in others. Expression [3.13] states that the desired real stock of money is simply a *constant proportion* of income. Given the emphasis on the role of money as a medium of exchange in the construction from which expression [3.13] has been derived, the role of real income here is a proxy to the quantity of real goods and services produced and exchanged by the economy during a certain period. Money is held for transactions purposes, and, the higher the level of real income, the more transactions are to be made and the *higher* the amount of *real* money to be held. The fallacy in this argument is that the convenience of holding money has to be weighed against the costs of holding it; this cost is ignored in expression [3.13].

There is a second shortcoming in [3.13], although it is not as serious as the one described above. With the coefficient $k = \bar{k}$, a constant, it may be easily verified that the income elasticity of demand for real cash balances is necessarily constrained to be unity.[7] It is a remedy of these two shortcomings (particularly the first) that the modern quantity theory of money has been developed.

The Modern Quantity Theory of Money.[8] The view of contemporary expositors of the quantity theory as a theory of the demand for money is that the Cambridge Form analyzed in the previous paragraph, $m^d = ky$, is a plausible one but that the coefficient k should no longer be considered as a constant. Rather it should be considered as a function, among other things, of the cost of holding money and of the level of real income itself; $m^d = k(i, y)\, y$ where now the notation $k(\ )$ means "a function of" or "is related to" whatever is within the parenthesis $(\ )$.

The cost of holding money (the nominal interest rate) is included because, *given any level of income, the higher the nominal interest rate, the lower the desired real money stock and therefore the lower the value of k.* The dependence of the coefficient k on the level of real income cannot be asserted without some prior evidence. Whether k will rise, fall, or remain the same when the level of real income rises depends on whether the income elasticity of the demand for money is larger, lower, or equal to one (as money demand expression [3.14] indicates).

The qualification made at the beginning of this chapter (to the effect that, strictly speaking, a measurement of wealth or "permanent" income would be better than just the level of current income) also applies here. The proponents of the modern quantity theory have consistently emphasized this point.[9]

Thus the form of the demand for money

$$m^d = k(i, y) y \qquad\qquad [3.14]$$

has all the normal features discussed at the beginning of this chapter. The *interest elasticity of the demand for money*, $(\Delta m^d/m^d)/(\Delta i/i)$, reflects the "sensitivity" of the coefficient k to changes in the interest rate.[10] Since the coefficient k is the inverse of velocity (V), the modern form of the quantity theory of money may also be expressed as

$$MV(y, i) = Py$$

Velocity will be larger (as its inverse, k, is lower), the higher the interest rate.

THE KEYNESIAN THEORY OF THE DEMAND FOR MONEY— THE "LIQUIDITY TRAP"

In the midst of the Great Depression, the British economist John Maynard Keynes wrote one of the most influential pieces of economic analysis of this century, *The General Theory of Employment, Interest and Money* (1936). The Keynesian theory of the demand for money summarized in this section is the one contained in that book.[11] The resulting demand for money function is, in general, not going to be different than the ones considered earlier. There is, however, a vast difference in the reasons why the demand for money function is written in the form $m^d = L(y, i)$.

The basic approach used by Keynes in his theory of the demand for money is to distinguish among the reasons, or "motives," for holding money. The first two of these motives recognized by Keynes do not depart from previous theory, namely, the *transactions motive* and the *precautionary motive*. People hold money because money is used for transactions, and in a world of uncertainty they will take the precaution of holding a bit more than what they will normally expect to use in those transactions. Then, the part of the money stock held by the public for these two motives can be made, basically, a function of real income, which is a measurement of transactions, and perhaps, also, the rate of interest. However, we shall soon see that the interest rate effect is not really important in this case, given the third motive. Thus,

$$m_1^d = L_1(y, i)$$

where m^d denotes the real stock of money to be held in account of the transaction and the precautionary motives, y is the level of real income, i is the nominal interest rate, and L_1 means "a function of."

The third motive is really what gives a particular character to the Keynesian formulation, and it is called the *speculative motive*. The argument here, in the simplest form, goes as follows. At any point in time there is some interest rate in the market; at the same time, individuals have some idea about what the long-run or "normal" interest rate should be. At every point in time there will be some individuals who expect the interest rate to rise, some who expect it to remain at the current level, and some who expect it to fall. For those who expect the interest rate to rise, the tendency will be to borrow, that is, to sell bonds. Why? Because an expected rise in the interest rate is equivalent to an expected fall in the price of bonds, and a capital gain can be made by selling bonds today and buying them back in the future at a lower price. For those individuals expecting a future rise in the rate of interest (a fall in the price of bonds), the tendency is to "hold on" to money in the expectation of lending it in the future rather than today at a higher interest rate. The opposite will be the tendency for those expecting a fall in the rate of interest, that is, a rise in the price of bonds. In this case, a capital gain might be made by buying bonds today (lending money) and selling them in the future at a higher price.

If individuals' expectations about what is the normal level of the interest rate follow approximately what can be called a *normal distribution* (that is, few individuals expect the normal level of the interest rate to be very low or very high and most individuals expect some intermediate value), for lower and lower levels of the *current* interest rate more and more individuals will believe that the current level is "too low" and therefore will expect it to rise in the future, so that more and more individuals will be willing to "hold on" to money, planning to lend it (buy bonds) in the future. If this pattern holds, we can denote the real money stock held for "speculative" purposes by m_2^d and say that

$$m_2^d = L_2(i)$$

with the qualification that, as the nominal interest rate, i, falls, m_2^d rises as more and more individuals believe that it is too low compared to what they believe is its normal level and therefore "hold on" to money in the expectation that it will soon rise. (L_2, of course, means "a function of.") Thus there will be some level of current interest rates low enough so that most (or all) individuals will expect it to rise later. This is the celebrated *liquidity trap* that Keynes did not emphasize but that many of his disciples did. It occurs at a very low value of the current interest rate, one so low that all individuals expect it to rise in the future. These individuals will hold on to whatever quantity of money there is in the system because to them it seems much more sensible to wait and lend it in the future at a higher interest rate (or buy bonds at a lower price).

Contemplate for a moment the intuitive reasons for the existence of a liquidity trap and on the implications of such a "trap" for policy. The essential idea behind monetary policy is to "give" money to individuals (in the real world, the money is not given but "sold" in exchange for bonds or for goods and services, but the results are very much the same) so that they go out and spend it trying to restore the proportions among different assets in which they hold their wealth. In a liquidity trap situation individuals will simply accumulate new money (under their mattresses, if you wish) so that the effect is exactly as if the money had not entered the system at all.[12] Thus, if the economy were in fact in a liquidity trap situation, monetary policy would be completely ineffective.

The only way out of the dilemma would be to rely on fiscal policy. If individuals will not spend the new money introduced in the system, then the only way to increase expenditures is that government to spend directly. This is a sketchy but accurate description of the *perceived* economic conditions in the late 1930s and early 1940s.[13]

Adding together the desired real cash balances corresponding to the transaction and precautionary motives (m_1^d) and to the speculative motive (m_2^d), we obtain

$$m^d = m_1^d + m_2^d = L_1(y, i) + L_2(i) = L(i, y) \qquad [3.15]$$

That is, the desired real stock of money is, as before, a function of real income and the interest rate, but with the particular twist that at some very low level of the interest rate, the interest elasticity of the demand for money can become equal to infinity.

Figure 3–4 describes the resulting Keynesian demand for money functions, where i_0 is some interest rate so low, that any future increase of the

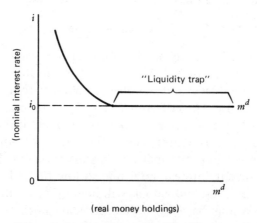

Figure 3-4. The Keynesian "liquidity trap."

stock will be willingly absorbed by money holders and kept in the form of money in the expectation of a rise in the interest rate (the liquidity trap).

CONCLUSION

In this chapter we have traced the development of several theories of the demand for money up to and including the modern version of quantity theory. The discussion has been kept at a fairly simple level, but the *concepts* are of crucial importance. These concepts provide the necessary stepping stones to an understanding of how money works in influencing important economic variables, including inflation. The next three chapters will integrate this notion of the "demand for money" into the framework of a simple but complete model of the economy.

FOOTNOTES

[1] This is, for example, the way in which judges determine compensation to be paid for an accidental loss of life.

[2] But it could. Negotiable orders of withdrawal (NOW) accounts and other "transaction accounts" can pay interest but are transferable as demand deposits (see Chapter 2).

[3] Equation [3.2] is associated with the famous contributions of the British economist John Maynard Keynes (1883–1946).

[4] An alternative would be to record all transactions; this procedure is an alternative form that yields the so-called transactions form of the equation of exchange.

[5] In particular, in our formulation it is called the *income velocity*, as opposed to the so-called *transactions velocity* that is obtained in the transactions version, where all (rather than just final) transactions are included.

[6] In the United States, under conditions of no inflation, the average holdings of money (currency plus demand deposits) have been estimated as being the equivalent of ten weeks income. If we take the year to have approximately fifty weeks, we can conclude that $V = 5$, and $k = 0.20$ on an annual basis.

[7] The income elasticity of demand for any good (including the services of money) is defined as the ratio between percentage changes in the quantity demanded (m^d) and percentage changes in income, and this ratio is always equal to unity in a demand function as [3.13].

[8] The standard exposition on this point is Friedman, "The Quantity Theory of Money—A Restatement," in M. Friedman, ed., *Studies in the Quantity Theory of Money* (Chicago, University of Chicago Press, 1956). There, the coefficient k is assumed to be a function of the expected cost of holding money relative to other assets, the level of wealth, and the ratio of human to nonhuman wealth.

[9] This *expected permanent income*, in turn, is usually measured as a weighted average of past levels of income, where the weights decline backward with time. It is assumed that the public forecasts future income by looking at past income, giving more importance to more recent past income. When current rather than expected future income is used, it can be interpreted as an assumption that the public forecasts future income only by its current level, without looking at the past. In other words, it is equivalent to an assumption that the public expects the *current* level to prevail forever.

[10] Money demand elasticity may also be expressed as

$$\eta_i = \frac{\Delta m^d/m^d}{\Delta i/i} = \frac{\Delta k/k}{\Delta i/i}$$

that is, the interest elasticity is equal to the elasticity of the coefficient k with respect to changes in the interest rate. The symbol η_i simply denotes *money demand elasticity*. In the usual graph plotting the desired real stock of money as a function of the interest rate for some given level of income (as in Figure 3–3b), the magnitude of this elasticity measures the response of the desired stock of money to changes in the nominal interest rate. In general, the greater this response, the "flatter" the curve and the lower the response to interest rate charges, the "steeper" the money demand curve. In the particular case of the original Cambridge Form of the demand for money with k constant, $\eta = 0$, and the curve is a vertical line.

Income elasticity of money demand may also be analyzed. The "income elasticity" of the demand for real cash balances, $(\Delta m^d/m^d)/(y/y)$ or η_y, is given by

$$\eta_y = \frac{\Delta m^d/m^d}{\Delta y/y} = 1 + \frac{\Delta k/k}{\Delta y/y}$$

that is, one plus the elasticity of the coefficient k with respect to changes in real income. In the original Cambridge Form, with k constant, the second term is zero so that $\eta_y = 1$.

[11] Before the *General Theory* (1936) the writings of Keynes were very much within the classical tradition.

[12] In the Keynesian system it is assumed that the alternative for individuals is to hold either money or bonds. In other words, any excess of actual over desired real cash balances

is resolved by purchasing bonds. Purchasing bonds tends to lower the interest rate and increase expenditures in a particular type of goods-investment goods. In the classical system, the other extreme position is taken: any excess of actual over desired real cash balances is resolved by buying goods and services. The liquidity trap equivalent for this last case would be a situation in which individuals expect the price of goods and services (rather than the price of bonds) to fall in the future, so that they may receive and hold money but postpone their expenditures in goods and services, expecting prices to be lower in the near future.

[13] An interesting fact, historically, is that for several years economists took it for granted that during the Great Depression the economy was indeed experiencing a liquidity trap and that monetary policy over the period was ineffective. Later, more careful research investigated the evidence and found that during those years the Federal Reserve System (in charge of controlling the stock of nominal money) followed a contractionary or only a midly expansionary monetary policy—just the opposite what it should have in the circumstances prevailing at the time. At the same time, no carefully executed empirical study has been able to detect a liquidity trap in the demand for money. Both circumstances appear to redeem monetary policy, and today it is considered a very powerful (although sometimes dangerous) instrument for stabilization purposes. We shall return to these important points in future chapters.

KEY CONCEPTS

demand for money (desired real stock of money)

wealth (nominal and real)

assets
   real assets
   financial assets
   money

stock of money held by an individual

costs of holding money
   opportunity cost
   inflation

income elasticity of demand

quantity theory of money
   equation of exchange
   Cambridge equation
   modern quantity theory

velocity of circulation

Keynesian theory of the demand for money

money demand elasticity
   transaction motive
   precautionary motive
   speculative motive
   liquidity trap

QUESTIONS FOR DISCUSSION

1. Why will an individual not choose to hold his wealth all in money? What about holding all of his wealth in real or financial assets?

2. When determining the stock of money held by an individual, why do we refer to average holdings? Why is an average figure not necessary when we speak of the stock of money for *all* individuals?

3. Outline the differences between the old quantity theory of money, the new quantity theory of money, and the Cambridge version of the quantity theory.

4. Explain why the demand for money depends (a) on income and (b) on the interest rate.

5. Using the table below, find velocity (*V*).

(a)

Transaction Number	Beers Exchanged	Price
1	6	0.50
2	3	1.00
3	4	0.75
4	7	0.60
5	2	1.25

$V = ?$

(b) After long-run adjustments have occurred and the velocity found in (a) is assumed constant, the stock of money increases. What will the effect be upon the right side of equation (3.10)? What does this mean for the economy?

6. An individual wishes to maintain desired holdings at some real level. The desired level is $145, the price level is currently $156. How much must the individual have added since the base year of the price index? What are nominal holdings?

7. Draw a demand curve for the services of money. Show graphically what will happen when the nominal interest rate declines from 13% to 10%. What will happen when this individual's income decreases?

8. For an increase in income, what will be the difference between a high and a low income elasticity of demand for the services of money? Show this graphically.

PART II

MONETARY THEORY
A Modern Approach to Income, Employment, and Inflation

CHAPTER 4

BASIC MONETARY PROPOSITIONS: Classical, Keynesian, and Monetarist

The quantity theory of money discussed in Chapter 3 provided economists with a simple but powerful tool of analysis for over two hundred years. Classical and neoclassical economists, from the philosophers David Hume (1711–1776), John Locke (1632–1704), and Richard Cantillon (1680–1734) to the twentieth century economists Irving Fisher (1867–1947) and A. C. Pigou (1877–1959) derived, with that simple tool, some very perceptive long-run and short-run propositions. These classical propositions have been reworked, redefined, and reinterpreted over many years. Many of these modified short-run propositions are currently the basis for the methods and policy recommendations of an important group of economists, the so-called *Monetarists*.

Chapter 4 provides a brief and elementary account of some of those classical propositions. In the first section the long run is discussed, wherein the classical writers established elementary principles that are even today central to much of monetary economics. Next, the short-run or the adjustment process, is analyzed. In dealing with the short run, problems arise with respect to the ability of the economy to adjust automatically to a full employment of productive resources. It is precisely the questioning of this *automatic mechanism* that brought about the so-called Keynesian revolution in the 1930s and led to the development of what we call "the modern analysis." The chapter is concluded with an account of the Keynesian critique so that we can understand the motivations behind the modern analysis, which is the subject of Chapter 5.

The word classicals should be interpreted in a very comprehensive, general way. By classicals, and sometimes neoclassicals, we mean the writers who, from the very beginning of economic analysis through the 1930s, contributed to the building blocks of what, by then, was the conventional wisdom of macroeconomics. It is not that such conventional wisdom was without its critics, but just before the 1930s it could indeed be said that a certain body of received doctrine was widely accepted by academicians and policymakers alike. The very architect of the revolution of that time, John Maynard Keynes, was a prestigious recipient and expositor of the classical tradition before breaking with it.

THE CLASSICAL ANALYSIS OF THE LONG RUN

Classical economists excelled at analyzing the very long run, that is, a "run" or conceptual time period long enough for all adjustments in the economy—prices, labor supply, output and so forth—to have taken place. Indeed, some classical propositions survive as the cornerstone of monetary economics when prices are perfectly flexible in the long run.

Classical economic analysis made a definite separation between particular markets (for example, for shoes, for beer, or for credit), and the forces determining the general price level, that is, an index of the prices of all commodities in terms of money. On one side, *real* forces of supply and demand in each and all individual markets would determine relative prices; on the other side, very different forces would determine the general price level, and here the quantity theory of money was called into play.[1] Not only would real, as opposed to *monetary*, forces determine relative prices among all commodities, but also, in the long run, real forces would determine the total level of output (real income) and the interest rate. Relative prices, except for occasional, short-lived deviation, would be determined by a level at which all factors of production, and particularly labor, are fully employed, in the sense that their markets would be in equilibrium. Take, for example, the market for labor, with a demand for labor by business firms and a supply of labor, both depending, among other things, on the real wage rate. The real wage rate, as opposed to the nominal (or money) wage rate, is simply the money wage divided by an index of the price level. If there is unemployment, the nominal wage rate would fall (and, initially, so would the real wage) and it would continue to decline until workers are no longer unemployed. Whether such an increase in production and output would bring about a corresponding increase in aggregate demand for goods and services depends on another further assumption.

The interest rate also depends on real considerations. Because the interest rate is simply the "price" in the market for lending and borrowing, it would be determined by the equilibrium in that market, the supply and demand for credit. These, in turn, are given by the public's taste for thrift (the extent to which consumption today is preferred to consumption tomorrow), and by the so-called *marginal productivity of capital*, that is, how much it will pay businessmen and others to invest instead of consuming.

Separation of the determination of relative prices, or the real part of the economy, and the determination of the general price level, or the monetary part, is called the *classical dichotomy* by economists. If in the long run this separation is valid, then several propositions follow. The first is that in the long run the *nominal money stock* does not matter. Money is only a "veil," or in Hume's words "not the wheel but the lubricant of trade."

The second proposition (which is really implied by the first one), is that in the long run the general price level is determined by the nominal quantity of money. Consider any of the versions of the quantity theory presented in Chapter 3, for example, equation [4.1].

$$M \cdot V = P \cdot y \qquad\qquad [4.1]$$

Even if velocity (V), in expression [3.14], depends on the level of real income and on the interest rate, these two real magnitudes do not change in the long run. Velocity will remain the same in the long run and will be independent of the nominal money stock (M). The only item that will change in the quantity theory expression when M changes is the general level of prices (P). If M, the money stock, rises by 5 percent, prices will also rise by 5 percent; if M doubles, P will also double. None of the real magnitudes changes and neither does the real stock of money, M/P in the long-run formulation of the quantity theory of money.

Alternatively, the same conclusion may be reached by considering the demand for money equation. The *desired real money stock* is equal to the actual stock in the long run, or

$$M/P = k(y, r) \cdot y \qquad\qquad [4.2]$$

If the right-hand side does not change in the long run (because real income, y, and the real interest rate, r, are determined by real forces), then the left-hand side cannot change in the long run. The result is obtained when proportional changes in the nominal money stock are matched by equal and proportional changes in the level of prices.

These two propositions are often summarized in a general dictum: in the long run money (the nominal money stock, that is) is *neutral.*[2] It does not matter how many pieces of paper (dollars, in the case of the United States) are in circulation: the only difference that the quantity of that paper will make is that each quantity will correspond to a different price level. In this case, "the price level" includes the price of everything, including wages, salaries, nominal value of physical and financial assets, and so on.

The rationale behind the neutrality proposition may become clearer after the following conceptual experiment. Suppose that one night the prices of all things, as well as the nominal money stock in the economy, double: if an individual had 20 dollars in bills at night, the next morning he or she would have 40 dollars in bills; if the individual's salary (the price of labor services) was 200 dollars a week, it would now be 400 dollars a week. If the market price of the person's used car was 600 dollars, it is now 1,200 dollars. After such a change nothing has actually changed in *real* terms: the real value of the individual's wealth (including money holdings) is the same as before in terms of its real purchasing power; that is, the *real* value of his salary is the same, and so on.

The conceptual experiment assumed a simultaneous change in *both* the nominal money stock and the price level, both in the same proportion. The classical experiment by which the long-run neutrality of money was investigated consisted, instead, of imagining a once-and-for-all change in the nominal money stock. Proportional change in the price level was in this case the *outcome* of market forces, and the manner in which it takes place is discussed in detail later in this chapter.

Because the idea of changing prices and the nominal money stock overnight appears rather artificial, it is interesting to note that many real historical episodes have essentially duplicated such an experiment. These are the so-called "monetary reforms" that took place in several European and Latin American countries in the present century.[3]

A *monetary reform* is simply a change in the monetary unit, usually a transformation such that the new monetary unit is worth some multiple of ten units of the old one. Invariably such reforms take place after prolonged periods of severe price inflation, where prices have been rising so much that they end up being at very high levels. The purpose of a monetary reform is simply to facilitate transactions, both from the physical viewpoint of not having to carry so many pieces of paper, and from the accounting viewpoint of not having to insert so many zeros in records and calculations.[4] In France, for example, such a reform took place on January 1, 1960; before that date, a cheese sandwich was priced at about 800 francs. The government announced that starting in 1960, 100 "old" francs would be worth only one "new" franc. Naturally, the manner in which the Central Bank of France could assure this equivalence was by exchanging 100 units of the old money for one unit of the new one. At the same time, all legal contracts and documents were to be written in terms of the new monetary unit. Everyone understood, of course, that the result would immediately be for prices quoted in terms of the new unit to decrease by a factor of one hundred. The old francs circulated for some time until people got accustomed to the new system, with merchants quoting prices in terms of the two monetary units. The cheese sandwich was now priced at 8 new francs, or 800 old francs. A few months later all of the old money had been replaced, there was no room for misunderstanding, and everyone spoke simply of "francs." Nothing had changed in the economy other than the nominal money stock and the level of all prices, both in the same proportion.

The classical proposition of neutrality carries with it the theory that the general price level is determined by the nominal money stock. The classical economists were well aware that price response in the economy was not instantaneous and that, during the adjustment process, redistribution effects would occur and many real magnitudes could change. Let us consider the adjustment process in greater detail.

THE CLASSICAL ADJUSTMENT PROCESS AND THE LEVEL OF REAL OUTPUT AND EMPLOYMENT

The manner in which changes in the money stock are translated into changes in prices in the classical world can be explained in rather simple terms. However, implicit mechanisms in this adjustment process are of significance not only for the experiment, but also for some other far-reaching propositions.

Assume an initial situation where all markets are in equilibrium and where the public is holding their desired real stock of money. Suppose, additionally, that all resources in the economy are fully employed. As before, assume that overnight the nominal money stock is doubled, so that the following morning everybody finds twice as many dollar bills as he or she had the previous night. After such a change, the real money stock has immediately doubled because prices are exactly what they were before. Everyone feels, and indeed is for the moment, "richer," but the cash recipients are in disequilibrium—they hold too much of their wealth in the form of money. Faster or slower, individuals will try to convert this increase in wealth (which they have received in the form of money) into other forms (consumption and durable goods, financial assets, and so on). In other words, individuals will *increase their expenditures* on all kinds of things,[5] in spite of the fact that resources are fully employed.

Producers of most items will face an increase in the demand for their products, and they may try to increase production to meet the additional demand. Indeed, for a short time and to a limited extent, they might be able to do so. For some time, for example, workers may be willing to work overtime or machines can be used for an extra "shift." But increases in demand will bring about an increase in wages, as producers compete among each other for a larger amount of inputs that are in fixed supply and cannot be permanently increased. The result is that prices must rise in order to allocate the supply of commodities among competing demanders.

The increase in prices, in turn, will lower the *real* value of the larger nominal money stock, and this step in turn will *decrease* expenditures. The increase in prices will continue for as long as total demand for commodities (expenditures) exceeds output produced; that is, for as long as there is excess demand, the real money stock and with it the level of expenditures will continue to fall. The end of the process is predictable: a fall of the real money stock back to its initial level, an increase in prices and wages by the same proportion as the initial increase in the nominal money stock, and a final level of production equal to the exact level before the change.

Although this is basically a simple process, it includes some **subtleties**. The adjustment process involves a chain of cause and effect that goes from **real** money stock changes to a change in individual's expenditures, and from this **to** a change in prices. A change in prices means, in turn, a change in the **real** money stock, so that from there on the "cycle" repeats itself. The two **links** (a) between changes in the real money stock and changes in the level of expenditures, and (b) between changes in expenditures and changes in prices **are** very important, especially relationship (a). Much of past and present controversy among economists concerning macroeconomic and monetary theory and policy centers around these links. These matters will emerge in a number **of** later chapters.

In the first conceptual experiment, the response to an initial change in the real money stock brought about by a change in the nominal money stock was investigated. But this closed loop of cause and effect suggests that other experiments could be performed. For example, imagine what would happen if overnight, starting from an equilibrium situation, everyone decides to hold a *larger real money stock.* Individuals will, for some time, spend less than their income, so that over a certain period of time they may accumulate cash balances and, in the future, reach their goal of a higher real stock. Under these circumstances expenditures fall short of income, and producers of most goods and services find that the demand for their products has fallen and that inventories begin to pile up. What would producers do? They could lower their prices, and/ or reduce production, by laying off workers. In the latter case unemployment begins to rise and wages would start to fall. Falling wages mean lower costs of production and lower prices. The fall in prices would increase the real value of the existing nominal money stock and this process would, in turn, tend to increase expenditures. The fall in wages and prices (and the resulting increase in the real money stock and in expenditures) would continue for as long as output falls short of full employment output. Again, the bottom line is predictable: a final situation of full employment with a lower level of wages and prices, the same nominal money stock (which is unchanged throughout the process), but a higher real money stock as desired by money holders. The initial decline in expenditures, after some short-lived adjustment pains, has worked itself out with no lasting consequences on the level of economic activity and employment.

In this second experiment we should pay special attention not only to the link between the real stock of money and expenditures, but also to the manner in which the level of employment and output is kept (except for possible transitory fluctuations) at the full employment level. The essential assumption here is that wages and prices are completely flexible in both directions, up and down. (The validity of this assumption will be considered later in this chapter.)

We should note an additional point in connection with the dependence of expenditures on the real stock of money. The real money stock might change either because the nominal stock changes (a policy that, at least in principle, government decides), or because the price level changes (an occurrence that no one individually decides, but which is the outcome of market activity). Thus presumption that the real money stock influences people's expenditures suggests two possible and important conclusions: first, that there is an *automatic mechanism* for adjusting the economic system to equilibrium (that is, changes in the level of prices); second, that whenever changes in prices do not take place changes in the stock of nominal money might substitute for price changes in restoring full employment equilibrium. The second implication opens the possibility for active, *compensatory monetary policy*, that is, monetary control by an authority such as the Federal Reserve System in the United States in order to affect employment, output, and inflation. Policy matters will be discussed in detail in later chapters, especially Chapters 10 through 16. Analysis of the first proposition will be expanded in Chapters 5 and 6, but first it is instructive to understand how, over forty years ago, a very influential economist argued that the automatic equilibrating forces in the economy would not work.

THE KEYNESIAN REVOLUTION

The elementary description of the last section was very much at the heart of macroeconomics by the early 1930s. It is not that there were no dissonant voices up to that time; nor was it the case that the classical writers were naïve fools. Rather the above description is simply a synopsis of a detailed analysis that was subjected to rigorous polishing over a long period of time. Real world events have always influenced economic theory, but in the 1930s, these events became too dramatic for economists to ignore. In 1929 the percentage of the total labor force unemployed was 3.2 (a very acceptable figure); two years later, it was 16 percent, while the consumer price index had fallen by 10 percent in comparison with 1929. Four years later, in 1933, while prices were 25 percent lower than in 1929, *one quarter* of the labor force was unemployed; about 13 million people were willing to work but were unable to find jobs. By contemporary standards, a similar *percentage* of unemployment would mean about 25 million persons out of work. As late as 1939 almost 10 million people (17 percent of the labor force) were unemployed. Similar figures were commonplace in much of the rest of the Western world.

Whether the persistent recession was the result of the lack of a self-adjusting mechanism (a slap on the face to classical thinkers) or whether it was the result of mismanagement by monetary authorities, everyone was ready for

a change.[6] The change came at the hand of an already prestigious British economist brought up in the best of the classical tradition, John Maynard Keynes.
Keynes was born in 1883 and, until his death in 1946, he was a man of many
interests—one of those fortunate individuals who excel effortlessly at almost
everything they do. From an aristocratic family, he was educated at Eton and
at Cambridge, where he later taught. He was a civil servant and an influential
policy adviser; he even wrote a highly appraised work on the theory of probability and was successful at making a fortune by speculating in foreign exchanges. He patronized the arts (to the rather practical extent of marrying a
prima ballerina), and was the editor for 34 years of the most prestigious professional economic journal in Europe. His work made him the most influential
economist of the twentieth century, at least in terms of policy prescriptions.

The advent of the *Keynesian revolution* may be marked by the publication of Keynes' book *The General Theory of Employment, Interest and Money*
in 1936. (In the last twenty years much of the "new macroeconomics" of
Keynes, and especially the macroeconomics of his followers, has in turn come
under attack. As with all revolutions, the Keynesian revolution inspired a
counterrevolution, by a group now called the Monetarists.) There is no doubt
that the *General Theory* forced a reexamination and a reappraisal of all of the
basic tenets of the classical system. Whether one accepts Keynes' ideas or not,
they present a grave challenge to orthodox concepts.

What was the Keynesian revolution all about? The *General Theory* is a
rather complex book and, in fact, much of its meaning is still open to controversy and interpretation. For our purposes, however, only two points are necessary for discussion.

First, and perhaps less important for the viewpoint of the methodology,
there was a denial that, at least in the short run, wages (and therefore prices)
are flexible in the downward direction. Workers, in the scenario of the *General
Theory*, would not "accept" lower nominal wages even if, at the same time,
prices fell and caused their real wages to remain unchanged. Their refusal
may be caused either by the presence of labor unions, or by workers' "money
illusion," or both. If nominal wages cannot fall, then prices will not fall either,
circumstances creating the possibility for the automatic tendency toward full
employment not to operate, at least not in the short run. The assumption
of wage and price rigidity, and of adjustments taking the form of changes in
real income instead, has come to be a standard feature of much of the Keynesian
analysis. A prominent monetarist has recently interpreted this assumption as
being the main difference between classical and Keynesian analysis.[7] But this
possibility, if wages and prices are assumed to be inflexible, is a conclusion that
would also follow from classical macroeconomics, except perhaps for a question of emphasis.

A more substantial proposition from the Keynesian revolution is the proposition that, even if wages and prices are completely flexible, so that they could therefore fall in the presence of unemployment (as, in fact, they did in the 1930s), an increase in the real value of the money stock (under certain circumstances) would not have the effect of increasing the level of expenditures, so that a state of *chronic unemployment* can persist.

The latter proposition has far-reaching implications. On one hand, it means that the *automatic mechanism* for ensuring that expenditures will reach a level associated with full employment will simply not work. (A fall in prices would increase the real money stock, but an increase in the real money stock would not influence expenditures.) On the other hand, the proposition implies that changes in the nominal money stock (the other manner in which the real money stock can change) would not be successful at inducing an increase in expenditures. That is, there are here twin propositions, both the result of the same reasoning: (1) the economic system will not adjust automatically to a full employment equilibrium, and (2) changes in the nominal quantity of money (that is, monetary policy) will be ineffective at influencing the level of demand in order to bring about such an equilibrium.

What can the government do in order to increase expenditures in the face of unemployment, so that producers would be induced to increase employment and output? The only option left is that government *spend directly*, that is, undertake *fiscal policy*. This was the practical message of Keynesianism during the late 1930s, and the rationale behind most macroeconomic policy measures of the post-World War II era in the United States.

Finally, Keynes' theory of the determination of the interest rate departed substantially from established wisdom. In Keynes' view, in the short run, the interest rate was determined solely by the demand for money and the existing money stock. The interest rate is, in the short run, a purely monetary phenomenon. This *liquidity preference* theory of interest is of tremendous importance for the analysis of disequilibrium and for the short-run effects of monetary and fiscal policies. It will be featured and analyzed at length in Chapters 5 and 6.

THE MONETARIST COUNTERREVOLUTION

Keynesian theories and policy prescriptions become widely and quickly accepted and were soon considered the conventional wisdom. Managing the money stock was *not* important for stabilization purposes in this view, and active fiscal policy was the cure for departures from full employment. But in some quarters Keynesianism was not quite accepted, and the early 1950s saw the beginning of what today is called Monetarism, usually associated with (but not restricted to) Milton Friedman and The University of Chicago. If a benchmark is to be set, perhaps the publication of the *Studies in the Quantity*

Theory of Money in 1956 may be used as the formal beginning of the monetarist counterrevolution.

The nature of Monetarism and how it compares to Keynesianism has been the subject of an endless series of technical, and not-so-technical, works since the 1950s. Agreement on these matters by either the main participants or their interpreters has not been reached. It is enough to report, for example, that in 1970 and 1971 two important papers by Friedman, intended to spell out basic differences and to formulate a common framework, were followed by invited criticisms by some of the most prominent Keynesians. The exchange of views aroused more disagreement than consensus.[8]

In short, Monetarism is a return to a reinterpretation of, and a refinement of, much of the pre-Keynesian monetary economics. A good example of this reworking of the old theory is the new formulation of the quantity theory as a theory of the demand for money, which was analyzed in Chapter 3. At the Monetarist policy level, the emphasis is that monetary rather than fiscal policy is effective in controlling economic fluctuations. Chapter 14 will discuss and analyze many of these issues.

CONCLUSION

After a revolution and a counterrevolution, synthesis follows, and while extreme versions of both approaches may be found today, much cross-breeding has taken place. In Chapters 5 and 6, a coherent method of analysis general enough to accommodate differences within, and even the polar extremes, of both Keynesian and Monetarist approaches will be presented. Much of the controversy concerns technicalities that do not matter for general theoretical conclusions on which most, if not all, economists today agree.

FOOTNOTES

[1] Of course, in a monetary economy all prices are *quoted* in terms of money. But when, say, the market for shoes determines a certain price of shoes in terms of money, what it has really determined is the price of shoes relative to all commodities included in the general price index. If all prices change in the same proportion, say by 10 percent, both the money price of shoes and the general price index change by 10 percent, but the price of shoes relative to all commodities will remain the same as before.

[2] Claiming that "money is neutral" is very different from saying that "money does not matter." The latter expression is often used to mean that in the short run monetary policy is not an effective stabilization tool.

[3] Among them, France and Italy not so long ago, and Germany before World War II. In South America (Argentina, Brazil, and Chile), several monetary reforms took place during the 1960s.

[4] This is really the only immediate purpose. Besides, these monetary reforms are often

undertaken at the beginning of stabilization programs, in which case they are linked to an effort to stop or diminish the rate of price increase.

[5] During this process, in which individuals increase their demand for everything (including financial assets), the increase in lending will put downward pressure on the interest rate, stimulating expenditures on capital goods. This "indirect" mechanism, first described by the British banker Henry Thornton in 1802,

implied that, in the short run, the interest rate would also depend on monetary, and not only "real," conditions.

[6] Chapter 16 discusses some interpretations of the real causes of the depression.

[7] Milton Friedman's contention has not been accepted by the Keynesians.

[8] See *Milton Friedman's Monetary Framework. A Debate with his Critics*, edited by Robert J. Gordon (Chicago: The University of Chicago Press, 1974).

KEY CONCEPTS

long-run economic phenomena

short-run economic phenomena

classicals (neoclassicals)

marginal productivity of capital

classical dichotomy

relative and real prices

"neutral" money

monetary reform

adjustment process
  automatic mechanism
  links in adjustment process

Keynesians

monetarists

fiscal policy

QUESTIONS FOR DISCUSSION

1. Why do you think there is a preoccupation with short-run mechanisms in government? Why would Congress and the President implicitly pursue a policy known to be inflationary?

2. The monetary authority has contracted (decreased) the money supply. Compare the possible chain of events for the Keynesians and the Classicals.

3. Using the table below, determine whether real or nominal, prices have changed.

	P_x	P_y	P_z
Year 1	10	8	20
Year 2	11	8.8	22

CHAPTER 5

THE MODERN ANALYSIS OF EXPENDITURES, INCOME, AND PRICES (I) Expenditures

In Chapters 5 and 6 the modern analysis of expenditures, income, and prices will be presented and the role of money and of monetary policy in the economy will be investigated. In Chapter 5 we are concerned with the determinants of total expenditures and with being able to summarize this important concept with a very general expression. In Chapter 6 we can then use this expression to discuss not only the effects of changes in the quantity of money (monetary policy) and in the level of government expenditures (fiscal policy), but also to characterize some contemporary conflicting views on how the economy works, and what to do when it misbehaves.

We call this analysis modern in a very specific sense: it is a synthesis of the revolution in macroeconomics that started in 1936 with the work of Keynes and has incorporated important developments that took place later. The controversy between Keynesians and Monetarists mentioned in Chapter 4 will reappear often in this book. The framework that we present in Chapters 5 and 6 will be useful in providing a general scenario with which to understand why Keynesians and Monetarists hold different views concerning the working of the economy and the role of monetary and fiscal policies. Chapters 5 and 6, in other words, will examine the implicit assumptions behind those views. Later on, in Chapter 14, the controversy will be reexamined as will other important differences concerning less abstract, more practical issues related to the implementation of policy. It will be shown there that the Keynesian–Monetarist policy views are built upon general, but contrasting, political philosophies concerning the role of government in economic affairs.

Several clarifications are in order before we turn to the simple macro-economic model of the system. *Monetary policy* and *fiscal policy* or simply "policy" are, for now at least, general terms meaning alterations (increases or decreases) in the money stock or in aggregate tax and spending (budget) policies or changes in both. The *manner* in which these changes are effected and the *institutions* through which they work are the subjects of Chapters 9 through 14. Mechanisms of the Federal Reserve System, which conducts monetary policy in the United States as well as the fiscal policies of public finance, are discussed in these chapters. For the present discussion and that of Chapters 6, 7, and 8, simply keep in mind the fact that monetary policy means "changing the money stock" and fiscal policy means "changing government expenditures" and/or taxes.

A SIMPLE MODEL OF THE ECONOMIC SYSTEM: SECTORS AND MARKETS

Figure 5-1 shows a simple but comprehensive scheme of the functioning of a monetary economy with a financial market. Notwithstanding its simplicity, such a map is useful for visualizing the interaction of magnitudes such as income, expenditures, and consumption, and also for understanding the conditions under which the economic system is said to be *in equilibrium*.

There are three *sectors:* households, business firms, and government; and three *markets:* the market for commodities, the market for loanable funds (that is, for borrowing and lending), and the market for factors of production. For simplicity, it is assumed that only households hold money, and, further, that there are no taxes on households and businesses.

First, observe the arrows connecting these sectors and start with *households.* Households sell factors of production (mostly the services of labor, but

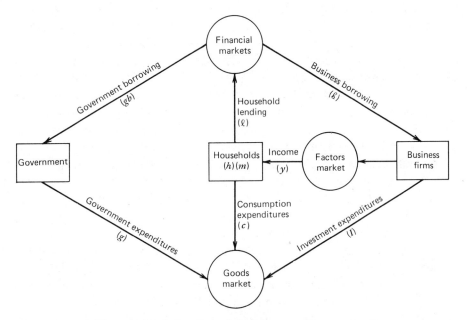

Figure 5-1. A simple model of the monetary economy.

also the services of physical capital) to business firms and, in exchange, receive a total payment, per period, equal to the value of the flow of production during the same period. This flow is necessary if payments to *all* factors of production are to be accounted for (including dividends, or business profits).[1] We call this *income*, and use the letter y as its symbol when income is expressed in real terms. In this simple framework, of course, income in real terms is also *output*.

With their flow of real income, households may dispose of their income in three ways: they spend part of it on *consumption goods* (which in real terms is denoted by c), they lend part of it (denoted by the symbol ℓ, in real terms), and they may keep it in order to increase their holdings of money (that is, they hoard it, designated by h). To stress the connection between these flows of income, consumption, lending, and hoarding by households, and also the fact that in a monetary economy all of these flows take a monetary form, there is a box for the household sector containing the letter m (the symbol for real money stock). Such a box may be visualized as a pool of water; income, which is received in the form of money, is analogous to a faucet that increases the water in the pool. Consumption and lending, which also take place through monetary payments, are outlets in the pool which decrease the stock of water. Obviously, the difference between the rate at which the stock of water is being increased through income and the rate at which it is being decreased through consumption and lending is the net rate at which the water in the pool is rising (hoarding) or falling (dishoarding, or negative hoarding). From the viewpoint of the effect of these flows generated by households on the various markets, we say that households supply factors of production (in the market for factors of production), demand consumption commodities in the market for goods and services, and supply funds in the market for loanable funds.[2]

Look now at the second sector, *business firms*. Business firms pay to factors of production (households) an amount equivalent to the real value of production (y). They receive, from their sale of finished products in the commodities market, an amount equal to the total spent by households (consumption), and by the third sector, government (the letter g is used for government expenditures in real terms). They also receive payment, and pay, for the purchases of investment goods (I, in real terms), and do so by financing those purchases through borrowing in the loanable funds market (ℓ is the symbol for borrowing).[3]

Finally, let us turn to the third and last sector, *government*. Through the analysis, it is assumed that government expenditures are entirely financed by borrowing (gb, for "government borrowing," in real terms). Of course, we all know that in the real world this is not necessarily so: most government expenditures, in fact, are financed via taxation, and sometimes just by printing money. (For simplicity, taxes are assumed to be nonexistent.) Besides most of the discussion among economists about the effects of changes in the level of government expenditures assumes that those expenditures are indeed financed by borrowing. Government, then, receives a flow gb per period, equal to the flow of their expenditures in the commodities market, g.

These matters may be summarized by the *budget constraints* of the three sectors involved (households, firms, and government) in the following manner:

$$y = c + \ell + h \qquad\qquad\qquad [5.1]$$

$$I = \ell \qquad\qquad\qquad [5.2]$$

$$g = gb \qquad\qquad\qquad [5.3]$$

Expression [5.1] indicates that households' income must be equal to the sum of their consumption, their lending, and their accumulation of real cash balances. Expression [5.2] argues that business firms will borrow at a rate equal to their desired investment, and expression [5.3] says that government expenditure is financed exclusively through borrowing from the public.

The linkages between these sectors have been discussed. Let us now examine each market. In the *commodities market* the total demand for commodities (or "total expenditures") is made up of consumption (demand by households), investment (demand by firms), and government expenditures (demand by government). For the market for commodities to be in equilibrium, total demand or expenditures must be equal to the amount of output being produced by the economy, that is,

$$y = c + I + g \qquad\qquad\qquad [5.4]$$

Notice that this expression [5.4] is not an identity (that would always be true) but an equilibrium condition that *may or may not* hold in the short run. What would happen if the commodities market is not in equilibrium? If total expenditures fall short of output (that is, if there is "excess supply" of commodities), business firms will be accumulating inventories. If, instead, the flow of expenditures is larger than the flow of output or income (that is, if there is "excess demand" for commodities), then inventories will be decreasing.

What about the *financial market?* The demand for loanable funds is made up of funds demanded by business firms (ℓ) and by government (gb). The supply of loanable funds is given by the flow of lending on the part of households (ℓ). For equilibrium in this market, then, expression [5.5] is required

$$\ell + gb = \ell \qquad\qquad\qquad [5.5]$$

where the left-hand side is the demand for loanable funds, and the right-hand side the supply of loanable funds.

For the time being the third market, or the market for factors of production, will be ignored. At this point it is enough to say that for that market to be in equilibrium the supply of factors of production (mostly labor) must equal the demand for those factors by business firms. The market for factors is neglected now because it relates to the conditions determining the total supply of commodities in the economy and, in the present chapter, the determinants of total demand or expenditures are of primary concern.

From the viewpoint of expenditures, the conditions that must be met in equilibrium are important. Real cash balances must be at a stationary value, neither rising nor falling; that is, hoarding must be zero, or

$$h = 0 \qquad\qquad [5.6]$$

Expressions [5.4], [5.5], and [5.6] are then conditions for equilibrium. By using the identities provided by the three budget constraints, [5.1], [5.2], and [5.3], we can write these conditions in an equivalent, but more interesting form, as

$$y = c + I + g \qquad\qquad [5.4']$$

$$y = c + I + g + h \qquad\qquad [5.5']$$

$$h = 0 \qquad\qquad [5.6']$$

These three expressions are, again, the equilibrium conditions given before. The first is identical to the previous expression [5.4], and so is the third, [5.6']. We can write the second one, [5.5'], or the equilibrium condition for the loanable funds market, in a different way by using the three budget constraints. The interesting thing about writing the equilibrium conditions in this manner is that it becomes apparent that, for the long-run analysis, we can drop any one of them. *When any two of them holds, the third also holds.* In other words, if both the commodities and the financial markets are in equilibrium, it will also happen that hoarding will be zero. Or, if hoarding is zero and there is equilibrium in the market for commodities, the market for loanable funds will also be in equilibrium. This is obviously an extremely useful feature for macroeconomic and monetary analysis.

Given the manner in which all three sectors are connected in this simple economy, and the conditions that may be expected to hold when the system is in equilibrium, we need to analyze the context within which all of these people (consumers, investors, and producers) make decisions. We have already discussed one important theory about people's behavior at length. The theory of the demand for money (Chapter 4) revealed something about the conditions for the public to be holding their desired real money stock and, presumably, for not intending to hoard or dishoard. Two others must now be analyzed: how households determine their level of consumption, and how business firms determine their desired level of investment.

THE COMPONENTS OF TOTAL EXPENDITURES:
CONSUMPTION AND INVESTMENT

As mentioned before, in this chapter we are primarily concerned with the question of what determines total expenditures. The three components of total expenditures are consumption expenditures (by households), investment expenditures (by business firms), and government expenditures. The latter, which is determined by policy, is sometimes called *an exogenous variable:* the level of government expenditures is whatever government decides it will be. We are left with the other two components, and a very brief account of how these two magnitudes are determined is necessary. Begin by considering households and their expenditures on consumption goods.

CONSUMPTION EXPENDITURES

What are the determinants of household expenditures on consumption goods during a certain period? The answer to the question may be complex and even controversial, but at a level sufficient for this discussion one component may be singled out—the level of income. That is, real consumption at some period will depend on the level of real income at that same period.

Of course, other obvious magnitudes will influence the level of consumption. In particular, any theory of consumption expenditures cannot ignore the role of the interest rate. Since the interest rate is essentially the real relative price of current versus future consumption, it must play a role in the decision of whether to consume today or lend and postpone consumption until later. In particular, a high interest rate means a relatively high level of future consumption that an individual is giving up every time he or she decides to consume today. Then one would expect that, for the same level of income and of the other variables involved, a higher interest rate would bring about a lower level of (present) consumption. In spite of the clear influence of interest upon consumption, this dependence of consumption on the rate of interest will be ignored. None of the important conclusions is changed in any significant way if we do so.

We should note another important factor concerning the exclusive dependence of present consumption on the level of present or current income. The *shorter* the period to which the analysis refers, the less sense it makes to say that consumption during the period will be independent of the income that individuals expect to receive at later periods. In other words, it makes more sense to say that consumption at some period depends not only on the level of income at the same period (current income) but also on the future path of the stream of income that individuals expect to receive in the future. This is the so-called *permanent income hypothesis* (invented by US economist Milton

Friedman), in which permanent income refers to some measurement of the permanent income stream that individuals expect to receive in the future. By saying that current consumption depends only on current income we must assume, implicitly, that individuals consider their current income as a good predictor of what their future, permanent income will be.

After these qualifications, we can then return to the simplest hypothesis. This simple hypothesis indicates, once again, that consumption in any period will depend on income at the same period. As income rises, consumption rises, and vice versa, but if income rises consumption will rise by less than income, and if income falls consumption will fall also by less than income. The so-called *marginal propensity to consume*, or ratio of changes in consumption to changes in income, is positive but less than one. We can write the simplest form of such a relationship—the consumption function—as

$$c = \bar{c} + c_y y \tag{5.7}$$

Notice that expression [5.7] is a linear relationship—the simplest expression that can be used. In this relationship, consumption will be equal to some constant term, $\bar{c}$ (sometimes called the *autonomous* component of consumption), plus the level of income (y) multiplied by a number, c_y, which is the marginal propensity to consume. A less simple form would be one where this marginal propensity to consume is not constant and the same for every level of income; for our purposes, the simple form is sufficient.

Economists have tried to measure this coefficient c_y, and to be on the safe side one can think of it as a number around 0.8; a marginal propensity to consume of 0.8 means, of course, that, if real income rises by one (real) dollar, then consumption will rise by 80 (real) cents. Or, equivalently, one can say that 80 percent of any increase in income is spent on consumption goods. Expression [5.7] is an elementary theory of what determines the first component of total expenditures (consumption expenditures). Let us now analyze the second component, expenditures on investment goods by business firms.

INVESTMENT EXPENDITURES

Expenditures by business firms on investment goods depend on many variables, such as expectations concerning prices of the product firms intend to produce, prices of inputs such as labor, and the level of demand for the product. But, if these items are assumed constant, we can examine the influence of one interesting variable: the interest rate.

Even though a rigorous derivation of the relationship is complicated, the rationale behind the connection between the real interest rate and the level of business firms expenditures on investment goods is easy to visualize intuitively. The interest rate is one of the costs of holding physical capital (the other being maintenance costs, depreciation, and so on). The interest rate is one of the costs of holding physical capital because it represents the costs of having an outstanding loan taken for the purchase of that piece of capital. Alternatively, it can be thought of as the *opportunity cost* of owning the piece of capital, that is, the interest that could be obtained by selling the machine (or by not having bought it) and lending the proceeds. The latter is interest that is forgone by *not* selling the piece of capital, that is, by holding it.

At every period of time, business firms have a list of possible investment projects, with different expected *rates of return*. The decision to undertake or not to undertake a single investment project is then the outcome of the comparison between the rate of interest (that is, the rate at which funds can be borrowed for undertaking the project) and the expected rate of return on the project. The firm will then undertake all the projects for which the rate of return is higher than the rate of interest on loans, and abandon those projects that do not qualify because they yield a rate of return lower than the rate of interest on loans. That is, investment in every period will proceed up to the *marginal project*, the one for which the rate of return is equal to the rate of interest.

Under these circumstances a lower rate of interest will bring about a larger number of investment projects to be undertaken, since now new projects will qualify which previously did not. This relationship is depicted in the graph of Figure 5–2, in which the vertical axis measures the interest rate and the horizontal axis measures the flow of investment at every period. Notice that the slope of this *investment schedule* will depend on how the rate of return on the various investment projects falls as more and more projects are undertaken. If firms have a long list of projects with very similar rates of return, the investment schedule will be very flat and investment expenditures will be very sensitive to changes in the interest rate. A small decrease in the interest rate at

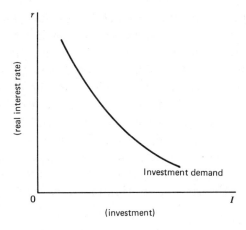

Figure 5-2. The investment schedule.

which firms can borrow for financing the projects would now qualify a lot of projects that previously could not be funded. Likewise, if the rate of return of alternative investment projects falls considerably as we go down the list, a big fall in the rate of interest would be required to bring in additional projects. Investment expenditures, in other words, will be very insensitive to changes in the interest rate, and the investment schedule will be very close to a vertical line. Alternatively, in the extreme case in which other considerations dominate business investment decisions to such an extent that the rate of interest becomes but a very unimportant factor, the investment schedule will be very close to a vertical line, indicating an almost complete insensitivity of investment expenditures with respect to the interest rate.

Like the consumption function, the investment relationship can be expressed in a simple, linear form, as

$$I = \bar{I} - I_r r \qquad\qquad [5.8]$$

Expression [5.8] indicates that the level of investment is equal to some constant, $\bar{I}$, minus the interest rate multiplied by a number, I_r, which indicates the *sensitivity* of investment to changes in the rate of interest. The extent to which the level of investment will change when the rate of interest changes is given by the size of the coefficient I_r. If I_r is zero, in one extreme case, then the level of investment is independent of the interest rate (and always equal to the number $\bar{I}$). If I_r is infinite, in the other extreme, then the investment schedule is a perfectly horizontal line, indicating that all possible investment projects (at least in a certain range) would yield the same rate of return.

As we will see later, the size of the coefficient I_r plays a very important role for the overall results of the model developed in this chapter, and hence for economic policies. In fact, it is one of the elements that help shape some of the differences between Keynesians and Monetarists. Even though Keynes paid much attention to the dependence of investment expenditures on the level of the interest rate, he believed that, more than on the interest rate, investment depended on producers' expectations about the future course of the economy—entrepreneurs' "animal instincts," which in turn were quite unpredictable and a source of instability. In much of the Keynesian and post-Keynesian literature, therefore, the influence of the interest rate is simply ignored, and the investment schedule is simply a vertical line. On the other side (even though this is often not made explicit), Monetarists tend to think in terms of a rather *flat* investment schedule; that is, they assume a very sensitive response of the level of investment expenditures to changes in the interest rate. In the extreme case, a perfectly horizontal investment schedule results. A horizontal schedule reflects the belief that (in the long run, at least), there is a large quantity of projects for which the rate of return is the same, a position taken by the American economist Frank Knight in his theory of capital.

THE TOTAL EXPENDITURES SCHEDULE

We have now considered each of the three components of total expenditures: consumption, investment, and government expenditures. If we add these three components using the simple forms of expressions [5.7] and [5.8], then expression [5.9] may be obtained.

$$te = c + I + g = (\bar{c} + \bar{I}) + c_y y + g - I_r r \qquad [5.9]$$

Expression [5.9] indicates that total expenditures is the sum of (1) three autonomous or fixed terms, $\bar{c}$, $\bar{I}$, and the level of government expenditures, g; (2) a term that depends on the level of income (through consumption), $c_y y$; and (3) a third term, $I_r r$, which depends on the interest rate (via investment). For a better understanding of the fourth term in the total expenditures expression, we must investigate the manner in which the interest rate is determined.

A discussion of the immediate determination of the interest rate must include two competing theories. For the long-run equilibrium, both these theories yield the same answer; the same is not true, however, for the short run. On the one hand there is the Keynesian "liquidity preference" theory, invented by Keynes and widely used today by Keynesians and some non-Keynesians alike; on the other hand, there exists the so-called "loanable funds" theory, which is associated with the classical, pre-Keynesian tradition, but which, in some general form, is implicitly used by some Monetarists today. Taking the mainstream approach, we will follow the liquidity preference theory and reserve a discussion of the loanable funds theory for the Appendix to this chapter. The extra time necessary to learn the loanable funds theory of the Appendix will be rewarded, because this theory facilitates a neat interpretation of the main differences between Keynesians and Monetarists, and a clear definition of some much discussed side effects of fiscal policy (that is, changes in the level of government expenditures). It also better illuminates some topics discussed in Chapters 13 and 14.

HOW THE INTEREST RATE IS DETERMINED: THE LIQUIDITY PREFERENCE VIEW

One of Keynes' major contributions was the idea that the interest rate is, in the short run, a purely monetary phenomenon, determined by the stock of money people wish to hold (the demand for money) and by the existing stock (the supply of money). In the Keynesian world, individuals make choices between holding a stock of money or a stock of bonds, and they can switch from one to the other quickly, so that the interest rate adjusts to assure that actual and desired stocks of money and bonds are equal.

Figure 5–3 shows how the interest rate is determined, and what variables will affect its level. Suppose the demand for money is L_0 for the level of real

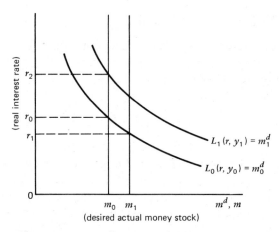

Figure 5-3. *Interest rate determination: the liquidity preference view.*

income y_0, and the stock of (real) money is m_0. Then, the interest rate that makes the actual stock m_0 and the desired stock equal, is r_0.

The items that can change the level of the interest rate are all those affecting either the supply or the demand for money. Suppose, first, that the stock of real cash balances increases to, say, m_1; the interest rate that now brings equilibrium is r_1. An increase in the money stock decreases the equilibrium interest rate, and vice versa. The extent of the change depends, of course, on how sensitive the desired money stock is to changes in the interest rate. The more sensitive moneyholders are to changes in the interest rate (or the flatter the schedule is), the smaller the change in the interest rate brought about by a change in the money stock, that is, the smaller the change in the interest rate to convince or to induce the public to hold the additional amount of money.

What are the factors that can change the demand for money? There are many, including a change in tastes (as in the demand for popcorn), but the most important factor (as with popcorn) is the level of real income. Recall from Chapter 3 that an increase in the level of real income shifts the demand for money schedule to the right. Suppose that in Figure 5-3 real income goes up to y_1, and that the demand for money schedule corresponding to such higher level of real income is L_1. For the original stock of money m_0, the rate of interest in equilibrium is r_2; *an increase in the level of income increases the interest rate.* In different words, at a higher level of real income money holders wish to hold more money. For any fixed stock, the cost of holding money needs to go up in order to allocate the existing stock. The extent of the change in the interest rate depends on two things; (1) the magnitude of the shift of the schedule (how much people wish to increase their money holdings at every interest rate), and (2) the slope of the schedule (how sensitive their desire to hold money is with respect to the cost of satisfying their desire—the interest rate).

Thus, in this approach the interest rate, always at the level that makes actual and desired money stock equal, depends on (1) *the stock of money* (when the stock of money goes up, the interest rate goes down, and vice versa); and (2) *the level of real income* (when real income goes up, the interest rate goes up, and vice versa).

The above verbal and graphical explanation has a useful and simple analytical counterpart. The demand for money schedule can be written in linear form, as

$$m^d = \overline{m} + L_y y - L_r r \qquad\qquad [5.10]$$

Expression [5.10] says that the desired real money stock (m^d) is equal to some constant term, $\overline{m}$, plus a term that depends on the level of real income, $L_y y$, where L_y is simply a coefficient indicating how sensitive the desired money stock is to the level of real income, minus a third term, $L_r r$, or the interest rate times a coefficient L_r, which indicates how sensitive the desired money stock is to the level of the real interest rate. In the extreme Keynesian case of the liquidity trap, L_r would be infinite (and the demand for money would be pictured, at least in the relevant range, as a horizontal line), while in the other extreme case of the primitive quantity theory, in which the demand for money does not depend on the interest rate, $L_r = 0$, the demand for money schedule is a vertical line.

If we assume that the interest rate at all times adjusts to make the actual and the desired real money stocks equal, or $m = m^d$, then expression [5.10] can be written as

$$m = \overline{m} + L_y y - L_r r$$

Solving for the interest rate in this expression, we obtain

$$r = (\overline{m}/L_r) + (L_y/L_r) y - (1/L_r) m \qquad\qquad [5.11]$$

Here, the term (L_y/L_r) indicates how much the interest rate will rise per unit increase in real income, and the coefficient $(1/L_r)$ indicates how much the interest rate will fall per unit increase in the real money stock. This expression helps to make obvious what is clear from the graph in Figure 5.3, that is, the importance of the sensitivity of the desired money stock to changes in the interest rate (the coefficient L_r). The larger this coefficient, L_r (that is, the *flatter* the demand for money), the smaller will be the effects of changes in the money stock and the level of real income on the interest rate. In the extreme case of a perfectly horizontal demand for money (the liquidity trap case), changes in the level of real income, and, more important, in the quantity of money, will have no effect on the rate of interest.

PUTTING IT TOGETHER:
THE TOTAL EXPENDITURES SCHEDULE
Expressions [5.9] and [5.11] reproduce our two main conclusions.

$$te = (\bar{c} + \bar{I}) + c_y y + g - I_r r \qquad\qquad [5.9]$$

$$r = (\bar{m}/L_r) + (L_y/L_r)y - (1/L_r)m \qquad\qquad [5.11]$$

The first of these two equations indicates the manner in which total expenditures will depend on the level of real income and the interest rate (for a given level of real government expenditures). The second expression shows how the interest rate will be determined by the level of income and the real money stock. Thus we can say that the level of total expenditures (for a given level of government expenditures) is given by real income and the real money stock. Real income, y, appears as a direct, explicit determinant of total expenditures, to the extent that it will influence consumption expenditures. The magnitude of this influence is given by the *marginal propensity to consume*, c_y. But the level of real income will also help to determine the level of the interest rate (expression [5.11]). To the extent that investment expenditures are sensitive to the level of the interest rate, the level of income also influences total expenditures in an indirect way. In particular, an increase in real income increases total expenditures through the first, direct effect via consumption expenditures; but, to the extent that the increase in real income also increases the interest rate, it will bring about a fall in investment expenditures. That is, these direct and indirect effects work in the opposite direction. The real money stock does not appear explicitly in expression [5.9] and therefore does not influence total expenditures in a direct manner. But to the extent that the level of the real money stock influences the level of the interest rate, it will have an indirect effect on total expenditures through the level of investment expenditures. Finally, the third element in expression [5.9], the level of government expenditures, directly increases total expenditures (by the same amount) with no indirect effect, since it plays no role in the determination of the interest rate.

All of these direct and indirect effects can be easily visualized in Figures 5-4, 5-5, and 5-6. At the left in each of these figures is the representation of the demand for money and the real money stock, describing the determination of the interest rate. At the right of these figures is the representation of the sum of consumption, investment, and government expenditures ($c + I + g$). Notice that the slope of this last schedule is given by the coefficient I_r, showing how sensitive investment expenditures are to changes in the interest rate. Consider, first, the effects of changes in the level of real income (Figure 5-4). At the right side of Figure 5-4 the ($c + I + g$) or *total expenditures schedule* shows that for a given level of income (say, y_0), total expenditures increase when the interest rate falls. The initial situation assumes a level of real income

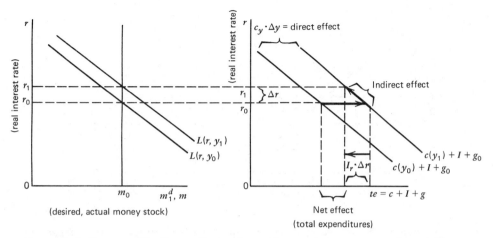

Figure 5-4. *Direct and indirect effects of a real income increase on total expenditures.*

y_0, an equilibrium interest r_0, a real money stock m_0, and a resulting level of total expenditures te_0. If real income increases to y_1, two things occur. First, the total expenditures schedule shifts to the right, the extent of the shift given by the change in income, Δy, times the marginal propensity to consume, c_y. This is the explicit or *direct effect*, or increase in consumption expenditures. Second, the demand for money schedule shifts to the right, bringing about an increase in the rate of interest. Then, the implicit, *indirect effect* can be seen as an upward movement along the new $(c + I + g)$ schedule, as a response to the change in the interest rate from r_0 to r_1. The magnitude of this second effect is given by two factors: the change in the interest rate (which in turn depends on how sensitive the demand for money is to interest rate changes) and the slope of the $(c + I + g)$ schedule (which measures the sensitivity of investment expenditures to changes in the interest rate). The indirect effect is precisely the last term, $I_r r$, in expression [5.9].

Consider now the real money stock, which does not appear explicitly in expression [5.9]. There is no explicit or direct effect now. But if the money stock rises, for example, and if the demand for money schedule is not completely flat, the interest rate will fall. To the extent that the investment component of expenditures shows any reaction to the fall in the interest rate, total expenditures will in turn rise. In Figure 5-5 this can be seen as the movement along the schedule $(c + I + g)$, which is again the graphical representation of the last term in expression [5.9]. There is no direct, explicit effect of money on total expenditures, it occurs only through a change in the interest rate and, hence, through a change in investment.

Finally, consider what happens if the level of government expenditures increases. Figure 5-6 shows the effect of such a change. There is an explicit,

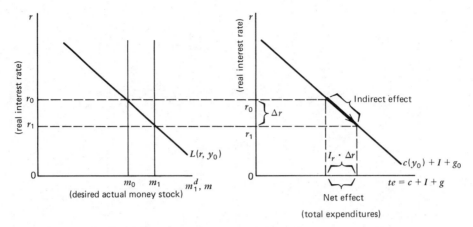

Figure 5-5. *Indirect effect of a real money stock increase on total expenditures.*

direct effect given by the shift to the right of the $(c + I + g)$ line (equal in magnitude to the change in g) but no implicit or indirect effect: the interest rate has remained the same because the demand or the supply of money has remained stationary.

All these effects can be summarized compactly by substituting expression [5.11] into [5.9], to obtain

$$te = [\bar{c} + \bar{I} - \bar{m}(I_r/L_r)] + [c_y - (L_y I_r/L_r)] y + g + (I_r/L_r) m \qquad [5.12]$$

In spite of the formidable look of this expression, every one of the coefficients reflects the simple reasoning we have been following.

Let us examine the effects on total expenditures in an organized and orderly fashion. Basically we are interested in how *changes in income* (Δy),

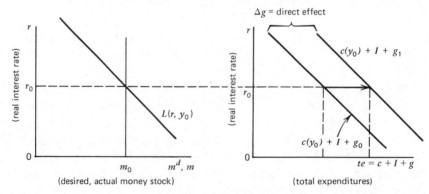

Figure 5-6. *Direct effect of an increase in government spending on total expenditures.*

the real money stock (Δm), and *government expenditures* (Δg) affect *changes in total expenditures.* In order to understand these relationships, refer to expression [5.12]. For our purposes the first term on the right-hand side of [5.12], $[\bar{c} + \bar{I} - \bar{m}(I_r/L_r)]$ can be ignored. The term is a constant and any changes in income, the real money stock, or government expenditures are assumed to have no impact on the first (bracketed) term. But, in order to observe the influence of these variables on total expenditures, let us recall the basic determinants of a change in expenditures. In other words,

$$\Delta te = \Delta C + \Delta I + \Delta g$$

and

$$\Delta C = c_y \Delta y; \quad \text{i.e., } \Delta y \text{ affects } C \text{ directly}$$

$$\Delta I = -I_r \Delta r; \quad \text{i.e., } \Delta r \text{ affects } I \text{ directly}$$

$$\Delta g = \Delta g; \quad \text{i.e., } g \text{ is autonomous}$$

All of these *direct* effects were discussed earlier in the chapter. We must also consider, however, the *indirect* effects. Changes in income (Δy) and changes in the real money stock (Δm) affect changes in the rate of interest (Δr), and in turn cause changes in investment (ΔI). The specific nature of these changes follow: A change in income may change the rate of interest by an amount (L_y/L_r), or

$$\Delta y \longrightarrow \Delta r = (L_y/L_r) \Delta y$$

Furthermore, a change in the real money stock may change the rate of interest by an amount equal to $-(1/L_r)$, or

$$\Delta m \longrightarrow \Delta r = -(1/L_r) \Delta m$$

As a result we can summarize the direct and the indirect effects of *changes* in income, the real money stock, and government expenditures on the three components of spending. Consider the effects of a change in income (y) on consumption, investment, and government spending. They are

$$\Delta c = c_y \Delta y \qquad \text{(a direct effect)}$$

$$\Delta I = -I_r \Delta r = -I_r(L_y/L_r) \Delta y \quad \text{(an indirect effect)}$$

$$\Delta g = 0 \qquad \text{(no effect)}$$

Therefore, the effect of a change of income on total expenditures is summarized as

$$\Delta te = [c_y - (I_r \cdot L_y/L_r)] \Delta y$$

which accounts for the *second term* in expression [5.12].

Next consider a change in the real money stock. The effects on consumption, investment, and government are summarized:

$$\Delta c = 0 \qquad\qquad\qquad\qquad\qquad\qquad\qquad \text{(since } \Delta y = 0\text{: no effect)}$$

$$\Delta I = -I_r \Delta r = -I_r(-1/L_r)\,\Delta m = (I_r/L_r)\,\Delta m \qquad \text{(an indirect effect)}$$

$$\Delta g = 0 \qquad\qquad\qquad\qquad\qquad\qquad\qquad \text{(no effect)}$$

Therefore the change in total expenditures from a change in the real money stock is

$$\Delta te = (I_r/L_r)\,\Delta m$$

which is the *last* term in expression [5.12].

Finally, the effects on the components of total expenditures of a change in autonomous government expenditures can be summarized:

$$\Delta c = 0 \qquad \text{(since } \Delta y = 0\text{: no effect)}$$

$$\Delta I = 0 \qquad \text{(since } \Delta r = 0\text{: no effect)}$$

$$\Delta g = \Delta g$$

Thus, a change in government expenditures alters total expenditures by the same amount, or

$$\Delta te = \Delta g$$

Figure 5–7 is a useful picture of the manner in which changes in the levels of real income (Δy), the real money stock (Δm), and real government ex-

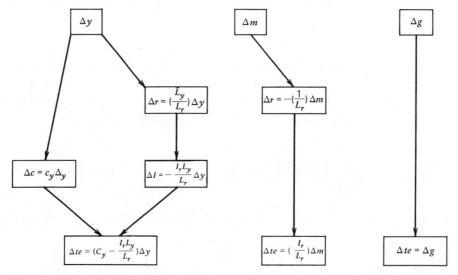

Figure 5-7. A summary of the effects of income, money stock, and government spending changes on total expenditures.

penditures (Δg) influence total expenditures. A unit increase in real income (y) increases consumption (and hence total expenditures) directly by c_y units. Simultaneously, increases in real income increase the interest rate by (L_y/L_r) units; since every unit increase in the interest rate decreases investment expenditures (and hence total expenditures) by I_r units, it will decrease total expenditures, indirectly, by (L_y/L_r) times I_r, or by $(L_r/L_r)I_r$ units. The net effect of an increase in real income on total expenditures will then be the first minus the second, or $[c_y - (L_y/L_r)]$—the coefficient of real income in expression [5.12]. Next, every unit increase in the real money stock decreases the interest rate by $(1/L_r)$ units; since every unit decrease in the interest rate increases investment (and hence total expenditures) by I_r units, the effect of a unit increase in the real money stock will then be to increase total expenditures by $(1/L_r)$ times I_r units, or (I_r/L_r)—the coefficient of the term m in expression [5.12]. Finally, real government expenditures influence total expenditures only directly, and by a factor of one; that is, a unit increase in real government expenditures increases total expenditures by the same amount.

A GENERAL (AND A PARTICULAR) FORM OF THE TOTAL EXPENDITURES SCHEDULE: KEYNESIANS AND MONETARISTS ONCE AGAIN

Again consider expression [5.12], which summarizes the determinants of total expenditures. As a step toward simplicity, notice that the term (I_r/L_r) appears three times in that expression. At the same time, note that the first term $[\bar{c} + \bar{I} - \bar{m}(I_r/L_r)]$ is a constant and can be written in a much shorter manner. Let this constant equal a_0, and the term (I_r/L_r) be represented by α. Expression [5.12] can then be written as

$$te = a_0 + (c_y - L_y\alpha)y + g + \alpha m \qquad [5.13]$$

The term $\alpha = (I_r/L_r)$ is an important one, for it summarizes some of the crucial differences between the Keynesian and the Monetarist viewpoints. First, there is a difference of opinion about the size of the coefficient I_r: it is high in value for a Monetarist, but very low for a Keynesian. I_r, of course, represents the sensitivity of investment expenditures to changes in the rate of interest. Second, there is controversy related to the size of the coefficient L_r: it is assumed to be rather high for a Keynesian (that is, a high response of the demand for money to changes in the interest rate, infinite in the very extreme liquidity trap case), and low for Monetarists (zero, in the other very extreme case of the original, primitive quantity of money theory). On both accounts, a Keynesian would tend to think of the coefficient α as being very low because, for most Keynesians, the numerator (I_r) is considered low, and because the denominator (L_r) is high. A Monetarist, for exactly the opposite reasons, would tend to think of such coefficient α as being very high because the numerator (I_r) is high and because the denominator (L_r) is low.

The Appendix to this chapter demonstrates that the liquidity preference approach to the immediate determination of the interest rate which is followed here, an approach yielding expression [5.13], is not very conducive to the representation of the very extreme Monetarist position (an α coefficient of infinite value). Expression [5.13], though, is very adequate for representing the very extreme Keynesian position for, if the coefficient α is zero, expression [5.13] reduces to

$$te = a_0 + c_y y + g \qquad [5.14]$$

That is, the marginal propensity to spend is the marginal propensity to consume, c_y, and (what is far more important) changes in the real money stock do *not* influence real total expenditures at all. The conclusion follows because changes in the quantity of money do not change the interest rate in the extreme liquidity trap case and, even if it did so, changes in the interest rate would not change the level of investment expenditures (the extreme vertical line investment schedule case). As will be shown in the next chapter, this "Keynesian conclusion" would be of far reaching consequences. (Expression [5.14] is the very simple form encountered in most Principles of Economics courses.)

Of course, most Keynesians and Monetarists do not take extreme positions on these matters. And in order to consider the very general case, where the difference between the two approaches results in conclusions that are different only as a matter of degree, it is useful to express [5.13] in a more general and shorter way,

$$te = a_0 + a_y y + g + a_m m \qquad [5.15]$$

where the coefficients $a_y = (c_y - L_y \alpha)$ and $a_m = \alpha$ represent the influence of real income and the real money stock on total expenditures. This very general expression will serve as the foundation for the theoretical issues discussed in Chapter 6.

CONCLUSION

In Chapter 5 the determinants of total expenditures have been investigated, and findings have been summarized in a general expression—either [5.13] or [5.15]. These expressions tell us that total expenditures depend upon the level of income, government expenditures, and the real money stock. Of course, they are not sufficient to solve the system in any formal sense; that is, they cannot reveal what the level of the variables involved will be in equilibrium. As we will see in Chapter 6, the final result depends not only on this demand or expenditures side, but also on the supply side of the economy.

In Chapter 5 one particular theory for explaining the immediate determination of the interest rate—the liquidity preference theory—has been used. The Appendix to this chapter considers an alternative, the loanable funds theory, which yields some additional insights.[4]

Appendix 5
THE LOANABLE FUNDS THEORY AND THE DETERMINATION OF TOTAL EXPENDITURES

As indicated in Chapter 5, there are two competing theories of the *immediate*, short-run determination of the interest rate: the liquidity preference and the loanable funds theories. Following a mainstream approach the first theory was used in deriving the total expenditures schedule. In this Appendix the second theory is investigated for several important reasons. First, a general form for the total expenditures schedule can be derived which is even more general than that derived in Chapter 5, and which lends itself to a clear statement of the limiting, extreme forms of both the Monetarist and the Keynesian views. Indeed, in the form derived in this Appendix a familiar effect that often is referred to in the literature—the *crowding out effect* of government expenditures on private expenditures—can be discussed. This effect refers to the fact that, when government expenditures are financed by borrowing from the public, such borrowing tends to increase the interest rate and therefore to discourage private borrowing and, with it, expenditures on investment goods. In the liquidity preference view of total expenditures, the interest rate does not depend on the flow of government borrowing; it depends solely on the supply and demand for money. Furthermore, the demand for money is unrelated to government borrowing. In the liquidity preference model, such an important effect is absent; that is, an increase in government expenditures financed through borrowing always has a one-to-one effect on total expenditures. Second, the loanable funds view allows some additional insights on topics that will be examined later

in this book, such as financial markets (Chapter 13) and the implementation of monetary policy (Chapter 14), although the loanable funds discussion in these chapters is self-contained.

The Loanable Funds View and the Concept of Hoarding

The distinction between the theories of liquidity preference and loanable funds essentially refers to the basic difference between stocks and flows. In the first, discussed in Chapter 5, the assumption is that the level of the interest rate, at each point in time, is the one that will make moneyholders (and bondsholders) satisfied with holding the stock of both money and bonds that exist in the economy. Thus there is an assumption that there is an *instantaneous adjustment* among those stocks. In the loanable funds view, alternatively, it is possible for the public to be holding, for some period of time, a stock of real cash balances different from the desired stock. Over each period the flow of the public's lending will be regulated so as to approach their desired long-run money stock over several periods. According to this view, the interest rate equates this flow of lending to the flow of borrowing (in the simple world depicted here, the borrowing by firms is to finance investment expenditures, and the borrowing by government is to pay for its expenditures). Therefore, in the loanable funds view the flow of desired hoarding, and hence of lending, is a well-defined magnitude that will in turn depend on other variables. In the liquidity preference view examined in the body of this chapter, hoarding (and therefore lending) were just residuals; the interest rate was at each point in time the exact rate that made the actual and the desired real money stocks equal. Hoarding and lending were simply the flows required for the market of loanable funds to be in equilibrium. Thus the condition of equilibrium in this market was useless in deriving the total expenditures schedule.

Once we accept the possibility that the public may at some times be holding a stock of real cash balances different from their desired stock, the idea of desired hoarding, that is, the desired rate at which they wish to accumulate (or deaccumulate) cash balances in order to approach their equilibrium, comes up naturally. For example, it makes sense to say that money-holders will try to accumulate cash balances at a rate that depends on the difference between their desired and their actual stocks. The simplest manner in which this can be expressed is

$$h = b\,(m^d - m) \qquad [5.16]$$

Expression [5.16] states simply that the flow of desired hoarding in real terms (h) will equal some fixed coefficient (b) multiplied by the difference between the public's desired real money stock (m^d) and the stock they are holding, or actual stock (m). Of course, if the actual stock happens to be higher than the desired stock, there will be negative desired hoarding; i.e., dishoarding.

If we express the desired money stock in the simplest form (that used in the text of Chapter 5), hoarding becomes

$$h = b\,(\bar{m} + L_y y - L_r r - m) \qquad [5.17]$$

From this expression it is easy to verify that: (1) a rise in the level of real income will raise hoarding because it increases the desired money stock and creates (or increases) excess of desired over actual money holdings; (2) a rise in the interest rate decreases hoarding because it decreases the desired money stock; and (3) an increase in the actual money stock decreases hoarding because it creates an excess of actual over desired cash balances so that the public will try to lower this actual stock. The coefficient b is a measurement of how fast the public wishes to adjust to their target, the desired amount of real cash balances: the higher the coefficient b, the faster this adjustment and the higher the flow of desired hoarding (or dishoarding) for any stock disequilibrium. In the limit, a value of infinity for the coefficient b would mean that the public is willing and able to adjust at an infinite speed. The adjustment of actual to desired money stocks would be instantaneous, as would be the case in the liquidity preference theory.

The nature and the determinants of the *hoarding function*, as the simple expression [5.17] may be called, the lending function, the market for loanable funds, and the determination of the interest rate according to the loanable funds view, can now be treated.

How the Interest Rate is Determined: Borrowing and Lending Schedules

In the text of Chapter 5 the flow of loanable funds demanded was characterized as the sum of borrowing by firms (ℓ), equal to their investment expenditures (I), and the borrowing by government (gb), equal to government's expenditures (g). The supply of loanable funds by households, ℓ, must now be examined. If we use the household's budget constraint this is an easy task.

The budget constraint faced by households given in expression [5.1] is repeated here for convenience,

$$y = c + \ell + h \qquad [5.1]$$

From [5.1], it is obvious that lending must equal income, minus consumption, minus hoarding, or

$$\ell = y - c - h$$

Utilizing the simple expressions for consumption and hoarding developed earlier, we conclude that

$$\ell = y - (\bar{c} + c_y y) - b(\bar{m} + L_y y - L_r r - m)$$

or

$$\ell = -(\bar{c} + b\bar{m}) + (1 - c_y - bL_y)y + bm + bL_r r \qquad [5.18]$$

Expression [5.18] indicates that the flow of lending by households will depend on the level of real income (y), the level of the real money stock (m), and the interest rate (r). The influence of these variables will depend upon the magnitude of the corresponding coefficients. If real income rises by one unit, lending will rise by $(1 - c_y - bL_y)$ units; if the real money stock rises by one unit, lending will rise by b units, and if the interest rate rises by one unit, lending will rise by bL_r units. The interpretation of the last two is immediate for, if the real money stock increases, lending increases immediately by b units, because consumption does not change (it depends only on income). The desired money stock does not change either, so that the increase in lending is just a fraction of the monetary stock disequilibrium. If the interest rate rises consumption does not change, and the increase in lending corresponds to the dishoarding induced by the fall in the desired money stock. The interpretation of the coefficient for the level of income, $(1 - c_y - bL_y)$, is a bit more involved: an increase in real income increases the desired money stock and hence hoarding (by the magnitude bL_y per unit increase in income), and, likewise, increases consumption (by the magnitude c_y per unit increase in income). The remainder is one minus the sum of these two coefficients, so that the total change can be negative (and the increase in income result in a fall in lending) if the increase in consumption and hoarding is high enough. We will assume that a rise in real income *increases all three*, consumption, hoarding, and lending, so that the term $(1 - c_y - bL_y)$ is greater than zero but less than one.

Notice, also, that the coefficient (bL_r), indicating the sensitivity of lending to changes in the rate of interest, is the product of b, the speed at which the public wishes to adjust their actual to their desired real cash balances, and L_r, which indicates the sensitivity of the desired money stock to changes in the interest rate. This last term plays a crucial role in lending—the higher it is, the higher the response of lending to changes in the rate of interest rate. In the extreme cases of a perfectly vertical demand for money schedule (that is, in the

crude version of the quantity theory, with L_r equal to zero), this coefficient is equal to zero and lending is *not* influenced by the interest rate. In the other polar case, of a perfectly horizontal demand for money schedule (the extreme Keynesian case of the liquidity trap), the coefficient is equal to infinity. We will see the importance of this immediately.

In order to gain some generality and to simplify the notation, let us substitute the coefficients in expression [5.18] to obtain

$$\ell = \ell_0 + \ell_y y + \ell_m m + \ell_r r \qquad [5.19]$$

where ℓ_0 stands for the (negative) constant term $(\overline{c} + b\overline{m})$, and $\ell_y (= 1 - cy - bL_y)$, $\ell_m (= b)$, and $\ell_r (= bL_r)$ are the coefficients indicating the influence of real income, the real money stock, and the interest rate on lending.

Figure 5–8 is a graphical representation of the lending schedule of expression [5.18] or [5.19]. The interest rate is represented on the vertical axis, and the flow of lending corresponding to each level of the interest rate is displayed on the horizontal axis. Of course, any such schedule is drawn for a *given* level of the other two variables (the real money stock and the level of real income), such as m_0 and y_0. The slope of the schedule is given by the coefficient $\ell_r = bL_r$. In the extreme case of the primitive quantity theory, with $L_r = 0$, $\ell_r = 0$, and the lending schedule would be a vertical line, indicating a total insensitivity of lending to

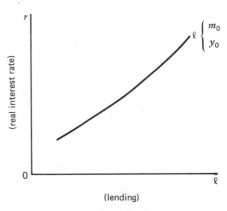

Figure 5–8. The lending schedule.

the interest rate. In the extreme case of the ultra-Keynesian liquidity trap situation, L_r (and therefore ℓ_r) are equal to infinity, and the lending schedule would be a horizontal line.

Notice also that the coefficients ℓ_y and ℓ_m, which indicate the amount that lending would increase per unit increase of real income or the real money stock, are a measurement of the lateral shift in the lending schedule (to the right, for increases in either real income or the real money stock) per unit change in any of these two variables. Figures 5–9 and 5–10 show the extent of these shifts (denoted by the symbol $\Delta\ell$) for the cases of an increase in real income (Δy) and in the real money stock (Δm), respectively.

The lending schedule has now been developed, and the determination of the interest rate according to the loanable funds theory can be analyzed. Before we do this, recall that the borrowing schedule (or the demand for loanable funds) is simply equal to $\ell + gb = \bar{I} - I_r r + gb$, that is, the sum of borrowing by firms for investment purposes, and borrowing by government. The borrowing schedule will be just the investment schedule described in Figure 5–2, with the lateral addition of government borrowing. Therefore, the slope of the borrowing schedule will be the same as the slope of the investment schedule (I_r): the higher the sensitivity of investment expenditures to changes in the interest rate and the

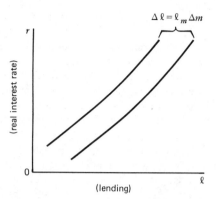

Figure 5-10. An increase in the real money stock shifts the lending schedule to the right.

flatter the investment schedule, the flatter will be the borrowing schedule. In the two extreme Keynesian and Monetarist cases suggested when we discussed the investment schedule, the borrowing schedule is a *vertical* or a *horizontal* line.

Figure 5–11 shows both the lending schedule (for a given level of real income, y_0, and a given level of the real money stock, m_0) and the borrowing schedule, $\ell + gb_0 = \bar{I} - I_r r + gb_0$, for a given level of government borrowing, gb_0. The equilibrium interest rate is r_0, and the equilibrium level of borrowing and lending, $\ell_0 = \ell_0 + gb_0$.

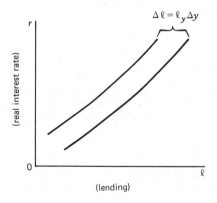

Figure 5-9. An increase in real income shifts the lending schedule to the right.

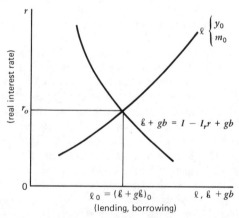

Figure 5-11. Equilibrium real interest rate.

How might this instantaneous equilibrium of the interest rate be altered or changed? Simply, by any of the items affecting either the lending or the borrowing schedule: real income or real cash balances, for the former, and the level of government borrowing, for the latter. A change in any of these three magnitudes shifts the schedules and brings about a change in the level of the interest rate and a change in the equilibrium level of private borrowing, that is, in investment. The indirect dependence of the level of private borrowing (and therefore of investment expenditures) on those three magnitudes (government borrowing, real income, and the real money stock) is precisely what we are concerned about in deriving the total expenditures schedule. From a viewpoint of problem separation we should investigate here how the equilibrium level of the interest rate is affected by changes in these magnitudes, and then analyze how investment expenditures react to those changes in the interest rate. This method was used in Chapter 5 when the liquidity preference approach was utilized. But, in the case of the loanable funds theory, the lending and borrowing schedules determine the interest rate, and the fundamental component of the borrowing schedule is the investment schedule, so that investment is determined simultaneously with the interest rate. We will then investigate the direct dependence of investment on the three magnitudes (government borrowing, real income, and the real money stock).

Interest Rate Determination, Investment, and the Total Expenditures Schedule

Any change in real income, in the real money stock, or in government expenditures will induce shifts in the lending or borrowing schedules. The equilbrium level of the interest rate, borrowing and lending, and hence (and simultaneously) the level of investment is thus changed. There is a very simple manner for investigating the market for loanable funds and for showing how the level of investment expenditures will depend indirectly on those three magnitudes.

To do so in the simplest manner, a minor change in the characterization of the demand and supply of loanable funds (the borrowing and lending schedules) must be introduced. Recall that the demand for loanable funds, or borrowing schedule, is made up of private borrowing by firms for investment purposes, $\ell = \bar{I} - I_r r$, plus government borrowing, gb, and the supply of loanable funds (the borrowing schedule) is ℓ. That is, for equilibrium in the market for loanable funds, which we will assume is fulfilled at all times, expression [5.20] is required

$$\ell + gb = \ell \qquad [5.20]$$

But, if we transpose a term, we can write this condition as

$$\ell = \ell - gb \qquad [5.21]$$

where the left-hand side is *borrowing by firms*, and the right-hand side is *total lending minus government borrowing*, that is, the supply of loanable funds (lending) left over to private borrowers. (This latter function may be called "net lending.") This small change eliminates an unnecessary step and the mechanics of the adjustment are apparent graphically in Fig. 5–12. If we let $\ell^* \equiv \ell - gb$ (the net lending function) and b equal borrowing by firms, Figure 5–12 shows that the adjustment described above has no effect on the interest rate, r_1. That is, simultaneous elimination of government borrowing from the $\ell + gb$ function, which results in a ℓ schedule of *private* borrow-

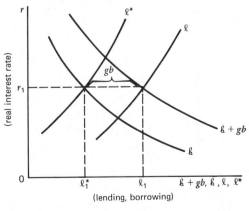

Figure 5–12. The "net lending" adjustment.

ing, and the "netting out" of public borrowing from the total lending function, which likewise displaces the lending function by $-gb$, produces a private market equilibrium at the same rate of interest r_1 (see Figure 5–12). The intersection of the two schedules ℓ^* and ℓ take place, in other words, at the same interest rate as the intersection of ℓ and $\ell + gb$.

Figure 5-13 is the representation of the two schedules $\ell = \bar{I} - I_r r$ and $\ell - gb$. Its purpose is to help us investigate how changes in real income, the real money stock, and the level of government borrowing (all of which would now induce shifts in the second of these schedules) will influence the equilibrium level of borrowing by firms, ℓ, and hence of investment expenditures. Consider a shift in the net lending schedule by the magnitude $\Delta(\ell - gb)$, which could be induced by changes in either government borrowing, real income, or the real money stock. Notice that such a shift is equal to the sum of segments A and B, or $\Delta(\ell - gb) = (A + B)$. Notice also that the change in the equilibrium level of borrowing by firms and investment expenditures brought about by such a shift is equal to segment B, and the change in the interest rate equal to segment C. These segments are necessary in order to show how magnitude B is related to magnitude $(A + B)$. More precisely, we are interested in knowing by how many units borrowing

by firms (investment) will change the per unit shift of the net lending schedule, or the ratio $B/(A + B)$, which we call β. From the graph, it is clear that $I_r = (B/C)$ (the slope of the borrowing schedule), or the change in borrowing by firms (investment) per unit change in the interest rate, and that $\ell_r = (A/C)$ (the slope of the net lending schedule) or change in lending per unit change in the interest rate. From these two expressions, $B = CI_r$, and $A = C\ell_r$, so that the ratio, β, is equal to

$$\beta = \frac{CI_r}{CI_r + C\ell_r} = \frac{I_r}{I_r + \ell_r} \qquad [5.22]$$

The coefficient β is extremely important and useful. It is *the ratio of the change in the level of investment to the horizontal shift in the net lending schedule*. Changes in the level of investment, then, are

$$\Delta I = \beta\Delta(\ell - gb)$$

Since we know how shifts in the net lending schedule are induced by changes in real income (ℓ_y) and the real money stock (ℓ_m), the coefficient β permits us to relate changes in these last two magnitudes to changes in investment. What about the effect of government borrowing? Simply, a change in government borrowing causes a lateral shift in the lending schedule by the same magnitude, but of opposite sign: an increase in government borrowing of one dollar brings about a shift to the left of the net lending schedule of one dollar, and vice versa. The changes in borrowing by firms, and hence of investment expenditures can be related to changes in real income, the real money stock, and government borrowing by the following expressions[5]:

$$\Delta I = \beta\ell_y(\Delta y) \qquad [5.23]$$

$$\Delta I = \beta\ell_m(\Delta m) \qquad [5.24]$$

$$\Delta I = -\beta(\Delta gb) \qquad [5.25]$$

The coefficient β may be utilized in several interesting ways. First, the magnitude of β may be between zero or one. It will be zero when either I_r is zero or ℓ_r is infinite; it will be one when ℓ_r is zero or when I_r is infinite. In order to verify this last property, divide the

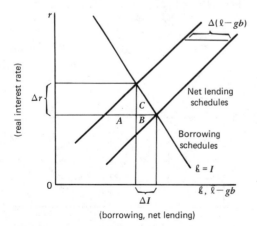

Figure 5-13. A shift in the net lending schedule.

numerator and the denominator by I_r, to obtain

$$\beta = \left(\frac{1}{1 + \left(\frac{\ell_r}{I_r}\right)}\right)$$

In general, β will be larger, the larger the coefficient I_r and the smaller the coefficient ℓ_r. To illustrate the significance of β, Figure 5-14 shows the effects of a given lateral shift in the net lending schedule for the case where I_r is very large (a very flat borrowing schedule, corresponding to a very flat investment schedule) and ℓ_r is very small (a very steep net lending schedule, which in turn corresponds to a very low sensitivity of the desired money stock to changes in the interest rate, L_r) the coefficient β is very large or close to one, and the effects of the shift on investment expenditures are very large. Figure 5-15 shows the opposite case, that is, when investment is not very sensitive to changes in the interest rate (I_r is very low) and the coefficient $\ell_r = bL_r$ is very high (that is, when the desired money stock is very sensitive to changes in the interest rate). In Figure 5-15 the coefficient β is very low (close to zero) and the change in invest-

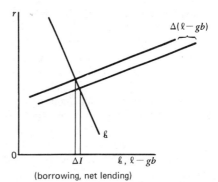

(borrowing, net lending)

Figure 5-15. A relatively steep borrowing schedule combined with a relatively flat lending schedule (a small β coefficient—the Keynesian position).

ment borrowing by firms and hence investment expenditures induced by the same shift of the net lending schedule is minor.

These two very different cases correspond to the Keynesian and Monetarist views of general macroeconomic relationships. In the Keynesian view the coefficient β is very small both because I_r is low, and because $\ell_r = bL_r$ is high (in the extreme, $\beta = 1$). In the Monetarist view the coefficient β is relatively high, and L_r (and hence ℓ_r) is very low. Thus the coefficient β is invaluable in summarizing differences between the two prevailing views of aggregate economy.

Another important element concerning the effects of changes in the level of government borrowing can be analyzed within this framework. In all but the extreme case in which β is zero, an increase in government borrowing brings about an immediate fall in the level of private borrowing and investment expenditures. This is so because to the extent that an increase in government borrowing raises the interest rate, and to the extent that investment expenditures are at all sensitive to the interest rate, private investment expenditures will decrease. This is the so-called *crowding out effect*: increases in government borrowing crowd out private borrowing, and hence investment. The coefficient β is a measure of such crowding out; for each dollar of additional government borrowing, β dollars of private borrowing and

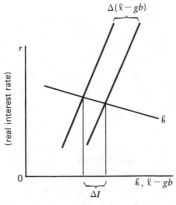

(borrowing, net lending)

Figure 5-14. A relatively flat borrowing schedule combined with a relatively steep lending schedule (a large β coefficient— the monetarist position).

investment expenditures will be crowded out. In the extreme (Monetarist) case of $\beta = 1$, crowding out will be complete. This is a very important effect when government expenditures are financed by borrowing (such as we have assumed in our model), because it tends to diminish the extent to which changes in government expenditures can affect total expenditures. On one side total expenditures will change by the amount of government expenditures, but on the other side private expenditures on investment goods will change by some amount in the opposite direction. In the extreme case, when $\beta = 1$, changes in government expenditures financed by borrowing have a zero net effect on total expenditures, and bring about only a substitution of one type of expenditures for the other. This effect of course does not exist if (according the the liquidity preference theory) the interest rate is determined exclusively, at every point in time, by the actual and desired money stocks.

We can now write the total expenditures schedule. Total expenditures are the sum of consumption expenditures, government expenditures, and investment expenditures. Consumption expenditures depend only on the level of income, and the investment expenditures depend directly on the interest rate, or indirectly (through the mechanism just developed) on the level of income, on real cash balances, and on government borrowing (expressions [5.23], [5.24], and [5.25]). We can write total expenditures as

$$te = \bar{c} + \bar{I} + c_y y + g + \beta \ell_m m + \beta \ell_y y - \beta(gb)$$

The first two terms are the constant components of consumption and investment expenditures; the third, $c_y y$, the part of consumption expenditures that depend on the level of real income; the fourth, g, government expenditures. The next three terms, in turn, reflect the indirect dependence of investment expenditures on the real money stock, the level of real income, and the level of government borrowing. If we recall that in this simple model $g = gb$, that is, government expenditures are financed entirely through borrowing, collecting terms, and calling the first constant term a_0, we can

write the basic expression as expression [5.26]

$$te = a_0 + (c_y + \beta \ell_y)y + \beta \ell_m m + (1 - \beta)g$$

$$[5.26]$$

Expression [5.26] indicates that real total expenditures will be given, at every point in time, by the levels of real income, the real money stock, and real government expenditures. The levels of real income and of real government expenditures have direct and indirect effects. When real income changes, it affects total expenditures directly, through changes in consumption expenditures (depending on the magnitude of c_y, or the marginal propensity to spend), and indirectly, through changes in the lending schedule, in the interest rate, and therefore in investment expenditures (depending on the magnitude of $\beta \ell_y$). When real government expenditures change, total expenditures are affected directly by the same amount (the coefficient one), and indirectly in an opposite direction, depending on the magnitude of the coefficient β. The effects of changes in the real money stock are *only* indirect, through shifts in the lending schedule, and depending on the magnitude of the coefficient ℓ_m. All these connections are described and summarized in Figure 5–16 in a manner so simple that it does not require further elaboration.

Finally, consider (once again) the characterization of the Keynesian and the Monetarist views as being captured by the magnitude of the coefficient β. In the Keynesian view, the coefficient β will be quite small. In the extreme form $\beta = 0$ and the total expenditures schedule reduces to

$$te = a_0 + c_y y + g \qquad [5.27]$$

This is the same simple expression developed for the extreme Keynesian case in the text of this chapter (expression [5.14]). In this case there is no crowding out, so that government expenditures affect total expenditures directly and by the same amount. Changes in real income do not have any indirect effects so that the coefficient for real income is simply the marginal propensity to consume, and the real money stock does not even appear.

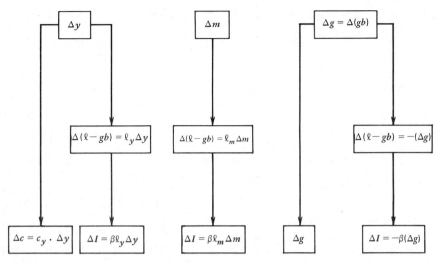

Figure 5-16. A summary of direct and indirect effects of real income, real money stock, and government spending changes upon the components of total expenditures.

In the Monetarist view the coefficient β is large and, in the extreme, equal to one. If this is the case, expression [5.26] becomes

$$te = a_0 + (c_y + \ell_y)y + \ell_m m \quad [5.28]$$

That is, the real money stock does have an effect on total expenditures, and there is complete crowding out, so that the level of real government expenditures does not even appear. Also, for this extreme Monetarist case, since $\ell_y = (1 - c_y - bL_y)$, and $\ell_m = b$ (expressions [5.18] and [5.19]), then [5.28] can be written as

$$te = a_0 + (1 - bL_y)y + bm \quad [5.29]$$

This manner of expressing total expenditures for the extreme Monetarist case lends itself to another illuminating interpretation.

Comparison of Liquidity Preference and Loanable Funds Theories, and the Keynesian and Monetarist Views

Differences between liquidity preference and loanable funds theories of the immediate determination of the interest rate have already been characterized. At the risk of repetition,

let us elaborate on some of these concepts. The suitability of each of the two theories for expressing the Keynesian and the Monetarist views of macroeconomic–monetary relations is of particular interest.

An initial point concerns the suitability of each theory in regards to Keynesian or Monetarist views about the shapes of the demand for money and the investment schedules (that is, the magnitudes of the coefficients L_r and I_r). Any view about the shapes of these schedules can be expressed with either of the two theories of the determination of the interest rate. In the text we derived a general expression for total expenditures by using the liquidity preference theory. Keynesian and Monetarist views concerning the magnitudes of the coefficients in that expression were discussed (in particular, the extreme Keynesian form, expression [5.14], was analyzed). In this Appendix, in turn, by using the loanable funds approach, the particular forms that would reflect the extreme Keynesian and Monetarist positions (expressions [5.27], [5.28], and [5.29]) were shown. But it happens that one of the theories (the liquidity preference approach) makes explicit the magnitudes that

Keynesians believe stronger and more relevant, while the other (the loanable funds view) treats more explicitly the magnitudes that Monetarists believe to be stronger and more relevant.

To see why this is so, let us recall a couple of expressions. The total expenditures schedule was derived by starting with its definition, as the sum of consumption, plus investment, plus government expenditures. By writing each of these components in simple, linear form, expression [5.30] was obtained.

$$te = \bar{c} + \bar{I} + c_y y + g - I_r r \qquad [5.30]$$

From this point, when the liquidity preference approach was used, the determinants of the interest rate were investigated to "plug in" the determinants in expression [5.30]. If one were a believer in the loanable funds theory, a different line of attack could be used. By assuming (as we have done) that the loanable funds market is always in equilibrium, and by recalling that, in this case, hoarding is not simply a residual (as in the liquidity preference theory) but a well-defined relationship as in expressions [5.16] and [5.17], one could use, as a point of departure, the equilibrium condition in the market for loanable funds (expression [5.5′], or

$$y = c + I + g + h \qquad [5.5']$$

In this expression, the term $(c + I + g)$ is equal to total expenditures, so that it can be written as

$$te = y - h$$

or, using the characterization for hoarding, as

$$te = y - b(\bar{m} + L_y y - L_r r - m) =$$
$$-b\bar{m} + (1 - bL_y)y + bm + bL_r r$$

By writing the negative, constant term first as a_0, the expression for total expenditures becomes

$$te = a_0 + (1 - bL_y)y + bm + bL_r r \qquad [5.31]$$

Expressions [5.30] and [5.31] can now be compared. In [5.30], there are direct effects on total expenditures of real income and real government expenditures; any indirect effects are summarized in the last term, $I_r r$. In the second, there are also direct and indirect effects, but through a different channel. First, income will influence total expenditures directly to the extent that it is not hoarded; the coefficient bL_y denotes the part of any increase in real income that is neither consumed nor lent, and there is hence hoarding. The term $(1 - bL_y)$ therefore is the part that, out of any increase in income, will not be hoarded. Second, the real money stock appears explicitly, indicating that changes in the real money stock will affect total expenditures directly to the extent that lending is changed. All indirect effects (of real income, of the real money stock, and of government expenditures and borrowing) are summarized in the last term, $bL_r r$, which indicates the extent to which changes in the interest rate will change hoarding.

Why would a Keynesian choose to use an expression such as [5.30] to attack the problem of singling out the determinants of total expenditures and choose a liquidity preference approach to interest rate determination? If the demand for money schedule is very flat (that is, if the coefficient L_r is very high), the interest rate will not change much, and whatever changes may occur will not matter in regard to total expenditures, because in the Keynesian view the term I_r is very small; that is, investment expenditures do not react much to changes in the interest rate. Furthermore, in the Keynesian view the demand for money is not only flat (the extreme being the liquidity trap case, of course) but also quite unstable. That is, the demand schedule itself may change frequently in an unpredictable manner. If this is so, changes in the quantity of money will not be very closely related to changes in total expenditures, because the interest rate depends only on the demand and the supply of money.

If one is in the policymaking business of manipulating total expenditures, the best that one could hope is that changes in the quantity of money keep the interest rate at some stable level, while changes in government expenditures take care of influencing total expenditures, on which it has a direct, predictable effect. Moreover, if there is any item that might provide a stable relationship between the level of real income and the level of total expenditures, it is the coefficient c_y, the marginal propensity to consume. This is the *reliable relationship* in the Keynesian world. The last term in expression [5.30] is negligible, and at most unreliable, and might as well be dropped; the result is expression [5.14]. Thus we can see why expression [5.30] and the liquidity preference view are the most suitable to express the Keynesian view. No wonder that Keynes invented the liquidity preference theory!

What about the Monetarist view, and the adequacy of the loanable funds theory and expression [5.31]?[6] In the Monetarist view, in which the level of investment is very sensitive to changes in the interest rate and the demand for money is very inelastic (that is, the coefficient I_r is very high, and the coefficient L_r is very low), effects treated as secondary in the formal presentation [5.31] will in fact be unimportant and can all be summarized in the same *last term*. The interest rate is rather constant, given by the narrow range determined by a very flat borrowing (investment) schedule,

and whatever changes occur in the interest rate will affect hoarding, and therefore total expenditures, by very little, because the term L_r is very small. The last term in expression [5.31] is, on both accounts, very unimportant. Likewise, if there is any stable link between income and expenditures, it is given by the *speed at which the public wish to adjust their real money stock, b*, and by the *demand for money*—more precisely, by the response of the desired money stock to changes in the level of income, L_y. And what is the term L_y? L_y is the *inverse of velocity*, or the term "*k*" that was discussed in Chapter 3 when the quantity theory as a theory of the demand for money was studied. Velocity becomes the *reliable, dependable* connection between income and expenditures.[7] What about the manipulation of total expenditures by the policy maker? Government expenditures do not count, or count very little, and whatever reliable influence the policymaker may have on total expenditures is that through changes in the money stock. Thus, the emphasis upon monetary policy is a hallmark of the Monetarist.

FOOTNOTES

[1] This is true even if there were undistributed profits retained by business firms; when this is the case, there is an explicit income accruing to households in the form of an increase in the value of their shares.

[2] Of course, during some periods some households will not lend, but will borrow. However, the symbol represents households *net* lending, that is, the difference between lending and borrowing by households.

[3] Viewing the business sector as a whole, these investment goods are items that firms "sell to themselves"; but from the viewpoint of individual firms these items are intermediate goods (machines) that each firm sells to other firms.

[4] Readers are encouraged to survey the Appendix to the present chapter, although there is no lack of continuity without it.

[5] The shift of the curve may be gauged

using the following method. Substitution of expression [5.19] into [5.21] yields

$$\ell = \ell_0 + \ell_y y + \ell_m m + \ell_r r - gb$$

Since we know that $I = \ell$,

$$I = \ell_0 + \ell_y y + \ell_m m + \ell_r r - gb$$

so, for example, if m (the real money stock) changes, the change in investment (ΔI) may be expressed,

$$\Delta I = \ell_m(\Delta m)$$

[6] Modern Monetarists envision a somehow more complex theory of the immediate determinants of the interest rate than the *loanable funds* view sketched in the Appendix to Chapter 5. Rather than only in terms of flows of borrowing and lending, they cast their view also in terms of stocks (as in the liquidity preference theory), but stocks of money,

bonds, and real capital (machines). Nevertheless, consider the following quotation from Milton Friedman: "We have not worked out the formal theory of a more sophisticated adjustment process in either detail . . . The one aspect we have considered is the effect of changes in M on interest rates. In the analysis, we have in effect regarded interest rates as adjusting very rapidly to clear the market for loanable funds, the supply of loanable funds as being possibly linked to changes in M. . . ." Milton Friedman, "A Theoretical Framework for Monetary Analysis," in *Milton Friedman's Monetary Framework* (Chicago, The University of Chicago Press, 1974), p. 54. In this quotation, Friedman is referring to work done with Anna Schwartz for the National Bureau of Economic Research.

[7] In 1963, Friedman and Meiselman published an influential (and controversial) study in which they take the consumption function (for the Keynesian view) and velocity (for the Monetarist view) as being the key relationships to test in their connection between expenditures and income. See Milton Friedman and David Meiselman, "The Relative Stability of Monetary Velocity and the Investment Multiplier in the United States, 1897–1958," *Stabilization Policies: A Series of Research Studies Prepared for the Commission on Money and Credit* (Englewood Cliffs, N.J., Prentice Hall, 1963).

KEY CONCEPTS

monetary policy	hoarding	consumption function
fiscal policy	permanent income hypothesis	marginal project
three sectors of the economy: households, business firms, government	present income	liquidity preference theory
	expected future income	loanable funds theory
markets: commodities, loanable funds, factor	marginal propensity to consume	"crowding out"
		liquidity trap

QUESTIONS FOR DISCUSSION

1. Must markets always be in equilibrium? Explain the adjustment process in the commodity and the loanable funds markets if they are out of equilibrium. Is this true for both the short run and the long run?

2. Why must hoarding be 0 in order for equilibrium to be attained from an expenditures approach?

3. How do Keynesians view the investment schedules slope, compared to Monetarists?

4. Explain the difference between the liquidity preference theory of interest rate determination and the loanable funds theory of interest rate determination in the short run.

5. Explain the factors that affect the interest rate according to the liquidity preference approach (in our simple model) and how they affect the interest rate.

6. What effect does real income have on total expenditures? Remember both the direct and indirect effects. Also explain the effects of interest rates, government spending, and the real money stock.

7. How do Monetarists and Keynesians view the slope of the investment schedule? How do they view the slope of the demand for money? What does this imply about the effects of a change in the interest rate on each?

8. Explain the role of hoarding in both the liquidity preference and the loanable funds theories of interest rate determination.

9. How can the β coefficient be used to measure crowding out in our simple model?

10. Describe the role of the economy's household and business sectors and explain how the existence of one is necessary to the survival of the other. Is the government sector vital to the survival of the other two? Could the government sector exist without households and businesses?

11. In terms of the "pool of water" example, explain why hoarding must equal zero (equation [5.6']) for equilibrium to exist in both the commodities and the loanable funds market simultaneously (equations [5.4'] and [5.5']).

12. Explain the notion of "opportunity costs" as it applies to the relationship between interest rates and both consumption and investment expenditures.

13. Explain the significance of the "sensitivity" term, I_r, in equation [5.8]. What can it tell you about the priorities of a firm in its decision-making process? What is its significance in the Keynesian–Monetarist debate? With what term in equation [5.7] does it coincide and how are the two terms similar?

14. True or False: Explain.
   According to the liquidity preference theory, there is a positive relationship between interest rates (r) and the money supply (m) with every percentage increase in m being matched by an equal percentage increase in r.

15. As incomes rise people wish to hold greater amounts of money in cash balances. Given a fixed supply of money, show graphically how this affects the interest rate. Without reference to your graph, explain why your results are logically consistent with the basic laws of supply and demand as they apply to loanable funds.

16. Show graphically the direct and indirect effects on total expenditures of both positive and negative changes in income, government spending, and the money supply.

CHAPTER 6

THE MODERN ANALYSIS OF EXPENDITURES, INCOME, AND PRICES: (II) The Supply Side

Chapter 5 concluded with a general expression for total expenditures, or *aggregate demand*, as it is sometimes labeled. Chapter 6 puts the expression to use and analyzes the determination of the price level and real income, and the effect of monetary and fiscal policies on those magnitudes. Expression [6.1] and the condition for equilibrium in the market for commodities (total expenditures equal to income) will be emphasized along with the importance of the supply side of the economic system (which has barely been mentioned up to now). After using two extreme and unrealistic, but very useful assumptions (that either real income or prices are fixed), we will analyze a more realistic and satisfactory view, namely, the one wherein there is some "full employment" level of output but from which there may be short-run departures. We will discover that there is an automatic adjustment mechanism of sorts in the economy, but that such a mechanism may not be so automatic or quick enough to counter deviations from full employment. Further, we will see that there are ways in which monetary and fiscal policies may be used to overcome the effects of undesirable shocks on the economic system.

EXPENDITURES, REAL INCOME, AND PRICES: THE MISSING EQUATION

Consider the familiar expression (from Chapter 5) for total real expenditures,

$$te = a_0 + a_y \cdot y + a_m \cdot m + a_g \cdot g \qquad [6.1]$$

The expression identifies total expenditures for a certain level of real income, provided that the levels of real money stock and government expenditures are also known and given. (Loanable funds *equilibrium* is built into the total expenditures function [6.1].) Government expenditures are a policy variable in that these expenditures will be whatever government decides they will be. But the levels of real income or the real money stock remain unknown. We do know that, if the economy is going to be in equilibrium, total expenditures (the amount of goods and services that consumers, firms, and government wish to purchase per period) must be equal to what the economy is producing, that is, to the level of real output or income. Only in this case will there be no un-desired changes in business inventories. This is the condition for equilibrium in the market for commodities,

$$te = y \qquad\qquad [6.2]$$

Expression [6.2] provides some help, although one cannot use it to deter-mine what the value of all these magnitudes will be in equilibrium. In the language of the mathematician, there are two equations ([6.1] and [6.2]) and three unknowns: total expenditures (*te*), real income (*y*), and the level of the real money stock (*m*). There is, so to speak, a *missing equation*.[1]

The problem is shown in Figure 6-1, where total expenditures schedules (for a given level of government expenditures, g_0) are shown for different levels of the real money stock (m_0, m_1, m_2, and so on). The higher the real money stock, the higher the level of total expenditures corresponding to every level of real income, and to each real money stock there will correspond a different real income and a different *te* schedule. The condition of equilibrium in the market for commodities, *te = y*, is also shown in Figure 6-1; it is represented by the line from the origin, with a 45 degree angle (a slope equal to one). Even if the analysis is restricted to points where there is equilibrium in the

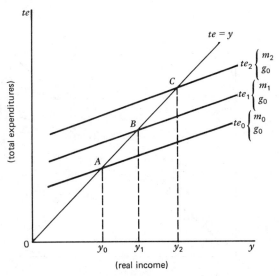

Figure 6-1. Total expenditure function shifts with changes in the real money stock.

commodities market, such as points A, B, C, and so on, there are still many points (one for each level of the real money stock), rather than just one.

Consider the *real money stock*, which is the nominal money stock (M) divided by the price level (P), or

$$m = M/P \qquad [6.3]$$

The nominal money stock, M, is also a policy variable since it will be "chosen" by the monetary authority. Prices are determined in the market, however. A more explicit form of the total expenditures schedule [6.1] can be written

$$te = a + a_y \cdot y + a_m \cdot (M/P) + a_g \cdot g \qquad [6.4]$$

Once more, the nominal money stock is whatever the monetary authority decides it to be, but the price level is a variable determined by the economic system. The problem of the missing equation can then be repeated but with reference to the *price level* rather than to the real stock of money. For a given nominal money stock and for a given real level of real government expenditures (both decided by government), there will be as many total expenditures schedules as there are possible price levels. Figure 6–2 shows essentially the same thing as Figure 6–1; for a given M_0 and g_0, the different total expenditures schedules $te_0, te_1, te_2, \ldots$, correspond to different levels of prices, $P_0, P_1, P_2, \ldots$, and so on. The lower the price level for a given nominal money stock M_0, the higher the real money stock and the higher the position of the total expenditures schedule.

One more equation is required. The *supply side of the economy*, which

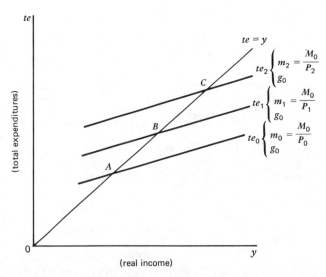

Figure 6–2. Total expenditure function shifts with price level changes.

has been ignored up to this point, must be combined with the total expenditures function. Real output must be related to the quantity of resources in the economy, the stock of physical capital, land, and natural resources, and the labor force. The equilibrium levels of real income as output cannot be discussed without the attempted reference to these factors. The concept is identical to a determination of the equilibrium price and quantity for tomatoes with knowledge about only the demand curve for tomatoes and information about the supply curve. Up to this point we have identified only a total expenditures schedule (akin to the demand schedule for tomatoes) and the equilibrium condition in the market for commodities (total expenditures equal to income), similar to the equilibrium condition in the market for tomatoes (quantity demanded equals quantity supplied).

There are two extreme, and very unrealistic, ways to describe the supply or production side of the economy and to solve the problem of the missing equation. Before presenting a more realistic framework, let us look at these two extreme assumptions by expanding the framework already developed. They are interesting because there are situations when such extreme assumptions may not be an inaccurate approximation to the real world.

The first of these two extreme approximations is an assumption that *at all times* the level of real income (output) in the economy is fixed at some level (for example, some rigid concept of full employment), while prices are completely flexible. In this very extreme case, there are no departures whatsoever from the full employment level of output—the level of production forthcoming when all of the factors are employed at their maximum capacity. Here nothing that might happen to total expenditures (the demand side) can affect the level of output, not even in the short run. In an analogy with the market for tomatoes, we might say that the supply of tomatoes is fixed at some level, at all times, no matter what. This is, certainly, the simplest theory one could have about the supply side of the economic system.

The alternative extreme assumption is to say that the price level is fixed at some level, and that real income (output) can be produced at whatever amount people wish to purchase. In the tomatoes case, this would be the equivalent to saying that the supply curve of tomatoes is a horizontal curve, at some price, and that the quantity supplied will depend only on the amount demanded at that price. Let us consider in some detail what would happen in each of these two cases.

AN EXTREME CASE: FIXED REAL INCOME (OUTPUT),
FLEXIBLE PRICES

Take, first, the case in which real income (output) is kept continuously at some rigid full employment level and prices are completely flexible. Suppose, in Figure 6–3, that $\bar{y}$ is the fixed level of real income. We can see that for a given

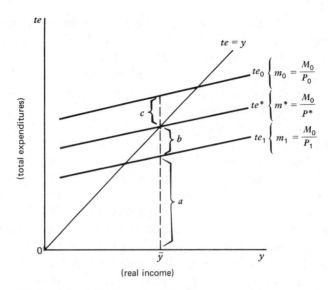

Figure 6-3. *Adjustments with constant real income and flexible prices.*

level of real government expenditures (g_0) and the nominal money stock (M_0) there is only one price level that will satisfy all the equilibrium conditions: in Figure 6-3 this price level is designated P^*. Of all three price levels shown in the figure (P_0; lower than P^*; and P_1, higher than P^*), only P^* is the price level for which, given the nominal money stock M_0, the real money stock (m^*) at the fixed level of real income, $\bar{y}$, total expenditures are equal to income.

What would happen if in fact the price level happens not to be P^* but, say, P_1 ("too high")? In this case, the real money stock will be "too low" (at the level m_1) and the relevant total expenditures schedule will be $(te)_1$. At the level of real income $\bar{y}$, total expenditures will be lower than what is being produced at every period in the economy: real income, $\bar{y}$, is equal to the sum of the two segments $(a + b)$.[2] As expenditures in this case are only what is indicated as segment a, segment b is the excess of output over expenditures. In this situation producers observe the unintentional accumulation of inventories and they might attempt to fire workers and to produce less. But, as soon as this starts to happen, nominal wages begin to fall and so do prices. The fall in prices starts to increase the level of the real money stock and the expenditures corresponding to every level of real income. That is, the total expenditures schedule starts shifting upward, thereby reducing the gap. Wages, costs of production, and prices will continue to fall as long as such a gap exists, and as long as prices keep falling the real money stock will keep rising and the total expenditures schedule will continue shifting upward. The result will be the disappearance of the gap, and total expenditures schedule will return to position te^*. And at total expenditures position te^*, the price level must be P^*.

What if the price level was "too low," like P_0? At that price level, the real money stock (m_0) is "too high," the total expenditures schedule is positioned at $(te)_0$, and at the prevailing level of real income, $\bar{y}$, total expenditures is given by the sum of the three segments, a, b, and c. The gap (now an excess of what people wish to buy over what is being produced) is given by the segment c. As inventories begin to fall, producers will try to produce more. But, since every resource is completely employed, producer efforts to hire more factors of production (mostly labor) will result only in an increase in wages and costs of production, and therefore in prices. Prices rise, and will continue rising for as long as the excess of total expenditures over output continues. But as prices rise, assuming the same level of the nominal money stock, the *real* stock of money falls and the total expenditures schedule (at the same level of income, $\bar{y}$) will start shifting downward. Such a process will continue until the real money stock is equal to m^*, and for this to happen prices must be at the equilibrium level P^*.

The assumption of such a rigid level of real income is unrealistic and will soon be modified, but it can be a good approximation to situations in which the flexibility of prices and wages assures a very quick adjustment in the market for factors of production—the *supply side of the economy*. Indeed, this was the way in which the classical economists sometimes visualized the workings of the system. Notice that this discussion resembles very much the preview offered in Chapter 4 concerning the adjustment process in the pre-Keynesian, classical world. In fact it is the same analysis except that we now know more about the determinants of total expenditures. Finally, notice not only that flexibility of prices (and wages) is necessary for this process to take place, but also that the real money stock must be one of the determinants of total expenditures. It is through the real value of money that the total expenditures schedule shifts up or down (closing the gap) as a response of changes in prices. Later on, after a more realistic consideration of "full employment," we will see that all kinds of problems emerge if the real money stock has no influence over total expenditures (or even if such influences are minimal). But, to conclude the analysis of this first extreme case, consider a sudden change (say, an increase) in the nominal money stock. This is, of course, what is called *monetary policy*.

In Figure 6–4, assume that the money stock is M_0 and the price level P^* so that the whole economy is in equilibrium. Suppose that there is a sudden increase of the nominal money stock, from M_0 to M_1. At first such a change translates, on a sudden increase in the real money stock, to $m_1 = M_1/P_0$, because prices are still what they were before. The total expenditures schedule therefore shifts abruptly upward to position $(te)_1$. There is an initial increase in total expenditures, and a gap (segment a). Producers are not able to increase production, and their efforts to do so result only in bidding up the price of factors of production (wages) so that costs of production and prices rise. As

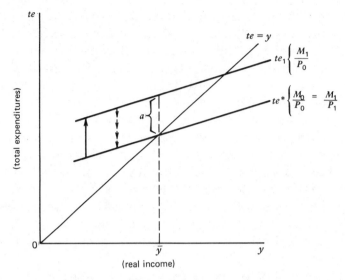

Figure 6-4. Effects of a money stock increase.

this happens, the real money stock begins to return to the original level as does the level of expenditures corresponding to the level of income $\bar{y}$. The story proceeds along familiar lines: prices rise for as long as the gap exists between total expenditures and income, and the total expenditures schedule is the same as the original one. For this to happen, the real money stock must be the same as before the change of the nominal money stock (m^*), which requires the price level to be higher than before the same proportion as the nominal money stock increased. This is, of course, the familiar *neutrality of money* proposition of the classics discussed briefly in Chapter 4.

A similar experiment can be conducted with a change in the level of real government expenditures rather than a change in the nominal money stock. The analysis of such a change is reserved for the next section, however, where the other extreme assumption about the supply side will be used.

A SECOND EXTREME CASE: FIXED PRICES, COMPLETELY VARIABLE REAL INCOME

The opposite view is the assumption that for some reason prices and wages are fixed but that real income always responds to changes in total expenditures. Even though we are imposing these assumptions rather arbitrarily here, we should realize that such a case would not be too extreme as an approximation of situations of widespread unemployment. Indeed, this was the case considered by Keynes when writing his most influential work at the time of the Great Depression. Later on, factors that may account for such an occurrence will be analyzed.

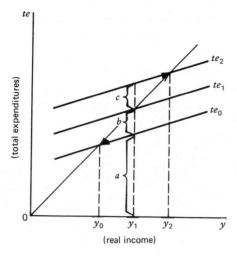

Figure 6-5. *Real income adjustment with prices constant.*

Figure 6-5 describes such a case. There, all three levels of real income (y_0, y_1, and y_2) are possible equilibrium levels, depending on which is the relevant total expenditures schedule (te_0, te_1, or te_2). In turn each of these schedules corresponds to certain levels of the real money stock and real government expenditures.

Suppose that the real money stock and government expenditures are those for which the relevant total expenditures line is te_1, so that the equilibrium level of real income is y_1. Assume, further, that something happens so that the total expenditures schedule suddenly shifts upward, say, to te_2. This "something" could be an increase in the nominal (and real, since prices are fixed) money stock, or an increase in government expenditures, or a change in autonomous expenditures (the number a_0, in expression [6.1]). As in the fixed income, flexible price change, there is now a gap, in this case an excess of expenditures over income. Expenditures have suddenly risen to a higher level (in Figure 6-5, the sum of segments $a + b + c$), so that the gap is segment c. As in the previous case, producers find that their sales are higher than what they are producing and there is an incentive for them to produce more. But in this case they are successful in doing so, presumably because there is *widespread unemployment.* Wages and prices will not change. Real income (output) will start to rise and the change of real income over time may be visualized as a movement along the 45 degree line. Expenditures will also rise above their initial level as a movement along the new total expenditures schedule, te_2. How is the gap closed? Real income will rise up to the level y_2, where once again total expenditures are equal to income. Note that during the adjustment both real income and real expenditures rise, but the change per unit of time of total expenditures is less than the same change in income. This is the case because the *marginal propensity to spend out of income* (the coefficient a_y

in expression [6.1]) is less than one, so that as income climbs along the 45°
line, expenditures increase by less along the total expenditures line. Eventually
(at $y = y_2$), income "catches up" with expenditures.

What if, instead, there is a fall in total expenditures—more precisely, a
shift downward of the total expenditures schedule, from the initial te_1 to,
say, te_0? Such a fall could result from a fall in autonomous expenditures (the
term a_0 in expression [6.1]), or a reduction in either the nominal money stock
or government expenditures. In this case there is an initial fall in total expenditures, at the initial real income level y_1, an excess of output over expenditures,
involuntary accumulation of inventories, and a desire by producers to produce
less. As they proceed to do so, wages and prices do not change; the total expenditures schedule remains at the new, lower position te_1, and the system can
eliminate the gap only by a reduction of real income to a lower y_0 level.

In this extreme case real income is given by whatever position the total
expenditures schedule takes, which, in turn, will depend only on its "autonomous" component. The autonomous component includes the coefficient
number a_0 and the levels of the policy variables, that is, the money stock and
government expenditures. If we are interested in the equilibrium points rather
than the adjustment process, we can formulate the dependence of real income
on these three factors. In equilibrium, points such as the three we just analyzed,
total expenditures will equal income; if we substitute this equality (that is,
expression [6.2]) into the left-hand side of [6.1], we obtain

$$y = a_0 + a_y \cdot y + a_m \cdot m + a_g \cdot g$$

so that, solving for the level of real income, we obtain

$$y = \frac{a_0}{1 - a_y} + \frac{a_m}{1 - a_y} m + \frac{a_g}{1 - a_y} g \qquad [6.5]$$

Expression [6.5] relates changes in a, m, and g to the final resulting changes in
real income. The coefficients of each of these terms are sometimes called
multipliers. We can develop the simple Keynesian multiplier by recalling that
in an extremely basic version of the Keynesian model $a_g = 1$ and $a_m = 0$. The
marginal propensity to spend out of income, a_y, is simply the marginal propensity to consume, c_y, and the autonomous component is equal to the autonomous parts of investment and consumption expenditures, $\bar{I}$ and $\bar{c}$. Then,
expression [6.5] reduces to

$$y = \frac{\bar{c} + \bar{I}}{1 - c_y} + \frac{1}{1 - c_y} \cdot g$$

where the multiplier for government expenditures or of autonomous private
investment, for that matter, is $(1/1 - c_y)$. This simple Keynesian multiplier is
larger than one. If the marginal propensity to consume (c_y) is 0.8, the multi-

plier is $(1/1 - 0.8) = 1/0.2 = 5$, and the change in the level of income resulting from an increase in government expenditures of, for example, 100 million dollars will be $(100) \cdot (5) = 500$ million dollars.

Let us also consider the other extreme, the Monetarist case. Here, too, there is a multiplier, but now it relates the change in the *money stock* to the resulting change in *real income*. In the most extreme monetarist form, $a_m = b$ (the coefficient of adjustment of actual to desired real cash balances), $a_g = 0$ (government expenditures do not influence total expenditures), and the marginal propensity to spend out of income $a_y = (1 - b \cdot L_y)$, so that $(1 - a_y) = b \cdot L_y$, and the expression [6.5] reduces to

$$y = \frac{a}{bL_y} + (1/L_y) \cdot m$$

The Monetarist multiplier is thus the *inverse of velocity.*

These multipliers should not be taken too seriously. The important thing to be learned from the foregoing section on the extreme case of fixed prices and variable real income is the manner in which equilibrium between expenditures and income is reached. After considering these two extreme assumptions, we can analyze more realistic cases.

A MORE GENERAL VIEW—THE CONCEPT OF FULL EMPLOYMENT

In order to overcome the missing equation problem two extreme assumptions concerning the behavior of the real sector or supply side of the economy were made earlier in this chapter. Both assumptions were very unrealistic, and applicable at best only in very special situations. On the one hand, prices and wages are not fixed and do change in response to shocks; on the other, the assumption of a fixed level of employment and output is obviously too rigid. Employment and output also change in response to shocks and there will be short-run departures from whatever point we take full employment to be. The purpose of the present section is to define a level of full employment in a more precise, flexible, and realistic way.

At any point in time there exists in the economy a given level of productive resources—physical capital such as buildings and machines, land and other natural resources, and a labor force. Also, at each point in time all of the factors of production will be used more or less intensively and a certain percentage of the labor force will be employed. The higher the percentage of the labor force being employed, the higher the level of production of goods and services in the economy.[3]

A meaningful definition of full employment is not easy. Obviously "full employment" does not mean that everybody in the labor force is employed. In a dynamic economy, with geographical mobility and continuous change in all sectors, some people ordinarily in the labor force are *temporarily* unemployed and in the process of changing jobs at any point in time. And this will occur even in times when all aggregate sectors are in long-run equilibrium and all expectations are fulfilled. The rate of unemployment that prevails in the long-run equilibrium is called the *natural rate of unemployment.*[4]

The natural rate of unemployment depends on many factors that do not tend to change too often or too abruptly. For example, the natural rate of unemployment depends on how efficiently and how quickly the labor market works, on how fast vacancies and workers are matched, on the costs of hiring and firing and of changing jobs, on regulations affecting structural changes in labor markets, and so forth. In official US government statistics, 4 percent used to be the rate of unemployment that is the equivalent of the natural rate. After 1977, the benchmark was increased to 5 percent.

The natural rate of unemployment is defined here as the reference point; thus full employment exists when the rate of unemployment is equal to the natural rate. In turn, the *full employment output* or potential output (or real income) is the level of real income-output forthcoming when there is full employment.[5]

It is possible for the rate of unemployment to be other than the natural rate. This occurs at times when there is disequilibrium in the economy and while employment and output adjustments are taking place. Indeed, one characteristic of the adjustment process is that the unemployment rate in fact departs from its natural level. For example, there are times when employment is at a higher level than the full employment level, that is, when the rate of unemployment is below the natural rate. We shall use this more flexible and realistic concept of full employment in the model of this chapter.

FULL EMPLOYMENT EQUILIBRIUM, THE AUTOMATIC ADJUSTMENT MECHANISM AND WHEN IT CAN FAIL

The definition of a full employment equilibrium level of output and income as one corresponding to the natural rate of unemployment provides a solution to the missing equation, in a manner similar but far more flexible than the assumption of a level of output fixed at all times. If full employment level of income is denoted as y^f, then the expression

$$y = y^f \qquad [6.6]$$

is not a condition that will be fulfilled at all times, but is rather an *equilibrium condition* that will be true under certain circumstances. When [6.6] is fulfilled and when [6.2] also holds—that is, when the level of income is equal to the level of expenditures—then full employment (or "global") equilibrium may be said to exist. Let us investigate departures from global equilibrium in addition to whether there is any mechanism in the economic system for eventually reaching global equilibrium.

Suppose the economy is in a position of full employment equilibrium, as shown in Figure 6-6. The level of output and income is equal to full employment income, total expenditures are in turn equal to the level of income, and the total expenditures schedule is $(te)_0$, for M_0, P_0, and g_0. Suddenly there is a change in the autonomous component of total expenditures (the term a_0 in the expression for total expenditures, [6.1]), so that total expenditures will be at a lower level than before for each level of income, real money stock, and real government expenditures. The change that could occur because of the fall in the autonomous component of investment, is visualized in Figure 6-6 as a shift downward of the total expenditures schedule.[6] At the same level of income as before (y^f), expenditures fall short of income; the gap is depicted in Figure 6-6. Business inventories start to accumulate since total purchases of goods and services (expenditures) are less than what is being produced. Producers will have an incentive to produce less in reducing output, and, they lay off some of their workers.

After a while real income is at a level lower than full employment and the rate of unemployment is higher than the natural rate. As these changes occur, nominal wages start to fall as a response of the labor market to the excess supply of labor, and as wages fall so do prices. With a fall in prices the real stock of money begins to rise (since the nominal stock remains at its initial level) and, to the extent that the real money stock influences total expenditures, total expenditures start to rise. Graphically, the total expenditures schedule starts to

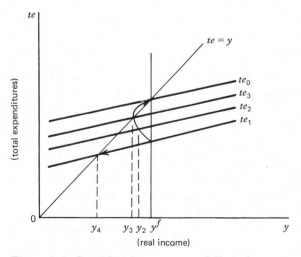

Figure 6-6. Possible adjustments to full employment equilibrium.

shift upward. For example, it could become schedule te_2. But, at the level of real income y_2 and with the total expenditures schedule $(te)_2$, an excess of output over expenditures remains, so that output falls still more. As this happens, prices go on falling, and the real money stock goes on rising, as do expenditures. At some point [for example, at the level of income y_3, and a level of prices and of the real money stock such that the total expenditures schedule is $(te)_3$], expenditures and output are once again equal and output stops falling. But, because output is now at a level lower than full employment, wages and prices continue to fall and the real money stock and total expenditures to rise.

The end of the process is a return to the level of full employment output. In Figure 6–6 an arrow shows the path of real income (falling at first, and then rising to its full employment level).

Consider once more the mechanism bringing the economy-wide equilibrium at full employment, namely, the influence of the real money stock in total real expenditures. For this mechanism to be operative, wages and prices must fall. Two conditions are required for the automatic mechanism to operate: (1) wages and prices must be completely flexible, and (2) the real money stock must be a determinant of total expenditures. Should either of these two conditions not be met, the economy would be in trouble. And it just happens that the message of Keynes' work was, precisely, that these two conditions might not be met. First, wages and prices might not be flexible in the downward direction, partly because of all sorts of institutional constraints (such as labor contracts fixing nominal wages for some time), and also because of union behavior (that is, union refusal to accept cuts in nominal wages even if there were unemployment and even if prices were lower). Workers, to some extent, suffer from *money illusion.*

Figure 6–6 shows what would happen if wages and prices were totally rigid in the downward direction. The adjustment would not proceed as previously described but would act according to the arrow, moving along the total expenditures schedule $(te)_1$, continuously pulling income down to a level y_4 and remaining there. Such a reduction in income and employment occurs exactly in the manner of the extreme "variable output, fixed price" case that was considered earlier in the chapter.

Rigidity of wages and prices was an eventual fact of life that could not be considered a significant blow to the theories of the classical economists before Keynes. The classicals always knew that a necessary condition for markets to work was that prices be flexible. Moreover, the problem of wage and price rigidity, although prohibiting the economic system from automatically reaching a full-employment equilibrium, did not very much alter the prescription for the kind of policy that would be sufficient to restore that global equilibrium, that is, monetary policy. If the automatic mechanism did not work only because wages and prices did not fall, the increase in the *real* money stock necessary for bringing total expenditures back to their initial level could be equally provided by increasing the *nominal* money stock. In other words, if wages and prices cannot fall, the real money stock would not rise automatically, but a rise can be brought about equivalently by increasing the nominal money stock.

A far more profound question was the second contention emerging from the work of Keynes. Keynes argued that, even if wages and prices are perfectly flexible and fall when output and employment are below the full employment level, such a decline would do nothing to total expenditures since the resulting increase in the real stock of money would not affect total expenditures. This is the extreme Keynesian case of [5.27] in Chapter 5 (Appendix): the real money stock (for the reasons discussed there) is not a determinant of total expenditures. This point is a far more significant objection to the conventional view, from the viewpoint of both economic theory and policy remedies. From the standpoint of economic theory Keynes' view is important because it is not a matter of simply denying that an assumption (price flexibility) would be met, but of saying that even when markets are not disturbed by any rigidity the automatic mechanism of adjustment to full employment could not work. From the viewpoint of the appropriate remedial policy, the situation described by Keynes would render monetary policy unimportant.

Clearly, the same reasons why the adjustment mechanism would not work (even with perfect wage and price flexibility) were the reasons why the conventional policy prescription (an increase in the quantity of nominal money) would fail: the absence of the real money stock as a determinant of total expenditures. The economy would be situated at a level of real income y_4, with an expenditure schedule $(te)_1$, and unemployment would be something more than just a transitory episode occurring during the adjustment. It could be that a true *quasiequilibrium* situation would remain unchanged even while monetary policy was being tried. After all, both wages and prices fell substantially during the Great Depression of the 1930s and such a fall did not seem to get the economy out of the slump. The only solution was fiscal policy, that is, an increase in the level of government expenditures.

Keynes' argument was a strong blow to the economics of the classics, and it provided the foundation for the belief that the attainment of maintenance of full employment required active fiscal actions on the part of the government. In the years since Keynes' work, however, many Keynesian propositions have been questioned, as outlined in Chapters 4 and 5. But the initial impact was a strong reversal of views about the adequacy of traditional policies, and the implementation of massive fiscal programs to get the world economy moving once again.

After an analysis of the automatic adjustment mechanism, when it can fail, and what corrective policies can accomplish, let us consider in more detail the effects of shocks originating in policy. Much of the following section is simply an immediate application of earlier discussion.

THE EFFECTS OF MONETARY AND FISCAL POLICIES

Suppose that the economic system is at an initial equilibrium, that wages and prices are completely flexible, and that we wish to investigate the short- and long-run effects of changes in the policy variables, that is, in the nominal money stock and in the level of real government expenditures. There are four possible cases to consider: a fall in the money stock or in government expenditures (a *contractionary policy*), or a rise in the money stock or in government expenditures (an *expansionary policy*). Since these four exercises are a straightforward application of the previous analysis, we will concentrate on only two of them: an *expansionary monetary* policy (a sudden increase in the nominal money stock) and a *contractionary fiscal* policy (a fall in the level of real government expenditures). We will assume in both cases that both the real money stock and government expenditures do influence, to one degree or another, the level of total expenditures. That is, we will not consider either of the two extreme (Keynesian or Monetarist) cases.

EXPANSIONARY MONETARY POLICY

Assume, first, that the economy is in global full employment equilibrium, with a stock of nominal money M_0, a price level P_0, real government expenditure at g_0, and a real income at the full employment level y^f, as in Figure 6–7. If the nominal money stock increases from M_0 to M_1 in this circumstance, the immediate result is an increase in the level of real balances to m_1 and a rise in real expenditures. The situation is visualized in Figure 6–7 as an upward shift in the total expenditures schedule from $(te)_0$ to $(te)_1$, the schedule corresponding to the now higher level of the real money stock, $m_1 = M_1/P_0$.

There is now an excess of expenditures over income, an unexpected depletion of business inventories, and the incentive for producers to increase output. As they do so, and as output starts to increase, wages begin to rise because of the increased demand for labor and so do prices. The rise in prices starts decreasing the level of the real money stock from high level m_1, and the fall in the real money stock starts decreasing total expenditures, lowering the total expenditures schedule [for example, to $(te)_2$ when prices have risen to P_2 and the real money stock is $m_2 = M_1/P_2$]. At some point, as expenditures fall from their new higher level and real income rises, they are again equal [for example, when the level of output is y_3 and the total expenditures schedule is $(te)_3$]. But, since output is *higher* than full employment output and the rate of unemployment is lower than the natural rate, wages and prices continue rising,

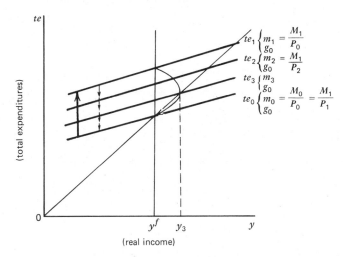

Figure 6-7. Effects of an expansionary monetary policy.

so that the real money stock falls (the total expenditures schedule shifts downward). The process continues until the initial equilibrium is restored at the same, full employment level of real income as before, but with a higher level of nominal wages and prices. Clearly, for equilibrium to reoccur the *real* money stock must be at the same level that it was before the policy change (m_0). Thus the price level must increase in exactly the same proportion as the nominal money stock so that $(M_1/P_1) = m_0 = M_0/P_0$. Once again, money is neutral in the long run, and we obtain the same long-run result as in the case of rigid, fixed output. The big difference is that the level of real income has changed in the short run: for some time, during the adjustment process, real income is *above* the full employment level.

CONTRACTIONARY FISCAL POLICY

Consider a second experiment, namely, a contractionary fiscal policy in the form of a sudden fall of government expenditures. Figure 6–8 shows a reduction in such expenditures from g_0 to g_1 producing an excess of real income and production over the level of total purchases or expenditures. Business inventories accumulate. As firms wish to produce less and to fire some workers, and as the level of real income starts to fall, nominal wages and prices also fall because of unemployment above the natural level. But, as changes occur, the real value of the existing money stock starts to rise and so do total expenditures. The effects are shown in Figure 6–8 as upward shifts in the total expenditures schedule. After some time (when real income is at the lowest level, y_1) total expenditures and output are once again equal, but wages and prices continue to fall because of the unemployment situation in the labor market. Real money

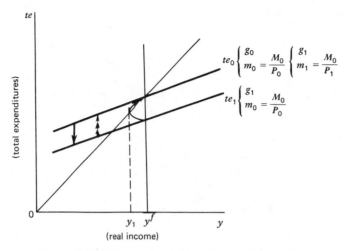

Figure 6-8. *Effects of a contractionary fiscal policy.*

stock and expenditures rise and there is now an incentive for producers to begin producing more. The end of the story will be a return to the same full employment equilibrium, but with a *lower* level of prices. Lower prices are required because, for total expenditures to be at the same level as they were before the policy change, the lower level of real government expenditures must be compensated by some higher level of the real money stock. Since the nominal money stock has not changed, prices must fall, as they do during the adjustment process.[8]

In this section we have analyzed two changes in policy, in both cases starting from a position of global equilibrium at full employment. We can study the results of other changes originating at full employment equilibrium or at disequilibrium points. In fact, in the real world most (but not all) changes in policy occur when the economic system is out of equilibrium as a means of "helping" the system to overcome stickiness in the automatic adjustment mechanism.

CONCLUSION

The determinants of total expenditures were discussed in Chapter 5, and the total expenditures schedule and the "real" or "supply" side of the economy were combined in a simple but realistic manner in Chapter 6. In additon, the chapter explained the presence of an automatic adjustment mechanism, how it can fail, and how policies can help to compensate for total failure or for a reaction that is too slow.

In Chapter 6 (as well as Chapter 5) *levels* of the nominal money stock and *levels* of prices have been discussed. A change in monetary policy, for example, is seen as a once-and-for-all change in the nominal money stock, and the system's response as a once-and-for-all change in the price level. Prices could change, but in equilibrium they could be at different (higher, or lower) levels, but *constant* levels. In other words, we have not been discussing *inflation* at all. There is inflation, for some time, while prices are rising from one level to a higher one as a consequence of an increase of the nominal money stock from a lower to a higher level. But this is not the study of inflation as a permanent and even long-run equilibrium phenomenon occurring when the money stock is *permanently increased at some rate*. We will concern ourselves with these issues in Chapters 7 and 8.

Appendix 6
A PICTORIAL REPRESENTATION OF THE ADJUSTMENT IN THE LEVEL OF REAL INCOME AND PRICES

There is a manner in which the adjustment process of the economy can be easily visualized, in a somewhat neater fashion than in the body of Chapter 6. As every point in this representation has already been considered in the text, we will learn no more economics from it. But the new representation is more explicit and may provide us some additional insights.

We are interested in following the path of adjustment of two variables: the *level of real income* (output) and the *level of prices*. In the text of Chapter 6 we assume, with the support of actual facts from the real world, that real income (output) reacted to the difference between real total expenditures and real income. When expenditures exceed income (output), business inventories fall and producers respond by hiring more labor and producing more, and vice versa. It is also assumed that prices reacted to the situation in the labor market. When output is above the full employment level (and consequently unemployment is below the natural rate), wages tend to rise as a result of the "tightness" in the labor market, and so do production costs and product prices, and vice versa.

We can see these two adjustment patterns easily in Figure 6–9, which plots the level of real income and of prices. Consider first the level of real income, which increases, or falls, or tends to remain the same, depending on

whether expenditures are large, small, or equal to income. As a reference line it is possible to find the combinations of the level of real income (y) and of prices (P) at which expenditures are equal to income. Consider, in Figure 6–9, a point such as the point A, with real income equal to y_0 and the price level equal to P_0, and suppose that this is a level of prices and income for which (given a certain nominal money stock, M_0, and a certain level of real government expenditures, g_0) total expendi-

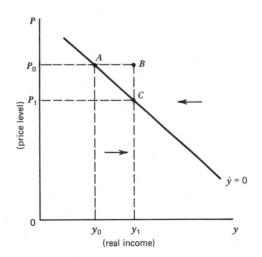

Figure 6–9. Direction of income adjustments.

tures are equal to income. Suppose now that we consider a point such as point B, for the same level of prices (P_0) but for a *higher* level of real income, y_1. We know that at such a point B total expenditures will be less than income because an increase in real income, other things being the same, increases total expenditures by less (that is, the marginal propensity to spend out of income is less than one). At point B, total expenditures fall short of income. What must happen to the price level to restore the equality between total expenditures and income? Prices must fall some for the real money stock and expenditures to be higher than at point B. Suppose the fall in prices necessary to restore this equality is from P_0 to P_1; then, point C will be another situation where (as in point A) total expenditures are equal to income.

If this experiment is repeated a few times, it will be discovered that, for higher and higher levels of real income, lower and lower levels of prices are necessary to maintain equality between total expenditures and income. By connecting all of those points together a line may be derived, such as the $\dot{y} = 0$ line, showing all of the possible combinations of real income and the price level for which total expenditures are equal to income.[9]

Two points must be noted. First, along the line $\dot{y} = 0$ in Figure 6–9 real income (out-put) will not be changing because total expenditures are equal to income. Second, points to the right of (or above) the line (such as point B) are points for which total expenditures are *less than income*, and therefore points at which real income will be *falling*. Points to the left of (or below) the $\dot{y} = 0$ line are, on the ohter hand, points for which total expenditures are *higher than income*, and therefore points where real income will be *rising*. This "falling" of real income on one side of the line and "rising" on the other can be graphically represented by arrows showing the direction of change of real income (measured on the horizontal axis).

Prices may also be considered in this framework. If prices are rising when real income (output) exceeds full employment out-put, and falling when real income falls short of it, then the direction of these changes can be shown in Figure 6–10, depending on whether real income is to the right or to the left of the vertical line positioned at the full employment level, y^f. This vertical line (showing the level of income at which prices will not be changing) is called the $\dot{P} = 0$ line.

Figure 6–10 puts all of these forces together. To remind us that the $\dot{y} = 0$ line was constructed for a given level of the two policy variables, these two magnitudes (say, M_0 for the nominal money stock, and g_0 for real government expenditures) are attached to

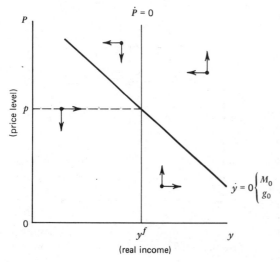

Figure 6–10. Adjustment pattern: prices and real income.

the line. In the upper-right quadrant, for example, real income will be falling and prices will be rising; in the lower-left quadrant, prices will be falling and real income will be rising; and so on. At the equilibrium point, $y = y^f$ and $P = P_0$, nothing changes and the system is at rest.

This simple apparatus can be used by tracing the path of prices and real income toward equilibrium following a policy change (that would change the line $\dot{y} = 0$) or a sudden, arbitrary departure from an initial equilibrium position. Suppose, for example, that for whatever reason prices are "too high" but the level of output is at the long-run equilibrium level (that is, at full employment). This situation is described in Figure 6–11, with an initial price level (point A) above the equilibrium level. The apparatus indicates that real income will start to fall, changing along a path that enters into the upper-left quadrant, where prices also start to fall. Both prices and real income continue falling until reaching a point such as B, where real income stops falling and starts rising again (at point B, incidentally, total expenditures are equal to income). From then on, income starts rising again, while prices continue to fall until equilibrium is restored.

Consider now one of the changes studied

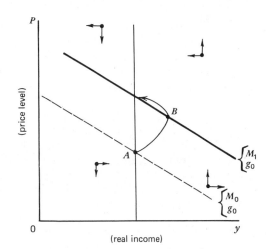

Figure 6–12. Possible path of adjustment for a rise in the nominal money stock.

in the text of Chapter 6, namely, the effects of a sudden increase in the nominal money stock. (Recall that the $\dot{y} = 0$ line was drawn for is given money stock, M_0, and for a real level of real government expenditures, g_0.) If the money stock suddenly rises from M_0 to, say, M_1, then the $\dot{y} = 0$ schedule shifts upward.[10] Figure 6–12 shows both old and new $\dot{y} = 0$ lines. The "old" line passing through point A is drawn for the former money stock M_0, which is now the initial point in the path of adjustment. The result of such a policy change, which has altered the equilibrium level of prices, is a path of adjustment as indicated by the arrow: first, real income (output) starts to increase and so do prices; at some point (such as point B) real income reaches a maximum and starts falling back, while prices continue rising. The equilibrium is restored at a higher price level.

Many more changes can be analyzed; for example, a sudden technological breakthrough or an increase in the labor force that would change the full employment output to a *higher* level (the one $\dot{p} = 0$). The changes can be analyzed with the apparatus of this Appendix or with the graphical framework of Chapter 6. All these methods are equivalent but there are always some economic insights to be gained from viewing the same process from different angles.

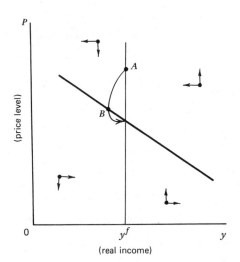

Figure 6–11. Possible path of prices and income.

FOOTNOTES

[1] The term missing equation refers to this situation and to the possible ways of solving the problem popularized by Milton Friedman and used later by many economists.

[2] This is so because the *te* schedule is the 45 degree line, so that the vertical line can be used to read the level of income as well.

[3] The *rate of unemployment*, then, is the percentage of the labor force which is not employed. The use of this rate of unemployment to measure the level of economic activity is often criticized on grounds that there are changes in the proportion of the population that is in the labor force. In particular, this has happened in the 1970s, during which a sizeable part of the population that before was not part of the labor force (teenagers and housewives) became part of it. Some economists argue that a better measurement would be the percentage of the total population that *is* employed, instead of simply the percentage of the labor force. The problem arises, basically, because of the methods through which these percentages are calculated. See, for example, Geoffrey H. Moore, "Lessons of the 1973–1976 Recovery," in *Contemporary Economic Problems*, William Fellner, ed. (Washington, D.C., American Enterprise Institute, 1977), pp. 117–158.

[4] The expression "natural rate of unemployment" was first used by Milton Friedman in "The Role of Monetary Policy," *American Economic Review*, 58 (March 1968), pp. 1–17.

[5] The relationship between the level of employment (or unemployment) and the level of output is given by the so-called *aggregate production function* for the whole economy, which relates the rate of use of productive factors to the rate of aggregate production.

[6] Notice that a similar result could have been brought about by a fall either in the nominal money stock or in the level of government expenditures.

[7] The argument fails to consider that the nominal money stock falls even more than prices and, as a consequence, engenders the collapse of a large number of commercial banks. Monetary policy was, so to speak, working in the opposite direction from the one it should have.

[8] The policy variable in the discussion has been identified as the real level of government expenditures. Of course, this is given by nominal government expenditures divided by the price level. One could analyze the case where government sets a nominal level of expenditures, and this would change the details of the discussion somewhat.

[9] The symbol $\dot{y} = 0$ for this line is simply a symbol and any other could have been used. There is some logic to its use. Sometimes a dot over a certain variable (real income, in this case) is used to denote the rate at which the variable is changing. Since real income will not be changing when total expenditures are equal to income, or the rate of change of income will be zero, the notation seems adequate.

[10] Why? Because to obtain equality between total expenditures and income we need, for any level of real income, the same real money stock as before the change, so that with a higher money stock this equality is accomplished with a higher level of prices.

KEY CONCEPTS

real money stock	multiplier	wage and price flexibility
nominal money stock	full employment	policy variable
total expenditures schedule	natural rate of unemployment	contractionary and expansionary policy
"autonomous component" of the total expenditures schedule	full employment output	
	full employment equilibrium	automatic adjustment mechanism

QUESTIONS FOR DISCUSSION

1. What is the relationship between the price level and total expenditure? Is it direct or indirect? Would a change in the price level constitute a shift in the total expenditure curve or a movement along it?

2. Discuss and show graphically the adjustment process involved in equilibrating total expenditures and income in both the "fixed real income" and the "fixed price" models. In each case discuss the effects of the process, if any, on employment, inventories, prices, output, and the real money stock. In which model does the MPC play an important part? Why?

3. The simplest expression of Say's law, that is, "supply creates its own demand," can be used to describe the "fixed income" model. What would be a comparable description of the "fixed price level" model?

4. Explain the difference between the Keynesian and Monetarist multipliers.

5. Show graphically the adjustment process in the equilibrium model. What is the importance of flexible wages and prices in this model? Discuss the Keynesian–Monetarist debate on this point. Why do Keynesians believe that the automatic adjustment process will not work in restoring equilibrium regardless of the extent to which wages and prices are flexible?

6. What would be the effects of a contractionary monetary policy and an expansionary fiscal policy in the equilibrium model? Show the effects graphically and explain the adjustment process.

CHAPTER 7

MONETARY EXPANSION AND INFLATION: The Long Run

In Chapter 6 the relationship between the level of the money stock (M), real income, and the level of prices (P) was analyzed in some detail. In particular, the short- and long-run consequences of once-and-for-all changes in the *stock* of money and its effects on prices were investigated. A related but different aspect was not discussed, that is, the response of the economic system to continuous, repetitive changes in the nominal money stock and the matter of inflation as a long-run, persistent phenomenon. This is the concern of Chapter 7. Instead of experiments in which the consequences of once-and-for-all changes in the nominal money stock (M) are analyzed, the response of the economy to changes in the proportional rate of change of the nominal money stock is the subject of Chapter 7. The proportional rate of change of the money stock, called the *rate of monetary expansion*, is symbolized as $\hat{M}$. The important relationship between the rate of monetary expansion, $\hat{M}$, and the inflation rate—that is, the proportional rate of change in prices per period, $\hat{P}$—is the principal topic of discussion.

Because the distinction between a once-and-for-all change in the *level* of the money stock (discussed in Chapters 5 and 6) and a change in the rate of monetary expansion is so important, let us make certain that we understand it. Figures 7–1 and 7–2 are helpful in clarifying the matter. Figure 7–1 shows the path over time of the level of the money stock (M), and of the change in that level at time t_0. The initial level is M_0, and at time t_0 there is an increase in the stock, to M_1. Figures 7–2a and 7–2b show what is meant by a change in the proportional rate of change of the money stock or the rate of monetary expansion. Figure 7–2a shows a level of the money stock (M_0) that, until time t_0, is not changing, but that at time t_0 begins to rise at a positive rate (say, for example, 4 percent per year) and from that time on continues to do so. Figure 7–2b indicates the path of the rate of monetary expansion corresponding to that change: zero up to time t_0, and constant (at 4 percent per year) after that period.

The analysis of the effects of alternative rates of monetary expansion is more interesting, empirically more relevant, and somewhat more involved than

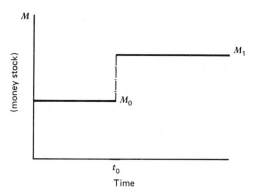

Figure 7-1. A once-and-for-all change in the level of M.

the analysis of the effects of alternative constant levels of the money stock. The rate of monetary expansion is the variable referred to in policy discussions. A glance at newspapers and other publications reveals that an often asked question relating to monetary policy concerns the rate at which the money stock is going to grow during, for example, the next six months. Moreover, the short- and long-run effects of changes in the rate of monetary expansion are issues making headlines today, and an understanding of the mechanics and the economics of inflation is crucial to understanding some of the most important worldwide economic events during many recent years. Inflation, a phenomenon that, after World War II was confined to some of the lesser developed countries of the world, has entered the American and the Western European economies, where it has proved to be both pervasive and persistent.

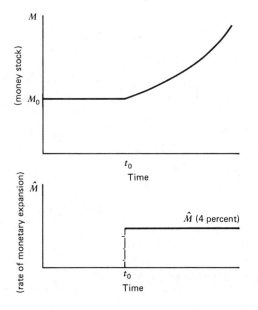

Figure 7-2a. A percentage increase in the nominal money stock.

Figure 7-2b. A change in the rate of monetary expansion.

A glance at Figure 7–3 indicates the reality and severity of the inflationary phenomena in the United States and in other developed economies in the world.

The effects of changes in the rate of monetary expansion are discussed in Chapters 7 and 8. The long-run effects of such changes on the rate of inflation, the real money stock, and the level of output and interest rates are analyzed in Chapter 7. Such an analysis, as with all discussions of long-run equilibrium, is perhaps not very realistic but it will be instructive as an important reference point. Additionally, a discussion of long-run equilibrium provides useful insights on events that *must* occur during the adjustment. Chapter 8 will be concerned with the short-run consequences of similar changes on the same variables.

The question to be answered in the present chapter is: *what will be the ultimate consequences of a change in the rate of monetary expansion from, say 2 percent per year to, say, 7 percent per year?* The important variables are the inflation rate, the level of the real money stock, and interest rates and real

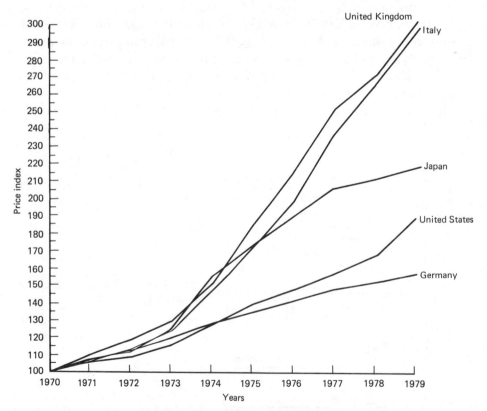

Figure 7-3. Price levels in five countries (1970–1979).

income (output). Since we are interested in long-run equilibrium, we will be comparing two economies identical in every respect, except by the fact that in one of them (which may be called the *stable economy*) the rate of monetary expansion is 2 percent while in the other (which may be called the *inflationary economy*), the rate of monetary expansion is 7 percent per year. A particular interpretation of the inflationary phenomenon will also be addressed, namely, the view that inflation is, to an important extent, a method by which the monetary authority (the government) can extract real resources from the economy. That is, the view that inflation is a tax will be investigated.

Although most of the present chapter (as well as Chapter 8) considers the case of a nongrowing, stationary economy (stationary in terms of *real output*), the conclusions are readily applicable to an economy that is growing over time, and one section of Chapter 7 shows the kinds of modifications that must be introduced in the analysis. Chapter 7 concludes with a discussion of the realism of a long-run equilibrium where the inflation rate is perfectly anticipated (that is, people correctly anticipate what the inflation rate will be) and whether, if it exists at all, such a state of affairs makes any difference to society's welfare.

MONETARY EXPANSION IN THE LONG RUN: INFLATION, INTEREST RATES, AND THE REAL MONEY STOCK

The discussion opens with a comparison of the relatively stable economy, with a rate of monetary expansion of 2 percent per year, to the inflationary economy, with a rate of monetary expansion of 7 percent per year. The relevant magnitudes are examined one by one.

THE INFLATION RATE

Consider, first, the rate of inflation. In the long-run equilibrium of the nongrowing economy the real stock of money, m, must be constant and equal to the desired real stock. Since the real money stock is the ratio of nominal money (which grows at the rate of monetary expansion) and the price level, for the real money stock to be constant prices must grow at the same proportional rate as the nominal money stock. That is, the rate of inflation must be equal to the rate of monetary expansion. The first and obvious difference between the stable and the inflationary economies is that in the first economy the inflation rate be 2 percent, and in the second 7 percent per year. In this long-run steady state all prices, wages, and—in general—nominal incomes are rising at the same rate of either 2 or 7 percent per year.

MONETARY EXPANSION, THE LEVEL OF REAL INCOME (OUTPUT) AND THE REAL RATE OF INTEREST

There will not be any difference in the long-run equilibrium between our two economies as far as the levels of real income and the real interest rate are concerned. If the economy is in overall equilibrium, real output will be at the full employment level.[1] The real interest rate in the long run, with a perfectly anticipated inflation, will not depart from its natural level. The natural level is given by real factors in the economy, such as the productivity of capital (which determines the investment schedule) and the public's preferences for consuming and saving.[2] Do the inflationary economy and the stable economy differ in any respect? The fact that both real income and the real interest rate are the *same* permits a clear examination of another real magnitude—the level of the real money stock, which will *not* be the same.

MONETARY EXPANSION AND THE REAL MONEY STOCK

In both the stable and the inflationary economy, the level of the real money stock will be constant in long-run equilibrium. The question is: constant, but at what level? The answer is easily provided by looking at the demand for money. The analysis of Chapter 3 indicated that the real desired money stock depends on the level of real income, the real rate of interest, and the expected inflation rate. The sum of the real rate of interest and the expected inflation rate is a measure of the cost of holding money rather than other assets. If the real interest rate is the same in the inflationary as in the stable economy, in the inflationary economy it will cost more to hold money and, for the same level of real income, the desired (and actual) level of real money holdings will be lower.

This principle is shown in Figure 7–4. If the real interest rate is, for example, 4 percent, and the expected (and actual) rate of inflation is 2 percent, the sum of the two (that is, the nominal rate of interest) is 6 percent, and the desired (real) money stock is m_0. In long-run equilibrium the inflation rate is perfectly anticipated. (By "fully anticipated" we mean that money holders—and market participators in general—correctly expect the inflation rate to be exactly what it turns out to be.) In the inflationary economy, with the same real interest rate and an expected (and actual) rate of inflation of 7 percent, the cost of holding money (the nominal rate of interest) is 11 percent, and the desired money stock, in real terms, is m_1.

This is an important conclusion from the viewpoint of economic theory and because it provides a clue for interpreting many real wolrd events that take place in inflationary economies. First, it reveals that different rates of monetary expansion, in the long run, do change at least one real magnitude: the *real money stock*. In other words, different rates of monetary expansion

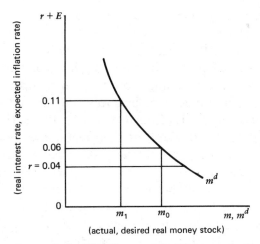

Figure 7-4. The "cost of holding money" and real money holdings.

are not neutral, because they *do* change something very real.[3] Changes in the rate of monetary expansion change a real, as opposed to a nominal, variable. Second, the fact that real money holding will be lower in an inflationary economy provides an important indication of what will happen to the rate of inflation during the adjustment period from one rate of monetary expansion to another (this will be discussed in Chapter 8). Third, it helps explain one seemingly paradoxical situation that is invariably encountered in many inflationary episodes—the often heard complaint about a *lack of liquidity* in the economy.

How can lack of liquidity occur in an economy where money is being produced at a high rate? The paradox is resolved once the nominal and the real money stocks are distinguished, and it is realized that in an inflationary equilibrium the real money stock must be smaller than in equilibrium of the stable economy. Indeed, it is true that liquidity is low in the inflationary economy, if by liquidity is meant the real value of the money stock. The most striking example of this situation is the phenomena of hyperinflation in Continental Europe in the early 1920s when in countries such as Germany, Austria, and Hungary the rate of inflation and the rate of monetary expansion were running at hundreds of percents per month. The seemingly paradoxical situation can be understood by contrasting German citizens who used money as wallpaper (because to do so was cheaper than purchasing wallpaper), with the common complaint in those days about the lack of liquidity or a scarcity of money. Of course, *nominal* money was increasingly abundant, but the level of *real* money was very low.[4]

What is the mechanism by which nominal money, being produced at a higher rate, will, in the long run, result in a lower real money stock? Even if this is a matter that belongs in Chapter 8, the issue is so important and so perplexing that it must be mentioned at this point.

When individuals wish to lower the level of their real money holdings, they *try* to do so by spending more than their income. In other words, they try to get rid of *nominal* cash balances. But all individuals together cannot do this, because money is circulated among them. How might all individuals simultaneously change the level of their real money holdings? Simply, through the ultimate market response to the excess of expenditures over income, that is, through a faster increase in prices than what would otherwise occur. It is not, of course, that individuals seek to modify prices; individually they seek only to lower their nominal money stocks, but the market responds through higher increases in prices. Individuals end up in equilibrium not because of a fall in their nominal money holdings (as they intended) but through price level changes.[5]

MONETARY EXPANSION AND THE NOMINAL INTEREST RATE

We have already noted in brief what will happen to the nominal interest rate in the new long-run equilibrium when there is a change in the rate of monetary expansion. Since the *real* interest rate is the same in the inflationary as in the stable economy, and since the inflation rate is perfectly anticipated in long-run equilibrium, the nominal interest rate will be higher in the inflationary economy by the amount of the difference between the corresponding inflation rates. (Real versus nominal rates are discussed in Chapter 1.) In the example related to Figure 7–4, with a real rate of interest of 4 percent, the stable economy will have a $(0.04 + 0.02 = 0.06)$, or 6 percent nominal interest rate, and the inflationary economy will have a $(0.04 + 0.07 = 0.11)$, or 11 percent rate.

This phenomenon, which in the 1970s and early 1980s is a feature of the American economy, has been an accepted fact of life for many years in countries with a chronic history of inflation. (More will be said about this in Chapter 8 when we look at the behavior of interest rates during the transitory adjustment process.) An important point to be noticed, however, is that the distinction between real and nominal interest rates is of tremendous importance not only for citizens in managing their private affairs, but for policymakers who, when faced with the distressing reality of "high" interest rates, might try to lower them through *further* and continuous increases in the rate of monetary expansion.

Another point refers to the connection between inflation and nominal interest rates, which is sometimes seen by bankers and the media as going from the latter to the former: high interest rates increase costs and prices, and therefore "produce" or "aggravate" inflation. The *causality is precisely the op-*

posite: high inflation rates (or the expectation that they will take place) increase nominal interest rates.

The effects of monetary expansion in the long run on nominal interest rates and the real money stock are thus fairly straightforward. But inflation also means revenues for the monetary authority. That is, the monetary authority receives revenues from the creation of money, and the manner in which those revenues are related to monetary expansion and to the inflation rate is the subject of the following section.

MONETARY EXPANSION AND REVENUES FROM THE CREATION OF MONEY: INFLATION AS A TAX

In Chapter 2 the concept of seigniorage was introduced. Seigniorage is the gain made by whoever owns the right to produce fiat money, where such gain is the flow of revenues given by the difference between the real cost of production and the market value of the new money being produced per period. In the case of US monetary arrangements and those in most other countries it is a good approximation to assume the real cost of producing money (paper and ink) to be zero, so that the seigniorage is equal to the real value of the money being produced. In a system like that in the United States, where a substantial part of the stock of money is made up of demand deposits and in which interest is not paid on most demand deposits (at least not in an explicit form),[6] seigniorage will be shared by the two groups who can produce money—the government and the banking system. In the present section the banking system, for the sake of simplicity, will be ignored and we will proceed as if all money were currency printed by the monetary authority. Thus our analysis is relevant for the part of the money stock made up of currency (around 25 percent in the United States).

The essential point behind the concept of seigniorage is that, in the real world, increases in the stock of nominal money do not occur miraculously by, for example, dropping money from airplanes. In the real world the government does not distribute the newly produced money as a gift, but "sells" it, that is, introduces it into the system in exchange for financial assets and goods and services. Even though both activities (acquisition of financial assets and acquisition of goods and services) amount to the same thing, the present analysis will proceed by assuming that the monetary authority increases the quantity of money by exchanging the newly printed money for goods and services (that is, by running a deficit in the budget).

Although seigniorage exists even in the absence of inflation when the economy is growing (later in this chapter this case will be discussed), the connection between inflation and government revenues from the creation of money has been recognized for a long time. But it is only relatively recently that cconomists have realized that inflation is, in essence, conceptually *identical* to a *tax on the holdings of cash balances*. In the present section, the nature of these seigniorage gains will be investigated as will the relationship between these gains and the rate of inflation. First, the logic behind the idea of identifying inflation with a tax on the holdings of money will be discussed.

INFLATION AS A TAX AND AS A SOURCE OF GOVERNMENT REVENUES

Consider in a summary form the analysis of Chapter 3, in which the situation confronted by an individual who is trying to decide whether or not to hold some part of his or her wealth in the form of money was discussed. If the economy is in long-run equilibrium and there is some constant rate of inflation that everyone predicts correctly, the nominal rate of interest is the sum of the real interest rate, plus the inflation rate, or $i = r + \hat{P}$.

There are two basic alternatives open to individuals besides holding such part of their wealth in the form of money. They could buy bonds (that is, lend) and receive the nominal interest rate i (and therefore a real rate r) per period, or they could acquire real capital, yielding a real rate of return r. If individuals decide to hold such part of their wealth in the form of money they will then pay a cost, which for either of these two alternatives will be the same: the cost per unit of time of holding a certain money stock m will be equal to $m \cdot (r + \hat{P}) = m \cdot r + m \cdot \hat{P}$.

The first component in the cost of holding money, $m \cdot r$, is the *opportunity cost* per unit of time, which measures the real flow of goods that could be collected if real assets were held and which is given up when cash balances are held instead. The second component of the cost of holding money is $m \cdot \hat{P}$, and this is the real cost incurred at every period since, with a rate of inflation $\hat{P}$, real cash balances "depreciate" by the rate at which prices are rising, so that there is a need for replacing this loss through the addition of new nominal balances. Thus such a cost may be interpreted as the depreciation of the real stock per period, or as the real value of the continuous flow of new nominal balances which must be added to the nominal stock so as to keep that stock constant in real terms. For real cash balances to remain constant it becomes necessary for the moneyholder to add nominal balances at every period at the same (proportional) rate as prices rise. The real value of these periodic additions is the depreciation cost.

The similarity of this situation with the case of physical capital (machines, houses, or automobiles) may be noted. If physical capital depreciates at a certain rate per period, one component of the cost of holding it is the cost of continuously adding to it so as to offset depreciation and to keep the stock constant. In our case the depreciation rate is the rate of inflation, $\hat{P}$.

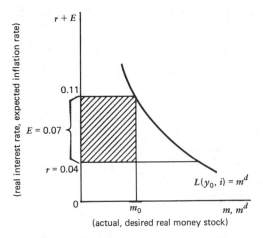

Figure 7-5. A tax on money holdings.

It should be clear why inflation is a tax on the holdings of money and why its effects on the holdings of money are identical to, say, a property tax on the "holding" or ownership of houses or land. The real tax paid per period is equal to $m \cdot \hat{P}$: m, the level of real cash balances held, is the "base" of the tax (as the number of houses held by whoever pays the property tax would be); $\hat{P}$, the inflation rate, is the *tax rate*, or tax paid per unit of real money held (the equivalent of the per house tax in a property tax example).

All of this can be easily visualized in Figure 7–5, which shows the demand for money for the level of real income y_0. If the interest rate is, say, 4 percent per year and the expected (and actual) inflation rate is, for example, 7 percent per year, the real money stock held by the public is m_0. The amount of the tax per period, in real terms, is the shaded area, or the real money stock, m_0, times the rate of inflation $\hat{P} = 0.07$. The analysis is then identical to the study of a tax on any other asset, such as houses.

This peculiar tax is paid by moneyholders, that is, through the continuous accumulation of nominal money necessary to keep the stock of real money constant. But how is the tax collected? In the case of a tax on the ownership of houses, the owner is under the legal obligation of filling out a form and making an explicit payment to the taxing authority at every period, but no one goes around asking moneyholders for the payment of the inflation tax.

To find out, consider the real value, per period, of the additional nominal money stock introduced by the monetary authority in exchange for goods and services. If we call ΔM the increase in the nominal money stock at every period, and R the real value of these increases (that is, the real value of the revenues from creating money), the *real revenues per period* are

$$R = (\Delta M)/P \qquad\qquad [7.1]$$

or the nominal revenue per period, ΔM, divided by the price level at that period. If the right-hand side of expression [7.1] is divided and multiplied by M, the nominal money stock, real revenues are equal to

$$R = (\Delta M/M) \cdot (M/P) = \hat{M} \cdot m \qquad [7.2]$$

or the rate of monetary expansion multiplied by the real money stock. Since in a nongrowing economy the inflation rate is equal to the rate of monetary expansion, it may be verified that the real "payment" made by moneyholders at each period (the real money stock times the inflation rate) is identical to the real revenues of the "tax collector" (the real money stock times the rate of monetary expansion).

Now the picture is complete, with taxpayers and the tax collector in place. Even so, the peculiar process by which the tax on real cash balances imposed by inflation is paid and collected deserves more elaboration. In the equilibrium situation depicted above, the public is holding the desired stock of real money, the constant and permanent rate of inflation is correctly antici-pated by everyone in the economy, and the monetary authority is increasing the nominal stock of money at a constant proportional rate by continuously buying a constant real amount of goods and services with newly printed money. The public, in turn, is receiving a flow of real income which is constant in real terms, so that their nominal income also rises at the same rate at which prices rise. At every period, total income received by the public equals the total value of the goods and services produced in the economy. Furthermore, the public needs to divert part of their total income away from expenditures in every period in order to accumulate nominal cash balances so as to keep real cash balances constant in the face of continuously rising prices. In other words, moneyholders need to refrain, period after period, from buying goods and services by a fixed real amount (and an increasing nominal amount) so as to be able to maintain their real monetary stock constant at the desired level. The part of total real output not being purchased by the public is then exactly compensated by purchases of goods and services made by the government.

This is, in a simplified but ultimately realistic manner, the way in which the transfer of real income from moneyholders to the money issuer takes place. This is the way in which the *proceeds of the tax* are paid by the public and collected by the government. Ultimately, there is no essential difference between this process and the case of conventional taxation, where taxpayers make an explicit payment at every period and government spends the tax proceeds by purchasing goods and services. Of course, this inflation tax is not treated as an implicit tax by policymakers or government officials, but this is not important. Conceptually the inflation tax is the same as any other tax— but it has not been voted for by society.

A clarification is needed. The inflation tax is completely different from a situation often described by the media, in which it is argued (and correctly so) that inflation increases the level of *real proceeds* from conventional taxes, because of the progressive nature of the income tax structure and the fact that capital gains are taxed in nominal terms. This situation is a distortion in the structure of conventional taxes, which has nothing to do with the concept of the inflation tax that we have studied.

THE REVENUE MAXIMIZING RATE OF INFLATION

If inflation is a means by which the monetary authority can impose a tax on holders of real cash balances, and in doing so extract resources from the private sector of the economy, a legitimate question is: what happens if government chooses to extract from the public a steady, permanent stream of real resources as large as possible by means of the inflation tax? Since the government can print as much money as it wishes and introduce it into the system in exchange for goods and services, is there no limit to the flow of resources it will be able to extract? Or, in other words, is it true that the higher the rate of monetary expansion (and, consequently, the rate of inflation), the larger the real value of this continuous transfer of resources will be?

If the analysis is confined to long-run situations (that is, with a constant rate of inflation equal to the rate of monetary expansion) there *is* a limit to the flow of resources it will be able to extract. In the long run there will be an inflation rate at which the real value of those revenues, at every period, will be a maximum, and from there higher and higher inflation rates will yield lower and lower real revenues. The reason for this limit is, of course, that higher rates of monetary expansion will eventually bring about prices rising not only at faster rates but also to a higher *level* than they would otherwise be.

This pattern can be seen by inspecting the definition of the real value of revenue per period, repeated here for convenience as

$$R = \hat{M} \cdot m = \hat{P} \cdot m \qquad [7.3]$$

It is of course true that the monetary authority can always establish a very high rate of monetary expansion, and hence a very high rate of inflation (the *tax rate*). But in the long run the real stock of money that the public is willing to hold certainly depends on the cost of holding it, so that increases in the rate of the tax ($\hat{M}$, or $\hat{P}$) always bring about reductions in the *tax base* (m). The situation is identical to the case of any conventional tax and also, for that matter, with the problem faced by a monopolist who is trying to decide what price to charge for a product—a familiar case in basic economics. In the case of any tax, where the proceeds of the tax are the tax rate times the tax base (for example, the quantity of beer demanded, if we refer to a tax on the consumption of beer), the higher the tax rate the smaller is the tax base, so that it is not always the case that an increase in the tax rate will increase the total revenue from the tax. In the case of the monopolist who tries to decide what price to charge for a product, total revenue is again the product of the number of units sold times the price of each unit. An increase in the price will normally bring a fall in the number of units sold, and again it is not always true that an increase in price will bring about a rise in the monopolist's revenues.

Consider Figure 7-6a, which depicts a simple demand for money schedule, a straight line for a given constant level of real income, y_0. In this case there are two rates of inflation, zero and $\hat{P}_0$, which yield a zero real revenue. At a zero inflation rate, revenues per unit of time are zero simply because the monetary authority is not "selling" any newly printed money (the rate of monetary expansion is zero). At the rate of inflation $\hat{P}_0$, the cost of holding money is so high that the public does not hold any money (that is, the monetary system is destroyed and the public resorts either to barter or to some other form of money) and the base of the tax disappears. It is easy to verify that, starting from the two extremes, either small increases in the rate of inflation starting from zero to some positive value, or small reductions in the rate of inflation from $\hat{P}_0$ to some lower value, will bring about increases in the flow of real revenue per period. This pattern is shown in Figure 7-6b, where the level of real revenue per period (R) is plotted for different inflation rates.

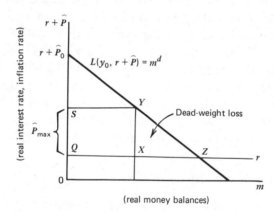

Figure 7-6a. Inflation as a tax.

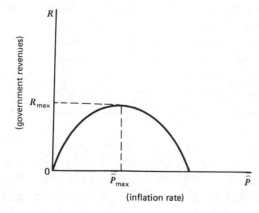

Figure 7-6b. Government revenues from an inflation tax.

To express the same concept in a slightly different form, when the inflation rate is increased in a certain proportion the level of the real money stock will always decrease. Whether such a change brings about an increase or a fall in revenues depends on whether the proportion by which the real money stock falls is smaller or larger than the proportion by which the inflation rate was increased. The point at which those two opposite changes exactly compensate corresponds to the maximum long-run level of real revenues attainable. In the analysis of the monopoly problem such a point corresponds to the part of the demand scheduled (for the monopolist's product, in that case) of elasticity equal to minus one. In the case of money and the inflation tax, the same is true: the revenue maximizing rate of monetary expansion (and consequently the inflation rate) is the one corresponding to the point where the elasticity of the demand of money is equal to minus one (assuming that the real marginal cost of holding money is zero).

The realization that there is a limit to the flow of real resources which the monetary authority can extract from the economy in the long run, and that an increase in the rate of monetary expansion (and therefore in the inflation rate) will not always result in an increase in the real flow of resources is an important conclusion regarding policy for many inflationary countries with a long history of inflation, if perhaps not for the United States at the present time. In fact, at various times such countries have run inflation rates well above those that would be their revenue-maximizing rates. Since the need for running budget deficits in those countries is usually declared to be the reason for justifying high rates of monetary expansion, one could argue that in the long run a higher real deficit could be financed by printing less money, while at the same time benefiting moneyholders, who now would be paying a lower "tax rate."[7]

MONETARY EXPANSION AND THE GROWING ECONOMY

Some of these conclusions concerning the long-run effects of different rates of monetary expansion must be modified slightly when the case of an economy where total real income (output) is growing is considered. Such growth can be the result of the accumulation of factors of production (more physical capital and a growing labor force) or of technical change (the knowhow that permits more output with the same amount of workers and machines) or, as it is mostly the case, of both. The sources of growth do not matter for the analysis. What matters here is the rate at which total real output is growing, and the effects that this growth has on the real money stock.

Why should the equilibrium real money stock grow when real income is growing? First, and to the extent that population is growing, new individuals need to be provided with their share of real cash balances. Second, and to the extent that real income per capita can also be growing, existing individuals will wish to hold larger and larger levels of real cash balances as their incomes go up (in much the same way as they wish to consume more and more goods and services). If the economy is going to be in its long-run equilibrium, the real money stock, m, must grow together with the desired money stock, m^d.

The relationship between the growth of real income and the growth of the real money stock will depend on the proportion of the growth in real total income that is per capita growth and the proportion that is growth in population and, given this proportion, upon what the income elasticity of the demand for money happens to be. But these technicalities are matters of detail. In the special case when such income elasticity is equal to one (that is, when a percentage increase in real income growth increases the desired money stock by the same percentage), the rate of growth of the equilibrium money stock is always equal to the rate of total real income and, for simplicity, we will assume this to be the case. Then, if total real income in the economy is growing, say, at a rate of 4 percent per year, the real money stock must be growing also at 4 percent per year.

Suppose that real income is increasing, year after year, at a constant rate, denoted by $\hat{y}$. If $\hat{m}$ symbolizes the percentage rate of growth of the real money stock, $\hat{m}$ must equal $\hat{y}$ in equilibrium. But the proportional rate at which the real money stock changes, $\hat{m}$, is equal to the rate of monetary expansion, $\hat{M}$, minus the rate of inflation, $\hat{P}$, or

$$\hat{m} = \hat{M} - \hat{P}$$

For the growing economy to be in long run equilibrium, $\hat{y} = \hat{M} - \hat{P}$, so that the resulting long-run inflation rate is

$$\hat{P} = \hat{M} - \hat{y} \qquad [7.4]$$

Expression [7.4] simply states that, in the long-run equilibrium, the rate of inflation is equal to the rate of monetary expansion minus the rate at which total real income is growing. If the economy is not growing at all, $y = 0$, and we return to the result of the first part of this chapter. In that case the real money stock is constant and prices rise at the rate of monetary expansion. What would happen if the economy is growing and the nominal money stock remains constant (that is, the rate of monetary expansion is zero)? Prices will need to fall at the same rate at which real income grows, and the growth in the real money stock is generated through a continuous *deflation* (or negative inflation). If stable prices are desired (a zero inflation rate), the nominal money stock must grow at the same rate as income.

The presence of growth changes the arithmetic relationship between the rate of monetary expansion and the inflation rate. It will still be true, as it was in the stationary economy, that higher rates of monetary expansion will bring about higher long-run rates of inflation, a higher cost of holding money, and therefore a real money stock lower than what it would be if the rate of monetary expansion and the inflation rate were lower.

The only other results that must be qualified are those related to the analysis of the real revenues accruing to government from the creation of money. If the economy is growing, the money producer will obtain a flow of real revenues that exceeds the tax on cash balances, and a real revenue accruing period after period would exist in the growing economy even if the inflation rate is zero. This is a remarkable and seemingly puzzling result, but one that has a simple explanation. In this case the revenue at each period has two components: first, the tax paid by moneyholders, or the real money stock at every period times the inflation rate, that goes to replenish the "depreciation" of the existing stock because of the rise in prices; second, the real value of the newly printed money that goes to increase the real money stock. Such a situation is exactly the same as that occurring when an industry sells refrigerators or automobiles to a growing market. A part of every year's sales makes up for the depreciation during that year; another goes to increase the stock. It will still be true that there is only one rate of monetary expansion (and a corresponding inflation rate) at which the flow of revenues will be a maximum, and beyond which real revenues will fall.

IS AN EQUILIBRIUM, PERFECTLY ANTICIPATED INFLATION HARMFUL?

The long-run consequences of alternative rates of monetary expansion and the resulting long-run, perfectly anticipated inflation rates were dealt with in the present chapter. Is there any harmful effect in such an inflationary equilibrium, rather than one where prices rise at a lower rate, or not at all? In Chapter 8 the important side effects of an unexpected inflation and the distortions that take place during the adjustment process will be discussed, but a perfectly anticipated inflation can be harmful, even when the overall inflation rate is constant.

First, such inflation is harmful because the *inflation tax* and the effects of the higher cost of holding money involve—as does almost any tax—a "welfare" or "deadweight loss." A deadweight loss due to an inflation tax is similar to that due to the monopolization of a product or service. When a monopoly price is charged, there is a transfer of "welfare" in the form of monopoly profits from consumers to producers. But, *output is also reduced* below the competitive level by the monopolist, causing a deadweight loss to society. (In graphical terms, this deadweight loss is a triangle formed by the difference between marginal costs and the demand curve beyond a vertical line at monopoly output.)

Likewise, not only does an inflation tax imposed by government involve a "welfare" transfer from moneyholders to government revenues, but it imposes an additional deadweight loss as well. Consider Figure 7–6a, for example, which depicts a money demand curve as a function of the costs of holding money (the real rate of interest plus the inflation rate). The inflation rate $\hat{P}_{\max}$ engenders a net revenue transfer from moneyholders to government in the amount of the rectangle $QSYX$. But note that there is a deadweight loss in welfare in the value of triangle XYZ exactly analogous to that of a private monopoly. The monopolization of money, in other words, permits a nonrecoverable welfare loss due to inflation rate $\hat{P}_{\max}$—one in addition to the welfare transfer from moneyholders to government revenues.

Second, constant and anticipated inflation is injurious because not all prices will rise smoothly and at an equal rate. As there is even a cost in the physical act of changing prices (consider all the prices to be relabeled on items at grocery or hardware stores), there will be a tendency for many prices to "jump" and remain at the same level until the next hike. Since those jumps will be simultaneous neither for all commodities nor for all firms, there will be permanent changes in relative prices, as well as a great deal of *dispersion* or difference in the price of the same commodity among firms. The costs of searching for the best price, which also exist in the case of price stability, become considerably larger.

Third, there is an additional danger to high inflation rates which is not the result of the inflation rates themselves, but of controls that either did not exist at times of price stability, or existed but were not binding. This has been the case with respect to regulations in financial markets concerning interest rates. Usury laws existing in many states have limited certain interest rates to levels of 10 or 12 percent. (These laws, in recent years of high interest rates, have been in flux.) Until very recently, bank regulations have prohibited commercial banks from paying above 5 or 6 percent interest rates on savings accounts (despite an inflation rate well in excess of 10 percent per year) and have effectively prevented the utilization of well-organized financial markets. Although these same controls and regulations existed before, they were not important because they established ceilings above what nominal rates were with lower inflation rates. The problem became so acute in the late 1970s that the Congress temporarily suspended usury laws and took action to remove interest rate ceilings in March 1980 (see Chapter 11 for details). The evidence from past experience, moreover, suggests that situations of a high but constant rate of inflation are short lived. High inflation rates also tend to be highly variable.

Finally, even if there are no surprises in the long-run equilibrium with a constant and well-anticipated inflation rate, a substantial transfer of wealth certainly occurs at the transition from a lower to a higher rate, and vice versa. This transfer takes place because all commitments and contracts are specified in nominal terms at a time when the expected inflation rate was a different one. Certain wealth transfers and capital losses and gains would occur even if the adjustment was instantaneous (in Chapter 8 we will see that there are transfers of the same nature that occur *only* during the adjustment process, because of the continuous error in predicting the inflation rate while such process takes place).

CONCLUSION

The long-run features of inflationary economies have been investigated in some detail in the present chapter. As was mentioned at the outset, such ideal long-run equilibria are not encountered very often in pure form in the real world, mainly because the rate of monetary expansion is in fact seldom kept at a constant level by the monetary authority. Still, the long-run analysis is very important. It permits a comparison of inflation rates in economies which, even if inflation rates are not constant, remain within certain range. Thus we can compare the American economy during the last ten years, with rates around 6–10 percent per year, with the Argentinian economy, with rates of around 8 percent *per month* (that is, about 150 percent per year) over the two-year period of 1978–1979. Moreover, the long-run analysis provides a necessary and convenient prelude to the study of what happens during the adjustment process—the subject of Chapter 8.

FOOTNOTES

[1] This matter will be examined more closely in Chapter 8 when we discuss the adjustment process. Some years ago there existed the belief that, in the long run, higher inflation rates would be associated with higher levels of output. The current view is that such an association is only a short-run, temporary phenomenon.

[2] It is clear from the framework of Chapter 5 that, since in the long run the levels of consumption and investment will depend only on the level of real income and on the real interest rate, for the full employment level of real income only one level of the real interest rate will correspond to overall equilibrium.

[3] This is expressed sometimes in the economic literature by saying that money is *neutral* but not *superneutral*. Thus it does not matter what the level of the money stock is, for as long as it remains at that level money is neutral; but if the money stock is continuously changing at a constant rate, the rate at which it changes does matter (money is not superneutral).

[4] It is true that in the hyperinflation episodes of the early 1920s both the rate of monetary expansion and the rate of inflation were not constant, as in our analysis, but were increasing rapidly during most of the process. Nevertheless, the conclusions of the text, which refer to stable rates of monetary expansion and inflation, are applicable to the so-called paradox of those days.

[5] Furthermore, as will be discussed in Chapter 8, a decrease in the demand for money in an inflationary environment is an adjustment in the money market to a higher expected rate

of inflation. There is a temporary burst of inflation due to the adjustment of expectations of price increases. This change in expectations can, as will be clear in Chapter 8, cause overshooting of the inflation rate; the decrease in the demand for money leads to a temporary burst of inflation which reduces the real money supply.

[6] See Chapter 11 for a description of some implicit forms of interest paid by commercial banks on demand deposits and for a discussion of NOW and similar accounts that pay interest but that are checkable in nature.

[7] This is a similar argument to the one made by some economists concerning the specific effects of the dramatic cut in property tax rates in the State of California. If the tax rates were high enough at the outset, the cut would, in the long run, bring about an increase in the total revenue from the tax.

KEY CONCEPTS

rate of monetary expansion

"neutral" money

superneutral money

lack of liquidity (during inflation)

seignorage

"depreciation cost" of holding money

QUESTIONS FOR DISCUSSION

1. Explain the effect of a decrease in the rate of monetary expansion from 8 percent to 3 percent on real income, inflation rates, nominal interest rates (suppose the real rate of interest is 4 percent), and the real money stock.

2. Answer question (1) assuming the economy is growing at a rate of 2 percent per year.

3. Why are there limits to inflation as a tax?

4. Explain the differences between inflation as a tax and increases in conventional taxes due to inflation. Explain how the former is collected.

5. Today Americans are earning higher salaries than ever before. How can there be complaints about not having enough money?

6. Much has been written about the "underground" economy. Instead of monetary transactions, people trade services, engaging in barter. Can you draw any conclusions from the increasing number of these transactions?

7. Name specific instances when inflation is beneficial.

CHAPTER 8

MONETARY EXPANSION IN THE SHORT RUN: Inflation, Unemployment, and Interest Rates

In Chapter 7 effects of alternative rates of monetary expansion in the long run, that is, after all of the adjustments had taken place, were discussed. In Chapter 8 the transition to the long run is analyzed. This is an important task because these effects, albeit transitory, can take a long time to be worked out and because they can be large in magnitude. The major issue addressed in Chapter 8 concerns the effects of *changing* the rate of monetary expansion. What will happen in an economy in equilibrium, with a given rate of monetary expansion (say, 4 percent per year), when the rate of monetary expansion is changed to a different one (say, 2 percent per year, or 7 percent per year)? Chapter 7 dealt, essentially, with the same issue, but the adjustment process in Chapter 8 takes the starring role.

A general discussion of the problem opens Chapter 8, after which the role of expectations is described. (Additions to the general theoretical framework in Chapters 5 and 6 will also be made.) Then, the transitory effects of changes in the rate of monetary expansion on the real money stock, the rate of inflation, inflationary expectations, real and nominal interest rates, output and unemployment, and government revenue from the creation of money are presented. Next the entire adjustment process and the problem of *stopping inflation* are reviewed. The chapter concludes by discussing the costs involved in unexpected inflation.

THE NATURE AND THE ROLE OF EXPECTATIONS

The expected rate of inflation was mentioned in Chapter 7, specifically when the demand for money and the distinction between the real and the nominal interest rates were discussed. In the study of the long-run equilibrium there is no need to distinguish between the *actual* inflation rate (the rate of inflation which is taking place, P) and the expected inflation rate (the rate of inflation that people expect to take place in the future, which we will denote as E). By definition, if the economy is in long-run equilibrium the public will be correct in their forecasts, and the expected inflation rate will equal the actual rate. This pattern does not take place during the adjustment, and the behavior of the expected rate of inflation is a crucial variable for explaining what happens over the adjustment period.

Why is the expected rate of inflation such an important matter? There are at least two reasons. First, such expectations are important because lending and borrowing will take place at nominal interest rates that reflect, for any given real rate the parties agree on, the expectations the market has about what the inflation rate will be during the period of the contract. Thus the nominal interest rate depends directly on the expected inflation rate.

Secondly, the expected rate of inflation is important in another, more straightforward way, as a direct determinant of the actual inflation rate. In the price formation process, one of the elements taken into account by those who post prices (business firms) is the rate at which they expect all other prices to rise during the immediate future.

There are several competing theories concerning how people form their expectations about the course of the future inflation rate. The most popular one is the so-called *adaptive expectations theory*. The adaptive expectations theory indicates that people form their expectations about the future course of the inflation rate by looking at past rates of inflation and "learning" little by little. Thus the rate of inflation expected today to occur tomorrow is an average of the current and past rates of inflation. The average is not a simple average, however, but what sometimes is called a *weighted average*. Not all past inflation rates entering in the construction of the forecast are given the same importance, or weight. More recent experiences are assumed to carry a larger weight than those more distant in the past. An alternative, but equivalent specification is to say that at every period the public "corrects" their expectation according to the mistake made in that period (that is, according to the difference between the actual inflation rate during the period, and the one that was expected *last* period for *this* period). Technicalities aside, the conclusion from the theory is that it will take time for people to get used to what is happening. Only after a long enough time will they be convinced that a certain inflation rate is a permanent, rather than just a temporary, occurrence. How long a time this will be depends upon how quickly people adjust their expectations or "correct" their prediction errors at every period.

To gain an understanding about the implications of such a theory, consider an example. Suppose that for a long time the rate of inflation was 2 percent per year, and that people's expectations are completely adjusted so that they also expect such a rate to occur in the future. Suppose further that one day (say, at time $t = t_0$) prices start rising at a higher rate, say, 6 percent

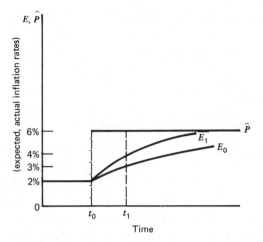

Figure 8-1. *Possible adjustment paths of expected to actual inflation rates.*

per year, and continue doing so for a long time. Figure 8-1 shows the two possible paths of the expected inflation rate, depending on how fast the public adjusts. In both cases expectations eventually catch up with the actual rate, but one of them is faster than in the other. For example, at time t_1, the slower adjustment path, E_0, indicates that the public believes the inflation rate will be 3 percent per year in the future, while the faster adjustment path, E_1, shows that people believe the inflation rate will be 4 percent. A limiting case would be one where the public adjusts so fast that they immediately catch up with what is going on.

The adaptive expectations theory has been widely used in the last twenty years in a variety of studies and it is a very "rich" theory in the sense that it can explain a number of results that would otherwise seem puzzling. Chapter 8 will, implicitly, use the main result of the adaptive expectations theory (namely, that it takes time for expectations to catch up). There are certain drawbacks in the theory, however. In particular, the theory implies that people are not too smart, because, if the theory is correct, people are *throwing away* information that could help them to better predict the future. Although the rate of monetary expansion is, sooner or later, an important determinant of the inflation rate, in this theory individuals do not look at the last (or the old, for that matter) rates of monetary expansion as an element in forming their anticipations. Certainly, higher rates of monetary expansion would eventually result in higher inflation rates, and at that point these higher inflation rates would be taken into account to form expectations about the future; but the public could anticipate those changes much earlier if they took account of the higher rates of monetary expansion in the first place. This is only one of the objections voiced by those who proposed what is called the *rational expectations theory*. Chapter 14 on monetary policy will return to some of the more sweeping implications of this latter theory. First, consider how expectations enter the whole process.

A PREVIEW OF THE ADJUSTMENT PROCESS

Chapter 6 concluded with a simple framework for the analysis of real income (output) and the level of prices, in final equilibrium as well as during the adjustment, to alternative levels of the money stock. Inflation was ignored.[1] The framework of Chapter 6 is not complete enough, then, to analyze the adjustment of the inflation rate, the level of real income, and some other magnitudes to alternative rates of change of the money stock—for example, rates of monetary expansion. The framework of Chapter 6 is not incorrect; it is only incomplete. Two simple additions must be made.

The first addition is fairly obvious. The desired money stock (the demand for money) must also depend on the expected rate of inflation or, alternatively, on the nominal interest rate, which in turn will depend on the expected rate of inflation. In the short run real total expenditures will depend on the expected inflation rate. An increase in the expected rate of inflation will decrease the desired money stock and increase total expenditures as people try to adjust to the lower desired level of their real cash balances.

The second addition concerns the process of price formation. An assumption has been used that prices would change according to whether real income (output) was higher, or lower, or the same as full employment real income. If, for example, real income (output) were at a level higher than full employment output, wages would be going up, and so would costs of production and prices, and vice versa. But the change in prices at every period is, of course, the rate of inflation. Chapter 6 concluded that in long-run equilibrium (at which real income must be equal to its full employment level) the rate of inflation would be zero. This assumption was of no major consequence in Chapter 6 because there the rate of monetary expansion was always zero, as was the inflation rate in the long-run equilibrium. Chapter 8 requires a more general formulation that allows for the possibility of a rate of inflation different from zero in the long run, when real income is equal to full employment income, and equal to whatever the rate of monetary expansion happens to be.

A simple formulation about the determination of the inflation rate is expression [8.1]. Expression [8.1] indicates that, at every period, the actual inflation rate ($\hat{P}$) is equal to what the public expected it to be (E), plus a term reflecting the difference between actual and full employment in real income (output), or

$$\hat{P} = E + \gamma(y - y^f) \qquad [8.1]$$

Two points concerning expression [8.1] are of interest. First, expression [8.1] is exactly the same as the theory about the formation of prices that was used in Chapter 6, except for the first term, E. In Chapter 6 we assumed that the public always expected an inflation rate equal to zero, and this was the case in analyzing the adjustment toward an equilibrium.

Expression [8.1] indicates that, at every period, the inflation rate will be equal, first, to the inflation rate the public expected for that period, plus a term reflecting the situation in the production side of the economy, being a coefficient that reflects the degree to which the level of unemployment influences nominal wages, which, in turn, affect product prices. Why would the expected rate of inflation (E) have such a direct effect on actual inflation rate? In the first place, many transactions in the economy are contracts involving the delivery of commodities at some later date, or a series of deliveries over a period, and prices in those transactions are set at higher levels when the parties expect other prices to rise in the future. Secondly, business firms post the prices at which they will sell over the period (or future periods); if they expect all other prices to rise at a certain rate during the period, then the way in which they can keep the relative price of their products (relative, that is, in relation to all other commodities) is to raise their prices at that same rate.

Expression [8.1], although simple, is far-reaching in its consequences. It is extremely important for clarifying the short- and long-run relationship between unemployment (or employment) and inflation. The framework is thus completed with these two additions. Unfortunately, even such a simple framework becomes too complicated to form a neat graphical representation that might keep track of all the magnitudes at the same time. It is too complicated because one more variable has been introduced (the expected inflation rate, E), and another equation (the theory that we might have concerning the formation of expectations—the *adaptive expectations theory*). Yet there are many insights to be gained by looking at each of the magnitudes involved and, occasionally, returning to each of the expressions that make up the framework.

Before doing so, however, we will gain from an overview of the whole adjustment process. Take the case of an economy in equilibrium where, suddenly, there is an increase in the rate of monetary expansion from, say, 2 to 8 percent per year. Such a change does not mean that the nominal money stock will be higher immediately, only that it will start to rise (see Figure 7–2b in Chapter 7). As the nominal money stock rises at the new rate of 8 percent per year, the real money stock also starts to rise (because the inflation rate does not react right away; in fact, at the beginning it will still be rising at only 2 percent per year). As the real money stock rises, so do real total expenditures (recall expression [5.9] for total real expenditures in Chapter 5). Total expenditures start to be higher than income, and real income (output) begins to rise as business firms find that people buy more than what they are producing and that their inventories start to fall. When real income (output) starts to rise above its full employment level, y^f, the inflation rate starts to rise (see expression [8.1]). Expectations have not yet changed, but they will soon start doing so, lagging behind the inflation rate.

Eventually [both because of the increased level of real income (output) above the full employment level, and because of achieved expectations], the inflation rate will catch up with the rate of monetary expansion, and surpass it, so that the real money stock will start falling, and with it the level of expenditures. Once again here, as in the simple noninflation case of Chapter 6, the real money stock as a determinant of total expenditures is the crucial link in the adjustment process. After a time for adjustments, the system will end up with a higher inflation rate, equal to the new rate of monetary expansion (8 percent, in this case), a lower level of the real money stock (now it costs more to hold money), and the same level of real income (output) at the "full employment" level. In the analysis of such a process, it becomes quite difficult to trace out these changes by looking at several magnitudes at the same time. Each magnitude must be analyzed separately. Much of what has happened in the United States during the last twenty years (and in many other countries in earlier decades) will become clearer as these variables are examined.

ADJUSTMENT TO AN INCREASE IN MONETARY EXPANSION

The course and direction of important magnitudes during the adjustment period can be plotted by analyzing the effects of an increase in the rate of monetary expansion. Later in Chapter 8 the opposite change (that is, a fall in the rate of monetary expansion) will be considered when the problem of stopping inflation is discussed.

As a starting point consider the situation of an economy in full equilibrium, with a rate of inflation equal to the rate of monetary expansion, real income (output) at the full employment level corresponding to the natural rate of unemployment, and fulfilled expectations. Numbers are useful as a reference. Suppose that the initial rate of monetary expansion and actual and expected rates of inflation ($\hat{M}$, $\hat{P}$, and E) are at a level of 2 percent per year. Suppose also that the real rate of interest is 4 percent per year. The nominal rate of interest would be equal to (4 percent) + (2 percent) = (6 percent per year). The initial level of the real money stock is equal to m_0. Suppose that one day (time t_0) the rate of monetary expansion rises from 2 to 7 percent per year and remains indefinitely at that level. The magnitudes can be evaluated one at a time.

THE RATE OF INFLATION AND THE REAL MONEY STOCK
First the consequences of the rise in money expansion on the level of the real money stock (m) and on the inflation rate (P) can be considered. From the

analysis of Chapter 7 we conclude that at the end of the adjustment process the real money stock will be lower (say, m_1) than the initial level m_0, because the inflation rate after the adjustment will be higher (7 percent) and individuals will wish to hold a smaller amount of real cash balances. (Remember that it costs more to hold money with a higher inflation rate.) Thus at least at some point during the adjustment period the real money stock will have to be falling (there is no way to go from the seventh floor to the third floor other than eventually going down the elevator). The fact that (at some point) the real money stock must be falling has profound implications. For the real money stock to be falling, the *rate of inflation needs to be higher than the rate of monetary expansion.* The real money stock is the nominal money stock divided by the price level, $m = M/P$, and in our experiment the nominal money stock (M) is rising at the rate of 7 percent per year. For real cash balances (m) to be falling, prices must be rising at a rate higher than 7 percent. At some time during the adjustment process, in other words, the inflation rate must over-shoot the rate of monetary expansion. This *overshooting* will always occur.

The extent of such overshooting will still be exaggerated by the fact that, initially, rather than falling, the real money stock will begin to rise. The more the real money stock rises (that is, the more the inflation rate lags behind the rate of monetary expansion), the more it will have to fall at a later stage in the process (and the more the inflation rate will later exceed the rate of mone-tary expansion). The fact that the initial lag is the response of the inflation rate, and therefore the initial increase of real cash balances, is clear from ex-pression [8.1]. The rate of inflation will begin to change only when expecta-tions change (but expectations themselves lag behind the inflation rate) or only until real income (output) starts to grow above the full employment level.

Figures 8–2a and 8–2b show what happens to the inflation rate and to the real money stock over time (measured along the horizontal axis). Figure 8–2a shows the rate of monetary expansion ($\hat{M}$) and the rate of inflation ($\hat{P}$). At the time t_0, the rate of monetary expansion rises from 2 to 7 percent per year and remains there. The inflation rate starts rising slowly, and only at time t_1 does it catch up with the latter. After that point the inflation rate temporarily overshoots the 7 percent per year value. It finally converges back at the rate of monetary expansion, probably in the *cyclical form* indicated in Figure 8–2a.

Real cash balances (shown in Figure 8–2b) start to rise at the very begin-ning of the process, reach a maximum at time t_1 (when the inflation rate has just caught up with monetary expansion, that is, when prices are rising as fast as the nominal money stock), and from there on start to fall and converge to their long-run equilibrium level, m_1 (smaller than their initial value, m_0).

The initial delayed reaction of the inflation rate to the higher rate of monetary expansion, and the overshooting that occurs after a while, has puzzled people many times. It has also helped shape some episodes of eco-

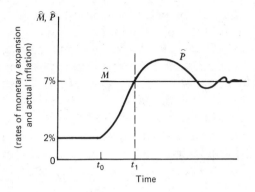

Figure 8-2a. *The inflation path when the rate of monetary expansion rises.*

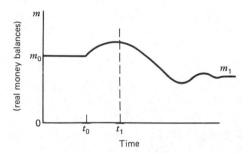

Figure 8-2b. *The effects of a rise in monetary expansion on real cash balances.*

nomic policymaking. For it is tempting to say, at the beginning of the process, that a higher monetary expansion does not cause inflation, and later on, when the inflation rate is above the rate at which money is being created, that inflation is caused by something other than changes in the nominal money stock. What the presence of these lags indicates is that the initial effects of changes in the rate of monetary expansion can be easily underestimated or overlooked, and that stabilization programs (a fall in the rate of monetary expansion) will take some time (and, most likely, a long time) to reduce the inflation rate.

EXPECTATIONS AND THE INTEREST RATE, REAL AND NOMINAL

The expected inflation rate and real and nominal interest rates must now be examined. We know that the nominal interest rate will always be the sum of the real rate borrowers agree to pay and lenders agree to receive, plus the inflation rate expected by the transacting parties. In order to understand the nominal interest rate, we must analyze these two components—the expected inflation rate and the real interest rate.

Since expectations about the inflation rate will "follow" the actual inflation rate itself, we can study the latter in order to analyze the former. Figure 8-3 reproduces the path of the inflation rate from Figure 8-2a and the same figure (8–3) plots the expected inflation rate. The expected rate will "lag behind" the actual rate, and it is only at a time such as t_3 (when the inflation rate has reached its maximum and is already falling) that expectations finally "catch up." After that, the expected rate actually "overshoots" the actual rate (that is, for a time people expect a higher inflation rate than the one that is actually taking place) before converging to the new 7 percent per year level.

The other component of the nominal interest rate is the real interest rate. In the framework of Chapters 7 and 8 the interest rate does not appear explicitly, but it is easy to find out what will happen to it by looking back at the discussion in Chapter 5.

As we will see later in Chapter 11, the manner in which the monetary authority, together with the commercial banking system, normally changes the money stock is to purchase securities in the open market, that is, to lend. An increase in the rate of monetary expansion has (as a first effect) a sudden increase in the flow of lending, and a gradual fall in the interest rate in financial markets. Since expectations about the future inflation rate are initially at the old level (2 percent per year), such a fall must occur through a *fall in the real interest rate.* In the new long-run equilibrium, after all adjustments have been completed, the real rate of interest will be at its initial level (in our example, 4 percent). This is enough to provide an idea of what will happen, and the graphical description appears in Figure 8–4: the real interest rate will fall immediately when the rate of monetary expansion is increased. Although the real rate will continue falling for a time, it will ultimately return to its original level, probably "overshooting" its final 4 percent equilibrium level.[2]

The nominal interest rate can now be analyzed by looking at (and adding up) its two components, the expected inflation rate and the real interest rate. This is what Figure 8–5 does. We know that in the final equilibrium the nominal rate will increase by the same percentage points as the inflation rate (in the numerical example, from 6 percent to 11 percent, since in the new equilibrium the real rate is 4 percent, and the inflation rate is 7 percent per year). But during the adjustment process the nominal interest rate at first falls because of the fall in the real rate (which expectations have *not* changed) and then starts to rise slowly, both because the real rate does so after its initial dip and because inflationary expectations start to go up as a reaction to the increasing inflation rate. It is only after a while that the nominal rate reaches its previous level (at time t_1, in the graph of Figure 8–5); it then continues to rise, overshoots its final equilibrium level of 11 percent, and finally converges to the long-run rate.

The short-run reaction of the nominal interest rate to a change (in our example, an increase) of the rate of monetary expansion is an important feature of the adjustment process because it is a reaction in precisely the opposite direction of what the long-run, permanent rate will be. Such behavior often misleads not only the public but also policymakers and, at times, even economists. The policymaker, unaware of the mechanics behind the scenes and con-

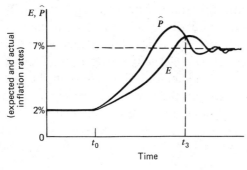

Figure 8-3. The effects of an increase in the rate of monetary expansion upon expected and actual inflation rates.

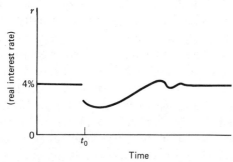

Figure 8-4. The rate of monetary expansion and the path of the real interest rate over time.

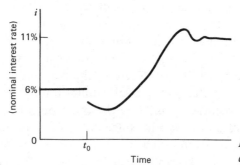

Figure 8-5. Nominal interest rate changes and the rate of monetary expansion.

cerned about "high interest rates" may feel tempted to continue to increase the rate of monetary expansion in order to bring interest rates down. Indeed, such an action will bring a short-lived *initial* fall in those rates, but sooner or later they will increase again, this time to a level still higher than what they were to start with. If the policymaker would insist on trying to keep those rates below their long run equilibrium level, *higher and higher* rates of monetary expansion would be necessary, without limit. This is one of the basic reasons why the interest rate (in particular, the nominal interest rate) may be a bad target for a monetary authority, such as the Federal Reserve System in the United States, to use.

Later in Chapter 8, when the problem of stopping inflation is considered, we see that the short-run response of the nominal interest rate to changes in the rate of monetary expansion is also an important occurrence when there is a fall, rather than an increase, in the rate of monetary expansion. In that case the immediate and short-run reaction is in a direction opposite than what will be in the long run.

Before the conclusion of this section, an important clarification is in order. The real interest rate is the rate expected by lenders and borrowers at the time they lend and borrow, but it is not necessarily the *ex post*, resulting rate. If, for example, the financial market clears (that is, the quantities supplied and demanded of financial assets are equal) at a real rate of interest of 3 percent for a one-year loan, and if the generalized expectation is that the inflation rate will be, say, 5 percent for that year, the nominal interest rate will be 8 percent. Since expectations during the adjustment process will in general turn out to be wrong, then the actual, resulting real rate in those loans will also turn out to be different. If inflation during that year is larger than expected (say, 7 percent), the resulting real rate will be smaller than intended (1 percent), and vice versa. It is not uncommon for this resulting real rate to be negative if actual inflation happens to be well above what was expected. Consider, for example, the real resulting interest rates paid during 1979 (a year when the inflation rate was around 13 percent) by borrowers who took a mortgage in 1978, at a nominal interest rate of 9.5 percent—a negative *real* resulting rate of almost 4 percent per year.

THE LEVEL OF EMPLOYMENT AND OUTPUT

The level of real income (output) during the adjustment process to a higher rate of monetary expansion may also be analyzed. After the adjustment has been completed, as in Chapter 7, the level of output will be the same as before the change: the level corresponding to the natural rate of unemployment, or full employment output. The path of output and employment during the transition is probably one of the most important single topics of public concern. In fact, the topic is so important that we must view it in historical perspective.

The Original "Phillips Curve." In 1958 a British economist, A. W. Phillips, published a piece of research that has had a tremendous direct impact on the economics profession as well as policymakers and political candidates.[3] Phillips presented the results of the analysis of data for the United Kingdom that showed what appeared to be a *long run-inverse relationship between the inflation rate and the rate of unemployment*; for periods of low inflation rates the data indicated high rates of unemployment, and vice versa.

The evidence shown in Phillips' original work, as well as in some later

Figure 8-6. The "Phillips relation" between the inflation rate and the unemployment rate.

works, looked more or less like Figure 8-6, where the rate of unemployment (u) is measured along the horizontal axis, and the rate of inflation, $\hat{P}$, along the vertical axis, and where each point corresponds to a single observation.[4] The resulting fitted curve that would summarize the apparent relationship has been baptized the *Phillips curve.*

If the Phillips curve shows a true long-run relationship, it indicates a very serious matter with all sorts of implications for policymaking. The existence of a long-run Phillips relationship would mean that there is a permanent tradeoff between two desirable goals, namely a high level of employment (or, equivalently, a low level of unemployment) and a low (or zero) inflation rate. If such a tradeoff existed, the policymaker would have to decide between two evils (inflation or unemployment), and the two desirable goals could never be achieved simultaneously.

The years following the original presentation of the Phillips curve kept economists very busy with two tasks. First, economists tried to find data for different years and different countries which would reproduce the original findings—and the results of these investigations were mixed. Second, economists sought a reason or reasons for such a tradeoff in the long run. Meanwhile, the Phillips tradeoff became commonplace among policymakers, economists, and the media.

A few years later an explanation was suggested that accounted for what is observed in the economy and that, in addition, had a theoretical rationale. This is the *natural rate of employment hypothesis,* or the "dynamic" or "expectations augmented" Phillips curve, or the "accelerationist" hypothesis. One should not be concerned about all of these names (which do have a rationale since all of them are related to the very same theory that we started using in this chapter with reference to expression [8.1]). We must now analyze how the natural rate hypothesis handles the trade off between inflation and unemployment.

The Natural Rate Hypothesis and the Dynamic Phillips Curve. The new explanation about the apparent "tradeoff" between inflation and unemployment was the result of several economists' work, notably that of Edmund S. Phelps and Milton Friedman.[5] Although not unanimously accepted by economists today (but by a large majority), the proposed resolution appears to give a reasonable explanation of the Phillips phenomenon.

The natural rate of unemployment hypothesis (see expression [8.1]) concerns the concept of full employment that was discussed in Chapter 6. There is a natural rate of unemployment (the same that was characterized in Chapter 6), but in the short run the actual level of output and employment might depart from it in such a manner that we can observe temporary associations between high levels of unemployment and low levels of inflation, and vice versa. There is not one but many Phillips curves, each corresponding to a given level of inflationary expectations, and each valid only for the very short run. In the long run the Phillips curve is simply a vertical line, and any inflation rate is compatible with the natural rate of unemployment. These statements must be discussed in some detail.

It is convenient to take expression [8.1] and to cast it in a slightly different, but equivalent, form. Remember that full employment real income (output), y^f, was the level of output forthcoming at the *natural rate* level of unemployment. Actual real income or output, on the other hand, can be related to the actual rate of unemployment (u): the higher the rate of unemployment, the lower the level of real output, and vice versa. There is a relationship between departures of the level of output from its full employment level ($y - y^f$) and departures of the rate of unemployment from its natural level ($u^f - u$). We can indicate the relationship equivalent to [8.1] as

$$\hat{P} = E + \delta(u^f - u) \qquad [8.2]$$

where u^f is our symbol for the "natural" rate of unemployment.

Expression [8.2] is exactly the same as expression [8.1] except that it makes reference to the labor market (by using rates of unemployment) rather than to levels of output forthcoming at each rate of unemployment. The economic interpretation is identical. Prices will rise at a given rate that is the sum of two components: (1) the rate at which people expect them to rise (E), and (2) a term reflecting departures of the rate of unemployment from the natural level. If unemployment is lower than the natural rate level, the term in the right-hand side of [8.2] is larger than zero and the inflation rate will exceed the expected inflation rate. The symbol δ simply indicates the speed with which the actual unemployment adjusts to the natural rate.

Consider what expression [8.2] indicates concerning the relationship that we might observe between the unemployment rate (u) and the inflation rate ($\hat{P}$). Expression [8.2] indicates that for a *given expected rate of inflation* (E) we will observe higher rates of inflation as associated with lower rates of unemployment, and vice versa. In Figure 8–7, as in Figure 8–6, the inflation rate is measured along the vertical axis, and the unemployment rate along the horizontal axis (in which u^f is the natural level of the unemployment rate). Expression [8.2] is represented in Figure 8–7 for a given level of the expected inflation rate. For example, if the expected inflation rate is E_0, the line labeled E_0 in Figure 8–7 would represent the relationship observed between unemployment and inflation. It is the *short-run* Phillips curve showing an *inverse* relation between the inflation and unemployment rates. If the expected inflation rate is higher (for example, E_1 in the graph), the line showing the inverse relationship between unemployment and inflation that one would observe is a higher one, as shown in the graph. The short-run Phillips curve would have shifted above and to the right. Thus there is one short-run Phillips curve for each expected rate of inflation. This is the *dynamic* Phillips curve suggested by the natural rate theory. Notice that if the inflation rate is, for example, E_0, then when unemployment is at its natural rate level the resulting inflation rate ($\hat{P}_0$) will be equal to the expected rate (E_0); this result is, of course, exactly what relationship [8.2] indicates.

Expression [8.2] shows, as did expression [8.1] for that matter, that in the long run when inflationary expectations have caught up with inflation (that is, when $E = \hat{P}$) the unemployment rate is equal to the natural rate. In long-run equilibrium any rate of inflation is possible (and given ultimately by the rate of monetary expansion), and in that equilibrium the unemployment rate will always be equal to the natural rate. It also indicates that in the short run, while expectations do not change, low rates of unemployment associated with high inflation rates might be observed (such as, for example, along any of the two

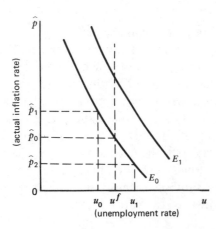

Figure 8-7. Actual and expected inflation rates and the natural rate of unemployment.

schedules shown in Figure 8–7, for either E_0 or E_1), but that this will be true only so long as expectations do not change.

Graphs such as Figure 8–2 (or expression [8.2]) show only the possible combinations of unemployment and inflation (for a given level of the expected inflation rate). They do not reveal the relevant short-run position of the economy. To find that out, we must return to our main theoretical framework.

Suppose, from the numerical example that has been used in this chapter, that the natural unemployment rate is 5 percent of the total labor force. Retain the assumption that the initial actual (and expected) inflation rate was 2 percent per year, equal to the initial rate of monetary expansion, and that we are studying the effects of an increase in the rate of monetary expansion from 2 to 7 percent per year. Figure 8–8 describes the initial situation (point A), the final equilibrium (point B), and the rates of unemployment and inflation during the adjustment. These changes may be traced out.

When the rate of monetary expansion rises from 2 to 7 percent per year, the real money stock, and with it total expenditures, begins to rise. As expenditures start to become larger than real income (output), real income starts to rise (that is, unemployment starts to fall) and the inflation rate rises. For as long as the expected inflation rate is the same as it was earlier (2 percent per year), the movement would be along the original, *short-run* Phillips curve. But soon expectations react to the inflation rate, so that the Phillips curve starts to shift upward. But the unemployment rate continues to fall, and it does so up to a point (say, the unemployment rate u_2 in Figure 8–8—in our example, perhaps 2 or 3 percent). In Figure 8–8, this pattern occurs when the expected rate of inflation is E_2. After that, unemployment rises again while the inflation rate goes on rising, reaches a maximum above its long-run level—the overshooting—and starts falling back to its new long-run equilibrium level (7 percent per year).[6] Before returning to its natural level of equilibrium, the rate of unem-

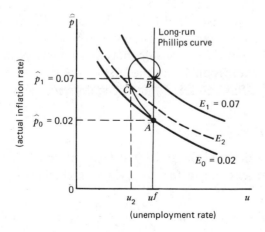

Figure 8–8. The "expectation's adjusted" Phillips curve: short-run and long-run relations.

ployment will for some time be higher than the natural rate (in our example, the 5 percent level). Such overshooting must take place.

There are several important additional points. The low level of unemployment (say, the level u_2 in this example) is a short-lived phenomenon. If policymakers wanted to keep unemployment below the "natural" level when the economy is at a point like point C in Figure 8-8, they would need to increase the rate of monetary expansion at a level higher than, in our example, 7 percent. In this way inflation would go on rising but unemployment would tend to remain for a while at the low level u_2. After some time a still higher rate of change of the money stock would need to follow, and so on. Thus to maintain unemployment at such low level[7] would require higher and higher rates of monetary expansion and inflation—the reason that the natural rate hypothesis is sometimes called the accelerationist hypothesis. To keep unemployment below the level of the natural rate prices would have to rise not merely at faster, but also at forever accelerating rates. The true tradeoff is not between unemployment and inflation rates, but between unemployment and increasing inflation rates.

The behavior of unemployment as a response to an increase in the rate of monetary expansion suggests that there may be a short-run incentive to engage in expansionary policies, as the initial effects on unemployment may seem attractive (see footnote 6, above). But it also implies (as we will see soon) that when the rate of monetary expansion is lowered there will be, for some time, an increase in the rate of unemployment—a transitory but painful price to pay for stabilization programs.

A second point is that the original Phillips curve treatment of inflation and unemployment is inaccurate in suggesting the possibility of long-run, equilibrium unemployment rates above or below the natural rate. The omission (if the natural rate theory is correct) is simply to forget the role of expectations. If the effects of alternative rates of monetary expansion were analyzed with the price adjustment theory used to analyze the effects of alternative *levels* of the money stock (where it was true that the equilibrium inflation rate is always zero, because the rate of monetary expansion is zero), we would also have concluded that there is a long-run relationship between unemployment and inflation. If, for example, in expression [8.2] the first of the two terms in the right-hand side (the expected inflation rate, E) had been deleted, we would have been left with

$$\hat{P} = \delta(u^f - u) \qquad [8.3]$$

or, equivalently, if we would have omitted the same first term in the [8.1] version (in terms of output levels rather than in terms of their corresponding unemployment levels),

$$\hat{P} = \gamma(y - y^f) \qquad [8.4]$$

Expressions [8.3] and [8.4] are really the ones used in the analysis of the effects of once-and-for-all changes in the nominal money stock, M. Prices would be rising (the inflation rate would be larger than zero) whenever output is above the full employment level (expression [8.4]) or, similarly, when unemployment is below the natural rate level (expression [8.3]). It is not that expressions [8.3] and [8.4] are wrong; they in fact reflect the assumptions from Chapter 6 about how the price level would behave. These assumptions are adequate simplifications for situations in which the rate of monetary expansion is always zero (as in Chapter 6), so that there is no possibility for the inflation rate to be other than zero in the long run. But, if either of these two incomplete expressions is used for cases when the rate of monetary expansion is *not* zero, and when therefore the rate of inflation is not zero either, we are bound to conclude that the employment and output levels can be permanently different from the natural rate levels, and higher than their natural levels when the inflation rate is positive. In graphical terms, expression [8.3] can be drawn in Figure 8–8, and it remains stationary independent of what happens to expectations.

The natural rate hypothesis is currently a well-known aspect of monetary policy. This hypothesis, which has been used and discussed extensively in Chapter 8, is still not completely accepted among some economists. The idea originated as a very Monetarist proposition, but over time it has gained wide support. There appears to be a growing consensus in recognizing the hypothesis as an excellent theory with which to explain some of the evidence.[8]

TAX REVENUES FROM THE CREATION OF MONEY

We have already looked at a number of interesting magnitudes and at their behavior during the adjustment to a higher rate of monetary expansion. There is an additional consideration—one that in some circumstances may provide a clue as to why certain policies are followed. It concerns the revenue received by the monetary authority from the creation of money during the adjustment period. Chapter 7 analyzed the reasons why inflation is the exact equivalent of a tax on the holdings of money, the particular way in which the "tax" is collected, and how, in the long run, there is a maximum flow of real revenues that government can collect by printing money. Let us now discuss the flow of real revenues during the adjustment to a higher rate of monetary expansion.

Expression [7.2] in Chapter 7 indicates that in any period the real revenue from the creation of money in a *nongrowing* economy was equal to

$$R = \hat{M} \cdot m \qquad [8.5]$$

that is, the rate of monetary expansion times the level of the real money stock at the period in question. Recall also that in the long run, in a nongrowing economy, the rate of inflation is equal to the rate of monetary expansion ($\hat{P} = \hat{M}$), and that in the long-run equilibrium the real money stock was always lower the higher the inflation rate. Thus in long-run equilibrium an increase in the rate of monetary expansion, and consequently in the inflation rate, always decreases the real money stock. After a certain level, further increases in the rate at which money is printed would result in a fall, rather than in an increase, in real revenues per period.

In the short run the indications of expression [8.5] are straightforward: the immediate response of the flow of real revenues is to rise when the rate of monetary expansion is raised, and to fall when the rate of monetary expansion is lowered. *This is so irrespective of whether in long-run equilibrium such a move would result in a rise or a fall of the flow of real revenues.* When the rate of monetary expansion increases, the real money stock does not decrease immediately; in fact, it will even rise for some time before starting to fall. Figure 8-9 depicts these results. The two "paths" depicted for the level of real revenues correspond to two possible cases: in the first one, the increase in the rate of monetary expansion brings about a long-run increase in the level of real revenues (from the original $R_0 = \hat{M}_0 \cdot m_0$ to $R_1 = \hat{M}_1 \cdot m_1$); in the second, the same change brings about a long-run level of real revenues smaller than the initial one (from the original $R_0 = \hat{M}_0 \cdot m_0$ to $R_2 = \hat{M}_1 \cdot m_2$). In both cases the rate of monetary expansion is the same ($\hat{M}_0 = 2$ percent per year for the initial rate, and $\hat{M}_1 = 7$ percent per year for the "new" one), but in the second case the level of the real money stock has fallen so much that revenues fall in the long run. *But in both cases real revenues initially jump to a higher level*, and in both cases revenues continue to rise for a while after the initial jump before converging to their new long-run equilibrium. Even if the long run effect is a fall in revenues, the initial effect is an increase.

As soon as the rate of monetary expansion is increased, more dollars per period are used by the money producer to purchase goods and services at the same prices as before, so that more goods and services can be purchased per unit of time. After that, and for a time, even though prices start to rise faster

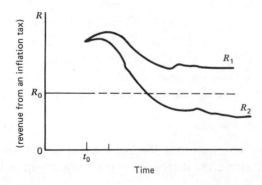

Figure 8-9. Alternative paths of government revenue from an inflation tax.

than before, the higher and higher price levels are still not high enough to compensate for the higher number of dollars per period used for those purchases. Only after some time are prices high enough for the higher number of dollars to buy less (and, in the second of the two cases shown in Figure 8–9, still less in the new equilibrium than before the change).

To use an analogy, the pattern here involves much the same economics as the case of, say, an increase of the tax rate on the ownership of houses. Even if in the long run a higher tax rate decreases the tax base (the number of houses) by so much that total revenues from the tax end up being lower with the higher tax rate than what they were with a lower tax rate, this result will happen only after a while as houses evaporate through depreciation and are not replaced. In the short run the houses are there, and somebody owns or holds them and pays the tax,[9] so that an increase in the tax rate will always increase tax revenues for some time. The only difference is that in the case of a house tax the number of houses will start to fall immediately after the increase in the tax rate, rather han still rising for some time as in the case of the real money stock.

The short run response also works the other way around. No matter what the result is with respect to the long-run final equilibrium, a fall in the rate of monetary expansion will always decrease real revenues immediately and only after a while those revenues will start rising again to reach their final value. All of this suggests that, from the viewpoint of financing part of the budget via the printing of money, an increase in the rate of monetary expansion offers the government the short-run attractiveness of allowing an increase in the level of real expenditures (or to decrease the level of conventional taxes). In contrast, a drop in the rate of monetary expansion imposes a disproportionate short-run burden on the budgetary situation.[10]

A REVIEW OF THE ADJUSTMENT PROCESS

We have now examined, piecemeal, all of the magnitudes involved in the adjustment process. In this section all of these magnitudes can be summarized so as to interconnect the behavior of all of them and to overview the process of monetary expansion. At the same time, a brief account of the most important overall features of what happens during the transition is offered so that details do not preclude an understanding of the broad and important characteristics.

Panels (a) to (f) in Figure 8–10 summarize what happens to the inflation rate (panel a), the real money stock (panel b), interest rates (panel c), unemployment (panel d), real income (output) (panel e), and the real revenues from money creation (panel f) with an increase in monetary expansion. We should note several things. Panels (d) and (e) are mirror images as they describe what happens to the level of unemployment and the resulting level of real income

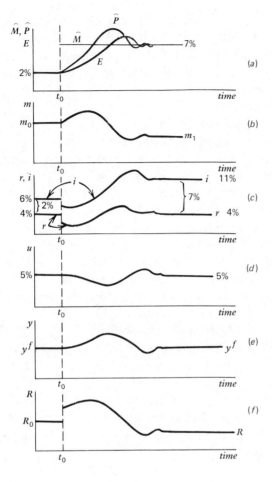

Figure 8-10. *A summary of the effects of an increase in the rate of monetary expansion.*

(output). The nominal interest rate is simply the sum of the real interest rate and the expected rate of inflation. Real revenues from the creation of money follow the path of the real money stock (because those revenues are always equal to real cash balances times the rate of monetary expansion, which remains fixed at 7 percent per year after the change). Panel (f) describes the case where revenues fall in the long run.

The simultaneous movement of all of these variables should not obscure the understanding of the chain of causality driving the forces of the economic system, that is, the understanding of "what causes what." The initial increase in the rate at which nominal money is introduced in the economy starts to increase the real money stock, which, in turn, increases total expenditures above income and encourages business firms to raise their level of employment and production. As production begins to be higher than the full employment level (or, similarly, as the rate of unemployment starts to be less than the "natural rate") there is pressure for nominal wages (and therefore for production costs and prices) to rise at a faster rate (see expression [8.2]); that is, the inflation rate starts to rise. Only then the expected inflation rate starts to respond. Meanwhile, interest rates, both real and nominal, have initially fallen, and perhaps continue to do so for a time before starting to rise again.

The final equilibrium is brought about because of the momentum that the inflation rate gains after a while, as a result of both the rising inflationary expectations and the lower and lower rates of unemployment (expression [8.2]). As the inflation rate rises above the rate of monetary expansion, the real money stock begins to fall and reduces total expenditures, the level of output, and eventually the inflation rate to their long-run equilibrium levels.

Important from the viewpoint of policy is a particular feature of the overall process, one that helps to explain why expansionary monetary policies are fairly easy to get into, and very hard to get out of. This feature can be appreciated by glancing at the six panels in Figure 8–10. At the beginning of the adjustment process, as the most immediate effect, (i) unemployment falls (that is, real income rises), a rather popular event; (ii) interest rates (both real and nominal) fall, another occurrence that usually is treated as "good news"; and finally (iii) a larger part of the government budget may be financed without resorting to additional conventional taxes. And all of this happens without a noticeable increase in the inflation rate.

Given the relatively long lags involved in the process, it is only much later that most of these results turn around: unemployment starts rising, as do interest rates and the rate of inflation, and the part of real government expenditures that can be financed by money creation begins to fall (in the case described in Figure 8–10, the latter ends up lower than before the change). These results occur late in the transition, with an inflation rate transitorily well above the level that the rate of monetary expansion would seem to justify. All of these events point in the same direction and suggest that is is easy (almost attractive) for governments to engage in expansionary monetary policies. As we will see in the coming section, the same, symmetric results operate in the case of a contractionary policy, that is, a *fall in the rate of monetary expansion.*

EXPECTATIONS AND THE PROBLEM OF STOPPING INFLATION

So far, Chapter 8 has analyzed the process of adjustment to a higher rate of monetary expansion. The results of the opposite experiment, that is, a fall in the rate of monetary expansion from an initial long-run equilibrium situation (for example, from a 7 to a 2 percent per year), is perhaps more important. The behavior of all the magnitudes involved, and for exactly the same reasons, is perfectly symmetric. The mechanics of the process are simple, but such an exercise has a great deal of relevance in its own right (particularly today, in the US economy), for it refers to policies that are most likely to take place when the monetary authority decides to implement a stabilization program.

In all stabilization attempts a great deal of time is spent by government officials (and rightly so) in trying to modify people's expectations about the future course of the inflation rate. Consider first a stabilization program consisting of a sudden and permanent decrease of the rate of monetary expansion (from 7 to 2 percent per year).

STABILIZATION PROGRAMS: THE ADJUSTMENT TO A LOWER RATE OF MONETARY EXPANSION

Panels (a) to (f) of Figure 8–11 show the result of a sudden fall of the rate of monetary expansion from an initial long-run equilibrium situation at which the

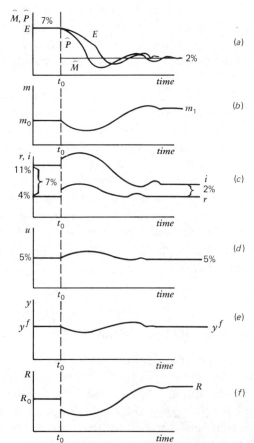

Figure 8-11. Stopping inflation: a summary of the effects of reducing the rate of monetary expansion.

rate was 7 percent per year. Assume, in other words, that at time t_0 the rate of monetary expansion falls from 7 to 2 percent per year. It is easy to realize that each panel in Figure 8-11 is exactly equivalent to its counterpart in Figure 8-10, except that it is "upside down." Following the change, the rate of inflation does not react very rapidly, but interest rates do—they jump up and keep on rising for some time before starting to fall. Unemployment starts to rise (and output to fall), and the real value of the part of the government budget that can be financed through money creation falls drastically. All of this is unpleasant news. It is only after a while that the long-run effects reveal themselves: the fall of the inflation rate, a return to the natural rate of unemployment and the corresponding full employment level of output, and the fall of the nominal interest rate to its new, lower, long-run equilibrium level (in our example, 6 percent per year). Eventually, an increase in the level of revenues from the creation of money—in the new long-run equilibrium, the level of these revenues can be higher as in the case shown in Figure 8-11, than before the lowering of monetary expansion.

The mechanism by which all of this is accomplished is exactly the same as before, but now it acts in an opposite direction. The first effect of the lower rate of monetary expansion is to begin lowering the level of the real money stock, which in turn lowers real expenditures below real income and output. Business firms find that inventories accumulate, and they start to reduce their level of production and employment. As unemployment rises above the natural rate level, wages start rising at a lower rate and so do prices. Meanwhile, here is a sudden increase in interest rates: since now there is a lower level of lending by the monetary authority, the real rate of interest goes up and so does the nominal rate. The increase in nominal interest rates starts softening (and will revert to a fall) as inflationary expectations begin to be revised downward. As the inflation rate falls, the real money stock stops falling and rises again, so that real expenditures also rise and unemployment starts adjusting back to the natural rate level.

The process is exactly the reverse of the adjustment mechanism that we discussed before. In both cases expectations were lagging behind the actual inflation rate, because the public looked only at changes in that rate to adjust their expectations, with a lag.[11]

We have seen that the adjustment process is exactly the reverse of the adjustment pattern that we discussed for monetary expansions. In both cases expectations were lagging behind the actual inflation rate, and those expectations depended exclusively on what happens to the inflation rate. The public looked only at changes in this rate, with a lag, to adjust their expectations. What if suddenly, at the very beginning or during the adjustment process, expectations had been influenced by other factors? This possibility deserves more attention.

THE IMPORTANCE OF EXPECTATIONS
IN STABILIZATION ATTEMPTS

As mentioned before, every stabilization attempt is usually accompanied by dramatic efforts to assure the success of the program, that is, that the inflation rate will indeed fall. There are reasons for this to happen other than the usual political rhetoric. It is true (as we just saw) that, if the monetary authority lowers the rate of monetary growth and keeps it at the lower level, inflation will eventually fall and the new equilibrium will be reached. This will happen whether the public "believes" in the success of the effort or not: all that is required is that the public eventually revises their expectations downward as the actual rate of inflation falls. But any program will have much quicker results (and much less painful in terms of the intensity and duration of the transitory rise in unemployment) if the public's expectations can be modified even before the actual inflation rate shows any change.

This hypothesis is so for two reasons: (1) because expectations determine directly, in the short run, what the rate of inflation is going to be (expressions [8.1] and [8.2]), and (2) because the stock of real money the public wishes to hold depends upon the expected inflation rate. The lower the expected inflation rate, the higher the real money stock desired by the public and the lower the level of expenditures forthcoming. In other words, a fall in the expected inflation rate induces the public to accumulate cash balances, and in order to do this they must reduce their expenditures.

As a concrete example, let us look at an ideal case in which, at the very beginning of the stabilization effort (that is, at the same time as the rate of monetary expansion is lowered from 7 to 2 percent per year) government announces a new policy, and the public believes that from that moment on the inflation rate will, at all points in time, be 2 percent per year.[12] Assume that the hypnosis of such an announcement lasts long enough so that people believe in such a 2 percent rate of inflation throughout the whole adjustment process. This is obviously an exaggerated case, but one that highlights the crucial importance of expectations and captures what, in a less extreme form, has happened on occasions.

Figure 8-12 (again, with six panels) shows what will happen in this case. Panel (a) shows the rate of monetary expansion and the expected inflation rate falling at time t_0, from 7 to 2 percent per year. The actual inflation rate will also decline immediately from 7 to 2 percent (expressions [8.1] or [8.2]). But the cycle does not end here, and in fact panel (a) shows that the inflation rate will need to fall still further after the initial "shock" because the public will also wish to hold a *higher level of money in real terms*. Real cash balances will rise only if prices rise at a lower rate than the 2 percent per year increase in the nominal money stock. Thus real expenditures will fall for a while and some temporary unemployment will take place.

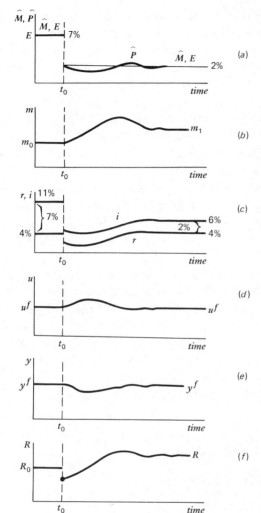

Figure 8-12. *A fall in the rate of monetary expansion and in the expected inflation rate—the policymakers' dream.*

Finally, observe what happens to interest rates. Because less money is being lent by the monetary authority, the real interest rate will rise and will create a higher nominal interest rate. On the other hand, since the expected inflation rate has dropped (from 7 to 2 percent) the nominal interest rate will decline. Panel (c) shows the second effect dominating, with an initial drop in the nominal interest rate and a gradual adjustment of both real and nominal rates to their long-run equilibrium values (the real rate = 4 percent, and the nominal rate = 6 percent per year). Since the expected inflation rate is always 2 percent following the announcement, 2 percent is always the difference between the real and the nominal rate throughout the adjustment process.

Nevertheless, in the policymaker's "dream case" there is a transitory cost of the stabilization program, in the form of a recession (though probably milder and shorter than what it would have been without the change in expectations). The policymaker may do something else that would eliminate this cost, but it is difficult to accomplish. If, at the time of the reduction in the rate of monetary expansion and the change in expectations, the *level* of the real money stock would be increased from m_0 (the initial, old equilibrium level) to m_1 (the final equilibrium stock, that is, the stock the public wishes to hold at the lower expected inflation rate), we would be in a perfect world with the whole adjustment taking place at once and without any transitory unemployment. This state would occur because the monetary authority would have provided the public with the additional quantity of real money it wanted to hold at the lower expected inflation rate and the public would not have needed to reduce the level of their expenditures in trying to accumulate these additional cash balances.

Why is the avoidance of recession difficult to achieve in practice? Because, even if government is initially believed in its announcements concerning the future course of inflation, this belief may not be very "robust." Furthermore, anything the monetary authority does other than keeping the money stock growing at the announced rate of monetary expansion could easily destroy such a belief and backfire in the form of a sudden upward revision of the expected inflation rate. In fact, there are several examples of such episodes that at times have occurred in many countries with rich inflation histories.

THE SHORT-RUN DISTORTIONS OF INFLATION

In Chapter 7 some of the effects of inflation in the long run were discussed. They were, first, the capital gains and losses to the parties committed to contracts specified in nominal terms, and the exaggerated "dispersion" that always occurs among product prices even if, on the average, those prices rise at a constant and perfectly anticipated rate. These were effects that occurred even if the adjustment to the new inflation rate took place overnight. But, as Chapter 8 has indicated, the adjustment is a relatively long process and it is during this process that some of the most serious distortions occur.

First, since the public will in general make mistakes in forecasting the inflation rate during the adjustment process, there will be continuous transfers among debtors and creditors, workers and business firms (because wage contracts are specified in terms of nominal dollars), fixed income recipients, and so on. Second, and still more important, it is during this long adjustment process that the largest variation in the rate of change of individual prices will occur. Take, for example, the case of the adjustment to a higher rate of monetary expansion. When total expenditures start to rise they normally do so by different amounts for different products: the demand pressure is uneven among sectors. Not all industries are equally speedy in increasing their production levels, or in exerting pressures on the labor market. Output responses will be uneven across sectors, as will price responses. The result is that during the adjustment the "signals" given by prices (which are supposed to alert producers and consumers about the real scarcity of goods) will be badly distorted.

The problems related to output and prices of final goods and services also apply to wages in different sectors. In the long run, with a perfectly anticipated average inflation rate, there is no reason to believe that there is a consistent and significant redistribution of income (for example, from labor to business firms, or vice versa), and most empirical studies confirm this view. But in the short run, while the adjustment process is taking place, almost anything can happen.

OTHER THEORIES OF INFLATION AND OTHER POLICIES FOR FIGHTING IT

In our analysis of the phenomenon of inflation we have described a mechanism in which the rate of inflation is, at least in the long run, a strictly monetary event. An increase in the rate of monetary expansion over and above what is necessary to keep the real money stock at the level desired by the public increases expenditures, and after some period of adjustment the inflation rate ends up matching the increase in the rate of monetary expansion. This phenomenon is described sometimes by saying that inflation is a *demand pull* event. Prices rise because expenditures (that is, the demand for goods and services) do. The monetary mechanism, and the view that there is a close correlation between the rate of monetary expansion and the rate of inflation, is indeed the dominant view nowadays.

It is nevertheless useful to review alternative explanations, some of which became popular several years ago, and others which today are still stressed by certain economists and hastily accepted by the layman. Most of these views do not deny the fact that a substained, long-run equilibrium level of the inflation rate is only possible when accompanied by a certain rate of monetary expansion—an equal rate, in the case of the nongrowing economy—but they tend to stress what may be viewed as *original causes* that tend to raise prices and somehow force the monetary authority to "match" the increase in prices with increases in the quantity of money. Even though the label does not strictly apply to all of these theories, most of them can be characterized by being *cost push* theories.

INFLATION AS A STRUCTURAL PHENOMENON
The structural view of inflation was first put forward in the United States by the former president of the Council of Economic Advisers Charles Schultze,

and about the same time by some Latin American economists. This view begins with the proposition that prices are rigid in the downward direction: they might rise, but they will fall only very slowly if at all. The result of the rigidity is substantial unemployment. Permanent changes in supply and demand conditions in different sectors bring about continuous changes in relative prices in a growing economy. If money prices cannot fall, the only manner in which relative price changes can take place is that through increases in some money prices. Suppose, for example, that a real change (a technological breakthrough, or a change in tastes) requires the real, relative price of corn (that is, the price of corn in terms of all other commodities) to fall by 20 percent. This can be accomplished either through a fall of the money price of corn by 20 percent, with all other money prices remaining at the same level, or through a 20 percent increase in all other money prices, or through a combination of the two. If the money price of corn cannot fall, equilibrium in the real sector of the economy can be attained only through a rise in the price of all goods except corn. If this is so, then in order to maintain the equilibrium level of the real stock of money it would be necessary for government to match the increase in the general price level with a rise in the nominal money stock. According to this view, changes in the quantity of money, rather than causing increases in prices, merely *validate* autonomous price changes in order to maintain the overall equilibrium.

The validity of the structural view depends on whether prices are in fact so resistant to reductions—a state that creates some amount of transitory unemployment—and on whether growth and the dynamism of the economy require frequent and important changes in relative prices. Empirical observation does not seem to be compatible with the structural view: certain economies have grown substantially over long periods of time with very little or no inflation (for example, West Germany after World War II), and others, while remaining stagnant, have suffered very high inflation rates (almost any Latin American country in the past thirty years).

MONOPOLY POWER BY UNIONS AND BUSINESSES, OR THE THEORY OF "UNREASONABLE DEMANDS"

Alleged monopoly of inputs and outputs supports still a different view of inflation, that could most accurately be called a *supply push* interpretation. Depending on what variation of the theory is accepted, inflation is here primarily generated either by wage increases demanded by unions above and beyond increases in the productivity of labor, or by price increases by firms that to some extent possess monopoly power. Increases in the quantity of money—as in the structural view—would do nothing else than *accommodate* those autonomous wage and price increases. The argument is particularly popular among consumers and firms. On the one hand, workers and consumers see changes in commodity prices as being "set" by firms, and their salary increases as merely matching those price increases. Firms, on the other hand, look at rises in their labor costs and consider their price increases as merely matching the rise in their costs. In fact, both price and cost increases are part of the same phenomenon.

Several objections can be raised against the view that *unreasonable demands* by unions and business are the ultimate culprit in creating inflation. First, there is the question of how many industries are actually monopolized by either business or labor; the empirical evidence shows that conditions very similar to perfect competition prevail in most sectors of the economy. Second, we know that when monopoly power exists in a sector there is an equilibrium level of the price of the commodity produced by such sector (or, for the wage commanded, if the sector is a particular union). Under monopoly conditions, a given equilibrium price will be higher than under competition but it cannot be increased indefinitely.

A particular form that this view has taken nowadays (particularly among government officials) is the argument that much of the current inflation is due to increases in the price of oil. There has been a real change (the operation of the cartel by oil producing countries) with a resulting higher price of oil in terms of all other commodities. If the real quantity of money is not going to fall (as the consequence of a rise in the money price of one product, in this case oil), an oil price increase would require either a fall in the money prices of all other commodities, so that the general price level would remain the same, or a rise in the nominal money stock, with all other money prices remaining constant. If the second policy is followed, as it has been, then the general price level rises. The "oil explanation" contains other complications. If oil prices are fixed by the cartel in terms of dollars, a way for the monetary authority "producing" dollars to eliminate the real increase in oil prices (in terms of all other commodities) is to increase the money stock sufficiently for all other money prices to rise by the same percentage as the price of oil. Oil sheiks would receive more dollars per barrel of oil but could buy only the same quantity of other commodities in the world market as before the change. Naturally, such a move by the major oil importing countries would bring about further increases in the dollar price of oil, and new matching increases in the quantity of money by the rest of the world: monetary policy in the United States would then be indirectly but ultimately dictated by the oil sheiks! A more direct and practical option for the oil cartel is to set the price of oil directly in terms of a basket of commodities, adjusting the dollar price automatically—a procedure that has indeed been followed.

Finally, the reader should notice that Switzerland, purchasing the totality of its oil consumption, has been (and continues to be) the country with the lowest inflation rate. If OPEC's price increases explains inflation in the US, why not in Switzerland?

SOME ALTERNATIVE POLICIES TO FIGHT INFLATION

Notice once more that in the two views about the ultimate causes of inflation described above, changes in the quantity of money (or in the rate of monetary expansion) were not the cause, but the consequence of price increases. If those views were to be accepted, then the usual prescription for stopping inflation by lowering the rate of monetary expansion would lose effectiveness and its application could bring more pain than relief. If prices rise first, and the increase in the rate of monetary expansion is the inevitable consequence, inflation would be better fought by precluding prices from rising in the first place. The two policies described below, in any of their variations, respond to this view.

DIRECT PRICE AND WAGE CONTROLS

Direct price and wage controls have a long history (dating at least to the Egyptians and to the Roman Emperor Diocletian) and have invariably failed, except for episodes during which, for a short time, they were able to influence expectations. The procedure consists of establishing maximum levels for either all or some prices and wages, and adopting some mechanism to enforce such levels. There is first, of course, the problem of effective enforcement and of avoiding the development of "black markets" in one or another form. Second, monetary expansion in the presence of such controls (which still create increases in total expenditures) creates higher levels of demand and lower levels of supply in various markets, and therefore longer and longer waiting lines. Finally, the inevitable removal of the controls usually brings about, over a very short period, the same increase in prices that would have otherwise been distributed over a longer period of time. Indeed, there is some evidence that anticipation of price controls do tend, in the short run, to make prices higher than they would otherwise be, since firms would rush to increase their prices before controls are put into effect.

A popular variation of price and wage controls is the so-called *guidelines* method. Whether established in a formal way or through "arm twisting" by government agencies or the President, such guidelines have the same effects as direct controls, the only difference being the extent of the penalty for not abiding, and the probability of being caught cheating.

Are price controls effective in any way? If inflation were due to the exercise of monopoly power by business or unions, direct controls would be the natural way to fight inflation. Prices and wages would not start to rise in the first place, and the quantity of money would not be forced to rise. However, experience with price controls shows that, while prices and wages are not allowed to rise, increases in the quantity of money continue taking place at the same time that the disequilibrium becomes more and more important. The only extent to which direct controls have proved somehow effective has been in the very short term, and only for as long as their imposition was able to reduce inflationary expectations. Under these circumstances, a fall in the rate of monetary expansion and concrete government actions showing the determination to keep the rate at the lower level have proved to have a better effect upon expectations.

TAX-INDUCED POLICIES (TIP)

Some recent proposals, all of which can be grouped under the name of *Tax-Induced Policies* (TIP) consist of devising a scheme under which prices would be allowed to rise at rates higher than the guideline, but with a penalty in the form of higher taxes, while increases below the guideline would be rewarded with the payment of lower taxes. Essentially, these are the same as direct controls, with some higher degree of flexibility. If we compare TIP with direct, rigid controls that are effectively enforced, the former are preferable to the extent that they would allow the markets to eliminate nonprice rationing; instead of paying the price in the form of longer waiting lines, consumers would do so through higher prices due to the part of the tax passed on to them. As such, TIP might have whatever positive effects direct controls have, with fewer market distortions. In the long run, the persistence of the ultimate source of inflation (high rates of monetary expansion), together with TIP, would bring about a situation of equilibrium with the same inflation rate that would exist in the absence of any controls or inducements, but with a higher level of taxation. The effects of TIP are similar to a generalized sales tax.

CONCLUSION

Monetary policy, or changes in the rate of monetary expansion, works upon the important economic targets—employment, prices, output, and so forth—through the important filter of expectations. Chapters 5 through 8 have presented a framework through which alterations in the money stock may be analyzed, but the principles and institutions through which the money stock itself is formed and changed have so far remained in the background. Before we turn to an extensive treatment of economic policy (Chapter 14) and policy history (Chapter 16), we must understand in detail the crucial roles of the commercial and central banking systems—along with those of financial intermediaries and markets in general. The process of money creation by commercial banks and other depository institutions in Chapter 9 initiates the discussion, after which central banks and financial institutions will be analyzed. These institutional details and processes will also contribute to an understanding of the actual workings of the theoretical processes described in Chapters 5 through 8.

Appendix 8
INDEXATION

The appearance of relatively high and variable rates of inflation in the United States and Western European countries during the last decade has brought a renewed interest in the adoption of *indexation* or *monetary correction* schemes that could soften some of the negative effects of inflation. To be sure, such interest is not completely new; the topic has been debated for many years in several less developed countries with a history of chronic inflation, and some have experimented with indexation in one form or another. In the United States, as far back as 1925, a private corporation issued bonds linked to a broad index of prices at the recommendation of the economist Irving Fisher.

In a general sense, to "index" a certain magnitude is to link it to the behavior of another magnitude—the "index"—which serves the function of a "yardstick," in such a way that changes in the latter are automatically translated into changes in the former. Specifically, a scheme of indexation (sometimes called "escalator clauses") involves the linking of future payments to some general index of prices in the economy. What magnitudes are indexed, what index or yardstick is used, and the manner in which the automatic adjustment takes place are crucial considerations for distinguishing between schemes and situations that are conceptually very different. Failure to recognize these distinctions has been the source of much confusion and misunderstanding among laymen and even among some economists. It is important to define indexation carefully because many of the most common objections to indexation arrangements are, in fact, objections to things other than what here (and in most of the technical literature) are considered true indexation.

Before we proceed, a clarification is in order. References are often made to indexation systems or schemes, and to the convenience or inconvenience of having them "adopted." The viewpoint taken here is that the adoption of indexation schemes—that is, those schemes that are efficient—will be the natural outcome of the market forces. Thus the role of government is

limited (at most) to the three following matters. First, the government may allow such private arrangements and assure that they will be enforceable in a court of law. Second, it may provide reliable price indexes. This function could be performed by private sector activity, as is the case, for example, in Brazil, but government's better access to data and the "public good" character of this kind of information indicate that a government agency is probably a better alternative. Third, the role of government concerning indexation is to specify taxes in real terms, so that changes in the price level do not bring about changes in the real tax bill, as is the case nowadays in the United States and in most countries with a progressive income tax system and taxes on nominal capital gains.

The Nature of Indexation

In any economy, a large number of transactions take the form of commitments to a payment or succession of payments to be made in the future, in exchange for goods and services delivered either at the time the contract is made, or later on as payments take place. Within a large variety of possible arrangements, *time* is involved in all of these transactions. Typical examples are the labor market, where the contract sets a wage to be paid in exchange for labor services during the duration of the contract, and the market for financial instruments, where contracts specify repayment of loans (plus interest) at some time in the future. Leasing or rental contracts on homes, land, and machinery are other examples.

During times of price stability, those future payments are usually specified in terms of the accepted monetary unit (dollars, in the case of the United States); because there is little or no uncertainty about the future purchasing power of money, money can satisfactorily perform its role as a unit account or standard of value for current as well as for future payments. Of course, even in this case there is risk involved to the extent that the particular price of the good or service to be delivered may rise or fall before the contract expires, imposing a capital gain or loss to the parties. The prospect of these gains is, indeed, the most powerful engine for both long-run economic progress and short-run adjustment to disequilibrium in a market-oriented economy. But there is no substantial risk concerning the *real value* (in terms of all goods and services in the economy) of the payments to be delivered in exchange for the commodity in question.

Things are different when the general price level is expected to change during the duration of the contract. If the direction and magnitude of the change is known with certainty, a mere adjustment of the nominal payments to be made will be sufficient, and the parties will specify those dollar or nominal payments in a manner such that their real value or purchasing power will reflect the real conditions of the contract. Thus the level of the inflation rate, or the extent to which the general price level changes is not the problem, but rather it is its variability and unpredictability. And it just happens that high inflation rates are in general associated with highly variable rates. If forced to specify future payments in nominal terms (that is, in terms of the monetary unit), the parties will again agree on some adjustment of those payments, and such an adjustment will reflect their expectations about the future course of the general price level, or the rate of inflation. Nominal payments will be fixed for a time, and they will have "built in" a certain inflationary expectation. Of course, any failure of either party's expectations to be fulfilled results in an unplanned transfer of wealth.

If allowed to do so, the parties may restore matters to the state that would have existed in the absence of uncertainty about the future course of the general price level by agreeing on a *real* level of future payments and leaving nominal payments to be adjusted according to changes in a general index of prices. Inflationary expectations would not enter in any way, and only the realized inflation rate would later on be reflected in nominal or dollar payments. This procedure is what we call (and is considered in the technical literature) "true indexation."

Two features of "true" indexation arrange-

ments deserve particular attention. The first one is that in such arrangements adjustments of nominal payments should take place as frequently as possible, so that these nominal payments might reflect the contemporaneous actual inflation rate, or at most the immediate past rate. Many "indexation" schemes call for a rather infrequent adjustment of future payments according to past inflation rates; the less frequently those adjustments take place, the more such a scheme is merely an equivalent of nonindexed contracts in nominal terms, with some specific formula by which the expected inflation rate is calculated. This is a crucial consideration, since much of the opposition to indexation, which argues that indexation tends to "perpetuate" inflation, is in fact an objection to this sort of ex ante arrangement.

The second feature deserving close consideration refers to the index to be used as a yardstick. The purpose of indexation is to secure the purpose of the contract, which is to fix in advance, and for a certain period, the general purchasing power of future money payments. Any price index suffers from bias, and an index of "general purchasing power" can be different for different individuals. But even with these limitations, true indexation requires the index to reflect movements of a large variety of goods in the economy, rather than a narrowly defined index or, in the extreme, the "spot" price of a commodity closely related to the activity in question. In this last case, the arrangement would bring about the *fixing* of a *relative* price that would be subject to uncertainty in the absence of inflation. An example is sufficient to clarify this point. In France, not long ago, indexation schemes became prevelant for the issuing of bonds by utilities companies operated (at least partially) by government, whereby the interest paid on the bonds was linked to the price of the output produced by the particular company. To the extent that such a price is related to the company profits, the arrangements meant that in fact the bondholder, instead of a lender, became a partner in the company's venture, very much like a stockholder. The effect, of course, is a hybrid that destroys the very nature of the lending–borrowing transaction and, at best, duplicates the role already played by the issuing of common stock.

What Indexation Is Not: Some "Nonobjections." The previous characterization helps to rule out of consideration many things often called "indexation," and consequently many misplaced objections (or "nonobjections"). Indeed, there are cases where such "nonobjections" turn out to be arguments for indexation as defined here, rather than against it. Consider some of the objections.

(a) *Indexation "freezes" relative prices, hence interferes with the resource allocation role of prices, and may bring about an "explosive" system.* The idea that indexation "freezes" relative prices can easily be dismissed because it refers to situations far removed from those involving true indexation. Most of the time, the argument refers to schemes in which the prices of certain commodities, in "cash" or "spot" transactions that do not involve time, remain fixed in terms of another commodity or group of commodities. A typical case is, for example, proposals for "indexing" the price of some primary commodities in the international markets, fixing their price in terms of manufactured goods.[13] In cases closer to what is properly defined as indexation, such a "freezing of relative prices" occurs when too narrow an index is chosen or imposed—the case just discussed in the previous paragraph. If this were the case, both objections are correct: prices would be deprived of their role in the process of resource allocation, and the system would be highly explosive. The system would be explosive because any change in the monetary price of any commodity would have to be matched by an equal change in the monetary price of all other goods. If the initial shock were due to changes in the underlying real conditions in the market, and such a shock needs to be worked out via a premanent change in relative prices, then such a system would become unstable.[14] The trouble with the argument, of course, is that it refers to a situation that may be called "indexation" but that has nothing to do with indexation properly defined.

(b) *The "indexation" of certain aggregates by government can be destabilizing.* The practice can indeed be destabilizing, but **again**, this "nonobjection" refers to nothing more than to certain "policy rules" by which the government may set certain targets. In particular, the "indexation" of the exchange rate is sometimes discussed.[15] This practice refers to a policy of making the nominal exchange rate whatever it needs to be to keep constant the "real" exchange rate (the nominal exchange rate divided by the domestic price level). This "nonobjection" may or may not be a valid criticism of a rule of stabilization policy, but it addresses, once again, a question far removed from indexation.

(c) *Indexation tends to perpretuate inflation.* This is probably the most frequent complaint against indexation, and the most dangerous one because it sounds intuitively correct. Consider the argument in a labor market context, that is, where nominal wages are automatically readjusted. The argument appears to imply that if this year the general level of commodity prices rises by 10 percent, next year wages will also rise by 10 percent, and prices will need to rise by the same proportion, and so forth. The process indicates that it becomes impossible to "break the circle" unless government and society are willing to pay a very high price in terms of unemployment. This misplaced objection is so generalized that it deserves closer consideration.

Consider the labor market. In the absence of indexation, nominal wages as specified in contracts will reflect some average of the inflation rate expected by both labor and management. Suppose, for example, that all involved parties expect a 10 percent per year inflation rate, and that the contract has a duration of two years. At any time during the contract the inflation rate will not be reflected in the nominal or money wage, and this will be so whether prices rise by more or by less than 10 percent per year. It is this case that we may properly identify as having "built-in" inflationary expectations. Indeed, this is one of the most powerful reasons why expectations about the future course of prices play such an important role in any inflationary process and, in particular, in any stabilization attempt.

Consider, instead, the case of the same

contract when salaries are specified in real terms (given the general price level at the time of the agreement) with the proviso that they will be periodically readjusted so as to keep that real value constant. In this case, inflationary expectations do not play any role in the determination of what nominal payments will in fact be, and whatever the inflation rate happens to be during the duration of the contract will determine nominal payments. The only thing that indexation will do is to assure that nominal wages keep up with actual, realized price changes. Of course, real wages will remain at the predetermined level only during the term of the contract, as in the case of price stability with no indexation. Any change in real underlying conditions will be reflected in the real wage rate emerging from negotiations at the time of a new contract.

We should see from this discussion that indexation, properly applied, facilitates rather than jeopardizes the return to price stability, by freeing nominal payments from "built-in" inflationary expectations, in turn being fed by past inflation rates. To this extent, the argument that indexation perpetuates inflation can be turned around to become an argument for indexation.

Some Objections. Consider now some genuine objections to indexation schemes as defined here. As such, they should not be dismissed and deserve closer examination.

The Stability Question. In a system where generalized indexation has been adopted, the transmission of price changes from one sector to another is faster than when future payments are fixed in nominal terms. It is legitimate to ask the general question of whether indexation would not bring about a tendency for the economy to "get out of hand," that is, to become highly unstable. In the case of the labor market, for example, the suspicion may exist that changes in prices that are immediately translated into changes in nominal wages might bring about an explosive or unstable sequence of events, with rises in prices causing rises in wages, increases in wages causing in turn further price hikes, and so on.[16]

In fact, economists do not know much about the comparative behavior of indexation versus nonindexed economies, because most models used to analyze "stability" questions are constructions implicitly assuming that there is perfect indexation; to "model" a system in which this does not occur is indeed a difficult task. Still, there is a strong presumption that generalized indexation does not bring about instability, but rather the opposite.

In the first place, it is not true that systems that adjust rapidly (as with generalized indexation) are necessarily more likely to be unstable. There is no general conclusion in economic analysis concerning the relationship between speed of adjustment and stability, but it is possible to present examples in which, in fact, a faster adjustment increases stability and decreases the likelihood of wide fluctuations.

Secondly, whatever specific literature exists on this issue—most of it referred to indexation in the labor market—indicates that if disturbances are originated in the money sector (such as changes in the rate of monetary expansion, or changes in inflationary expectations), a system with indexed wages may minimize fluctuations and increase the likelihood of stability.

A Problem of "Implementation": What Index to Use. Even sympathizers of generalized indexation often refer to a "physical problem of implementation," namely the question of what index to use as a yardstick. The answer to this objection is that for the bulk of transactions where indexation would take place—private contracts—the question becomes something of a red herring: the index to be used is simply the index chosen by the parties agreeing on the contract. Concerning the indexation of taxes and payments by government, it seems natural to select a broadly defined index of prices, such as the Consumer Price Index or the Wholesale Price Index, despite the biases inherent in these as in any index.

Lack of Incentives to End Inflation. This is the argument put forward recently by the late Harry G. Johnson, one of the world's most respected economists. The argument implies that, by making it easier to live with inflation, indexation schemes will tend to "tame" a public opinion that, otherwise, could exert strong pressure on the central bank to stop inflationary policies. Of course, this argument is difficult to assess; it relates to almost a matter of opinion. Here we wish only to point out that, whatever truth there is in the allegation, it must be weighed against the possibility (which is suggested below) that indexation might ease not only the effects of existing inflation, but also the return to price stability. Indexation, in sum, might lower the short-run price of a serious stabilization effort.

What Indexation Can and Cannot Do

As a general point, one should observe that there is a "general presumption" in a market economy that whatever solution the market generates is the optimal one. Of course, there are many circumstances in which the market solution can be shown not to be optimal; these are the cases of "market failure" due to the presence of externalities, monopoly, and so on. But such market failures are the exception and, as such, one needs to show in each case that they indeed exist. In the case of indexation none of the conditions for market failure has been shown to be present, and the natural conclusion is that to allow private arrangements concerning indexation and to make them enforceable are just other indications of the need to eliminate controls that cannot be explicitly justified. But this is a very general remark. Some of the things that indexation can do may be enumerated in a more concrete manner.

First, indexation can eliminate at least part of the "contrived" uncertainty brought about by inflation. The term "contrived" is used here to denote uncertainty that is imposed by policies, as opposed to that inherent in the natural unpredictability of the "natural" world. Whether the market will accept and demand a given quantity of a certain product, and whether this year's corn crop will be plentiful or small are uncertainties of nature. Large amounts of time and resources are used (and rightly so) by economic agents to predict future events and to cope with this uncertainty. In this process the prospects of profits and the fear of losses are, indeed, the motivation for costly prediction. In times of inflation there is the additional, "contrived" uncertainty of the future course of the general price level and therefore of the real value of future payments specified in nominal terms, and with it also the additional time and resources trying to cope with this uncertainty. The first thing that indexation can do is to eliminate such additional uncertainty.

Second, to the extent that indexation brings about faster propagation or "spreading" of rates of price changes among industries (and eventually a faster adjustment of the overall inflation rate to the rate of monetary expansion), it does allow for greater and quicker awareness about inflation on the part of the public. The "moment of truth" comes a little earlier, and this might tend to eliminate the easiness with which the economic authority is inclined to approach the possibility of too expansionary monetary policies. In a world where the rate of inflation, nominal wages, and nominal interest rates adjust slowly to expansionary policies (or "tight" policies, for that matter), and in which easy policies can be accompanied by a temporary increase in employment, there is a natural tendency by governments to underestimate the magnitude of the long-run consequences of their actions; this oversight, of course, is particularly true in a democracy where elected officials spend a limited period of time in office. A shorter time lapse between the action and the consequences seems to be, if that is indeed the effect of indexation, a desirable result.

Third, everything tends to indicate that indexation makes it easier to decrease or stop inflation, both because of the quicker transmission of the inflation rate among sectors (for lower, as well as for higher rates) and the possibily shorter lag between monetary expansion and inflation, as well as because of the smaller and shorter effect of "tight" monetary policies on the unemployment rate. This is interpreted here as an obvious benefit of indexation, withstanding the argument by Harry G. Johnson and others, in the sense that by "making it easier" to live with it, indexation might be a deterrent for the eventual public pressure on the monetary authority to end inflation.

Finally, there is the argument of equity. Here we have touched only on points related to an efficient allocation of resources, because equity questions are beyond the realm of the economist. There is, no doubt, a valid point in the argument of compensating those who may err in predicting the rate of price changes, in particular, when these changes are ultimately the result of policy (the most difficult thing to predict). Milton Friedman, among others, has endorsed this argument strongly.[17] He has, for example, pointed to the need for a government-issued indexed bond, which could be acquired by those who, if indexation in capital markets is not allowed, would be in no position to engage in speculation in the capital markets because of the small volume of their wealth and the high transactions costs.

What Indexation Is Not Expected To Do. First, indexation cannot avoid the occurrence of transitory but substantial changes in relative prices due to unexpected and uneven (among industries) changes in total expenditures generated by monetary policies. When, say, an unexpected expansionary policy takes place, increases in the demand for goods and services are not spread equally among all goods and services. Furthermore, the response to this increase in demand is not identical among productive sectors. The consequence is not only that for some time prices of different commodities will rise at a different pace and (what is more important) the allocation of resources among sectors will change, but also that the price of inputs in the production process (labor, for example) will also change unevenly. If the expansionary policy remains the same in the future, all of these differences will be worked out by the system and eventually disappear. But until this happens there will be a clear misallocation of resources, and a composition of total production different from what it would have been in the absence of the policy change. In the case of the wage rate, for example, indexation can do nothing (and had better not try to do anything!) to avoid fluctuations in the level of real wages set in new negotiations as contracts are being renewed.

Second, indexation cannot avoid some "price dispersion." Even if the inflation rate is constant on average for a long time, and if the public perfectly anticipates such average (and these are big "ifs"), one would expect the natural dispersion or differences in prices for the same commodity within a large market (which normally exists because of the presence of search and information costs) to be greater exaggerated. Indeed, the time and resources used in more intensive "search for the best price" will be greatly increased, since for producers and sellers it is not costless to change prices. Such changes will take the form not of a smooth, continuous flow, but of discrete, periodic changes in the form of "jumps." Of course, these "jumps" will not be simultaneous for all sellers of the same commodity, especially in markets covering a large geographical area.

Third, indexation cannot eliminate the "welfare cost" that occurs even when inflation is perfectly anticipated, as a consequence of the "tax on the holdings of money" that inflation implies.

Fourth, and at a less "technical" level, indexation cannot avoid some of the social conflict brought about even by perfectly anticipated inflation. When prices and nominal wages are all rising at a certain rate, labor finds that wages are rising, but that prices do also. Any "myopia" or failure to understand the whole process is likely to trigger the idea that, if it were not for business firms, who continuously raise prices, the *real* wage rate could be increasing, and that it is business that is precluding workers from improving their lot. Thus inflation is likely to be blamed on firms, which "set" prices too high. Businesses, in turn, see that the price of their products is rising, but that nominal wages are also, and again each business manager tends to believe that if it were not for continuously rising costs, profits would go up in real terms. Inflation is likely to be blamed upon rising costs (the so-called "cost push" explanation). What both firms and labor may not realize is that the increases in wages are in fact manifestations of the same phenomenon, and that if prices would stop rising, nominal wages would also, and vice versa.

A final observation is in order. One of the reasons why the indexation question is subject to so many characterizations (some people seeing it as a solution to many problems, and some treating it as an additional problem in itself) is that many economists still hold very different views from one another about the ultimate causes of inflation. In particular, there is the view that, in the last instance, inflation is due to the validation by government (through expansionary policies) of "unreasonable claims" by different groups to "shares of the pie" that together add to more than what the "size of the pie" allows. If this were true, it is obvious that indexation could be more of a problem than of a solution. But both economic theory and empirical observation strongly suggest that large increases in the quantity of money are the ultimate reasons for inflation, and not merely one more event in a line of causality ending in "unreasonable demands," which in any case have never been met by such increases.

FOOTNOTES

[1] More precisely, the rate of monetary expansion was assumed to be zero as was the rate of inflation in the final equilibrium. The public also always expected a zero inflation rate.

[2] This sudden fall will occur in the context of the loanable funds theory of the determination of the interest rate. If instead we adopt a liquidity preference approach, the interest rate, rather than falling immediately, will start to fall slowly. This difference does not alter our main conclusions, however.

[3] A. W. Phillips, "The Relationship Between Unemployment and the Rate of Change of Money Wage Rates in the United Kingdom, 1862-1957," *Economica* 25 (November 1958), pp. 283-299.

[4] Strictly speaking, the original formulation referred to rates of change in nominal wages, rather than in the general price level (inflation). The difference is not important, and later works were specified in terms of the latter.

[5] Edmund S. Phelps, "The New Microeconomics in Employment and Inflation Theory," in Edmund S. Phelps, ed., *Microeconomic Foundations of Employment and Inflation Theory* (New York, W. W. Norton and Co., 1970), pp. 1-23, and Milton Friedman, "The Role of Monetary Policy," *American Economic Review* 58 (March 1968), pp. 1-17.

[6] A supporting explanation for overshooting in a real-world context is that the monetary authorities at some stage in the adjustment process become overly concerned about the rate of inflation and *reduce* the rate of growth in the money supply (hence the rate of inflation) while expectations of inflation are still increasing. This action leads to severe overshooting and is a major source of the problem.

[7] It is not clear why the policymaker would want to keep unemployment below the "natural rate," although the natural rate may be associated with significant artificial barriers in labor markets. Also one could argue that there is something "bad" about an unemployment rate not only above the natural level but also below it, but these matters are neglected here.

[8] In Chapter 14 we will look at some of this evidence for the last twenty years, and the reader will recognize some short-run Phillips curves in the actual data.

[9] Houses would be abandoned, of course, when the tax per house is larger than the "rental" of the house. This is an extreme, but not altogether rare, case.

[10] This effect is perhaps one of the reasons why certain countries have persisted, in some cases for a long period of time, in maintaining rates of monetary expansion and inflation that correspond to long-run equilibrium levels of real revenues from money creation lower than what they would have been with lower inflation rates. At the same time these governments argued that they were forced to print money at high rates for the financing of the budget deficit. A stabilization program (a lower rate of monetary expansion) would, in the short run, have made things worse before making them better from a budget viewpoint.

[11] Many of the features of Figure 8-11

were part of the Federal government policy announced by President Carter in March 1980: necessary cuts in the Federal budget (panel (f)); the rise in interest rates (which was already dramatic during the first two months of 1980, as the Federal Reserve System was already reducing the rate of monetary expansion); the anticipation of a recession (panels (d) and (e)), and the statement to the effect that inflation would not fall substantially for several months (panel (a)).

[12] Of course, a sudden drop in the rate of monetary expansion (what is sometimes called shock or "cold turkey" treatment) is not the only, and sometimes not the best, manner in which a stabilization program can be implemented. The rate of monetary expansion, for example, could be brought down gradually—and this is, of course, *gradualism*.

[13] See, for example, the analysis of this so-called "indexation" in Gustav D. Jud, *Inflation and the Use of Indexing in Developing Countries* (New York: Praeger Publishers, 1978).

[14] Such an argument is often made in the context of the "structural" explanation for inflation which was discussed in Chapter 8.

[15] See, again, Jud (*op. cit.*), Chapter 1.

[16] See, for example, Walter Heller, "Has the Time Come for Indexation?" *The Wall Street Journal*, June 20, 1974.

[17] See, for example, Milton Friedman, "Using Escalators to Help Inflation," *Fortune*, July 1974, pp. 94–97.

KEY CONCEPTS

expected vs. actual rate of inflation

adaptive expectations theory

rational expectations theory

natural rate hypothesis (accelerationist hypothesis)

Phillips curve (dynamic Phillips curve)

adjustment process

gradualism

QUESTIONS FOR DISCUSSSION

1. Using the adaptive expectations theory, what are your expectations about inflation, considering current and past conditions?

2. Why do you think economists engage in so much effort trying to determine the current actions of the Federal Reserve?

3. Economists' attempts to predict a recession in 1979 were hampered by enormous, unexpected increases in consumer spending. Can you explain this?

4. Specifically discuss reasons why a decrease in the rate of monetary expansion is unlikely on the part of the government.

5. Compare Figure 8–11 and Figure 8–12.

Make sure you understand the differences between the paths.

6. Why do you think institutional arrangements have turned to such things as cost of living wage contracts and variable-rate mortgages?

7. Why is it said that the Phillips curve trade-off is not between unemployment and the inflation rate, but between unemployment and increasing inflation rates?

8. Discuss the chain of causality in the adjustment process for a decrease in the rate of monetary expansion. For an increase? Are the mechanisms different? Why or why not?

PART III

COMMERCIAL AND CENTRAL BANKING:
Theory and Institutions

CHAPTER 9

COMMERCIAL BANKS AS CREATORS OF MONEY

Earlier chapters of this book have considered many aspects of money. Why money is used, why its use is important for progress in any economy, why people demand money and, in Chapters 7 and 8, how the stock of money and how *changes* in the stock of money are translated into nominal prices and inflation. In the present chapter we return to the concept and definition of money outlined in Chapter 2 for the purpose of a detailed investigation of the unique role of commercial banks in the process of money creation.

Money consists of currency and demand deposits, and the latter component of the money stock can be created or destroyed only by the joint action of both the "public" (moneyholders) and the commercial banks. ("Checkable deposits" at nonbank institutions, described in Chapter 2, are not explicitly treated in this chapter, but may be lumped with demand deposits in the process of money creation discussed in this chapter.) Demand deposits are often called *checkbook money* since the holder of a checking account or one on whose account a check is drawn can *demand* from the bank, at any time, restitution of his currency. In particular, this "restitution" can take the form of an order given to the bank for a certain amount to a third party; this "order" is called a check and may be used as a means of payment. This unique feature of demand deposits permits us to include checkbook money as a component of money, that is, it permits us to define money as the stock of currency and demand deposits.[1] So-called "time deposits," which we do not include in the definition of money, have the requirement that the account holder give some notice in advance, but banks ordinarily waive this requirement. The checking account function along with making business loans, is a principle reason for a bank's existence, since there would be no essential need for banks if the public refuses to use checkbook money.

Thus, commercial banks are unique and crucial institutions in any society. They are the only institutions able to *create* money. With the exception of checkable accounts, such as NOW accounts and credit union share drafts, other financial institutions such as savings and loan associations and insurance companies, as well as departments other than "Checking Accounts" in Commercial Banks, act principally as transferers of funds from savers to investors. All these institutions are, in general, called "financial intermediaries." The reason that the banking system is singled out for study in a book on money is simply that demand deposits are one of two kinds of money (the other being currency) and that they are, far and away, the most important kind of money in terms of quantity held (at least in the United States). Moreover, commercial banks, at least for the present, are the primary producer of demand deposits in the United States. Although new laws may alter this state of affairs, an understanding of the current process of money creating activities within the context of the banking system is of vital importance.[2]

Given the definition we have established for money, this chapter addresses three important issues. First, it explains the process of money creation in a fractional reserve banking system. Second, it shows how alterations in the desires of the public or of bankers can change the total amount and the composition of the money supply. Finally, it suggests a simple analytical framework for a detailed discussion of how the government's central bank (the Federal Reserve System in the United States) may bring about changes in the stock of nominal money through the so-called instruments of monetary policy (open market operations, reserve requirements, the discount rate, etc.); this discussion is the topic of Chapter 11.

MONEY CREATION: THE CONCEPTUAL FRAMEWORK

Chapter 9 will develop a simple conceptual framework showing how the interaction of the public's and the bank's decisions yield a stable equilibrium of the stock of nominal money. The manner in which this equilibrium is attained, and the process by which money creation is described, is then analyzed in tabular and graphical terms in the following section. With these simple fundamentals in hand, let us explore various factors affecting the money stock such as changes in the quantity of high-powered money (to be defined below), in the desired ratios of currency to deposits and reserves to deposits, or in the institutional arrangements under which banks operate as, for example, would be the case in a 100% reserve banking system.

ASSUMPTIONS AND DEFINITIONS

In order to facilitate the understanding of these important concepts, we begin with some elementary definitions, several of which have been introduced earlier in the text. First, for the sake of simplicity, we assume the existence of a single bank (the "monopoly bank") operating in a closed and integrated community of moneyholders called the "public." The stock of nominal money is the sum of currency (C) and demand deposits (D), as in expression [9.1].

$$M = C + D \qquad [9.1]$$

Define *high-powered money* as the sum of currency in the hands of the public and currency in the hands of banks (the rationale behind such an exotic name will become clear later); in turn, "currency in the hands of banks," is technically called "reserves," so that definitionally,

$$H = C + R \tag{9.2}$$

where H is high-powered money, C is the total amount of currency in the hands of the public, and R is the total amount of currency in the hands of the monopoly bank.[3] High-powered money or currency plus reserves can be regarded as money that is used to produce other money. Its importance, and that of other variables affecting the money supply, can be analyzed by presenting a more specific identity for M. Dividing expression [9.1] by [9.2], together with a bit of manipulation, will provide a more specific identity for M.

$$\frac{M}{H} = \frac{C + D}{C + R} \tag{9.3}$$

Dividing the right hand side of expression [9.3] by D, where $c = C/D$ and $r = R/D$, we obtain,

$$\frac{M}{H} = \frac{C/D + 1}{C/D + R/D} = \frac{1 + c}{c + r}, \text{ or}$$

$$M = H \cdot \frac{1 + c}{c + r} \tag{9.4}$$

Thus, the money stock, as expression [9.4] shows, equals H, the quantity of high-powered money in existence, multiplied by a fraction containing c, the currency-deposit ratio, and r, the reserve-deposit ratio. Expression [9.4] is an identity, derived from mere definitions, and as such it will always be true.

Alternatively, equation [9.4] might be looked at in functional form. If, for example, expression $(1 + c)/(c + r)$ equals some constant k (for simplicity), the "production function" of money $M = kH$ is not totally unlike the production function for any good, say desks. Here money (the output) can be viewed as a function of input (the quantity of high-powered money). The input in this case is high-powered because one dollar of high-powered money will be multiplied by some factor k, which will ordinarily be greater than 1. (Later in the chapter, we will investigate a special case in which k is equal to 1.) The quantity of money (M) is affected by a multiplier (k) that produces a quantity of money larger than the stock of the high-powered input (H). Since the government, ordinarily through its central bank, determines the quantity of high-powered money in existence, the money stock, in this simple case, may be regarded in principle as a function of the quantity of high-powered money that the government chooses to produce.

Returning to the identity expressed in [9.4], several simple cases can be examined immediately. Should, for example, the public not hold demand deposits and the banks not hold reserves at all, the stock of money would equal the quantity of high-powered money in existence, that is, $(1 + c)/(c + r)$ would equal unity. A second (highly unrealistic) case would occur should the public choose to hold money only in the form of demand deposits. Hand-to-hand currency, which facilitates such everyday purchases as bus rides, a pack of cigarettes, or twenty-five cent candy bars, would no longer be used. In terms of expression [9.4], $c = C/D = 0$, and $M = H(1/r)$.[4] If the reserve-deposit ratio remained constant, the money stock would be a constant multiple of the stock of high-powered money, that is, $M = H/r$.

ACTUAL AND DESIRED RATIOS

Before analyzing aspects of the money supply equation in graphical terms, it is important to recognize the two contexts in which the ratios c and r may be viewed. The actual currency-deposit ratio is simply a calculation of total currency in the hands of the public, C, divided by deposit or checkbook assets, D, also owned by the public. Likewise, the actual reserve-deposit ratio is the total amount of currency on hand at the monopoly bank, R divided by deposit liabilities, D. Thus, if we are given values for C, D, and R, we can calculate actual ratios. But there is yet another manner in which to view these ratios.

The public's desired holdings of currency and demand deposits does not necessarily equal actual holdings at all times but only in equilibrium. The desired currency-deposit ratio, which we designate c^d, is a function of a number of variables, including, for example, confidence in banks, service changes on demand deposits, and the availability of alternative forms of transactions payments.[5] Here, the issue is not one of a choice between holding alternative kinds of assets, for example, between holding assets in government bonds, savings accounts, or money. Rather there will be a desired distribution of money holdings between currency and demand deposits (for any given quantity of money which the public would like to hold as an asset described by the relations discussed in Chapter 3).

Some practical considerations will help clarify this important concept. Suppose, for example, that the desired currency-deposit ratio (c^d) is 0.5. What does this mean? Clearly it does *not* mean that moneyholders wish to hold $1 in demand deposits for every dollar in currency. A c^d ratio of 0.5 means that for every one dollar of currency held, moneyholders wish to hold two dollars in demand deposits, that is, $c^d = \$1C/\$2D$. But why should the public desire this particular ratio and not some other?

Moneyholders' choice of a desired currency-deposit ratio depends on the advantages and disadvantages or, equivalently, on the costs and conveniences of holding money in the alternative forms. Some conveniences of holding money in the form of demand deposits are fairly obvious. There is, for example, the safety features of demand deposits. A lost check (that has not been endorsed) or lost checkbook, for that matter, is clearly not as catastrophic as a lost one thousand dollars in currency. Further, by holding checkbook money, money-holders earn other returns such as accounting services, which are a great convenience in personal finance. But there are costs to holding money in the form of demand deposits as well. Among them, service charges on checking accounts, the probability of bank failure, or even the somewhat mundane problem of cashing a check on Sunday. The holding of currency (as opposed to demand deposits) also has its costs and benefits. There is relative danger in carrying around fifty thousand dollars in cash versus the holding of ten dollars in order to purchase cigarettes, bus tokens, or a candy bar.

Similarly, the monopoly bank's desired reserve-deposit ratio, which we designate r^d, may not equal the actual ratio. The desired ratio of reserves to deposits will depend on numerous factors such as the return on bonds or alternative forms of loans, the central bank's discount rate—an interest rate at which banks, with proper collateral, may borrow from the central bank (where central bank control is assumed to exist)—and general economic conditions. In this connection, central bank imposition of a reserve requirement might simply express the minimum desired reserve ratio. The monopoly bank (or the banking system, as we shall see in Chapter 11) may, for some of the reasons discussed above, desire a higher reserve-deposit ratio than that imposed by the central bank. This was an especially important feature of our banking system during the Great Depression of the 1930s (see Chapter 16). At this point, however, monopoly bank equilibrium requires that the desired reserve-deposit ratio must equal the actual ratio. The public, in turn, is not in equilibrium unless the actual currency-deposit ratio equals the desired ratio. Symbolically, banks are in equilibrium when $r^d = r = R/D$ and the public is satisfied when $c^d = c = C/D$. How these ratios, along with the quantity of high-powered money, mutually determine the stock of money and its composition is the subject of the following discussion.

THE SYSTEM AT WORK: THE PROCESS OF BANK MONEY CREATION

With a firm idea of the mechanics of the model in hand, we turn to the major topic of the present chapter, bank money creation. In order to simplify the exposition of this important process we assume a single monopoly bank that makes loans only in *currency*. (The interest rate at which the bank borrows and lends is assumed fixed and is exogenously given in the capital market.) We might at first imagine an economy wherein the public holds currency in the amount of $1,000. Thus $M = H = C = \$1,000$. As the source from which the public initially got this currency is not important, assume that the public sold the government a bond and that the proceeds were $1,000 in high-powered money or currency. Furthermore, assume that a bank—*a monopoly bank*—is introduced for the first time (that is, no bank existed previously) and that the public's desired currency-deposit ratio is equal to 1 ($c^d = 1$). A desired currency-deposit ratio equal to 1 simply means that the public wishes to hold one-half of its money holdings in deposits and one-half in currency.

The monopoly bank, on the other hand, wants to hold (or the government forces them to hold) 20% of their deposits as cash reserves. (Recall that a government requirement can be a *minimum;* that is, the banks may choose to hold a greater percentage of deposits or reserves.) Thus, $r^d = 0.2$; 20 cents out of every dollar of deposits will be held as a currency reserve by the bank.

Table 9-1 uses the above data and summarizes the process of money creation.[6] Let us assume that the bank will open for business on Monday and line *A* of Table 9-1 summarizes the bank's and the public's situation on Sunday.

TABULAR ANALYSIS

On Sunday the bank has not yet been introduced. Hence, demand deposits, bank reserves, and outstanding loans are all zero. The money stock is, in this case, equal to the total amount of currency in the hands of the public, $1,000. Note also that the quantity of money just equals the stock of high-powered money ($C_0 = H_0 = M_0$) on line *A* of Table 9-1.

In order to more easily understand the process of money creation, an additional simplifying assumption is required. Specifically, it is assumed that *final* equilibrium is approached *discontinuously*. By this we simply mean that on alternate days, the bank and the money-holders act passively in the sense that one or the other is out of equilibrium on any given day. One might think of both banks and the public "balancing its books" at the end of each day. In this process, as we will see, one or the other will be out of equilibrium. (This unrealistic assumption is removed later in this chapter.)

Now, assume that the bank opens for business on Monday. Given that the public wishes to hold one-half of its money holdings in demand deposits, the monopoly bank receives cash deposits of $500. (The $500 in cash deposited in the bank is no longer included in the money supply when it becomes bank reserves.) On Monday night the monopoly bank looks at its accounts; Line *B* of Table 9-1 describes the situation. The bank holds deposits liabilities and cash reserves of $500. The money stock ($C + D$) still stands at $1,000, but this situation cannot last, as an examination of the last two columns of Table 9-1 will reveal. The actual currency-deposit ratio on Monday night is 1, which is *equal to the ratio desired by the public,* but the monopoly bank is clearly not in equilibrium: the actual reserve-deposit ratio is 1, but the

Table 9–1 A numerical example of money creation

Line	Day	R (Reserves)	(Loans)	R and L (Reserves and Loans)	D (Deposits)	C (Currency)	M (Money Stock)	C/D (Actual)	R/D (Actual)
(A)	Sunday	$ 0	$ 0	$ 0	$ 0	$1000	$1000	—	—
(B)	Monday	500	0	500	500	500	1000	1	1
(C)	Tuesday	100	400	500	500	900	1400	1.8	.2
(D)	Wednesday	300	400	700	700	700	1400	1	.42
(E)	Thursday	140	560	700	700	860	1560	1.22	.2
· · ·	· · ·	·	·	·	·	·	·	· · ·	· · ·
(N)		$166	$666	$833	$833	$ 833	$1666	1	.2

desired ratio is 0.2 or 20%. Given deposits of $500, the bank will want to hold only $100 as cash reserves. The bank promptly decides that it will remedy the situation on Tuesday.

On Tuesday, the bank "works off" excess reserves of $400 by making loans (for profit at some interest rate that is, for simplicity, not considered here). These loans of $400 are assumed to be made in currency. Line C gives us the situations facing the public and the banks on Tuesday night. Deposits held by the public are, again, $500, but the public has accepted loans in the amount of $400 (the quantity of excess reserves held by the bank Monday night). Cash reserves of the bank have fallen to $100, an amount that makes the actual value of reserves to deposits exactly equal to the desired ratio of 20%. Importantly, the money stock increases on Tuesday to $1,400, which is equal to the initial stock of high-powered money plus the $400 in cash loans made by the bank on Tuesday. The process of money creation does not stop on Tuesday, however. The banks are in equilibrium at the end of that day, since $r = r^d$, but the public is not: the actual currency-deposit ratio on Tuesday night, 1.8, is greater than the desired ratio, 1. Thus, conditions for further change exist in the system.

On Wednesday morning the public is in possession of "new money" in the amount of $400. The public wishes to hold one-half of the new money in deposits and one-half in currency, the monopoly bank receives a cash deposit of $200 on Wednesday. The public will thus hold deposits of $700 and $700 in currency, which will make the actual currency-deposit ratio just equal to the desired ratio. But on Wednesday evening the bank is again out of equilibrium, this time with an actual reserve-deposit ratio of 3/7 or 0.42. Since the bank wants to hold only $140 against deposits of $700, it finds that it has excess reserves of $160 ($300 less $140). On Thursday the bank will lend out $160, an action that puts the bank in equilibrium Thursday evening ($r = r^d = 0.2$). However, the public is again thrown out of equilibrium as the actual C/D ratio becomes 1.22 (860/700). The money-holding public again holds a surplus of currency and on Friday deposits $80 in the monopoly bank. On Friday evening the public's c ratio is in equilibrium, but the bank's is not.

The process continues in the manner described until the two actual ratios equal the desired ratios. Each step in the process brings the actual ratios closer to the desired ones. Thus the *process* of money creation can be described as the means by which the public and the bank simultaneously adjust desired and actual currency-deposit and reserve-deposit ratios given the existence of excess reserves in the monopoly bank. In other words, the process ends when there are no more excess reserves in the monopoly bank while, simultaneously, the public is holding currency and checkbook money in the desired proportion. The final line of Table 9–1 (Line N) shows the calculable results of the process. The money stock will equal $1,666, an amount that may be calculated immediately by "plugging in" or substituting the values given for H, c, and r into expression [9.4], that is, $1,666 = $1,000[(1 + 1)/(1 + 0.2)]$. Equilibrium currency and deposit holdings are equal to $833 [or (0.5) ($1,666)] and $833 [or (0.5) ($1,666)], respectively. Cash reserves will be held by the monopoly bank in the amount of $166 [or 0.2($833)], and loan assets (the public's liability) will be $666, the exact amount of the increase in the money stock.

THE CREATION OF MONEY: ALTERNATIVE DISCUSSIONS

The process of money creation described by the simple money supply equations and by the tabular analysis can be depicted using balance sheet analysis or in graphical terms. Both of these models of discussing money creation are fundamentally equivalent.

Balance Sheet Analysis: Money Creation in the Monopoly Bank. The traditional manner of viewing money supply expansion is the use of a simple balance sheet. This method, familiar to all students of basic accounting, employs the *accounting identity*, called the balance sheet equation, whereby the sum of all assets must always equal the sum of all liabilities and capital (or net worth) accounts. Here, for simplicity, the total assets and liabilities are not considered for the public and the monopoly bank, and capital accounts are eliminated altogether. In other words, only *changes* in the relevant accounts are considered; but, since the monopoly bank originally holds no assets or liabilities, the accounting identity holds for it in the tables that follow.

Returning to earlier tabular explanation of money creation, let us begin by considering the balance sheets on Sunday, which will be recognized as line (A) of Table 9-1. Table 9-2 summarizes the relevant asset holdings of both the public and the monopoly bank on that day. As we have seen, the public is in possession of cash in the amount of $1,000, and the bank is not yet officially in business. Cash reserves, loan assets, and deposit liabilities are zero for the bank.

Table 9-2

Public (Sunday)		Monopoly Bank (Sunday)			
Cash	$1,000	Cash reserves	0	Deposits	0
		Loans	0		
		$M = 1000			

Monday morning, however, the public deposits $500 in cash of its $1000 in cash assets into the new bank (see Table 9-3). The bank now has cash reserves of $500 and deposits liabilities of $500, with loan assets of zero.

Table 9–3

Public (Monday)		Monopoly Bank (Monday)			
Cash	500	Cash reserves	500	Deposits	500
Deposits	500	Loans	0		

$1 = \dfrac{500}{500}$

or $c^d = c$

$0.2 < \dfrac{500}{500}$

or $r^d < r$

Several important points should be noted relative to Table 9–3. First, the money stock is exactly the same as it was on Sunday, that is, it is still equal to $1000. More importantly, banks and the public are not equally happy with the existing state of affairs. The public's desired ratio of currency to deposit holdings is one and desired holdings are just equal to actual holdings. Thus the public is happy with the situation.

The monopoly bank, however, is unhappy with the state of affairs since its actual reserve to deposit ratio is higher (one) than it wants it to be (0.2). As the previous discussion implied, it is this dissatisfaction on the part of either party to the money creation process, which is the motive force of the process itself. This precept is clearly revealed in what the bank does on Tuesday (Table 9–4).

In looking at its reserve-deposit picture, the bank realizes that it has excess reserves of $400—reserves over and above its 20% desired amount against deposits—despite the fact that the bank is in "accounting equilibrium," that is, the sum of revenues and loans (assets) equals that of deposit liabilities. Being a profit-maximizing institution, the bank appreciates the potential income from lending these "superfluous" reserves, and it does so. After borrowing these funds, as noted in Table 9–4, the public has acquired new assets ($400 in cash) and new liabilities ($400 in notes payable). This action now puts the public out of equilibrium since the actual ratio of currency to deposits (9/5) exceeds the

Table 9–4

Public (Tuesday)			Monopoly Bank (Tuesday)			
Cash	900	Notes payable 400	Cash reserve	100	Deposits	500
Deposits	500		Cash loans	400		

$1 < \dfrac{900}{500} = 1.8$

or $c^d < c$

$0.2 = \dfrac{100}{500}$

or $r^d = r$

$$M = \$1,400$$

Table 9–5

Public (Wednesday)				Monopoly Bank (Wednesday)			
Cash	700	Notes payable	400	Cash reserves	300	Deposits	700
Deposits	700			Cash loans	400		

$$1 = \frac{700}{700}$$

or $c^d = c$

$$0.2 < \frac{300}{700}$$

or $r^d < r$

desired ratio (1/1), and the motive force for a new deposit at the bank on Wednesday is established. Most importantly, however, new money in the amount of $400 has been created! The bank has accepted something that is not money (a promissory note from the public) and gives the public something that is money, that is, cash. Thus, Tuesday's money stock stands at $1,400.

Dissatisfaction still reigns on Tuesday night. Though the bank is happy ($r^d = r$), the public is out of equilibrium ($c^d < c$). The public wishes to hold currency and deposits in a one-to-one ratio. On Wednesday, they rearrange their asset portfolio and deposit $200 in cash into the monopoly bank (Table 9–5), which puts their actual holdings in line with their desires. Banks consequently acquire additional cash reserves of $200 (now totaling $300) and additional deposit liabilities of the same amount. But after examining transactions on Wednesday evening the bank finds that its reserve-deposit ratio is again larger than it wants to be. The amount by which it is larger is easily calculated since the bank wants to hold only $140 or 20% of its cash reserve against deposits. The excess of $160 may be lent out at interest, which earns the bank some income. Table 9–6 shows what happens when the bank does just that on Thursday, increasing the money supply by an additional $160. Both the public's cash assets and note liabilities increase by $160, putting it out of equilibrium once more, and on Friday (not shown) $80 is promptly deposited with the monopoly bank, throwing it out of equilibrium. The bank then con-

Table 9–6

Public (Thursday)				Monopoly Bank (Thursday)			
Cash	860	Notes payable	560	Cash reserves	140	Deposits	700
Deposits	700			Cash loans	560		

$c^d < c$

$1 < 1.22$

$$0.2 = \frac{140}{700}$$

or $r^d = r$

$$M = \$1,560$$

Table 9-7

		Public (Day N)		Monopoly Bank (Day N)			
Cash	833	Notes payable	666	Cash reserves	166	Deposits	833
Deposits	833			Cash loans	666		

verts excess reserves into loans, and the process continues until, on Day (N), both the bank and the public are in equilibrium. As Table 9-7 shows, the public is in equilibrium when holding both cash and demand deposits of $833. The bank is in equilibrium when holding cash reserves of $166 in cash reserves against $833 in deposit liabilities. In the process, the money stock has increased to $1,666.

The balance sheet results may again be verified by "plugging" numbers into the equations developed earlier in the chapter. The money stock should rise as in [9.4], or

$$M = H\ \frac{1+c}{c+r} \quad \text{or} \quad \$1,666 = \$1,000 \cdot 1.66$$

Deposit expansion is given by multiplying the "money multiplier," [$(1 + c)/(c + r)$], by the amount of the initial cash reserve deposit, or

$$D = R\ \frac{1+c}{c+r} \quad \text{or} \quad \$833 = \$500 \cdot 1.66$$

Loans expand exactly by the increase in the money supply but by less than deposit expansion or by

$$L = D - r^d D \quad \text{or} \quad L = R\ \frac{1+c}{c+r} - rD$$

Money creation and loan expansion is less than the increase in deposits for a very simple reason. The public's deposit of cash does not alter the money supply, but it does force the bank to hold a fraction of the initial deposit created in desired reserves ($100). Consequently, all of the acquired reserves from the public's deposit are not "excess."[7] Only $R - r^d D$ or $400 is lendable on Tuesday. Money and loan creation is 1.66 times *excess* reserves ($400), however.

The Creation of Money: Graphical Analysis. This important concept discussed above in both tabular and balance sheet terms can be viewed graphically. For this purpose a simple graphical apparatus is developed. Again note that these methods are equivalent. Each method, however, has its own special usefulness in application to real world problems, as we will discover of the "graphical method" in Chapters 11 and 16.

As indicated in a previous section relating to actual and desired ratios, the monopoly bank and the moneyholding public will be in equilibrium when $\mathbf{r}^d = R/D$ and when $\mathbf{c}^d = C/D$, respectively. We now seek a method for showing the conditions under which both moneyholders and the bank will be in equilibrium. First, the public's equilibrium may be considered, using the equations developed earlier in the chapter. Specifically, the moneyholders or *public equilibrium function* will be developed with the use of our equilibrium condition $C/D = \mathbf{c}^d$ and the definition $M = C + D$. Since $C = M - D$,

$$\mathbf{c}^d = \frac{M - D}{D} \quad \text{or} \quad M = (1 + \mathbf{c}^d)D \qquad [9.5]$$

expression [9.5] is merely a formulation of the public equilibrium equation in terms of the money stock. The function may be depicted graphically. The public equilibrium function of Figure 9–1 features a zero intercept and is positively sloped (slope = $1 + \mathbf{c}^d$) with a value greater than one (except in the case where the currency-deposit ratio is equal to zero).

A similar formulation is given to a *bank equilibrium expression*. From previous definitions recall that in bank's equilibrium, $\mathbf{r}^d = R/D = (H - C)/D$. Since $C = M - D$,

$$\mathbf{r}^d = \frac{H - M + D}{D} \quad \text{and} \quad M = H + (1 - \mathbf{r}^d)D \qquad [9.6]$$

Thus expression [9.6] is an expression of bank equilibrium. The intercept of [9.6] is the quantity of high-powered money, H. The slope of the bank equilibrium function of [9.6] is positive with a value less than 1 (except, of course, in the case when $\mathbf{r}^d$ is zero).[8]

Consider Figure 9–2, which is constructed in the manner of Figure 9–1. Figure 9–2, however, depicts the bank equilibrium function with an assumed $\mathbf{r}^d$

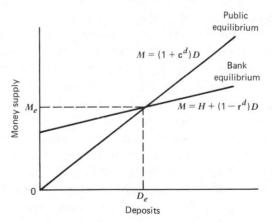

Figure 9–1. Money supply and deposit determination: a graphical analysis.

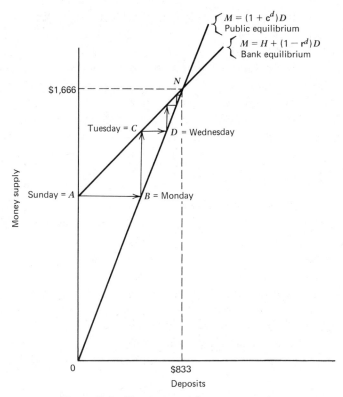

Figure 9-2. The process of money creation.

value of 0.2, while the public equilibrium function is drawn with an assumed c^d of 1. Thus, Figure 9–2 reproduces graphically the tabular analysis used in Table 9–1 and in the preceding balance sheet discussion.

Point A in Figure 9–2 corresponds to Line A of Table 9–1, which represents the situation facing the public before the bank is introduced in the system and is open for business. The total money stock equals the quantity of currency of high-powered money in existence. That is, reserves ($=0$) + currency = high-powered money = \$1,000 at point A. On Monday, however, the bank opens for business and begins accepting deposits. The public deposits \$500 in currency throughout Monday, an action that, by the end of the day, brings the combination of deposits and reserves to point B in Figure 9–2. At point B the actual currency-deposit ratio is equal to the desired ratio, and the public is in equilibrium. But, as should be clear from Figure 9–2, the banks are not in equilibrium. Thus, on Tuesday the banks take actions to achieve equilibrium. Loans in the amount of \$400 are made on Tuesday, putting banks in equilibrium on Tuesday night (the desired ratio of 20% equals the actual ratio). But the public is again holding too much currency to demand deposits (a ratio of 1.8).

On Wednesday the public acts to bring its desires into balance with actual holdings, depositing one-half ($400) of the cash loan it receives into the monopoly bank and holding one-half ($400) as currency. Point D of Figure 9-2 depicts this temporary state of affairs. The bank adjusts on Thursday, which brings the system to point E. And the process continues until point N is reached. Point N represents equilibrium since both the banks and the public are simultaneously holding actual ratios equal to those desired.

THE SYSTEM AT WORK: COMPARATIVE STATICS

The process by which the equilibrium of Figures 9-1 and 9-2 is attained *is* the story of the process of money creation. Before elaborating upon this important topic, which is the essential function of the present chapter, let us analyze some of the mechanics of the present model. This analysis—a "comparative statics" exercise—will help us understand the *effects* of once-and-for-all changes in the values of H, $\mathbf{r}^d$ and $\mathbf{c}^d$.

We can consider four examples. They are presented diagrammatically as Figures 9-3, a–d. First, we might consider the effects of a change, say an in-increase, in the quantity of high-powered money H. Just how this is accomplished in the real world will be discussed in Chapter 11, but for the present we might think of a mysterious government dropping high-powered money (currency) from airplanes. In terms of the model, imagine H being increased from H_0 to some larger quantity H_1. The intercept of the bank-equilibrium equation [9.6], is increased from H_0 to H_1, the slope, $\mathbf{r}^d$, remaining the same. (In Figure 9-3a, as in 9-3, b–d, the slopes and *not* the full equation for the equilibrium functions are given.) Such an increase is depicted in Figure 9-3a. An increase in the stock of high-powered money results in a larger money stock, that is, M_1 (or $C_1 + D_1$) $> M_0$ (or $C_0 + D_0$). But, since the public's *desired* currency-deposit ratio and the bank's desired proportion of reserves to deposits do not change in the new equilibrium, $C_0/D_0 = C_1/D_1$ and $R_0/D_0 = R_1/D_1$. (R_1 is calculated by subtracting new currency holdings C_1 from the new quantity of high-powered money.) Despite the fact that an additional quantity of high-powered money is introduced into the economy, the public will, in equilibrium, end up holding the same *fraction* of currency to deposits as before since $1 + \mathbf{c}^d$ remains the same. The same will be true for banks so long as $1 - \mathbf{r}^d$, the slope of the bank equilibrium function, remains constant.

But what if $\mathbf{c}^d$ or $\mathbf{r}^d$, due to a change in economic conditions, is altered? Our simple model is capable of giving us some insights into the effects of such changes. Consider Figures 9-3b and 9-3c in which changes in $\mathbf{c}^d$ and $\mathbf{r}^d$ are considered, respectively. Given a constant stock of high-powered money H_0, Figure 9-3b shows that an increase in the currency-deposit ratio from $\mathbf{c}_0^d$ to

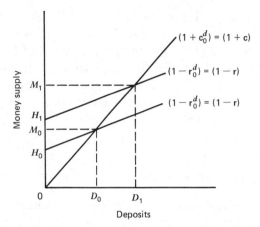

Figure 9-3a. An increase in high-powered money.

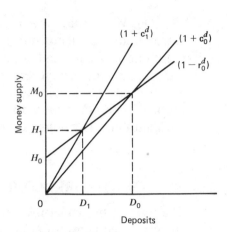

Figure 9-3b. An increase in the currency deposit ratio.

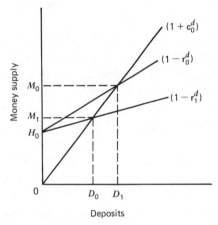

Figure 9-3c. An increase in the bank's desired reserve ratio.

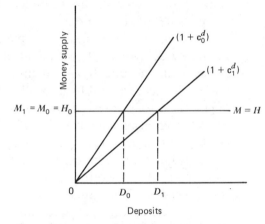

Figure 9-3d. The 100 percent Reserve banking case.

c_1^d results in the public reducing its holding of deposits (to D_1) and in a decrease in the money supply. An increase in desired $\mathbf{c}^d$, however, will always (at least, as long as $1 > \mathbf{r}^d > 0$) lead to an actual increase in *currency* holdings by the public. With respect to Figure 9-3b, the reduction in deposits held by the public is *greater* than the reduction in the money supply. The public must be holding more currency than before.

The case of change in the bank's desired reserve ratio is analyzed in Figure 9-3c. As depicted, the bank's desired reserve rises, producing a clockwise shift in the bank equilibrium function. Banks simply desire more cash reserves at every given level of deposits. (Note that the change in $\mathbf{r}^d$ is assumed to be voluntary since central bank control over $\mathbf{r}^d$ has not yet been introduced into the discussion.) The effects of an increase in r^d (from r_0^d to r_1^d) can be clearly seen in Figure 9–3c. The level of currency and deposits in our simple economy is reduced, and there is an unambiguous *reduction* in the money stock from M_0 to M_1. Although the proportion of currency to deposits remains the same ($C_0/D_0 = C_1/D_1$), the new equilibrium ratio of bank reserves to deposits has increased ($R_0/D_0 < R_1/D_1$). (R is calculated by subtracting C from H.) Thus any factor that increases (decreases) desired reserves as a proportion of deposits will decrease (increase) the money stock and the quantity of currency in the hands of the public.

A final case that might be considered in terms of the simple model is that of the so-called 100% reserve banking case. A variant of the case described in Figure 9–3b, r^d, in Figure 9–3d is assumed to equal one. In this case, the bank-equilibrium function is a horizontal line (since $r^d = 1$, from expression [9–6], $M = H$), and for every dollar of deposits the bank holds one dollar of cash reserves. The effects on the money stock of any change in c^d are clear when $r^d = 1$. *The money stock remains constant!* If, for example, the public reduced their desired ratio of currency to deposits from c^d to c^d, the money stock would remain the same: $M_0 = M_1 = H_0$. In the other cases considered in Figure 9–3, the money stock can be varied by changes in c^d and r^d. When r^d is fixed (or self-imposed) at a value of unity, however, the only factor that alters the money stock is the quantity of high-powered money. Although the case is largely of academic interest, a number of important economists, past and present, have proposed a 100% reserve requirement for monetary stability.[9]

CONCLUSION

In the present chapter the "statics" of how banks create money have been considered. It has been shown that the commercial banking system, in its attempt to turn excess currency reserves into loans and demand deposits, actually *creates* money. The public, on the other hand, participates in the process by its willingness to hold demand deposits as money. Moreover, interaction of the given desired currency-deposit and reserve-deposit ratios, in addition to the stock of high-powered money, has been shown to constitute limits to the process of money creation. One note of warning, however; we have explicitly assumed that the bank and the public act in discrete fashion. That is, until equilibrium is reached, one or the other participant (bank or public) but not both was out of equilibrium. We know that, in reality, banks and the public act *continuously* as forces propel the system toward equilibrium. Although this topic is unrelated directly to the main theme of this text, an introduction to these more realistic dynamics is presented in Appendix 9 to the present chapter.

After a brief introduction to the commercial and central banking systems in the United States in Chapter 10, we will show in far more specific terms how the limits to the money creation process discussed in the present chapter are prescribed and controlled by government agencies regulating banks, the main of which is the Federal Reserve System. After a brief discussion of commercial and central banking in the United States, we will return in Chapter 11 to a version of the model developed in the present chapter, one building more realism into our understanding of the important process of money creation.

Appendix 9
AN INTRODUCTION TO THE SIMPLE DYNAMICS OF MONEY CREATION

In Chapter 9, it has been explicitly assumed that the public and the bank adjust in what we might call discrete fashion. We have assumed, for example, that the two participants in the money creation process acted passively on alternative days. This assumption, though useful for expository purposes, is unrealistic. In the real world the public and banks act *continuously* to convert actual ratios into desired ratios.

Here the assumption of a single monopoly bank is dropped. The US banking system is composed of approximately 15,000 banks, some that are state chartered and some that are federally chartered. Banks, moreover, are heterogeneous in size, assets, capitalization, and in the degree with which and the level from which they are controlled. In the United States, the Federal Reserve System, the Federal Deposit Insurance Corporation (the deposit insurance agency of US banking), and the United States Treasury, not to mention state banking commissions and other regulatory agencies, affect banks and bank behavior. Though we postpone a discussion of the US commercial banking system, its development and regulation (by the Federal Reserve) until Chapter 11, we should note that commercial banks *as a whole* behave in a manner that is exactly analogous to our monopoly bank. That is, the banking system of the United States (or any country, for that matter) holds reserves of high-powered money in desired or imposed proportions, as indicated earlier in the present chapter. These currency reserves may be required for certain banks by state or federal regulations, but the important point is that the banking system, in an attempt

to maximize profits, will loan out excess reserves (those over and above desired and/or required reserves) in approximately the same manner as our single monopoly bank.[10] The fact that desired or required reserves might differ from bank to bank should not obscure the fact that the banking system, on average and at any given time, holds currency reserves and deposits in a given proportion.

The currency-deposit ratio of the public is also an abstraction. While it is clear that various segments of the public—high-income groups, low-income groups, businesses, and so forth—do not desire to hold currency and deposits in the same proportions, it is also true that, on average and at any given time, there exists a currency-deposit ratio in certain proportions. Thus, our abstractions concerning these ratios are representative of real world phenomena, and they affect the actual stock of money deposits, and currency in the manner described in the present chapter.

The process of money supply creation in terms of a model that does represent actual economic forces may now be described. These forces are summarized in Figure 9-4, which is merely a generalized version of Figure 9-2 from the text of the present chapter. The *banking system* and *moneyholders'* functions are identical concepts to the monopoly bank and public equilibrium functions of Figure 9-4. The arrows indicate what we might call "adjustment forces," which require additional explanation.

As we have already discussed, every point on the bank and public equilibrium functions indicates those combinations of M and D for

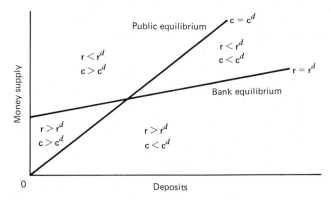

Figure 9-4. Adjustment forces in money supply determination.

which $r = r^d$ and $c = c^d$. At the point of intersection, N, these actual and desired ratios are simultaneously equal. Consider the situation in which there is disequilibrium for the public or for banks.

Public (Moneyholders) Disequilibrium. The public is in disequilibrium at all points to the left or to the right of the $c = c^d$ function in Figure 9–4. Disequilibrium can be analyzed by assuming that some combination of money and demand deposits places the public to the left of the equilibrium curve. If $M = (1 + c^d)D$ represents points on the curve, a position to the left of the $c = c^d$ curve would be represented as $M > (1 + c^d)D$. Since $M = C + D$, we can substitute, which yields $(C + D) > (D + c^dD)$. Canceling, it is apparent that all combinations of M and D to the *left* and upward of the public equilibrium function mean that $C/D > c^d$. (By similar reasoning, all points downward and to the left represent a situation where $C/D < c^d$.)

An economic interpretation may be given to all points above and to the left of the public equilibrium curve. The situation simply means that, for any M, the actual currency deposit ratio is "too high." The public will be substituting deposits for currency in their money holdings. Thus, to the left (right) of the $c = c^d$ function, there are behavioral forces that cause deposits to increase (decrease). The horizontal arrows introduced in Figure 9–5 pointing eastward to the left of the $c = c^d$ function and

westward to the right of the function indicate the directions of these changes.

Banking System Disequilibrium. The banks are in disequilibrium above and to the left and below and to the right of the bank equilibrium function. It may be assumed that some combination of M and D exists, placing the banks above the equilibrium function $r = r^d$. Since $M = H + (1 - r^d)D$ is the equation for the equilibrium curve, all points above the curve imply that $M > H + D - r^dD$. Given that $H = C + R$ and $M = C + D$, simple substitution means that at points above the bank function $r^d > R/D$. (Starting with $M < H + (1 - r^d)D$, points *below* the bank function clearly mean that $r^d < R/D$.)

Disequilibrium for the bank can now be given an economic interpretation. For any given level of deposits at all points above the $r = r^d$ function, the actual quantity of reserves is less than the desired quantity. Banks will attempt to build up cash reserves by "calling loans" from the public or by letting loans mature without making new loans, and in the process of doing so they will be draining currency from the public and therefore reducing the quantity of money. Banks, in short, begin to stockpile cash reserves, which in turn reduces the stock of money.

Analogously, when banks find themselves at any point (or combination of M and D) below their equilibrium function, economic forces

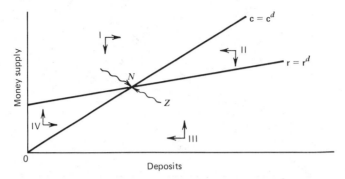

Figure 9-5. The dynamics of money creation.

cause the money stock to increase. At any such point and at any level of deposits, the actual reserve ratio is greater than the desired. In an attempt to achieve the desired ratio banks will lend out excess reserves, an action that engenders, as in Table 9-1, an increase in the money stock. These forces affecting the money stock are represented by northward- (southward-) pointing arrows below (above) the equilibrium bank function in Figure 9-4.

The dynamic aspects of money creation or destruction can be summarized in terms of quadrants, as in Figure 9-5. Equilibrium will be attained from any point in quadrant I, since there are economic forces causing the money stock to decline and deposits to increase. In fact, economic forces exist in any of the other quadrants that ensure a stable equilibrium at N. Take point Z in quadrant III. Equilibrium at N is assured since there are economic forces pushing the money supply upward and deposits downward. The *actual* path to the new equilibrium is not exactly predictable without some additional information.[11] Obviously, the path to

equilibrium from any of the quadrants will depend upon the *strength* of the alternative forces. We know the *direction* of the forces, however, and that these forces are sufficient to ensure that equilibrium at N will be attained.

The significance of dynamics and stability of equilibrium is easy to grasp. They simply mean that any displacement, such as changes in c^d, $\mathbf{r}^d$, or H (or indeed, any of the static shifts considered in Figures 9-3a to 9-3d), will result in the attainment of a new equilibrium money stock. An increase in high-powered money, for instance, will shift the bank's equilibrium function so that N is no longer an equilibrium point. Depending on the strength of deposit and money stock pressures, a path to equilibrium will develop through which both money stock and deposits increase. The directions of the arrows of quadrant IV guarantees this result. Under ordinary circumstances reestablishment of stable equilibrium may be expected for any parameter change (H, $\mathbf{r}^d$, $\mathbf{c}^d$) considered in the text of Chapter 9.

FOOTNOTES

[1] Demand deposits can be contrasted to time deposits in several respects. As noted in the text, withdrawal of most time and savings deposits, unlike the withdrawal of demand deposits, technically requires advance notice to the holder on the part of the owner. But this is not a basic difference in the character of these two types of deposits since, factually, most

banks do not enforce the requirement. Rather, the fundamental difference in the two types of deposits rests upon the fact that an order to transfer time deposits to some third party cannot be made. This ability to order the transfer of deposits to third parties is a unique characteristic of demand deposits or checkbook money. Some checkable deposits, such as the

NOW accounts, ATS accounts, and share draft accounts at thrift institutions, possess the characteristics of earning interest and transferability to third parties. These accounts are checkable, fulfill the criterion of money, and are included as demand deposits here.

[2] New regulations passed in 1980 affecting the ability of financial institutions other than banks to create demand deposits (and thus money) are analyzed in Chapters 11 and 12.

[3] The assumption that banks hold all reserves in the form of currency (or "vault cash") is an oversimplification. A large portion of bank reserves are held as bank deposits at the central bank (Federal Reserve Banks in the United States). Thus high-powered money is the sum of currency and reserves. See Chapters 10 and 11 for elaboration of these points.

[4] Most principles of economics texts, and many money and banking texts, identify the reciprocal of the reserve-deposit ratio (or the reserve ratio for short) with the *money multiplier*. The case in which the public holds no currency, as the model of the present text implies, is highly unrealistic. The simple model of the present chapter focuses upon the two most important determinants of the money multiplier, but there are still others. In Chapter 11 we discuss a more elaborate money multiplier—one used to analyze the direction of "k" in real world monetary policy.

[5] We should expect, for instance, that c^d rose after 1930 as confidence in banks' ability to function declined. Indeed the expectation is clearly verified in the actual statistical data from that period. See the discussion of monetary policy during the Great Depression of the 1930s in Chapter 16.

[6] Should the value of r^d equal 1, the case of 100% reserves, the quantity of money would equal the stock of high-powered money.

[7] If we had formulated a different money creation model based on the acquisition of $500 in reserves by the monopoly bank through the sale of securities, say to the government, the results would differ slightly from those represented above. In this case, the entire $500 would be composed of "excess" reserves. Both deposits and loans (money) would expand by $833 (again assuming that $r^d = 0.2$ and $c^d = 1$). In the case of the security sale, the expression for loan expansion in the text would understate loan and money creation. In either case, however, loans can be created in an amount equal to the money multiplier $[(1 + c)/(c + r)]$ multiplied by the *excess* reserves of the monopoly bank.

[8] The money creation example used in the text describes an increase in the nominal money stock caused by an injection of high-powered money into the system. (The real money stock depends upon both the nominal money stock and the price level.) The same effects on the nominal money stock could be shown if banks lowered their desired reserve-deposit ratio or the public decreased their desired currency-deposit ratio.

[9] Important twentieth-century economists such as Irving Fisher, Henry Simons, and Milton Friedman proposed 100% reserve banking as a means to economic stabilization.

[10] The model contains a slight oversimplification in that loans from banks in the real world are ordinarily transacted by a credit to the borrower's account. Inclusion of this feature of the process slightly alters the model developed in the text.

[11] The system, for example, may go from quadrant I to IV or II and from quadrant III into IV or II before converging to equilibrium.

KEY CONCEPTS

demand deposits	currency-deposit ratio (actual and desired)	balance sheet equation (accounting identity)
time deposits		
financial intermediaries	reserve-deposit ratio (actual and desired)	excess reserves
high-powered money		

QUESTIONS FOR DISCUSSION

1. What are some of the reasons moneyholders' desired c^d might change? Be specific.

2. Find c^d and r^d for currency = $10 billion, demand deposits = $4 billion, and reserves = $2 billion.

3. Given r^d and c^d above and high-powered money = $5,000, what is the money stock? What are equilibrium currency, deposit, cash reserve, and loan asset holdings?

4. Given $r^d = 1$ and $c^d = 0.5$, work through Table 9–1. Show the same process in bal-ance sheet analysis. Will changing r^d and c^d change the graphical analysis? If so, how?

5. Some critics of the money creation process have advocated drastically increasing reserve requirements for banks (for example, by 100%). Why do they express this viewpoint and what do the critics feel this change would accomplish?

6. What is the driving force behind the money creation process?

CHAPTER 10

THE FEDERAL RESERVE AND COMMERCIAL BANKING SYSTEMS: Structure and Institutions

Chapter 9 discussed, with the aid of a simple model of banking system behavior, the manner in which the money stock adjusts to changes in high-powered money, to desired reserves, and to the public's demand for different forms (currency and demand deposit) of money. The bare bones of our simple model of the commercial banking system must now be covered with the important institutional facts of banking in the United States, facts that, of necessity, blend elements of both commercial and central banking.

Chapters 10 and 11 investigate the major functions of a true central bank (the Federal Reserve System in the United States) as well as those of profit maximizing commercial banks. Historically, and especially in nineteenth century, these functions have often been combined in institutions that encountered major difficulties in providing a sound banking system. Accordingly, we present a brief historical account of these early attempts at "central banking" in order to introduce the reader to the institution of the Federal Reserve System.[1]

A brief discussion of these issues sets the stage for explaining the important facts and functions of the Fed (short for Federal Reserve System). Institutional structure and mechanisms of the Fed, some of them recently enacted, will be discussed in detail and the instruments of central bank monetary control will be emphasized (in Chapter 11). These three major "instruments" of Fed control are alterations in reserve requirements, securities purchases and sales (called open-market operations), and alterations in discount rate policy. (The discount rate is the rate at which member banks may, subject to Fed limits and controls respecting collateral, borrow reserves from the Fed). The role of the US Treasury in monetary control is also considered in this regard.

Much attention is given to the institutional and operational nature of the Fed System for good reason. These factual details are absolutely prerequisite to an appreciation of *how* the Fed controls the money stock that, as we have seen in Chapters 5 through 8, is intimately related to crucial economic variables such as prices, GNP, and employment. Once these institutional details of central bank controls have been mastered, we will discover—in Chapter 11 and in a more formal manner—how the money stock might be affected by changes in Federal Reserve policies. Specifically, this is accomplished by reexamining the simple money supply models that were developed in the previous chapter (Figure 9–1, for example). In Chapter 11 we investigate how the Fed's instruments of control affect the stock of high-powered money and the reserve requirement facing member banks and, hence, the money supply. The policy implications of this integration of institutions and analysis—extended to all financial intermediaries in Chapters 12 and 13—will become clearer at this point, although monetary policy is yet a more complex affair, as Chapter 14 will reveal.

CENTRAL BANKING: FUNCTIONS AND EARLY "EXPERIMENTS"

What are the essential functions of a central bank? Basically there are two. The first and oldest function of a central bank is to serve as a *lender of the last resort*. A second major function of central banks, developed only in the twentieth century, is what might be termed a *control function*, that is, one in which the monetary authority effects discretionary control over an important "product" of banks and other financial institutions, demand deposits. Control over money creation, it was discovered, is a powerful tool in mitigating or dampening swings in cycles of production, employment and prices.

THE DUAL ROLE OF A CENTRAL BANK
The control function of central banking will occupy us through most of the present and some of the succeeding chapters. An orientation to central banking would be less than complete, however, without some appreciation for the conditions under which the money market was conducted prior to 1913, the year in which the Federal Reserve Act was passed to establish the foundations for our contemporary central banking system. In other words, the formation of a central bank in the United States was closely related to the failure of any earlier institution to provide the old function of lender of the last resort.

What is a lender of the last resort and why is one needed? The problem is a simple one. In early times—before demand deposits gained ascendancy as a money component—*specie* (gold and/or silver) and bank notes circulated as a medium of exchange. Note-issuing institutions, such as commercial banks, exchanged notes for specie or specie for notes on a one-to-one basis. Notes circulated as a medium of exchange, but noteholders could instantly "repurchase" specie dollar for dollar. Bankers realized that only a proportion of notes outstanding were ever presented for specie redemption at a given time. Thus a portion of bank-held specie was kept as reserves against possible conversions and the remainder was invested, chiefly through loans, for profit. (Later, in somewhat analogous fashion, banks held cash reserves against demand deposits and lent the excess cash reserves for profit.)

The key point is that a miscalculation of specie or currency demands at any given time could, and often did, cause bank failure and financial panic accompanied by recessions and periodic economic disaster. The absence of a central bank where commercial paper of private commercial banks could be "discounted" for cash in times of heavy specie or currency withdrawals (or the absence of a lender of last resort) characterized early US banking and was also a major factor in the formation of the Federal Reserve System. All was not chaos in early US banking, however, and in this regard an examination of several American "experiments" in bank function is interesting.

A BIT OF HISTORY: CENTRAL BANK DEVELOPMENT IN THE UNITED STATES

The extensive controls over and regulation of the US commercial banking system is principally a development of the twentieth century. In fact, the United States was one of the last major nations of the world to adopt an "official" central bank, which is today known as the Federal Reserve System.[2] There were early private attempts at banking organization, however, arising out of conditions created by the heterogeneous state-chartered banking systems and institutions. We should not assume that all early banking was abortive, however. Many early commercial banks were successful in their operations.

Federal bank charters were also provided in two early banking experiments. The charters of the First and Second Banks of the United States were allowed to expire (the latter under the famous aegis of Andrew Jackson),[3] and the fundamental problems brought on by the absence of a true central bank continued to plague the state chartering system; namely, inadequate capitalization and reserves that led to specie inconvertibility in times of crisis, not to mention note overissue against specie by uncontrolled state banks.

The Federal government, wishing neither to re-enter the morass of banking activity nor to trust its accounts to commercial banks, or to a set of "pet banks," set up an Independent Treasury in order to collect and disburse funds, which were in the form of specie. The Treasury organized a number of branches throughout the country for this purpose, and the system operated effectively until the financial pressures of the Civil War forced the government to turn to the commercial banks once more. The result was the *National Banking Act of 1863.*

The exigencies of the Civil War brought the need for banking reform to the fore. Salmon P. Chase, the Secretary of the Treasury, proposed that national banks be established as a convenient outlet for government bonds that were, in addition to nonredeemable greenbacks, necessary to finance the War effort. His plan allowed the national banks to issue banks to issue bank notes against collateral in the form of government bonds (110% of bank notes issued). The bonds were then deposited with the Comptroller of the Currency.

Apart from its pragmatic aspects, the Act of 1863 was a distinct improvement in the commercial banking structure. First, the banks were required to observe a uniform minimum legal cash reserve requirement against deposits and notes. These requirements were fairly high by contemporary standards: 25% for banks designated reserve "city" banks and 15% for the smaller "country" banks (see Table 11-11 in the next chapter for a summary). Second, the Act established minimum capital requirements and provided for inspections by officials from the office of the Comptroller of the Currency, an official of the US Treasury. These inspections were generally more thorough and the inspectors more efficient than their state counterparts. Third, the notes issued by national banks and backed by government securities provided the economy with a uniform and secure paper currency.

The National Banking System, so organized, did not constitute a central bank. Originally many state banks refused to join the System, but in 1865 a tax of 10% levied on state bank notes effectively eliminated their source of profits (that is, loans in the form of state bank note issue) and forced the majority of these institutions either into the System or out of business. Table 10-1 shows that the number of nonnational banks fell drastically during this period. In 1865 the number of these banks fell to 32% of their 1864 level, a reduction of more than 700 banks. In 1868 both nonnational bank deposits (see Table 10-2) and the number of nonnational banks ebbed.

The situation was only temporary, however, for with the growth of deposits as the major component of the money supply in the late 1860s and 1870s the state banks again found an independent source of income. After

Table 10-1   Number of State and National Banks, 1863–1880

Year	National Banks	Nonnational Banks	Year	National Banks	Nonnational Banks
1863	66	1,466	1872	1,853	566
1864	467	1,089	1873	1,968	1,330
1865	1,294	349	1874	1,983	1,569
1866	1,634	297	1875	2,076	1,260
1867	1,636	272	1876	2,091	1,357
1868	1,640	247	1877	2,078	1,306
1869	1,619	259	1878	2,056	1,173
1870	1,612	325	1879	2,048	1,287
1871	1,723	452	1880	2,076	1,279

Source: US Bureau of the Census, Historical Statistics of the United States, Colonial Times to 1957, Washington, D.C., 1960, pp. 626, 628.

Table 10-2   Total Deposits, Nonnational Bank Deposits, and Bank Notes, 1863-1880

Year	Total Deposits[a]	Nonnational Bank Deposits	Bank Notes[b]	State Bank Notes
1863	504	494	239	239
1864	380	233	176	150
1865	689	75	180	48
1866	759	64	309	41
1867	744	58	329	38
1868	798	53	329	34
1869	772	56	329	36
1870	775	70	336	45
1871	888	97	370	62
1872	927	121	405	78
1873	1,625	789	339	c
1874	1,740	912	339	c
1875	2,009	1,111	318	c
1876	1,993	1,151	295	c
1877	2,006	1,188	290	c
1878	1,921	1,107	300	c
1879	2,149	1,059	308	c
1880	2,222	1,137	318	c

[a] All banks, includes both demand and time deposits.
[b] Notes issued by national and nonnational banks.
[c] Less than $500,000.
Source: US Bureau of the Census, *Historical Statistics of the United States, Colonial Times to 1957*, Washington, D.C., 1960, pp. 625, 629.

1872 state bank deposits grew rapidly, and the state banking system was revitalized despite the fact that state bank note issue declined to less than $500,000 per year. The result was a *dual banking system* with state bank charters and regulation existing alongside a national chartering system.

Control under the National Banking System was thus weakened not only by the growing number of nonmember banks but also by the resurgence of state banking permitted by the rise of deposits. The Act was "note" oriented rather than "deposit" oriented. With the gradual retirement of government bonds, and the consequent premium attached to them, national bank note issue became less profitable since national banks could issue notes only up to 90% of the *par value* of bonds held. National bank note issue stabilized at a yearly level of approximately $300 million throughout the 1870s and declined thereafter (until 1891). The steady rise of deposit banking continued to make national charters attractive, however, and the number of national banks continued to increase to a peak in 1929.

Crises, unfortunately, were not eliminated with the National Banking Act.

Pyramiding of reserves in large city banks was common practice, since country banks were allowed to count deposits in their city correspondents as reserves. Periodic demand for these funds by country banks forced liquidation (or *calling*) of loans and a general financial panic in the cities. Seasonal and cyclical demands for currency likewise often formed the crux of monetary crises. In short, there existed no lender of the last resort to adjust the money stock to the changing needs of businesses and consumers. Since the national banks were operated as private concerns, they were principally interested in maximizing profits and not in holding excess reserves for emergency lending in the public's interest. In this case private interests (profit maximization) did not necessarily coincide with public interest in a sound banking system. There was, in short, a general inelasticity of the money supply. (The form of this inelasticity or the "anatomy of a crisis" is considered at length in Chapter 16.)

A series of periodic crises in the late nineteenth century, but most significantly a severe debacle in 1907, led to the establishment of an institution to regulate the monetary system. After more than a century of experimentation and patchwork controls, the United States arrived at the threshold of institutionalized central banking.

THE FEDERAL RESERVE SYSTEM: THE STRUCTURE
OF US CENTRAL BANKING

Although much suspicion still surrounded the establishment of federal monetary control, the Congress passed the Federal Reserve Act, which was signed into law by President Woodrow Wilson on December 23, 1913. The System began operations in the fall of 1914 with the stated purposes of giving the country an elastic currency, providing facilities for the discounting of commercial paper, improving supervision of the banking system at the federal level, and enlarging facilities for check clearance.

FEDERAL RESERVE CONTROL: AN OVERVIEW

Reserve requirements, part of the National Banking Act, were continued by the Act of 1913 (for a summary see Table 11–11 in the following chapter). A new category of banks—the central reserve city bank—was established, and reserve requirements were lowered from their pre-1913 levels to 18%, 15%, and 12% for central reserve city banks, reserve city banks, and country banks, respectively.

The discounting facilities were (and still are) regarded as a prime instrument for emergency lending to commercial banks. It is at this level that the central bank fulfills its lender of the last resort function, and, true to its stated objectives, the Act was able to provide form elasticity to the money supply through the discounting facility and currency issuance. But, in the early days, these policies were oriented to the "needs of commerce and business," a philosophy of passive rather than active control.

Underlying this early philosophy of passive control was the "real bills doctrine." Broadly interpreted, the doctrine that the "proper" quantity of money in the economy should be governed by the quantity of currently produced goods. Loans, in this view, should be made by commercial banks only for the purpose of investing in circulating capital, for examples, raw materials or inventories. Thus the businessman's note would represent *real* current (or forthcoming) output on the market. In this way the quantity of money would be adjusted to output and the price level would be controlled thereby.

Such a view of adjusting credit and the money stock "to accommodate the needs of trade," a view that guided the banking system and the Federal Reserve in the early days, is in sharp contrast to the active countercyclical policies followed by the Fed today. The *activist view* has had a long, steady evolution from the 1920s when Benjamin Strong was chairman of the Board of Governors through the New Deal Banking Acts of 1933 and 1935. It involved the realization that variation of the discount rate and reserve requirements, as well as the open market purchase and sale of government securities, had predictable effects on commercial bank reserves and on the supply of money and credit. The broadened aims of monetary control, as outlined by the Employment Act of 1946, are to counteract inflation, to promote full employment and economic growth, and to balance international accounts. Commercial banks are thus regulated by the Federal Reserve in order to achieve these ends.

US CENTRAL BANK STRUCTURE

A knowledge of the formal structure of the Federal Reserve System is essential, and it will become apparent in the course of our discussion that concentrations of power and monetary policy have developed within the system. But first things first. What then is the formal structure of an institution that is one of the major instruments of economic policy in the United States? A simple schematic diagram such as Figure 10–1 will help us learn and remember that structure.

As we have already indicated, the Federal Reserve System is a creature of the US Congress. Congress has the power to alter the system it created but has seldom tampered with it. In fact the Fed System, unlike most governmentally created regulatory agencies, enjoys a quasiindependent position as an arm of government. Though the Congress has periodically threatened to bring the Federal Reserve System under closer control and scrutiny, the System (chiefly in the person of the Federal Reserve Board Chairman) has—fairly successfully—resisted threats to its independence, although it is presently required by Congress to regularly report its general economic policy plans (these reports are

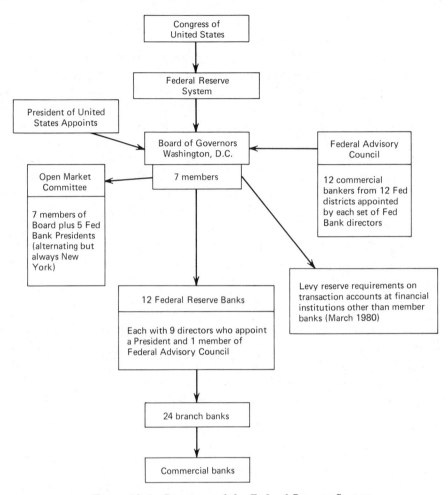

Figure 10-1. Structure of the Federal Reserve System.

reprinted in the monthly *Federal Reserve Bulletin*). Basically, however, the formal structure of the System remains as it was originally created in 1913.

The Board of Governors. At the apex of the Federal Reserve System is the Board of Governors located in Washington, D.C.[4] As Figure 10-1 indicates, the Board is composed of seven members appointed by the President of the United States with the "advice and consent" of the Senate. As a check on the President, members of the Board serve 14-year staggered terms. The President also appoints the powerful Chairman of the Board, who serves a 4-year term that does not necessarily coincide with the President's term of office. Theoretically, all members of the Board have an equal influence over monetary policy, but tradition and practice have established the Chairman as the person who speaks for the Board and for the entire system. The Board Chairman (along with the Secretary of the Treasury) is the concrete representative of monetary policy in the overall management of the economy. Bankers, industrialists, and economists, among others, serve on the Board, which is, theoretically, to represent the "public interest." The President is directed to create a fair representation of industrial, commercial, agricultural, and banking interests in his appointments, and he cannot appoint more than one Board Governor from any single Federal Reserve District. (There are twelve Federal Reserve Districts, each with a district bank; see Table 10–2.) The Board is, with appropriate advice, directly responsible for the determination of monetary policy. Most importantly, the Board is responsible for setting and administering (within Congressional limits) reserve requirements for member banks and other depository institutions, discount rates, and, as we shall shortly see, open market operations.

The Federal Open Market Committee. The Federal Open Market Committee (FOMC) is composed of the seven members of the Board plus five Presidents of the 12 Federal Reserve Banks, although *all* Fed Bank presidents attend meetings that are held at three- or four-week intervals. As indicated in Figure 10–1, the president of the New York Fed, principally because of close proximity to major money market activity, is always included and other presidents of the Fed Banks rotate on the committee. The Chairman of the Board is also the chairman of the FOMC, which adds yet another dimension to his influence over monetary policy. In this case, the instrument controlled is the buying and selling of government securities to the noncentral bank public.

Federal Reserve Banks. Though a single integrated system in action, the Federal Reserve System is geographically dispersed among 12 districts (see Figure 10–2). For example, the Federal Reserve Bank of Dallas, or the 11th district, is "banker" to member commercial banks in the dark-lined area indicated in Figure 10–2. Most of the districts have branches (there are 24 in all). The Dallas district, for example, includes three branches in Houston, San Antonio, and El Paso.

Each of the Federal Reserve Banks is privately "owned" by the member commercial banks in each district. Member banks pledge up to 6% of their own capital and surplus in Reserve stock. The analogy between corporate stockholders and Reserve Bank stockholders is not a good one, however, because the impact of members upon Reserve Bank policies and operations is necessarily minimal. Reserve Banks are not profit-maximizing firms. Rather, their object is to control and to discipline member commercial banks in their districts.

Each of the 12 Reserve Banks is managed by a nine-member Board of

The Federal Reserve System
Boundaries of Federal Reserve Districts and Their Branch Territories

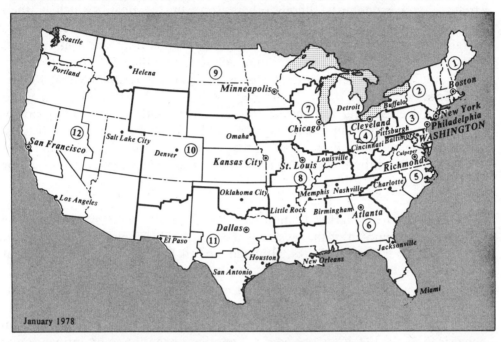

January 1978

HAWAII

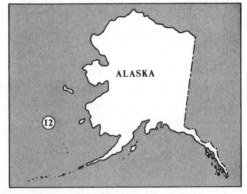

ALASKA

LEGEND

—— Boundaries of Federal Reserve Districts

—— Boundaries of Federal Reserve Branch
Territories

⭐ Board of Governors of the Federal
Reserve System

◉ Federal Reserve Bank Cities

• Federal Reserve Branch Cities

· Federal Reserve Bank Facility

Figure 10-2. The Federal Reserve System map.

Directors with staggered three-year terms. Some indirect, but miniscule, influence is exercised by the district member banks in the appointment of six of these Directors. Class A and B Directors (three in each category) are elected by the member banks of each district. Class A Directors are commercial bankers drawn from those banks that own stock in the Reserve Bank. Class B Directors are also elected by member banks, but they are drawn from commercial, industrial, and agricultural interests of the district. Finally, three Class C Directors, who represent the interests of the public, are appointed by the Board of Governors. The Chairman and Vice-Chairman are also appointed by the Board and are selected from Class C Directors. The role of the Directors is essentially threefold: (1) to appoint the "President" of each Fed Bank, *with the approval* of the Board of Governors in Washington;[5] (2) to appoint a commercial banker to the Federal Advisory Council; and (3) to serve in advisory capacity to the District Fed Bank on economic and financial conditions of the district.

Major Activities of Reserve Banks. The formal structure of the Federal Reserve System is decentralized, with each of the 12 banks controlling and ministering to the needs of the member banks in its district. In reality, however, as the reader has undoubtedly surmised, power and control have stabilized in the Board of Governors in Washington and, most particularly, in the Chairman.

Thus the banks act as one unified body with 12 regional offices and is properly termed a "System." Within the large realm of bank activities, each bank (1) owns cash and certain types of earning assets; (2) holds deposits of member banks, the Treasury, and foreign banks; (3) issue banknotes, that is, Federal Reserve Notes; (4) sets the discount rate *subject to* approval of the Board; and (5) enforces reserve requirements set by the Board of Governors.

Commercial Banks: Member and Nonmember Banks. There are approximately 14,700 commercial banks in the United States, but—given the "dual" banking system enshrined in the National Banking Act of 1863 and maintained by the Federal Reserve Act of 1913—two levels of government issue bank charters. The Comptroller of the Currency, an official of the US Treasury, issues charters to National Banks, while all the various states may issue bank charters for operation within each state. By law, *all* National Banks must belong to the Federal Reserve System, whereas state banks may join the System at their option subject, of course, to approval by the Fed. As of January 1980, there were 5,586 Federal Reserve members of which about 1,000 held state charters. Almost two-thirds of US banks do not belong to the FRS.

Tables 10–3 and 10–4 verify these facts. These two tables show member bank deposits and assets between 1966 and 1980 as a percentage of total deposits and assets of the commercial banking system. These percentages have been declining recently. As of January 1980, for example, a full 30% of banking resources lay outside the direct umbrella of System Control. A vast major-

Table 10-3   *Commercial Bank Assets (1966-1978)*
(in Millions of Dollars)

Date	Members	Total	Members/Total (Percent)
1966	$334,559	$ 403,368	82.9
1967	373,584	451,012	82.8
1968	412,541	500,657	82.4
1969	432,270	530,665	81.5
1970	465,644	576,242	80.8
1971	511,353	640,255	79.9
1972	585,125	739,033	79.2
1973	655,898	835,224	78.5
1974	715,600	919,600	78.0
1975	733,600	964,900	76.0
1976	772,900	1,030,700	75.0
1977	861,800	1,166,000	74.0
1978	945,200	1,284,000	74.0
1979 (April)	930,000	1,293,500	

Source: Federal Reserve Bulletin, various issues.

ity of banks in the United States did not belong to the System at this time, although most "nonmembers" were small "country banks."

Monetary Control and Fed Membership: An Aside on Present Structural Changes. Declining membership in the Federal Reserve System and, in par-

Table 10-4   *Commercial Bank Deposits (1966-1978)*
(in Millions of Dollars)

Date	Members	Total	Members/Total (Percent)
1966	$291,063	$352,287	82.8
1967	326,033	395,008	82.5
1968	355,414	434,023	81.9
1969	349,883	435,577	80.3
1970	384,596	480,940	80.0
1971	425,380	537,946	79.1
1972	482,124	616,037	78.3
1973	526,837	681,847	77.2
1974	575,600	747,900	77.0
1975	590,800	786,300	75.0
1976	618,700	838,200	74.0
1977	638,500	939,400	73.0
1978	716,300	993,100	72.0
1979 (April)	691,800	983,900	

Source: Federal Reserve Bulletin, various issues.

ticular, eroding control over bank reserves and deposit expansion have disturbed the Fed. The result, in March 1980, was passage of a far-reaching "omnibus" depository institutions bill entitled the Depository Institutions Deregulation and Monetary Control Act of 1980 (Public Law 96-221). Among many other alterations in *financial* (not only banking) *system* controls and regulations, provisions in the Act relating to nonmember banks may have an impact on the composition of membership. The costs and benefits of membership have been altered by the Act in that effective reserve requirements have been applied to all insured nonmember banks, along with providing official access to the discounting functions and to other advantages of the System membership.

Other provisions of the Act extend reserve controls to sections of the financial system previously unregulated by the Fed. Reserve requirements will be levied on all "transactions accounts" at thrift institutions such as savings and loans, credit unions, and mutual savings banks. The purpose of this extension of regulation is to control money stock expansions and contractions from all transactions accounts, that is, negotiable order of withdrawal accounts, savings deposits subject to automatic transfers, and share draft accounts, as well demand deposits at commercial banks. The entire matter of Fed membership and control—not to mention the sort of institution that is the subject of control—has been *blurred* by the "Depository Institutions Deregulation and Monetary Control Act of 1980."

The structure and nature of the Federal Reserve as a control institution may thus be expected to undergo major changes in the 1980s. The details of these changes and some of their probable effects will be considered in Chapters 11 and 12. We now return to still other structural issues.

COMMERCIAL BANKS: UNIT BANKS VERSUS BRANCHING

Unlike most other nations of the world, the structure of banking in the United States is dominated by a unit banking system (Canada, for example, has less than a dozen banks). A unit system means a single bank without branches. Whether branching—multiple bank offices acquired by merger or established *de novo*—is permitted or not is the affair of the various state governments. For the most part, unit banks are small country banks operating in 15 unit banking states in the Midwest and South. Over 68% of the banks in the United States are of this type, but as pointed out previously in this chapter the amount of assets held by these banks is small.

All other states allow some form of branch banking, with statewide branching the predominant form in the western part of the United States. States with limited branching ordinarily limit the establishment of branch offices to the country or the city of the main office of the bank. National banks are allowed to branch only to the extent allowed by the states in which they are operating. Branching is *not* allowed interstate, although the recent surge (after 1965) in bank holding companies has, in part at least, permitted some interstate organization.

Two important and related issues surround the question of whether branching should be permitted or not. The first is the political issue. Unit banking states are typically those with large rural populations. Small town bankers have perpetuated the "fear of bigness" and encroachment of "city bankers." Regular battles over branching take place in the legislatures of these states, but the second—and most important economic issue—is seldom brought out. It is the question of the efficient provision of banking services.

The issue amounts to this: would the branch of a large city bank in a city of small size be able better to serve the public than a unit bank? Evidence on this point is sketchy but that which exists seems to indicate that banks in the medium ($25–$50 million deposits) to medium–large ($100–$500 million in deposits) categories are the most efficient and profitable. Increase in bank size, moreover, is associated with branching, and here are some economies of scale although it obviously costs more to establish and to maintain bank branches. The range of services offered by larger branch banks also tends to be wider than that offered by smaller unit banks. Unit banks are protected from some competition that might tend to lessen or retard the introduction of new services or banking technology. Conversely, bigness or concentration—as reflected in a dozen or so giant banks existing, for the most part, in states that permit branching—may not be associated with the absence of competition. It is wise to remember that the number of firms in an industry (or its concentration ratio) does not always provide a correct picture of the nature of competitive conditions. A good deal more needs to be known before sound judgment on these issues can be posed. Until then, the issue of unit versus branch banking is highly debatable.[6]

COMMERCIAL BANKS: HOLDING COMPANIES

Restrictions or outright prohibitions on branch banking have provided the impetus to still other equally debatable developments in banking structure. Bank holding companies are corporations that control the stock of one or more banks (the one-bank holding company is a special case) and possibly that of other related corporations. The economic advantages and disadvantages are similar to those related to branch banking, but, unlike branch banking, bank ownership by the holding company may cross state boundaries. The majority of states do not regulate these corporations, but the Federal Reserve system was authorized to regulate them in 1956. This regulation relates to the types of businesses which the company may engage in and to the additional banks it may acquire under this form.

Of considerable recent interest is a form of "group banking"—the one-bank holding company. Again, this form of organization gained popularity in the 1960s, perhaps in part because of a certain regulation of the Federal Reserve System, Regulation Q. Although we defer major consideration of Regulation Q to Chapter 12, and although it will be eliminated by 1986 under the "Depository Institutions Deregulation and Monetary Control Act of 1980," it is the *maximum interest rate provision* on the payment of saving and time deposits at commercial banks (similar restrictions were applied to savings and loans in 1966). Banks were able to compete for these funds as long as the market rates are below the maximum, but market rates rose above this maximum beginning about the mid-1960s, a trend that meant a drying up of deposit sources of funds for many financial intermediaries, including banks.

As so often happens, the devices of banker-businessmen were employed to circumvent this regulation, and in the late 1960s we witnessed the development of the one-bank holding company. The 1956 Bank Holding Company Act gave the Fed the power to regulate only bank holding companies owning more than *one* bank. In the late 1960s, therefore, single-bank corporations including all of the largest U.S. banks—along with nonbank businesses—were reorganized within the holding company format. Banks could then be related to data processing, travel agencies, insurance, investment counseling activities, and so forth, which were formerly prohibited. In addition—and not the least important reason for the rapid development of this business form—was the ability of these related businesses to sell their own commercial paper at interest rates *not* controlled by Regulation Q. Deposits by nonbank businesses of the holding company could then be made at the bank, opening up a new source of bank funds for making high interest rate loans.

In the face of these developments the Congress in 1970 revised the 1956 Act to include one-bank holding companies. The Federal Reserve has attempted to confine holding company (both single- and multiple-bank) acquisitions to bank-related business and, in general, to monitor and control holding company bank purchases. By 1974 deposits in holding company bank groups amounted to more than 65% of all commercial bank deposits. This more flexible form of bank organization might continue to dominate banking structure in the future.

COMMERCIAL BANKS: A DIGRESSION ON CHECK CLEARING

Among other traditional advantages of belonging to the Federal Reserve System, member commercial banks are provided with a clearing house and, given recent banking legislation, nonmembers have open access to it (for a fee, of course). All member and nonmember banks, including small country banks, maintain *correspondent relations* with other banks in the system. Through correspondent relations some banks (member or nonmember) maintain deposits or deposit arrangements with other banks that provide services to them including regional and local check clearing—that is they are private (non-Fed) clearing houses.

The process of check clearance is so fundamental to the banking system that it deserves some special attention. For simplicity consider an example of Federal Reserve check clearing. As we will discover, checks written on banks anywhere in the country (say, one written on a Dallas bank in favor of an individual or company in San Francisco) can be "cleared" through appropriate adjustments in member bank and Federal Reserve Bank accounts.

Using a practical example of a Dallas bank we can illustrate the clearing house function with the simple T-accounts of Table 10–5. Assume a small producer in Dallas, the Acme Company, who buys $300 worth in an input from a small fabricating company, Ace Manufacturing, in San Francisco. Acme writes a check on its Dallas bank (Trinity National Bank) and sends it to Ace. The Acme Company receives the input and Ace Manufacturing deposits Acme's check. But what is happening behind the scenes? If we consider the bookkeeping for *this transaction only*, the deposit, $300, is offset by a reduction in Ace's holding of the input on its balance sheet. Bay City National's account with Ace is also affected. Specifically Bay City's liabilities (deposits of Ace) have increased by $300. But Acme's check has not yet been collected and Bay City National Bank deposits Acme's check in the Federal Reserve Bank of San Francisco, gaining an asset of "cash reserves" in the Fed of $300 (deposits of

Table 10–5   Check Clearing

Ace Manufacturing		*Bay City National Bank—San Francisco*	
+ Deposits in Bay City N.B. $300		+ Reserves in Fed— San Francisco $300	+ Deposits of Ace $300
− Input $300			

Fed Reserve Bank of San Francisco		*Fed Reserve Bank of Dallas*	
	+ Reserves of Bay City $300	− Deposits in FRB —San Francisco $300	− Reserves of Trinity National Bank $300
	− Deposits of FRB —Dallas $300		

Trinity National Bank—Dallas		*Acme Company (Dallas)*	
− Reserves in FRB —Dallas	− Deposits of Acme Company	− Deposits in Trinity National $300	
		+ Input $300	

member banks in the Fed are all called "reserves"). As we shall see shortly, Bay City may use these new reserves to support loan expansion, or they may (if they are excess reserves) convert them into cash in order to meet currency withdrawals. The important thing to notice at this point is that Bay City is credited with new reserves at the San Francisco Fed, which now holds a check written on a Dallas bank. What happens next?

Federal Reserve Banks, like most commercial banks, hold *interbank deposits*, that is, deposits in other banks. These deposits are held for a variety of reasons and one of them is for check clearance. Thus the Fed Bank of Dallas holds deposits in the Fed Bank of San Francisco. When the San Francisco Fed wants to "collect" on Acme's check, it simply reduces the Dallas Fed's account by $300 and sends Acme's check on to Texas. When Dallas receives the check and puts it through its electronic decoding device, it discovers that a check has been written on one of its member commercial banks, Trinity National. Trinity's reserves, which are a liability to the Dallas Fed, are reduced by $300, and its interbank deposit with the San Francisco Fed (an asset to the Dallas Fed) is reduced by a like amount. The check is sent on to Trinity National in Dallas, which adjusts its balance sheet appropriately by reducing Fed reserves and deposit liabilities to the Acme Company. Acme receives the "cancelled" or "cleared" check in its next monthly statement.[7] The process would be identical for a personal check sent from one individual to another or for any kind of transaction including payment by check. All such transactions are carried out without currency once changing hands, that is, solely through accounting entries.

Access to borrowing from the Fed and use of the Fed's clearing house function have been among the chief benefits of belonging to the Fed system. The Fed also supplies its members with a great deal of information on money and credit markets. But there were significant costs to membership as well. Member banks and other financial institutions must conform to many Fed-defined standards of operation and conduct, chief of which is the maintenance of a required reserve against deposit liabilities.[8] These reserves limit the extent to which banks and financial institutions may lend and earn interest, and thereby limit the profitability of banks and other financial intermediaries. Since most state bank reserve requirements are considerably lower, many state banks (which, prior to 1980, constituted 60% of all banks in charge of 25% of banking resources), chose to remain outside the Federal Reserve System. Whether these "maverick" banks posed serious problems for Fed monetary control is not resolved, but in 1980, in an "omnibus" Banking Act, the Federal Reserve gained control over all financial institutions that issue "checkable deposits." Benefits and costs to all institutions are being equalized so that the very distinction between members and nonmembers (and, eventually, between banks and nonbanks) is being blurred. These financial system reforms will be detailed in Chapter 12, but we should note here that another aspect of bank regulation has been a major bulkward against financial failures. Again, a brief look at history proves instructive.

THE FDIC AND BANK SAFETY

Although a detailed historical discussion of the role of money in economic fluctuations is postponed to Chapter 16, it is clear from an examination of twentieth-century bank data that the relative health of the banking system is closely related to the business cycle. Federal Reserve bank membership and assets climbed steadily during the post World War I period and through the spectacular boom of the late 1920s, although the number of member banks declined late in the decade. State nonmember banks were not so fortunate, and membership declined by over 5,000 banks from 1920 to 1930. The reduction was due, in small part, to the attraction of Federal Reserve membership. In the main, however, this large number of nonmember bank closings revealed underlying unsoundness in the entire economic system.

The facade of speculation was swept away by the stockmarket collapse of 1929, and the many ingredients of decline—including, some believe, mismanagement at the level of Federal Reserve itself—converged to produce the most severe depression of US history.[9] The effects of the depression on the commercial banking system were immediate, but they were of varying severity on member and nonmember banks. The number of member banks in 1933 fell to 67% of the 1916–1920 average, while total assets of these banks actually increased by 39% of the 1916–1920 average. Nonmember bank membership declined to 42% of the 1916–1920 average, while assets were reduced to 54% of the previous period's average.

The depression-inspired Banking legislation of 1933–1935 was designed to reduce the frequency of bank failures and to strengthen the Banking System. Some important changes wrought by this legislation were an increased governmental supervision of bank holding companies as well as the prohibition of the payment of interest on demand deposits. Although the desirability of the latter change is still being debated, a partial result of these reforms has been a marked reduction in the number of bank failures, which fell from an approximate 9,000 between 1930 and 1933 to about 300 in the 1934–1940 period. Failures have fortunately remained at a low level since that time (20 in the period 1951–1956 and a small number in the 1970s).

The most important depression development in US banking, not unlike the early New York Safety Fund System and various other state systems, was the installment of the Federal Deposit Insurance Corporation. Born of the Banking Act of 1935, FDIC was established as a protective device against losses to small depositors and, in addition, to provide additional supervision and examination of banks subscribing to the insurance. All national and state Federal Reserve banks were required to subscribe. Nonmembers, if approved, could join the system.

The US Treasury and the Federal Reserve Banks pledged the starting capital in the amount of $289 million, which was later retired. Assessments from the insured banks and interest earnings also contribute to the fund, which has developed a sizeable accumulated surplus. Depositors of insured banks have their deposits guaranteed in the event of a bank closing, and the impact of this institution on the confidence and stability of the banking system can hardly be overestimated. Depositors in banks holding well over 99% of all deposits in the banking system in 1980 were covered (only up to $100,000 for each deposit, of course) by deposit insurance.

The FDIC, moreover, is a factor in preventing financial mismanagement through its investigatory function. This safeguard is particularly applicable in regard to the small nonmember state banks, of which over 97% (a mere 253 out of 8,526 nonmembers chose not to join the FDIC) subscribed as of June 1975. Under certain conditions the corporation may also lend to distressed banks as well as provide other preventive functions. In short, the impressive record of the FDIC, as well as the implicit moral obligation of the government to stand ready to back the corporation in crises of the severest magnitude, is closely linked with the relative stability exhibited by our contemporary banking system.

CONCLUSION

The present chapter has dealt with many factual details of the US central and commercial banking systems. Although the important story of the interplay between the Federal Reserve and the commercial banks and other financial intermediaries in creating economic stability remains to be told in Chapter 14 (for recent monetary policy) and Chapter 16 (for a twentieth-century historical account), the present chapter has emphasized the development and present status of banking institutions. Our very brief excursion has underscored (1) the slow-but-ever-changing nature of banking *structures* and (2) the evolution of *functions* within the structure of banking institutions. More than a lender of the last resort, the Fed has taken on the crucial function of helping to orchestrate the stability of the entire US economy through monetary instruments of control. The nature of these instruments and the manner of their implementation are the subjects of Chapter 11.

FOOTNOTES

[1] We reserve a discussion of post-1900 history of the US monetary system until Chapter 16 of this text.

[2] The US Fed was preceded by the Bank of England (1694), the Bank of France (1800), and other central banks.

[3] President Jackson's famous opposition to the Second Bank of the United States originated in a fear that the corporation was gaining power over the public good owing to special privileges granted it by charter. The result was that monopoly-charter restrictions

and entry control began to fade as an element of the corporate form.

[4] At the time of the formation of the Fed there was a bitter fight with New York interests over the location of the Board. The enmity was considerable and may have vexed monetary operations in the 1929–1933 period as control centered in Washington D.C. See Chapter 16 for details on this issue.

[5] The Banking Act of 1935 strengthened the Board of Governors in this manner and, in fact, gave the BOG virtually all control over member commercial banks.

[6] Congress could allow national banks to branch without respect to state laws. If this action were taken, unit bank states would undoubtedly retaliate by permitting state banks the branching privilege. Such action does not seem likely, however.

[7] Note that aggregate member banks reserves are increased temporarily over the period of time it takes to "clear" the check. This is a form of reserve bank credit that is called *float*. In the example above, reserve float is $300 between the time that Bay City National Bank is credited with $300 in reserves and the time that Trinity National in Dallas is debited by $300. This point is brought out again in Chapter 12.

[8] The reader should notice that these required reserves are only part of what we called desired reserves, r^d, in Chapter 9.

[9] Because of the form of inelasticity of the money stock—or to an inability of the central bank to adjust to a rising currency/deposit ratio—the US lender of the last resort took a holiday right along with the commercial banks it was designed to keep open (see Chapter 16).

KEY CONCEPTS

reserve requirements

open market operations

discount rate

"lender of the last resort"

Federal Reserve System

National Banking Act of 1863 (national banking system)

dual banking system

Central Reserve city bank

Reserve city bank

Real Bills Doctrine

Employment Act of 1946

Board of Governors

Federal Reserve districts

Federal Open Market Committee (FOMC)

member banks

Federal Reserve Act of 1913

Depository Institutions Deregulation and Monetary Control Act of 1980

unit banking

bank holding company

interbank deposits

Federal Deposit Insurance Corporation

QUESTIONS FOR DISCUSSION

1. Where is most of the power centered in the Federal Reserve System? Is that by law or by custom?

2. List the major laws surrounding the monetary system in the United States and summarize the primary role and effects of each.

3. Why are central banks established? What was the significance of the National Banking Act of 1863? The Federal Reserve Act?

4. Do you think it would be possible to return to a private banking system? What about a return to passive monetary control? What would be the probable short-run and long-run effects of such a policy change?

CHAPTER 11

INSTRUMENTS OF MONETARY POLICY

In Chapter 10 the details of the US banking system were considered and some of the institutional interconnections between commercial banks, other financial institutions, and the Federal Reserve were analyzed. Before considering institutional aspects of banks and nonbank institutions further in Chapter 12, we concentrate upon the most important means of Federal Reserve management as it has currently evolved—the method (more properly, the methods) of monetary control.

Until recently (March 1980) the Fed's direct monetary control was limited, at least officially, to member banks. But, with the passage of the Monetary Control Act of 1980, the Fed has acquired some direct controls over nonmember banks and other financial institutions as well. "Checkable" accounts at financial institutions, NOW (negotiable order of withdrawal) accounts, and Automatic Transfer from Savings (ATS) accounts at all banks and at savings and loans banks, mutual savings banks and credit unions are now subject (after a "phase-in" period of six to eight years) to Federal Reserve controls. These institutions and the primary financial services they supply and demand will be considered in detail in Chapter 12, but aspects of the Fed's new controls will be discussed in a concluding section of the present chapter.

The primary objective in Chapter 11, however, will be to outline and to analyze the policy instruments through which Fed monetary controls are implemented. Quality and efficacy of Fed controls may be broadened by extending *coverage* of the individual controls (essentially the reserve requirements), as the Monetary Control Act of 1980 has done, but this fact does not alter the *nature* and workings of monetary control instruments themselves.[1] Commercial banks, at least for the present, remain the major institution through which Fed controls are effected and hence they receive the major share of attention in this chapter.

THE MECHANISM OF MONETARY POLICY: A PREVIEW

Before turning to the specific instruments or tools of the Federal Reserve, a brief overview of the chain of events through which monetary policy is conducted may be helpful. A thorough understanding of these matters awaits the following chapters of this book, especially Chapter 14, but a simple statement at this point conceptualizes this important and complex process.

The primary objective of central bank control, though not the only one, is to influence economic aggregates such as output (GNP), employment, and the rate of inflation. Chapters 5 through 8, especially, modeled the factors determining these important economic quantities and a major determinant of changes in these aggregates was "alterations in the money stock." Thus the process of monetary expansion (outlined in Chapter 9), which depends crucially upon the amount of high-powered money (currency and reserves) in the system, is at the heart of monetary policy. We can view the overall picture of monetary policy in the following manner.

MONETARY POLICYMAKERS (Fed's Board of Governors)

POLICY INSTRUMENTS
    Open-Market Operations
    Discount Rate Policy
    Reserve Requirements
    Selective Credit Controls

MONETARY TARGETS AND INDICATORS
    Reserves in the Financial System
    Monetary Aggregates (M-1A; M-1B, etc.)
    Market Interest Rates

ECONOMIC GOALS
    Price Stability
    Full Employment
    Economic Growth
    Balance of Payments

Monetary policymakers, and particularly the Board of Governors of the Federal Reserve System, act through policy instruments (sometimes simply called "credit controls") to attempt, ultimately, to affect employment levels, the rate of inflation, economic growth, and so forth. But there are *intermediate steps* through which these policy goals are affected. The Fed controls tools or instruments, such as open-market operations, discount policy, etc., but they do not directly control the monetary targets such as the money stock. Rather, the Fed attempts to control the money stock through the policy instruments' effects upon *reserves* in the monetary system. Control of the Fed over ultimate economic goals is thus indirect: the Fed uses instruments to affect reserves; the quantity of reserves in the system then can affect the money stock in a desirable manner, and alterations in the money stock (and, perhaps, the interest rate) can affect, say, inflation or unemployment in the economy.

To compound matters, there are time lags between the implementation of instrument changes and their effects. The policymaker's job is a particularly devilish one, since the length of lags are not exactly predictable either between the instrumental policy change and the targeted variable (money supply or interest rates), or between money supply rate changes, say, and the inflation rate. Add to this the fact that economic goals may not be complementary—for example, there *may* be a tradeoff between higher employment rates and higher inflation rates (in the short-run, at least)—and the role and responsibility of monetary controllers become staggering. These important and practical matters are discussed at length in Chapter 14. For now, the more mechanical issues of identifying and analyzing the tools of the Federal Reserve will be considered along with *some* of their effects upon reserves and, most importantly, the money stock.

For many years, the essential intermediate target of Federal Reserve control was interest rates (and especially the Federal Funds rate) through the various instruments of monetary policy.[2] But on October 6, 1979, the Fed announced a policy change to improve control over the various monetary aggregates (M-1A, M-1B, M-2, etc.). This change is significant for it means that the Fed now intends to place greater emphasis upon its day-to-day operations in the supply of bank reserves to the system (especially through open-market operations). As one observer noted: "This action represents both a fundamental change in the focus of monetary policy and a clearer recognition of the link between Federal Reserve actions that affect bank reserves and the monetary aggregates which it seeks to control."[3] Interest rates will not be ignored in the new policy, but the focus will be upon money supply changes as initiated by changes in bank and financial system reserves.

RESERVES: SOME USEFUL CONCEPTS

The money stock is "controlled" by discretionary alterations in member bank and financial system reserves. (For convenience, and unless otherwise noted, we will designate reserves affected by the Federal Reserve as *member bank reserves* (MBR) in spite of the fact that reserves must now be held at nonmember banks and at thrift institutions.) Actually we have already encountered two concepts of reserves in the form of "desired" and "actual" reserves as described in the banking model developed in Chapter 9. In Chapter 9 the commercial bank's major role in the money creating process was to adjust *actual reserves* against deposits held to the level of the bank's desired reserves against demand deposits outstanding. Although we will return to the technical aspects of this operation later in the chapter, recall that every time actual reserves were greater than desired reserves, bank loans and the money supply could be increased.

This simple model must be modified with some real-world facts. As should be apparent from earlier discussions of banking institutions, one of the major features of membership in the Fed system is the requirement that member banks hold reserves in the Fed bank of their district. These reserves are expressed as a percentage of demand and savings/time deposits outstanding at the commercial bank in question. If a member bank acquires $1 in new demand deposits and the required reserve is 15%, 15¢ must be held as a required (sometimes called "legal") cash reserve against the new deposit liability.[4] It is the *excess reserves* upon which the banking system may lend and create new money. Thus the amount of excess reserves in the system is a major factor determining the expansion or restrictiveness of the money stock in the economy. (Shortly we will consider whether excess reserves are a good indicator of the tightness or ease in monetary policy.) Simply put, control of excess reserves of commercial banks is the means by which monetary policy is *operationalized*, and there are several tools with which the quantity of excess reserves are controlled, namely, through changes in (1) the required reserve, (2) the discount rate, and (3) the volume of securities held by the Federal Reserve Banks.

THE FED'S BALANCE SHEET

One of the best ways to get at the overall operation of the Fed as it affects the commercial banking system is to analyze the Fed's consolidated balance sheet. The major assets and liabilities of the Federal Reserve System at the end of February 1980 are summarized in Table 11–1, taken from the *Federal Reserve Bulletin*. A brief examination of these items is in order.

The first three Asset items, gold certificates, cash, and cash items in the process of collection, should be defined. Legally the Fed cannot own gold, and in 1968 all connections between gold and the money stock were officially abandoned. (Today gold may be traded as any other commodity such as shoes on an open market, but the Federal Reserve still values gold certificates at the "official" price.) Prior to 1968, however, the Fed was required to hold a percentage of gold certificates against the System's note and deposit liabilities. Before this time, all gold was held by the US Treasury, which issued gold certificates (akin to warehouse receipts) and sold them to the Fed. Gold drains, chiefly through adverse balance of payments conditions, depleted the US gold stock (the Fed held 16 billion dollars in certificates in 1962), and the connection between gold and Fed liabilities was finally abandoned.

Coin items on the Fed's balance sheet represents all coin and paper money holdings—other than Federal Reserve Notes outstanding—of the System. Gradually all non-Federal Reserve note issues, such as Treasury currency issues, are being retired. These treasury notes represent a miniscule percentage of currency outstanding. The item "Cash in Process of Collection" includes the difference between checks received and checks cleared by the system. As implied in the example of check clearance described in Chapter 10, it takes time to clear a

Table 11-1   Federal Reserve Bank Balance Sheet (Consolidated), February 1980 (Millions of Dollars)

Assets

Gold Certificates		172
Special Drawing Rights Account		2,968
Coin	468	
Cash in Process of Collection		8,906
Earning Assets (Loans and Securities)		
Loans to Member Banks	3,364	
(Discounts and Advances)		
Acceptances	205	
Federal Agency Obligations	8,247	
US Government Securities	115,171	
	126,987	126,987
Bank Premises and Equipment		411
Other Assets		4,003
Total Assets		154,915

Liabilities and Capital Account

Federal Reserve Notes (Outstanding)		109,170
Deposits:		
Member Bank Reserves	31,725	
U.S. Treasury	2,417	
Foreign	450	
Other	733	
	35,325	35,325
Deferred-availability Cash Items		5,752
Other Liabilities and Accrued Dividends		2,106
Total Liabilities		152,353
Capital Accounts (including surplus)		2,562
Total Liabilities and Capital Accounts		154,915

check written on a Dallas bank and deposited in San Francisco. For that period of time (most often a few days) the check will appear on the Fed's bank as "cash items in process of collection."

The most important asset items—that is, those that have a direct impact upon member bank reserves, and thus the money supply—are listed as "earning assets." These items directly affect the reserve position of member banks and will be considered in detail later in this chapter. Loans to member banks may be made by the Fed to commercial banks via "discounts and advances." It is in part through this activity that the Fed performs its function as a lender of last resort. Commercial banks may be allowed to discount commercial paper or notes at a specified rate. More typically, however, loans to commercial banks are secured by putting up government securities as collateral. The Fed stands ready under these provisions to lend in emergencies, but traditionally the Fed has refused to become a limitless source of funds for commercial banks. The commercial banks have at times, but not recently, considered it something of an embarrassment to be forced to use the discounting privilege. An increase in loans to commercial banks causes an increase in member bank reserves and vice versa.

Far and away the largest item on the Fed's list of assets is US government securities. At the end of February 1980 the Fed held 115 billion dollars plus of this asset, which is traded on the open market. (The buying and selling of securities is called open-market operations.) Principally these securities have been acquired by Fed purchases from the US Treasury, which often utilizes them to finance debt and deficit operations. Increased holdings of these securities by the Fed via either purchases of new Treasury bonds or purchases on the open market, will increase member bank reserves, whereas reductions will decrease them. Lumped together, the loan and securities accounts are often called *reserve bank credit*, with increases (decreases) connoting an increase (decrease) in member bank reserves.

The major liabilities of the Fed Bank are composed of Federal Reserve Notes and Deposits held by the member banks, by the Treasury, and by foreign countries. The Federal Reserve Note Liability (the largest one) is self-explanatory. It represents all holdings of Federal Reserve notes outside the Fed Banks.

Member bank reserves are the second largest liability on the Fed's balance sheet. Both commercial bank deposits at the Fed and commercial banks' vault cash (since 1958) may count as reserves. These reserves—any excess of which may be instantly converted into currency—stand as the legal requirement against demand deposits. Importantly, it is on the basis of *excess reserves* that commercial banks can create money.

Other deposit liabilities are those held in the Fed by the US Treasury, which often uses the Fed as well as other banks as its checking account keeper, and by foreign countries. Deferred availability cash items are related to the asset "cash items in the process of collection" and to float. When banks present a check for collection, a period of time (several days) elapses before the check is "collected." Usually it takes the Fed longer than the deferred period to collect cash. This delay gives rise to what is called *float*. Float, which is clearly a form of Federal Reserve Bank Credit since it increases bank reserves (if only temporarily), is the difference between "cash items in process of collection" (what the Fed has not collected) and deferred availability cash items (credit that has been temporarily deferred).[5] An increase in deferred availability cash or in any of the liability items, except member bank reserves themselves, will tend to decrease member bank reserves and the money supply. But this notion should be treated more formally.

MEMBER BANK RESERVES: DEFINITIONS

Member Bank Reserves and Reserve Bank Credit are so important in assessing overall monetary conditions that they are presented (in weekly and monthly form) in the *Federal Reserve Bulletin*. In fact, the Fed's format for computing MBR utilizes the so-called "reserve equation" that expresses reserves as the difference between "factors supplying reserve funds" and "factors absorbing reserve funds." Sources of funds to the commercial banks are those "factors supplying reserve funds" and competing uses of funds to the commercial banks comprise those factors absorbing reserve funds. Expressions for MBR can be viewed, alternatively and equivalently, as follows:

MBR = Assets of Fed minus Liabilities of Fed (except MBR), or

MBR = Factors Supplying Reserves minus Factors Absorbing Reserve Funds, or

MBR = Sources of Commercial Bank Reserve Funds minus Competing Uses of Reserve Funds.

A "source of funds" is defined as any item of which an *increase* causes an increase in MBR, whereas a "use of funds" is any item of which an increase causes a decrease in MBR. Sources of funds are composed of (1) the sum of government securities held by the Fed and loans to commercial banks plus float and other assets; (2) the gold stock and Treasury Currency Outstanding; and (3) foreign and treasury deposits at the Fed and other Fed assets. Special Drawing Rights (SDRs) are a special kind of international reserve created by the International Monetary Fund in 1967 to supplement overall money reserves of IMF participants. (The function of these deposits will be treated in Chapter 15.) Unless the effect is "neutralized" by the Fed, an increase in any of these sources of funds will increase member bank reserves, which, along with currency, are a component of high-powered money.

Uses of funds, those factors that absorb funds in the monetary system, include: (1) currency in circulation (except vault cash); (2) treasury cash holdings; (3) treasury, foreign, and deposits other than member bank reserves held at the Fed; and (4) other Fed liabilities plus the Capital Accounts. An increase in any of these items indicates a reduction in member bank reserves.

Table 11-2 provides a summary of these factors affecting member bank reserves for February 1980 (based on monthly average of daily figures). The major source item is reserve bank credit outstanding, which is comprised of securities, loans, float, and other assets. Changes in reserve bank credit are often taken as a barometer of changes in member bank reserves. A repatriation of treasury currency—cash issued historically by the Treasury—would also in-

Table 11-2   Factors Affecting Member Bank Reserves (February 1980, Millions of Dollars)

Supplying Reserve Funds		Absorbing Reserve Funds	
Reserve Bank Credit	135,485	Currency in Circulation	121,591
US Government Securities	115,028	Treasury Cash Holding	477
Loan and Acceptances	1,722	Deposits (Treasury, Foreign,	
Float	5,617	and Other)	3,379
Federal Agency Securities	4,818		
Other Fed Assets	8,299		
		Other Fed Liabilities and	
		Capital Accounts	4,713
Gold Stock	11,172		
Special Drawing Rights Accounts	2,968		
Treasury Currency Outstanding	13,059	Member Bank Reserves	31,878

Note: Monthly averages of daily figures.
Source: Federal Reserve Bulletin.

crease MBRs, as would increases in the gold stock; but these occur slowly, having negligible effects on reserves, and are often "neutralized" by Fed policies. Currency in circulation is far and away the major factor absorbing reserve funds. Other things being equal, as noted in Chapter 9, an increased demand for currency to demand deposits on the part of the public will decrease member bank reserves.

The information in Table 11-2 shows actual values of the factors that determined or generated some 31 billion dollars in member bank reserves in February 1980. Before turning to a detailed analysis of the Fed's controls over these bank reserves (which give it actual control over the supply of high-powered money—currency *plus* bank reserves—in the system), let us consider two additional items.

Uncontrolled Reserve Changes. We should remember that the Federal Reserve has discretionary control over only some of the items in its balance sheet, that is, *over only those items composing reserve bank credit.* The many factors exogenous to Fed control, such as currency in circulation, shifts in international deposits or Treasury operations (tax collections or disbursements), could hamper the Fed's control over reserves, and the Fed must account for them in its control over the volume of bank reserves.

Figure 11-1, as an example, depicts the effects of tax payments upon member bank reserves. Ordinarily the public pays taxes through withholdings from current income, but the effects insofar as reserves go are the same as writing a check on one's commercial bank. The public's deposits are reduced by the amount of the tax, whereas the Treasury's deposits at the Fed are increased by the same amount. The Fed merely increases one liability (Treasury deposits) and reduces another (commercial bank reserve deposits). With a

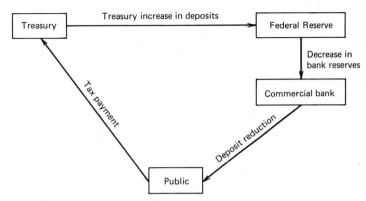

Figure 11-1. Treasury taxation.

reduction in reserves, the banking system's ability to lend has been reduced. Government expenditures on goods and services have the opposite effect on member bank reserves and on the public's deposits in commercial banks, so that any Federal government deficit or surplus could have a profound impact upon the reserve position of banks. Such changes in the exogeneous factors affecting MBR's make monetary policy an intricate art.

FEDERAL RESERVE CREDIT CONTROLS

Though "unplanned" or inexactly predictable factors can affect member bank reserves, the Fed has discretionary powers that constitute a mightly arsenal in the control of reserves and the money stock. Principally, these controls can affect either the stock of reserves (high-powered money) or the "powerfulness" of a given stock of bank reserves or both. The stock of reserves is altered chiefly through open-market operations (securities transactions) and via discount rate policy, and the degree of "powerfulness" of a given quantity bank reserves is changed by alterations in the legal reserve ratio. Each of these mechanisms will be investigated in detail before they are built into the model developed in Chapter 9.

OPEN MARKET OPERATIONS

Securities transactions—buying and selling bonds on the open market—is the most important and flexible tool of monetary policy. The Federal Open Market Committee (see Figure 10-1) is responsible for the conduct of open-market operations to affect reserves on a day-to-day basis. Depending on a wide array· of factors, such as (1) GNP, (2) unemployment, (3) the money stock and the rate of inflation, (4) interest rates, (5) the Treasury deficit to be financed, (6) balance of payments situation, and (7) the size of excess reserves and borrowings from the Fed, the FOMC makes policy decisions. These decisions are transmitted to the Account Manager, an officer of the Federal Reserve Bank of New York. This person controls the "Open Market Desk" of the New York Fed and operates directly with securities on Wall Street.

Until October 1979, explicit targets for the money supply were a central feature of monetary policy as directed by the FOMC, but the day-to-day operational guide to meet these targets was the Federal Funds rate. Because of rapid changes in the rate of inflation in the 1970s, short-term interest rates (depending, in part, on the demand for cash balances) became less predictable. In late 1979 basic operating procedures changed so that *reserves* in the banking system will be the day-to-day guide in controlling the supply of deposits and money. Formerly the Account Manager at the New York Fed was given a narrow target range for the Federal Funds rate by the FOMC and a wide range for monetary aggregates. Now this situation is reversed. Instructions are now more specific about bank reserves and monetary aggregates.

An example will help clarify the role of the FOMC in controlling reserves. Suppose the economy enters a mild recession—that is, industrial production and employment decline, and excess reserves of commercial banks are at a minimum. What should the Fed do? At such a time the Fed would wish to *increase* monetary aggregates, for example, the money stock. Given the theoretical analysis of Chapters 5 and 6 we should expect to see an increase in business loans, business activity, and employment "following" an increase in the money stock.

While some of the possible pitfalls of monetary policy between execution and result will be discussed in Chapter 14, it is important to understand fully how basic monetary expansion takes place. Essentially, the FOMC directed its Account Manager to "loosen up" on the quantity of money and excess reserves. The result is accomplished by the Federal Reserve's going into the open market and buying government securities. The mechanics of the effects on member bank reserves when the Fed buys government securities may be explained with simple T-accounts.

Although the Fed buys and sells through certain New York securities dealers, the mechanism can be viewed more simply if we assume that transactions occur directly with commercial banks and the nonbank public. (The Fed, of course, also buys securities from the Treasury to finance government expenditures and deficits, a practice that will ordinarily increase member bank reserves as well as prices at the grocery store.) First let us assume that the Federal Reserve buys 10 million in securities from the commercial banks. Reflecting only changes in the *relevant* T-accounts, Table 11–3 shows the commercial banks gain 10 million dollars in reserve assets and lose 10 million in government securities. The Fed obviously gains securities assets and new

Table 11-3   The Fed Buys Securities from Commercial Banks

Commercial Banks				Federal Reserve			
Assets		Liabilities and Capital		Assets		Liabilities and Capital	
(−) Securities	10			(+) Securities	10	(+) Reserves	10
(+) Reserves	10						

reserve liabilities in the amount of 10 million dollars. The important point is that excess reserves, the basis for making loans to individuals and businesses, have grown by 10 million dollars. In other words, the stock of high-powered money has risen as indicated in Table 11-3. Given that consumers and investors will respond instantly to lower interest rates (caused by an increase in the supply of loanable funds), the money stock will increase as will output and employment.

A second group from which the Fed may buy securities in times of an economic downturn is the public. In this case, contrary to the one described above, the money supply—or the demand deposit component of it—will increase immediately. As the T-accounts of Table 11-4 show, the public gains commercial bank demand deposits from the sale of securities, whereas commercial banks gain cash reserves at the Fed of 10 million dollars. In both of the cases described, the quantity of high-powered money ("H" of Chapter 9) has increased in the system. Depending upon the proportion of currency to demand deposits desired by the public as well as upon the required reserve percentage, the money supply might increase.[6]

Some idea of the volume and the maturity distribution of government

Table 11-4   The Fed Buys Securities from the Public

Public				Commercial Banks			
Assets		Liabilities and Capital		Assets		Liabilities and Capital	
(−) Securities	10			(+) Reserves	10	(+) Demand deposits	10
(+) Demand deposits	10						

Federal Reserve			
Assets		Liabilities and Capital	
(+) Securities	10	(+) Reserves	10

securities traded can be obtained by an examination of Table 11–5, which summarizes Fed open market transactions on an *annual* basis from 1975 to 1979. Most of the action of the Federal Reserve open-market account is in government securities as opposed to Federal Agency obligations and bankers acceptances and in short-term Treasury bills (less than a year maturity) as opposed to longer-term obligations.

The policy intent, that is, tightness or ease, of the Federal Reserve in open market operations is difficult to discern with annualized data. Indeed, open market operations have not traditionally been used as a tool to counteract large swings in economic activity but, rather, have been primarily employed as a "fine-tuning" day-to-day or month-to-month device. However, the gross purchases of securities have increased dramatically over the decade of the 1970s. Gross purchases of securities increased from about 10 billion dollars annually in 1972 (not shown in Table 11–5) to 24.5 billion in 1978, falling to about 23 billion in 1979. The overall effect has been to increase bank reserves and the stock of high-powered money, including currency in the hands of the public. (Whether this gross expansion in reserves and the money stock had any effect on the inflationary 1970s will be discussed in Chapter 14.)

The Federal Reserve's open market policy intentions comes into better focus when shorter time periods are analyzed. Table 11–6 presents monthly changes in open-market operations, bank reserves, and two alternative measures of the money stock from October 1979 to March 1980. High rates of inflation characterized the economy of the 1970s, but after a moderation in the rate of increase in 1977 prices began to rise dramatically in 1978 and 1979, reaching

Table 11–5 Selected Federal Reserve Open Market Transactions (Millions of Dollars), 1975–1979

Type of Transaction	1975	1976	1977	1978	1979
US GOVERNMENT SECURITIES					
Outright transactions (excluding matched sale-purchase transactions)					
Treasury bills:					
Gross purchases	11,562	14,343	13,738	16,628	16,623
Gross sales	5,599	8,462	7,241	13,725	7,480
Redemptions	6,431	5,017	2,136	2,033	2,900
All maturities:					
Gross purchases	21,313	19,707	20,898	24,591	22,950
Gross sales	5,599	8,639	7,241	13,725	7,480
Redemptions	9,980	5,017	4,636	2,033	5,500
Net change in Federal Agency obligations	978	882	1,383	−426	681
Total net change in System Open Market Account	8,539	9,833	7,143	7,743	6,896

Source: Federal Reserve Bulletin.

double-digit proportions in the second quarter of 1978. The Fed followed "stop and go" policies over much of the period, but during 1979 it began a concerted restrictive policy of monetary restraint. The open-market account data of Table 11–6 reflect these changes, showing net sales of securities in all but two months of the six-month period. Reserves grew very slowly and showed a slight decline in February. M-1A, currency outside banks plus demand deposits, held fast over the period, actually declining in March. M-1B—which includes NOW, ATS accounts at thrift institutions, credit union share drafts, and demand deposit accounts at mutual savings banks *plus* M-1A—grew by 24 billion dollars over the period. The latter may reflect a shifting from noninterest-bearing demand deposits to other interest-bearing types as these accounts become more widespread with Federal Reserve authorization. (ATS and NOW accounts were authorized in New York state in November 1978 and authorized nationwide in March 1980.) Although other factors might explain the monetary slowdown and great caution must be exercised in reasoning from cause to effect, it appears that the Fed's open market policies acted to retard inflationary growth over the period covered in Table 11–6.[7]

Two issues remain concerning the conduct of open market operations. How does the Fed buy and sell securities at will with commercial banks and the public? The answer is simply "supply and demand." When the Fed places a large order for government securities, there is, in effect, a large increase in demand for securities in certain maturity classes. *The price of these securities rises.* Given that the price of a security is inversely related to the interest rate, two things happen when the Fed enters the market. First, banks or the public might realize a capital gain by selling and, secondly, the yield from *holding* the bond to maturity declines with the interest rate. In order to maximize profits, the holders (commercial bank or public) of bonds will sell.[8] The Federal Reserve is able to negotiate successfully in the open market in this manner.

Table 11–6 Open Market Operations, Bank Reserves, and Alternative–Money Stock Measures (October 1970–March 1980)

	Total Net Change in System Accounts (Millions of Dollars)	*Member Bank Reserves (Billions of Dollars)*	*Money Stock (Billions of Dollars)*	
			M-1A	*M-1B*
October	−2,658	42.19	368	384
November	4,376	43.07	369	385
December	679	43.51	371	387
January	−2,345	43.51	372	389
February	−903	43.40	376	392
March	1,497	43.74	375	392

Source: Federal Reserve Bulletin.

A second minor point concerns interest earnings on bonds held by the Fed. Congress allows the Fed to earn income and, with interest-bearing assets, the Fed has been able to support itself and its operations. Any "excess" yearly income of this quasipublic institution is remitted to the US Treasury, which may use it to pay off debt or perhaps to increase government spending. Interest-earning assets of the Fed are not limited to securities, of course, which brings us to another major credit control—loans to commercial banks.

DISCOUNT RATE POLICY

When loads are made to commercial banks, bank reserves immediately increase. Thus "discounts" of various types of tradable paper, along with Fed security holdings, constitute a form of reserve bank credit. The *discount rate* is the percentage rate at which specified kinds of securities, notes, and loans in effect may be exchanged by commercial banks for additional reserves. Again, the simple effects can be discribed with T-accounts. This time, suppose that commercial banks are desirous of holding excess reserves perhaps because of an anticipated seasonal cash drain, or assume that banks have (temporarily) fallen below the legal reserve requirement. The T-accounts of Table 11–7 show that the implementation of a new 10 million dollar loan is accomplished by the creation of 10 million in bank reserves. If a bank has fallen below the legal requirement and if this is the reason for the loan, the bank will have time (ordinarily two weeks) to adjust its portfolio in order again to meet the required reserve.

Discounting was established as a principal role of the Fed ("lender of last resort") in the original Act of 1913, but it evolved as a tool of "activist" monetary policy control. Lending via the "discount window" is controlled by the Fed in several ways: (1) the Fed sets the rate or rates (technically the *rediscount* rate since borrowers have already *discounted* the commercial paper) at which commercial banks and others may borrow; (2) the Fed establishes the kind of collateral (mortgages, government securities, and so forth) that it will accept to support the loan, and rates differ according to both type of collateral and nature of the borrower; (3) the Fed has the option to lend or not to lend. Thus the *four discount* rates on April 30, 1980, ranged from 13% (the "loan rate" to *member banks* against collateral of high grade commercial paper or US

Table 11–7　The Fed Lends to Commercial Banks

Commercial Banks		Federal Reserve Bank	
(+) Reserves　10	(+) Due Fed res　10	(+) Loans　10	(+) Member bank reserves　10

government obligations) to 16% (the rate applicable to all other borrowers against US securities or US government granted securities).

The discounting process is initiated by member banks and other borrowers but it is a privilege and not a right. The Federal Reserve discourages continuous borrowing by commercial banks when such borrowing is for the purpose of meeting the legal reserve requirements. Rates are set by district banks with the approval of the Board of Governors and, though they may differ slightly between Fed districts, rates tend to follow those set by the Federal Reserve Bank of New York. Table 11–8 presents a summary of discount rates at the New York Fed between 1970 and April 1980 on high-grade paper discounted by member banks. Changes have, at times, been fairly frequent with rates ranging from 4.5% in late 1971 to 13% in April of 1980. Some rate changes may be related to some alterations in economic conditions. It is often unclear whether the rate leads or follows business cycle fluctuations or whether it acts to reinforce other tools of monetary policy.

Up until late 1979 and early 1980 one of the largest single jumps in the rate—a full 1% increase—occurred on November 1, 1978. It was an attempt to save the besieged dollar on international markets where its value in terms of other currencies was falling because of inflationary pressures in the United States and other factors. Additional changes may not be so clearly related to economic events.

A look at the reserves and borrowings of member banks also proves instructive. Table 11–9 presents *annual* figures on reserves and loans to member banks from 1967 to 1978 plus *monthly* data between October 1979 and March 1980. On an annual basis, fairly wide fluctuations in member borrowing between 1967 and 1978 can be noticed with 1.3 billion dollars in reserves borrowed in 1973 and 107 million dollars loaned by the Fed in 1971. But look again at Table 11–8. A reduction in the discount rate does not necessarily mean an increase in member bank borrowings and an increase may be accompanied by high loan demand. Between December 1970 and December 1971 the rate fell by one whole percentage point, but borrowings were at a 10-year low in 1971. Likewise the discount rate rose by $2\frac{1}{2}$% over 1973 (from 5 to $7\frac{1}{2}$%) while borrowing reached 1.3 billion dollars over that year.

The key to analyzing these situations lies, in part, in the fact that commercial banks are profit-maximizing institutions. Just as individuals will borrow from banks if the interest payment is less than the interest they may receive on investments, so commercial banks will borrow from the Fed when the rate that they receive in the market sufficiently exceeds the discount rate, that is, when the *spread* becomes profitable. Indeed, as profit-maximizing firms, commercial banks are *expected*, other things equal, to borrow in markets where interest rates are lowest; however, as suggested above, the Fed may (ultimately) discourage such borrowing.

Table 11-8   Federal Reserve Bank Interest Rates—Summary of Changes (1970-1980)

Effective Date	Federal Reserve Bank of New York	Effective Date	Federal Reserve Bank of New York
In effect Dec. 31, 1970	5½		
1971—Jan. 8	5¼	1976—Jan. 19	5½
15	5¼	23	5½
19	5¼	Nov. 22	5¼
22	5	26	5¼
29	5	1977—Aug. 30	5¼
Feb. 13	5	31	5¾
19	4¾	Sept. 2	5¾
July 16	5	Oct. 26	6
23	5		
Nov. 11	5	1978—Jan. 9	6½
19	4¾	20	6½
Dec. 13	4¾	May 11	7
17	4½	12	7
24	4½	July 3	7¼
		10	7¼
1973—Jan. 15	5	Aug. 21	7¾
Feb. 26	5½	Sept. 22	8
Mar. 2	5½	Oct. 16	8½
Apr. 23	5½	20	8½
		Nov. 1	9½
1973—May 4	5¾	3	9½
11	6		
18	6	1979—July 20	10
June 11	6½	Aug. 17	10½
15	6½	20	10½
July 2	7	Sept. 19	11
Aug. 14	7½	21	11
23	7½	Oct. 8	12
		10	12
1974—Apr. 25	8		
30	8	1980—Feb. 15	13
Dec. 9	7¾	19	13
16	7¾	In effect April 30	13
1975—Jan. 6	7¾		
10	7¼		
24	7¼		
Feb. 5	6¾		
7	6¾		
Mar. 10	6¼		
14	6¼		
May 16	6		
23	6		

Source: Federal Reserve Bulletin.

Table 11-9 Reserves and Borrowings of All Member Banks (Selected Periods 1967-1980, in Millions of Dollars)

Period		All Member Banks				
		Reserves			Borrowings	
		Total Held	Required	Excess	Total	Seasonal
1967		25,260	24,915	345	238	—
1968		27,221	26,766	455	765	—
1969		28,031	27,774	257	1,086	—
1970		29,265	28,993	272	321	—
1971		31,329	31,164	165	107	—
1972		31,353	31,134	219	1,049	—
1973		35,068	34,806	262	1,298	41
1974		36,941	36,602	339	703	32
1975		34,989	34,727	262	127	13
1976						
1977		36,471	36,297	174	558	54
1978		41,572	41,447	125	874	134
1979	(Oct.)[a]	42,279	42,007	272	2,022	161
	(Nov.)	42,908	42,753	155	1,906	146
	(Dec.)	43,972	43,578	394	1,473	82
1980	(Jan.)	45,170	44,928	242	1,241	75
	(Feb.)	43,156	42,966	190	1,655	96
	(Mar.)	43,352	42,907	445	2,828	152

[a]Monthly data not seasonalized.

Source: Federal Reserve Bulletin.

As with open market operations, a look at monthly data proves instructive. Consider the reserve picture (Table 11-9) and borrowing over the period October 1979 through March 1980, a fairly clear period of monetary restraint. The prime rate of interest, that is, the rate charged by banks on highest quantity short-term business loans, remained (on average about 11.75 percent from January 1979 through August of that year). But Table 11-10 shows what happened from August 1979 through April 1980. Business activity and, specifically, loan demands in the commercial banking and financial system—together with earlier "tightness" in monetary policy and actual inflation and inflationary expectations—created a rise in prime rates by almost 8 percent between August 1979 and April 1980. (The rate fell dramatically in May.) To help stem the inflation and, perhaps, to bridge the spread between the discount and prime rates, the Fed continued upward pressure on discount rates, but at a more dramatic pace and in bigger amounts. On September 19, 1979,

Table 11-10 *Prime Rate Charged by Banks on Short-Term Business Loans (August 1979–May 1980, Percent per Annum)*

Month	Average Rate	Month	Average Rate
August (1979)	11.91	January (1980)	15.25
September	12.90	February	15.63
October	14.39	March	18.31
November	15.55	April	19.77
December	15.30	May	16.57

the rate was increased one-half of one percent and on October 8, 1979, and again on February 15, 1980, the Fed raised the discount rate by one full percentage point.

Borrowing from the Fed over this period continued unabated as Table 11-9 reveals, reaching very high levels. The Fed was probably responding to higher market rates in raising discount rates, but market rates were rising more quickly, too quickly to make borrowing from the Fed unattractive. Another possible factor concerned conditions in the Federal Funds market—a rapidly growing market in which banks (and others) supply and demand temporary funds (often for one day). The Federal Funds market is often a source of reserve funds for banks, especially over high periods of loan demand, but over the period October 1979 and March 1980 the rate of interest on Federal Funds *exceeded* that obtainable at the discount window on loans with prime collateral.

Did the Fed use discount policy to tighten reserve, loan, and money expansion over the period? The volume of borrowing over the period would not seem to indicate this, but monetary policy is an intricate affair. Clearly, the volume of loans to commercial banks over the period would have been larger without large increases in the discount rate. But a more fundamental point is that the Fed often utilizes more than one tool to control reserves, money aggregates, and economic activity. We have seen that vigorous open market operations *accompanied* changes in the discount rate. These combined policies were apparently sufficient to severely restrict growth in reserves and in M-1A (see Table 11-6).

Thus discount rate policy is certainly an arm of overall Federal Reserve control, but it has been used relatively sparsely in controlling severe cyclical swings in business activity. Consideration of a brief period of monetary policy suggests that open market operations (the most important day-to-day tool of the Fed) were the "choice" tool of the Fed in controlling reserves and monetary aggregates, with an assist from discount rate policy. Use of one policy tool does not preclude use of others, and this fact makes Fed policy detection difficult. The Fed's decision (October 1979) to focus on money supply measures, moreover, might mean that interest rate targets are actually giving way to reserves and the money aggregates as the (intermediate) objects of monetary policy. Both open market operations and the discount rate policy affect excess reserves and high-powered money and both will continue to be used to implement monetary policy.

RESERVE REQUIREMENTS: CHANGING THE POWER
OF HIGH-POWERED MONEY

Reserve requirement changes are a third important tool in monetary control. The Federal Reserve's alteration of the legal reserve requirement is of dual importance to the banking and monetary system. Such an alteration not only produces once and for all changes in the *stock* of bank excess reserves, but makes high-powered money either more or less "high-powered." This mechanism can be easily verified if we recall equation [9.4] from Chapter 9, which is reproduced again as equation [11.1].

$$M = H \; \frac{1+c}{c+r} = \frac{H+cH}{c+r} \qquad [11.1]$$

Here the stock of money is seen to be dependent on H, the stock of high-powered money, c, the currency-deposit ratio, and r, the reserve-deposit ratio. Given the same stock of high-powered money, a reduction in r, which we now interpret as a required or legal reserve ratio, would clearly reduce the value of the denominator $(c + r)$ and increase M. Likewise, an increase in r would decrease M, the money stock. Thus a reduction in the legal reserve requirement "frees up" a greater quantity of excess reserves out of a given stock of high-powered money. The money stock, therefore, may increase for two reasons: because r declines and because excess reserves out of a given quantity of reserves held by the banking system. The quantity of high-powered money does not change with a lowering of r, but its ability to support an increased stock of money has.

What of the actual levels of reserve requirements? Table 11–11 summarizes past and current reserve requirements of member banks. Under the National Banking Act of 1863 statutory requirements were relatively high at 25% for large banks. Under the Federal Reserve Act of 1913 legal reserves were considerably lower, although the distinctions between "reserve bank cities," "reserve cities," and "county banks" were preserved. (Banks were originally classified by size of the city in which they operated.) Between 1917 and 1936, statutory requirements were fixed at even lower levels than those of 1913. Over this period, the "powerfulness" of high-powered money was also fixed. A banking act passed in the midst of the Great Depression gave the Federal Reserve power to alter reserve requirements. In effect, this gave the Fed a discretionary countercyclical tool for affecting economic conditions within statutory limits (currently at 10% minimum and 22% maxi-

Table 11–11 *Reserve Requirements for National and Federal Reserve Banks*

Type of Deposit	National Banking Act of 1863	Federal Reserve Act of 1913	Amendment of 1917	1971	February 1976	April 1980
Demand deposits						
Central Reserve cities	25%	18%	13%	—	—	—
Reserve cities[a]	25%	15%	10%	17% first $5 million, plus 17.5% over $5 million	7.5% first $2 million, plus 10% next $8 million, plus	7% first $2 million, plus 9.5% next $8 million, plus
Country	15%	12%	7%	12.5% first $5 million, plus 13% over $5 million	12% next $90 million, plus 13% next $300 million, plus 16.5% over $400 million	11.75% next $90 million, plus 12.25% next $300 million, plus 16.25% over $400 million
Savings deposits[b]	Same as demand	5%	3%	3%	3%	3%
Time deposits				3% first $5 million, plus 5% over $5 million	3% first $5 million, plus 6% over $5 million	3% first $5 million, plus 6% over $5 million[c]

[a]Effective November 9, 1972, reserve cities were redefined. A bank having net demand deposits of more than $400 million is considered to be a reserve city bank and the location of the head office of such a bank is designated as a reserve city. Also cities containing a Federal Reserve office are defined as reserve cities.

[b]Effective January 5, 1967, time deposits open account, such as Christmas and vacation club accounts, became subject to the same reserve requirements as savings deposits.

[c]Savings deposits maturing in 180 days and over carry lower reserve requirements.

Source: *Federal Reserve Bulletin* and Federal Reserve Bank of Kansas City, *Monthly Review* (April 1974).

mum for reserve city banks). Clearly, a lowering of the reserve ratio increases the availability of excess (lendable) reserves to member banks while raising them reduces the quantity of excess reserves. But, more importantly, a legal reserve ratio alteration changes the amount of deposits that a given quantity of high-powered money will support.

Since 1936 the reserve requirement has been changed often (about 60 or so times) reaching a high of 26% (for central reserve city banks) in 1937, 1941, and again in 1948. Since 1948, however, reserve requirements for all classes of banks have in general declined, almost reaching their 1917 levels. Indeed, as the notes to Table 11–11 indicate, the classification of banks as "city" and "country" has no more meaning, since uniform percentage of deposit requirements apply to all banks, large or small.

How do member banks react to reserve requirements? Without doubt, alteration of reserve requirements is the most powerful tool of monetary policy. An alteration, say an increase, of $\frac{1}{4}$ or $\frac{1}{2}$ of one percent in the requirement—especially when banks are loaned up—can cause a reduction of several billions of dollars in loans and a severe "credit crunch." Obviously the impact of reserve requirement changes will vary from region to region and from bank to bank depending upon the reserve situation of the locale or the bank. Thus the impact of an alteration may not be so easily predictable.

Minute variations of the requirement are not practiced since portfolio adjustments over the entire banking system are very costly. Small changes in bank reserves producing moderate tightness or moderate ease in the money and capital markets are much more easily and efficiently produced by open-market operations. Alterations in reserve requirements are not really suitable, in other words, for "fine tuning" on a day-to-day or week-to-week basis, but they may be of great value in inducing large changes in bank reserves. We can safely surmise that reserve requirement changes will be used far less than any other major credit control and, barring an economic catastrophe, they will likely only move in a downward direction.

THE MARGIN REQUIREMENT

At various times in the past, usually in wartime situations, the Fed has been given temporary authority by the Congress over certain areas such as terms of credit on consumer durables and mortgage credit. These controls are regarded as affecting selected areas of credit and not overall conditions (hence "selective controls"). For example, between 1941 and 1947, and again during the Korean conflict, the Fed helped suppress consumer spending by specifying an increased amount of downpayment on consumer durables together with a reduced period for which such credit could be extended. The result was a (temporary) curb on inflation, an increase in savings, and a reallocation of materials and labor to the war effort.

The Fed does not especially like having such powers, however, since they affect particular markets selectively and therefore hint of discrimination. (Consider the protest from the construction industries when interest rates and terms are tightened on residential mortgages.) At present, one such official control—the margin requirement—remains in the hands of the Fed.

Born of the speculative binge of the 1920s which spawned pyramiding of collateral and other kinds of questionable bank practices, the Securities and Exchange Act of 1934 prescribed that the Fed be able to specify the downpayment required when borrowing to finance a stock purchase. For example, a margin requirement of 30% means that 30% of the purchase price of a stock must be put down in cash and that 70% may be borrowed from a financial institution. Unlike all other credit controls, the margin requirement of the Fed applies to all lending institutions (not just commercial banks). Presently the rate is 50% on margin stocks, on convertible bonds, and on short sales.

How does the requirement work in practice? Suppose you decide to buy a stock in Fly-by-Night enterprises for $100. Ordinarily you would purchase the stock through a broker who has access to prime rate margin credit at a bank or other lending institution (you would probably pay the prime rate plus 1% transactions cost). Suppose (as is so often the case) that you have bought a loser. As the market price of your stock falls further and further toward $50, say around $58, the broker begins to get nervous. Although the broker exercises considerable discretion, he might at this point "call" for additional margin. If you cannot come up with it, your stock will be forfeited, that is, the broker will sell.

Clearly, the margin requirement is an important control over speculative frenzies in stocks, but the Fed's other powers over monetary variables such as the money stock, interest rates, and bond prices also have profound influences in the market. At high interest rates (low bond prices) bonds and government securities become competing sources of investment. Stock prices and bond prices have, in recent times, followed each other rather closely. A general tightening upon the money stock and credit, moreover, tends to dampen and restrict stock purchases. Although a study of the relation between stock market and monetary aggregates is a specialized issue and would be out of place in a discussion of the major monetary controls of the Fed, it is worth noting that such a correspondence exists and that it appears to be a by-product of the Fed's major functions.

AN ANALYTICAL VIEW OF THE INSTRUMENTS
OF FED CONTROL

The origin, structure, and actual workings of the Federal Reserve System have now been discussed. The Fed influences interest rates, credit, and the money stock and utilizes open market operations and the discount rate to affect the quantity of reserves and high-powered money. Alterations in the reserve requirement, on the other hand, influence not only the quantity of excess reserves held by banks but also the power of a given stock of high-powered money.

With these real-world details in mind, we can interpret the activities of the Fed in terms of the model of money and deposit creation developed in Chapter 9. Two items require preliminary comment. First, the banking system of the United States is composed of a large number of banks, member and nonmember. It is worth remembering that the model we developed in Chapter 9 does not deal with the operations or money creating activities of any bank or set of banks. Rather it deals with the entire banking system as a *monopoly bank.* In the check-clearing model of Chapter 10 deposits and reserves were shifted out of one bank (Trinity National–Dallas) and transferred to another (Bay City National–San Francisco). Deposits and reserves were shifted from one bank to another, but the lending and deposit capacity of the banking system remained unaffected. Thus, the money supply model of Chapter 9 does not pertain to the activities of any individual bank but to the banking system as a whole.

A second definitional point should be recalled. As definition [9.2] revealed, high-powered money is composed of currency in the hands of the public and bank reserves. Thus total reserves of the banking system are composed of vault cash (currency) and reserve deposits held at the Fed. The total amount of reserves in existence determines the level of deposits which the system can support, whereas the amount of excess reserves (total minus the legal amount) determines the amount of additional loans and deposits that can be created or must be destroyed. High-powered money, the *monetary base* of the economy, is composed of reserves plus currency in the hands of the public and banks.

Recall now the model developed in Chapter 9, which we reproduce here as Figure 11–2. The public (money demanders) was said to be in equilibrium at all combinations of M and D which make M equal to $(1 + c^d)D$, where c^d is

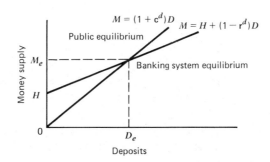

Figure 11–2. Public and bank equilibrium again.

the *desired* currency-deposit ratio. When the desired currency-deposit ratio does not match the actual ratio, forces are at work to return the public to a point on the "public equilibrium" function (see Figure 9–4 and the discussion of the system's dynamics). Similarly, banks are in equilibrium at all combinations of M and D which make M equal to $H + (1 - r^d)D$, where H is the stock of high-powered money and where r^d is the desired reserve ratio. But the desired ratio of reserves to deposits may differ, as in our previous interpretation, from the actual ratio. In this case, the banking system (note that in Figure 11–2 the monopoly bank equilibrium function of Chapter 9 is relabeled) will tend to return to equilibrium, given that the forces described in Chapter 9 are at work.

Something must certainly be said of our concept of high-powered money and of desired reserves. In Chapter 9 the monopoly bank was assumed to be a completely independent agency operating in a totally integrated community. There was no Federal Reserve System in our simplified treatment. Thus, we were unable to explain adequately several crucial points. Specifically, we could not explain where high-powered money came from in the first place. We simply assumed that the public was in possession of 1,000 dollars in high-powered money (currency). As discussed in the present chapter, high-powered money is injected or withdrawn from the system by the Fed, and that fact will be accounted for in a modified model.

The simple and crude concept of "desired reserves" no longer makes much sense by itself. Why did the monopoly banker desire to hold a certain portion of demand deposit liabilities in the form of cash reserves? Ostensibly, the monopoly banker wished always to be able to honor the "instant repurchase clause." This is certainly the same reason why commercial bankers today keep quantities of vault cash on hand (of course, proportions vary depending upon proximity to cash supplies). A review of the conditions for Fed membership also revealed that member banks must hold a *legally specified proportion* of their deposit liabilities in the form of cash reserves. Thus the concept of "desired reserves" must now be understood in a broader context to include both the legal reserve ratio plus any additional amount of reserves that banks may wish to hold for use in honoring the "instant repurchase clause."

CHANGING THE STOCK OF HIGH-POWERED (H):
OPEN MARKET OPERATIONS AND THE DISCOUNT RATE

How might an increase in the stock of high-powered money engendered by a purchase of government securities or by a lowering of the discount rate be viewed? In terms of the static model developed in Chapter 9 it is a simple matter to describe the result of a change in either of these instruments. As shown in Figure 11–3, the "bank equilibrium function" shifts upward by the amount of the increase in H. Naturally we must assume that the desired reserve

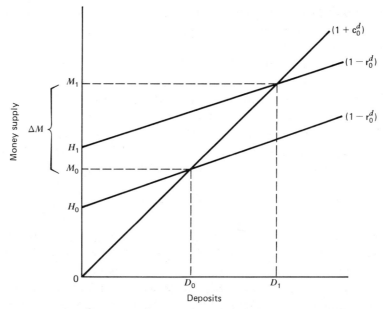

Figure 11-3. A change in the stock of high-powered money.

ratio (legal plus any additional cash reserves desired by banks) as well as the currency-deposit ratio remains constant. The money stock (and the demand deposit and currency components of it) will increase. Assuming a value of 0.15 (15%) for r^d and a value of 1 for the currency-deposit ratio, we can interpret a 50 million dollar injection from either (or both) open-market operations or new loans to commercial banks as follows:

$$\Delta M = \Delta H_{O,D} \; \frac{1 + c}{c + r}$$

$$\Delta M = 50 \cdot 1.739 \qquad \qquad [11.2]$$

$$\Delta M = 86.95 \text{ million dollars}$$

A reserve injection of 50 million dollars via purchasing securities or by lowering the discount rate, under the assumptions made, would produce a once-and-for-all 86.95 million dollar increase in the money stock. New deposits $(1 - c^d \Delta M)$ and new currency holdings $(c^d \Delta M)$ would be equal to approximately 43 million each. Bond purchases would obviously have the reverse effects.

Unfortunately, using a static, partial equilibrium approach to the matter causes serious difficulties in the translation of theory to what would actually happen with a high-powered money injection. The first difficulty may be best understood as the "other things are seldom equal" problem. Changes in one (or two) of the instruments of monetary policy seldom take place in a vacuum, as demonstrated earlier in this chapter. At a time when the aforementioned injection takes place and over the period when the effects of it are worked out, banks may not be fully loaned up, loan demand may be deficient, currency demands may be changing, the Treasury may be reducing reserves through fiscal policies, or a host of other factors may come into play. The amount of "float" that extends or reduces Federal Reserve Bank credit changes daily. The conduct of monetary policy is hampered by these many difficulties, though most factors are fortunately predictable. The point is that the bank equilibrium function is hardly stable vis-á-vis changes in high-powered money. Day-to-day, week-to-week and month-to-month changes in H are bound to occur, and the Fed must be able to account for all of them in determining policy.

There are other "slips" in policy implementation. Should the economy be undergoing a severe recession, for example, or if banks already hold large quantities of excess reserves, an expansionary discount rate policy might be totally ineffective. Banks simply cannot borrow at the discount window because they do not view it as profitable. Likewise, increases in the discount rate can have psychological effects on member banks without affecting the quantity of high-powered money at all. Member banks often view the discount rate as a "bell-weather" of Fed policy. Increases in that rate often portend things to come insofar as tightness or looseness in money and credit conditions go. Banks may act accordingly in anticipation even though their reserve position remains essentially unchanged. As Table 11–9 shows, increases in the discount rate might even be accompanied by active borrowing from the Fed.

CHANGING THE RESERVE RATIO

Excess reserves can be injected into the banking system through yet another route—by an alteration in the legal reserve requirement. Again the model will help us interpret the effects of this change. Figure 11–4 depicts a change in the requirements as a rotation of the bank equilibrium function, that is, as a change (increase) in its slope. The new legal reserve ratio $\mathbf{r}^d$ is lower than the previous ratio $\mathbf{r}^d$, and both the money supply and the level of deposits and currency rise. Consider the problem numerically. Suppose $\mathbf{r}_0^d$ is originally 15%, $\mathbf{c}_0^d$ is 1, and H_0, the stock of high-powered money, is 30 billion dollars. Furthermore, assume that banks are fully lent up. We know (from Chapter 9) that M_0, the initial money supply, can be expressed as

$$M_0 = H_0 \; \frac{1 + \mathbf{c}_0^d}{\mathbf{c}_0^d + \mathbf{r}_0^d}, \text{ or in our problem,}$$

$$M_0 = 30 \text{ billion } \frac{2}{1.15}$$

$$M_0 = 52 \text{ billion (approximately)}$$

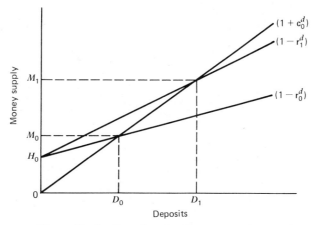

Figure 11-4. Changing the Reserve requirement.

Since the currency-deposit ratio is assumed to be 1, the public holds half of its money holdings in cash (or 26 billion dollars) and half in demand deposits (or 26 billion). Since the stock of high-powered money (30 billion) is composed of currency in circulation plus reserves, the banks must be holding 4 billion (30 minus 26 in reserves at the Fed or in vault cash). Since 4 billion in cash reserves are exactly required to support 26 billion dollars in deposits (4 is approximately 15% of 26), the banks are lent up.

What happens when the Fed decides to lower the reserve requirement to 10%, leaving the stock of high-powered money unaltered? Again the numbers are instructive. Now r_1^d is 0.10, and a new value for D, C, and R can be derived.

$$M_1 = 30 \text{ billion } \frac{2}{1.1}$$

$$M_1 = 30 \times 1.818$$

$$M_1 = 54.5 \text{ billion}$$

Clearly the money stock grows (see Figure 11–5) by 2.5 billion dollars as it attains the new equilibrium. Deposits grow to 27.25 billion and currency holdings of the public grow by the same amount. Since currency holdings have grown by 1.25 billion, bank's cash reserves must have declined by a similar amount (to 2.725 billion, just sufficient to cover 27.25 billion in deposit liabilities with 10% requirement).

The principles developed in Chapter 9 verify this point. When the reserve requirement was lowered banks were lent up. A 10% reserve would mean that banks were holding *excess* reserves (4 billion less 2.6 billion dollars required). The money creation process took place by a conversion of these 1.4 billion dollars in excess reserves into new money deposits and currency holdings. It is the identical process described in Table 9–1 and Figure 9–2.

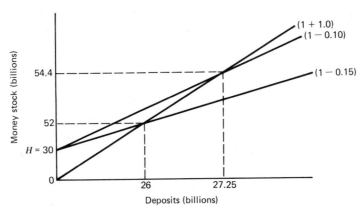

Figure 11-5. Changing Reserve requirements: a numerical example.

The theoretical process described in the foregoing model is subject to some of the same problems related to the implementation of open market operations and the discount rate. The impact of a change in reserve requirements again depends on the reserve position of banks as well as on general economic conditions and on the demand for loans. The excess reserve position of banks fluctuates significantly at times and monthly and weekly fluctuations can also be quite erratic. When borrowings from the Fed and Federal Funds transactions are *subtracted* from excess reserves of selected large US banks, banks hold over 100% of average required reserve for only one or two weeks a month. Reserve positions by size of bank also vary widely. Thus the overall impact of a change in the reserve requirement, or any of the other credit controls, might not be the same across the banking system. A lowering of the requirement can produce a rapid increase in the money supply in some sections of the economy (cities, regions, and so forth), with a small or not-so-rapid change in others. Nevertheless, the record of the Fed in influencing the monetary aggregate has been fairly good in the post-World War II period. Figure 11-6, for example, compares seasonally adjusted annual rate of growth in the money supply (M1-A and M1-B) with the growth of Reserve Bank Credit over the period 1960–1980. Note that legal reserve requirement changes, while not explicitly reported in Figure 11-6, are reflected in the degree of power of bank credit to create or to destroy money. Indeed reserve requirements were changed many times (usually lowered). Surely there is a close correspondence between reductions in the rate of growth of reserve bank credit and rates of decline in the money stock. Positive growth in bank credit does not correspond so well with growth in the money stock for numerous reasons, some of them outlined above.

One obvious problem is that the Fed has not aimed its controls solely at the money stock, although recent changes in Federal Reserve policy place

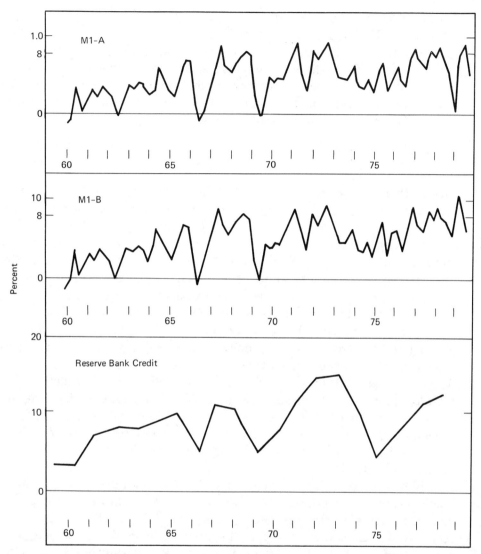

*Figure 11-6. Growth of monetary and banking aggregates (*Source: *Federal Reserve Bulletin).*

short-period fluctuations in bank reserves and money aggregates as the object of policy. (Historically, interest rates and net reserves have been the prime target.) Moreover, the money multiplier—$(1 + c)/(c + r)$ in our simple model— has itself been the source of instability in the Fed's control of the money stock. Let us briefly consider some of the particular exogeneous influences upon the Fed's control of reserves and the money stock. The impact of the currency-deposit ratio, c, is crucial; along with it, a slightly more elaborate money multiplier we will consider.

THE CURRENCY-DEPOSIT RATIO AND OTHER
EXOGENEOUS INFLUENCES UPON M

It is mainly through alterations in reserve bank credit (purchase and sale of securities, use of the discount window, and so forth) that the Fed influences the amount of high-powered money or the "monetary base" in the system. Reserve requirements, on the other hand, change the "power" of high-powered money. Consider the money supply equation again.

$$M = H \left[\frac{1 + c}{c + r} \right]$$

Clearly there is a factor $(1 + c)/(c + r)$ that, when applied to H, changes the money stock. In some of our discussion we have treated, for simplicity, $(1 + c)/(c + r)$ as a constant; that is, if $(1 + c)/(c + r) = k$, $M = Hk$, where k, the *money multiplier*, is a constant. But treatment of k as a constant will not stand up under the light of facts. Indeed, the value of k, the money multiplier, changes when r, the reserve ratio, changes. The important point is that some of the divergence we have seen between reserve bank credit and the money supply (refer to Figure 11–6) is explained by a changing money multiplier. Consider the record of the early 1970s. Over this period reserve bank credit, H, was growing and the growth in the money stock was declining! This seemingly inconsistent phenomenon can be explained partly in terms of changes in k. Annual changes in k between 1959 and 1980 are plotted in Figure 11–7. For instance, Figure 11–7 indicates that in 1974 a \$1 injection of H, high-powered money, would increase the money supply (M-1B) by approximately \$2.75, in 1980 by \$2.55, and so on. Also notice that the money multiplier is most certainly not a constant historically; it has varied significantly over the 20 years covered in Figure 11–7.

Before we consider the elements of a more complex money multiplier, a comment on its computation would be helpful. The multiplier is simply a measure of money stock (in the case of Figure 11–7, M-1B), divided by the *monetary base*. In constructing Figure 11–7 we have used a seasonally adjusted annual average of M1-B and the seasonally adjusted annual average of the St. Louis Fed's monetary base. The monetary base is very similar to the concept of high-powered money, that is, currency in the hands of the public and vault cash plus bank reserves, with one notable exception. We have used (and will use) the two terms interchangeably, but the calculation of the monetary base contains an adjustment for charges in reserve requirements (r) which, as stated earlier, affects the "power" of high-powered money. Since the reserve requirement has fallen over recent years, the "power" of reserves and currency to support levels of demand deposits has risen. Simply looking at the stock of high-powered money over the years will understate that stock's ability to support demand deposits, and the monetary base adjusts for this fact.

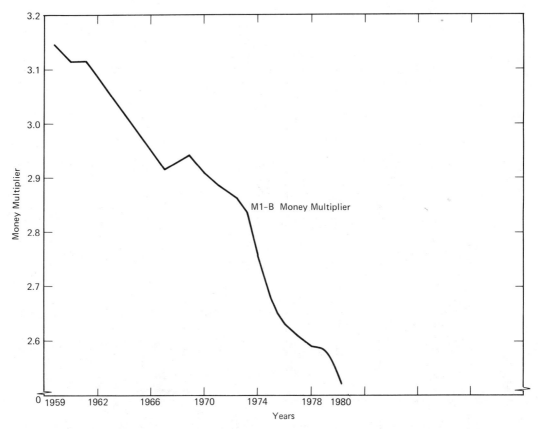

*Figure 11-7. The (M1-B) money multiplier, 1959–1980 (*Source: *Federal Reserve Bank of St. Louis).*

ELEMENTS IN THE MONEY MULTIPLIER

The discussion in Chapters 9 and 10 used an expression that focused upon the two most important elements determining the money multiplier, the reserve-deposit ratio, and the currency-deposit ratio, that is, $k = (1 - c)/(c + r)$. Two other factors should be introduced into the real-world multiplier, which is defined as k'.

$$k' = \frac{1 + c}{r(1 + t + g) + c} \qquad [11.3]$$

Instead of simply writing k, two factors are added; t and g must be explained, but r and c retain their previous definitions. The symbol t that appears in the denominator of [11.3] is equal to the ratio of time (savings) deposits to private demand deposits. Inspection of [11.3] tells us that a rise in t will cause the money multiplier to fall. Why? A rise in t implies that people are switching out

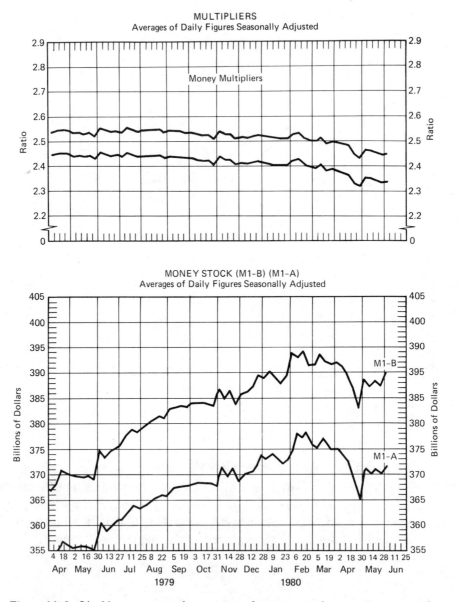

Figure 11-8. Weekly money stock measures, the monetary base, and money multipliers (April 1979–June 1980) (Source: Federal Reserve Bank of St. Louis: US Financial Data, June 11, 1980).

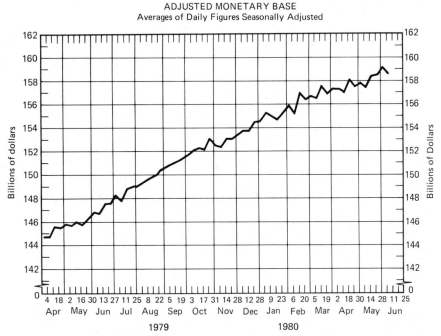

ADJUSTED MONETARY BASE
Averages of Daily Figures Seasonally Adjusted

Source: Federal Reserve Bank of St. Louis: US Financial Data, June 11, 1980.

Figure 11-8. (*Continued*)

of demand deposits into some form of time deposits, that is—given our defini-tion of money (currency + demand deposits: old M-1 or new M-1B)—reserves or high-powered money available to support demand deposits is declining.

Similarly, the **g** ratio is interpreted as the ratio of government demand deposits to private demand deposits. An increase in that ratio would *reduce* the money multiplier applicable to high-powered money used to support private demand deposits. In general, the **r** ratio has declined over the period 1959–1980. The **g**-ratio has remained fairly constant and close to zero and thus can be neglected. These two factors, by themselves, would seem to indicate a gradual *rise* in **k′**, the money multiplier. But Figure 11–7 clearly indicates that this has not been the case.

The explanation for the decline in the money multiplier over this period lies with changes in the two other factors of equation [11.3]. Both the cur-rency-deposit ratio and the time-demand deposit ratios have grown steadily over this period, a trend indicating that the public is demanding more currency relative to checkbook money and, simultaneously, has shifted assets from money (demand deposits plus currency) to the many forms of time deposits. Principally for these reasons, we have observed a decline in the money multiplier.

MONEY MULTIPLIERS IN THE SHORT-RUN

Alterations in the money multiplier, an element in the Fed's control of the money stock, should not be terribly disturbing for control if they are predictable. For the most part, they have been, and the growth (or decline) in the money stock has closely followed the growth or change of high-powered money. This parallel has certainly taken place during periods of one year or longer. But at times, especially over shorter periods, unpredicted changes in the money multiplier can be the "joker" in Fed control over the money stock.

Weekly data on M-1A, M-1B, the monetary base, and the averages of daily figures M-1A and M-1B multipliers between April 30, 1980, and June 4, 1980, are reported in Table 11–12, which is plotted (along with weekly data on these items from April 1979 through the first week of June 1980) in Figure 11–8. The monetary base has grown steadily over the period with some weekly variations. The money multipliers (M-1A/monetary base and M-1B/monetary base) have shown weekly variations but have in general been declining over the period, thereby exhibiting the trend shown in Figure 11–7. The M-1A and M-1B multiplier differs due to different definition of money. Money reserve M-1B contains all "transactions deposits" at thrift institutions along with currency and demand deposits, M-1A (see Chapter 2 for the alternative definitions of the money stock). As "transactions deposits" grow over time the two measures and their multipliers will diverge. The multipliers simply indicate that, for example, on October 31, 1979, a $1 addition to the stock of high-powered money to "the monetary base," would have supported about $2.50 in M-1A money and about $2.40 in M-1B money, but that this $1 injection would have had varying effects on the different money stocks at differing weeks over the period. The multipliers of Table 11–12 show this to be the case for the weeks April 30 to June 4, 1980. Changing currency demands relative to deposit holdings of the public, as well as changing proportions of time to transactions deposits, explain these variations. Between May 7 and May 14, a 4 million dollar reduction in the monetary base resulted in a 1.4 billion

Table 11–12 Multipliers, Money Stock Measures, and the Monetary Base (April 30, 1980– June 4, 1980, in Billions of Dollars)

Dates	M-1A	M-1B	Adj. Monetary Base	Multiplier (M-1A)	Multiplier (M-1B)
April 30	365.3	382.9	157.5	2.319	2.431
May 7	371.2	388.6	157.8	2.352	2.463
May 14	369.9	387.2	157.4	2.350	2.460
May 21	370.9	388.3	158.4	2.342	2.451
May 28	369.8	387.3	158.5	2.333	2.444
June 4	371.8	389.9	159.2	2.335	2.449

Source: Federal Reserve Bulletin.

dollar reduction in M-1B, whereas a 1 billion dollar increase in base money the following week resulted in a 1.1 billion dollar increase in M-1B.

The variability of these effects is partly explained by changes in the elements of the short-run money multipliers. In an interesting and serious study of factors influencing the money stock in 1974 and early 1975, Albert E. Burger has concluded that "throughout much of the period from late 1973 to early 1975, the currency behavior of the public was the major factor restraining the growth of money below the growth rate of the monetary base [the growth of high-powered money]."[9] Thus, the task of the Fed controllers can be rendered more difficult by untoward and unexpected changes in the short-run determinants of the money multiplier.

AGGREGATE RESERVE CONTROL: RECENT DEVELOPMENTS IN THE FED'S COVERAGE OF THE FINANCIAL SYSTEM

Alterations in the money multiplier can hamper the short-run ability of the Fed to control reserves, money stock, and economic aggregates, but institutional developments in the banking and financial sectors over the 1960s and 1970s have provoked a crisis in Federal Reserve's overall control over the monetary system. The structural details of other institutions in the monetary system will be analyzed in Chapter 12, but in the remainder of this chapter, important recent developments related to the expansion of the coverage of Federal Reserve monetary instruments will be considered and, tentatively, evaluated. We must remember that the expansion of Fed control is over both commercial banking and other financial institutions.

New developments and regulations, enshrined in the "Depository Institutions Deregulation and Monetary Control Act of 1980," will significantly alter the structure of monetary policy and control over the next six to eight years. We begin with a background to the "control crisis."

MEMBERSHIP AND CONTROL PROBLEMS

As noted earlier in this chapter, changing reserve requirements is not the most often used or popular tool of the Fed system. But the *existence* of a reserve requirement for banks implies that an amount of required reserves—a reserve base—exists which can be manipulated by the Federal Reserve to affect or to control money aggregates and other targets.

Consider the notion of required reserves from a bank's viewpoint. Reserves must be held in a noninterest-bearing form, either as deposits at Fed banks or as vault cash. This is, in effect, a noninterest loan to the Federal Reserve System. But the major cost of Fed membership—that is, earnings foregone—must be weighted against the benefits of membership, which, in the main, have been ready access to the discount window and to a lower discount rate (than non-members) and low-cost clearing house privileges.

In a competitive banking environment, however, banks subject to lower costs in the form of lower reserves will, with other things equal, be more profitable. In the past, the Fed has recognized and acted upon part of the problem. The institution in 1972 of uniform percentage requirements for all members of the Fed (see Table 11–11) resulted in the disappearance of one source of differential treatment of member banks regarding legal reserves. That is, all members of the Fed are given equal treatment with respect to reserves required.

The major issue remained unresolved, however. State-chartered non-member banks on average have been subject to lower legal reserve requirements than state- and nationally chartered member banks. Illinois, for example, has had, in the past, no statutory reserve requirement at all on either demand or time deposits! Rhode Island, Massachusetts, and Louisiana required no reserve requirement on time and savings deposits.[10] Perhaps the most important difference between treatment of member and nonmember banks has been in the form or kind of assets that will serve as reserves. Many states have allowed interest-bearing assets, such as Federal, state, and local government securities and Federal funds, and even certificates of deposit (CDs), to count, along with vault cash, as part of legal reserves. Not surprisingly, the number of member banks as a percentage of the total number has been declining over the past ten years or so (see Tables 10–3 and 10–4). It has simply been more profitable for a bank to be subject to state regulations.[11] The costs to member banks of remaining in the Fed system began to outweigh the benefits and the flight from the Fed reached high proportions. In 1979 a full 30 percent of banking deposits were out of Fed control and in the fourth quarter of 1979 and in January 1980, 69 banks with 7 billion dollars in deposits gave notice of withdrawal from membership.

CHECKABLE DEPOSITS AT THRIFT INSTITUTIONS

A second issue related to the control actually exercised by the Fed was that of the growth of "checkable" or "transactions" accounts at depository institutions other than commercial banks. "Transactions accounts" include demand deposits, negotiable orders of withdrawal accounts (NOW accounts), savings deposits subject to automatic transfers, and share draft accounts. "Transaction account" is simply a deposit or account on which a depositor or account holder may make withdrawals by negotiable or transferable instrument, telephone transfer, or similar items for making payments or transfer to third parties. These items bear interest, are money (see Chapter 2), and are principally means whereby interest may be paid on what are functionally demand deposits. Growth of these deposits has been dramatic from one-tenth of one billion dollars in deposits in 1972 to almost 3.5 billion in 1979. The point here is that items performing the same medium-of-exchange services at nonbank institutions were not subject to the same reserve requirements or to Fed control at all.

In early February 1980 Paul Volcker, Chairman of the Federal Reserve Board, summed up the whole matter in a statement before the Senate Banking Committee:

> The need for legislation is strongly reinforced by the decision of the Federal Reserve to adopt new operating procedures on October 6. These new procedures place much greater emphasis on reserves as the instrument for controlling money growth. Thus far, the procedures have worked reasonably well. But their effectiveness will be undercut as the share of money not subject to reserve requirements set by the Federal Reserve increases. Legislation to keep Federal Reserve control over the nation's reserve base from atrophying further is, in that context, an essential element in our anti-inflation program.[12]

Thus the Fed demanded monetary controls over the entire banking and financial system, arguing that reduced percentages of reserves may discourage "flight from the Fed" but that simply reducing reserve requirements would produce an insufficient quantity of reserves to control monetary aggregates adequately.

THE "OMNIBUS" BANKING ACT OF 1980

The result was the "Depository Institutions Deregulation and Monetary Control Act of 1980." The range of the Act and all of its provisions is very broad; its concerns extend from reserve requirement legislation to deregulation of interest rates, mortgage usury laws, and modification of "Truth in Lending" provisions. The (ultimate) elimination of Regulation Q will be discussed in Chapter 12. Here we focus upon the provisions relating to the extension of reserve controls to nonmember institutions. The following are the major provisions.

System Reserve Control. Reserve requirements are applied to all "transactions accounts" at FDIC-insured banks (including nonmembers eligible to be insured), mutual saving banks, all savings banks (savings and loans), and credit unions. The reserve requirement will be 3% on transaction accounts of 25 million dollars or less with a 12% rate on over 25 million (the latter rate's legal minimum is 8% and the maximum at 14%), and the amounts are to be indexed. All depository institutions will be required to hold reserves of 3% (with a legal **maximum of 9%**) against *nonpersonal time deposits*. Nonpersonal time deposits are transferable time deposits or simply time deposits not held by individuals. The Board of Governors may also impose a supplemental reserve requirement up to 4% in order to bring the aggregate amount of reserves maintained "to a level essential for the conduct of monetary policy."

Other Provisions of the Act. A gradual eight-year "phase-in" transitional adjustment will be permitted nonmember institutions to reach the ultimate amount of required reserves. A three-year phase-down adjustment for member banks whose reserve requirement exceeds those under the new Act was also provided. (The Board also received the power to permit depository institutions to maintain all or part of the required reserve in the form of vault cash, but the portion permitted must apply to *all* depository institutions.) *All* depository institutions in which transaction accounts or non personal time deposits are held will obtain the same discount and borrowing privileges as member banks. Furthermore, access to all Federal Reserve services, such as currency and coin services and check clearing and collection services, will be provided to all depository institutions at implicit cost-based fees.

The "Consumer Checking Account Equity Act of 1980," passed within the overall legislation, (1) permits all banks to establish automatic withdrawals from personal savings accounts or transfers from saving to demand deposits; (2) allows all depository institutions to issue NOW accounts nationwide; and (3) authorizes credit unions to pay dividends on share drafts and to allow owners of share drafts to make withdrawals by negotiable or transferable drafts.

Monetary Control: Some Observations. The "Omnibus" Banking Act of 1980 was a clear response to the attrition of member banks and to the emergence of new competitive financial instruments at institutions other than commercial banks. With the new legislation, financial institutions other than banks come under close supervision of the Fed. The attrition of member banks will also cease to be a problem since all banks, member and nonmember, will be subject to identical requirements. In fact, it is difficult to say whether "official" Fed membership will ultimately increase or decrease given the provisions of the new act. A blurring of "banks" with other institutions because of the emergence of "transactions accounts" at the latter is also recognized in the Act. (Congress and the Fed are here only acknowledging new deposit structures that have been evolving for some time.)

Basically the Act will establish competitive conditions by equalizing reserve requirements for all depository institutions offering comparable accounts and will eliminate interest rate ceilings (which we will consider in Chapter 12). Along with the homogenization of the banking and financial system the Federal Reserve (with Congressional approval) has attempted to consolidate a new reserve base in order to conduct efficient and effective monetary policy. The Fed's ability to achieve this objective will unfold over the decade of the 1980s.

CONCLUSIONS

Basic operations of the Federal Reserve in controlling reserves and monetary aggregates have been discussed and analyzed in Chapter 11. Just how successful the Federal Reserve has been in achieving the objectives is a matter for debate. Although some recent policy history has been considered in the present chapter, more information on the question is required before entering the debate over the efficacy of monetary policy. (Chapter 14 will discuss still other difficulties associated with monetary control and Chapter 16 provides a historical assessment of twentieth-century monetary policy.)

The ability of the instruments of Fed control to alter reserves and monetary aggregates, which was the principal topic of the present chapter, is not really in question. What is a matter for discussion is how well the Fed is able to "fine-tune" the effects of these tools on reserves and the money stock and, equally as important, how well the Fed is able to predict the effects of money aggregates upon inflation and employment. The mechanics of Fed control are simple, but the art of applying open market operations, discount policy, and so forth, to get the desired effects on reserves, money stock, and, ultimately, economic activity is not. Part of the problem has been, at least in the Fed's view, a loss in its reserve coverage due to a flight from Fed bank membership and the emergence of "transactions accounts" at other financial institutions. A massive legislative remedy designed to correct the situation has been enacted. In short, there might be hopeful signs that controls will improve in the 1980s.

FOOTNOTES

[1] The Depository Institutions Deregulation and Monetary Control Act of 1980 is composed of a number of "Titles" or sections, one of the most important of which is called "The Monetary Control Act of 1980." The title dealing with deregulation of interest rates, to be considered in Chapter 12, is the "Depository Institutions Deregulation Act of 1980." Still other titles deal with covering loans and truth-in-lending. A good summary of the provisions of this legislation can be found in the *Federal Reserve Bulletin*, June 1980.

[2] The Federal Funds rate, once a favored "target variable" of the Fed, is simply an interest rate determined by market forces, on short-term (one day and longer) borrowing and lending with commercial banks as the major participants. Banks have used federal funds as a short-term source of reserves or as a short-term investment for idle reserves.

[3] John A. Tatom, "Money Stock Control Under Alternative Definitions of Money," *Review, Federal Reserve Bank of St. Louis* (November 1979), p. 3.

[4] Since 1958 commercial banks may count vault cash, along with member bank

deposits at the Fed, as part of their legal reserve requirement. Vault cash along with currency in the hands of the public plus reserves held by banks at the Fed are the "high-powered" money of Chapter 9.

[5] Float exists for the individual also. One's bank balance temporarily "increases" by the amount of outstanding checks written to others but not yet collected.

[6] The effects of an alteration in H can be unpredictable depending on economic conditions. In recession, increases in H, according to one version of events, can result simply in additional holdings of money balances. Reductions in H, however, must be met by contraction of the money stock and reductions in the rate of increase in the price level.

[7] Time lags between open market operations and changes in the money stock measures, as well as lags between money stock changes and the rate of inflation and employment, are a large consideration in interpreting data like that in Table 11–6. These problems are analyzed in detail in Chapter 14.

[8] These relationships are treated extensively in Chapter 13.

[9] Albert E. Burger, "Explanation of the Growth of the Money Stock: 1974–Early 1975," *Review, Federal Reserve Bank of St. Louis* (September 1975), pp. 5–10.

[10] Laws vary widely; Louisiana, for instance, has applied a higher reserve requirement than the Fed on state member banks.

[11] For equity and in order to build and maintain membership in the System, the Fed could have paid interest on reserve deposits. But the Fed System and the Treasury have vetoed this solution, favoring a legislative requirement to subject all banks (and other financial institutions) to its legal reserve requirement.

[12] Statement by Paul Volcker, Chairman, Board of Governors of the Federal Reserve System, before the Committee on Banking, Housing and Urban Affairs, US Senate, February 4, 1980, reprinted in *Federal Reserve Bulletin*, February 1980, p. 143.

KEY CONCEPTS

policy instruments
    open market operations
    discount rate policy
    reserve requirements
    selective credit controls
    margin requirement

monetary targets and indicators
    reserves in the financial
        system
    monetary aggregates (M1A,
        M1B, etc.)
    market interest rates

economic goals
    price stability
    full employment
    economic growth
    balance of payments

excess reserves

float

assets and liabilities of Fed
member banks

Reserve equation

source of funds

use of funds

competing uses of fluids

SDRs

Federal funds market

exogenous influences upon M

monetary multiplier

transaction accounts

Depository Institutions
Deregulation and Monetary
Control Act of 1980

QUESTIONS FOR DISCUSSION

1. Which tools of the Fed are used the most and why? Why are the other tools not employed more often?

2. Which tools affect high-powered money and which affect the power of the money?

3. Suppose that the Fed wishes to combat inflation. What would be the policy followed with open market operations? What about a coordinated policy for all tools?

4. What circumstances would be likely to precipitate a change in the reserve requirement?

5. Briefly summarize the mechanics of each tool of the Fed.

6. Work through the problem in the text where $M_0 = 52$ billion dollars for $r_1^d = 0.20$. How will reserves and the money stock change?

7. Suppose the public shifts its holding of time deposits to demand deposits. What changes would we expect to see?

PART IV

FINANCIAL INTERMEDIARIES AND MARKETS IN THE ECONOMIC SYSTEM

CHAPTER 12

FINANCIAL INTERMEDIARIES: Commercial Banks and Other Depository Institutions

In Chapters 10 and 11 the institutions of the banking system, particularly the instruments of monetary control exercised by the Federal Reserve, were investigated. The Fed's instruments of control affect the stock of high-powered money (or the monetary base) and hence the money supply. In the past the Federal Reserve focused their direct controls only on member banks, but recent institutional developments—and particularly the Monetary Control Act of 1980 (discussed in Chapter 11)—have brought a number of new bank financial institutions under direct Fed control. The development of "transaction accounts" at nonbank financial institutions means, in fact, that the distinction between "banks" and "nonbanks" is itself beginning to lose meaning. Differences remain, however, in that many nonbank intermediaries ordinarily specialize in different kinds of financial instruments than banks. Both banks and financial intermediaries deal in specialized financial markets. (An analysis of financial markets is the subject of Chapter 13.) Contraction and expansion of the money supply by the Fed affect economic activity *through* these financial markets (consider the effects of "tight" money on the mortgage markets and the housing construction portion of investment spending). In order more fully to understand monetary policy, the institutional workings of all intermediaries, banks, savings and loan associations, mutual savings banks, credit unions, and others, must be analyzed.

The present chapter will introduce the *concept* of and economic justification for financial intermediaries and the process of intermediation. Financial intermediation is the process of buying and selling of credit or debt instruments (in the physical form of securities, bonds, insurance policies, mortgages, and so forth). A study of the principles underlying the buying and selling of these debt instruments is what we call an analysis of financial markets.) Next, we turn to a discussion of specific types of intermediaries—commercial banks, savings and loans, and mutual funds—and of the types of instruments bought and sold through them. Finally we will investigate some of the major regulations affecting financial intermediaries with particular emphasis upon the effects of the recent *deregulation* of interest rate ceilings imposed by governmental agencies on depository institutions.

Chapter 13 will also devote itself to the question of financial intermediaries and markets, but it then turns to a generalized discussion of the bond market focusing upon the concepts of the supply and demand for loanable funds and upon bond prices and bond yields. In Chapter 13, moreover, the principles of "money markets" (obligations less than one year) and capital markets (all obligations more than one year to maturity), including "bond yield curves" and the term structure of interest rates, are introduced. Finally, in Chapter 14, the role that financial intermediaries play in monetary policy will be highlighted.

FINANCIAL MARKETS AND INTERMEDIARIES: CONCEPTS

Why do financial intermediaries and instruments exist? Basically this question can be answered in the same manner as the question, Why do we use money?

TRANSACTIONS COSTS AND FINANCIAL INTERMEDIARIES

Transactions costs explain the existence of the industry of financial intermediaries.[1] Consumers derive satisfaction from consumption today and consumption tomorrow. The purchase of financial assets or securities enables individuals to transfer consumption through time or "intertemporally." But the purchase of these claims against the future involves both information and transaction costs. Throughout history many types of financial intermediaries have evolved to reduce these costs.

At one end of the spectrum one may view a stock exchange—for example, the New York Stock Exchange—as an intermediary that provides a physical locale for intermediation between buyers and sellers to take place. No assets are created, but the *information costs* of buyers and sellers of stocks are greatly reduced. If this marketplace were not provided, transacting costs would be gigantic with the result that the quantities of stocks traded would be greatly reduced.

At a far more sophisticated level, however, let us consider financial intermediaries that produce new financial instruments. Mutual funds or savings and loan associations sell shares or claims against all sorts of diversified assets. Small investors-savers (or postponers of consumption) could not possibly obtain these services for themselves except at (often prohibitively) high costs of transacting. The intermediary, however, is able to purchase large blocks of securities and other assets and to put together these assets in a form desired by consumers, thereby eliminating a large amount of transaction costs. Consequently, information costs, transaction costs, and indivisibilities explain the existence of financial intermediaries. In a purely competitive world where these costs or "frictions" did not exist, financial intermediaries would not exist. In a real world of frictions, however, specialized profit-making financial intermediaries have arisen and undergone many modifications to meet the specialized needs of groups of consumers of financial products. (Note again that these consumers of financial products are postponers of physical consumption).

SECTOR ANALYSIS: THE FLOW OF FUNDS

A financial intermediary may also be viewed as an agency or institution that serves as a conduit, or transformer, for funds as they move from ultimate suppliers to ultimate users. The economy can be pictured as divided into two sectors at any point in time: an "excess funds" sector and a "short of funds" sector. The "excess" sector will be composed of all households, businesses, and governments that have more funds available than they plan to use for current consumption or wish to hold as additions to cash balances. The "short" sector is also composed of households, businesses, and governments with the opposite problem—those that wish to consume or maintain cash balances in excess of their current level of funds. (A member of the excess sector during one time period can be a member of the short sector during another period.)

Another way of viewing the problem would be that members of the excess sector buy financial instruments (such as stocks, bonds, or treasury bills) that are written by members of the short sector. We shall call this type of transaction a "direct flow of funds." With the direct flow, there is no need for financial intermediaries.

The major problem with the direct flow of funds is that the financial instruments written by the members of the "short sector" are not always compatible with the needs of the members of the "surplus sector." Some major areas of incompatibility are *liquidity*, *risk*, *time to maturity*, and *denomination*.

Suppose, for example, that a large enterprise such as General Motors is "short of funds" in the amount of 100 million dollars for some new investment project. Thousands of individuals in the household and business sector may collectively be willing to supply "excess funds" to General Motors in the amount of 100 million dollars. A direct transfer of funds in this amount would be most difficult to accomplish, however. First, the transaction costs of getting so large a number of lenders together—not to mention the costs of dealing separately with each lender—would be phenomenal. Not all of the potential lenders would desire the same term to maturity, much less the term probably desired by General Motors. Problems such as these give rise to the institutions we call *financial intermediaries.* The role of these institutions is to obtain funds from the surplus sector and to supply funds to the short sector. In so doing,

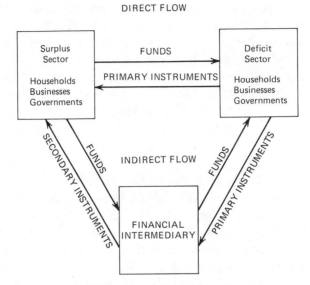

Figure 12-1. Flow of funds.

they buy primary instruments from the short sector and sell their own financial instruments, which are called secondary instruments, to the surplus sector. The flow of funds concept described above may be depicted as Figure 12–1.

In the process described in Figure 12–1, a financial intermediary is similar to any firm engaged in an intermediate level of production. A shoe factory will buy leather for money, transform the leather into shoes, and sell the shoes for money. The "leather" in the case of intermediaries is the primary financial instrument, the shoe factory is the intermediary, and the shoe is the secondary financial instrument. The "shoe" must be designed to "fit" the member of the surplus sector in which it is being sold.

PRIMARY AND SECONDARY SECURITIES

A hypothetical T-account or balance sheet for financial intermediaries is reproduced as Table 12–1. Clearly the balance sheet records the financial claims between deficit and surplus sections in our economy just as described in Figure 12–1. Primary instruments, which are *assets* to the financial intermediary, are issued by businesses and households (and by governments, such as municipal obligations). These include, for example, corporate bonds, home mortgages, and auto notes, that are received by the intermediary in return for lent funds. These primary claims are interest earning assets of the intermediary and are the source of its income.

On the other side of the balance sheet the secondary securities issued by the intermediaries are listed. These are the sources of funds to the intermediary

Table 12-1   *Financial Intermediaries–Typical Assets and Liabilities*

Assets	Liabilities and Net Worth	
Primary Securities	Secondary	Mutual funds shares
(Claims against business)	Securities	Time (savings) deposits
Bonds		Demand deposits
Loans		Insurance fund reserves
Mortgages		Pension fund reserves
Stocks		Stocks
(Claims against households)		
Home mortgages		
Consumer installment loans		Net Worth
Real Assets		Retained Earnings

and constitute its "specialized" liabilities. Ordinarily, interest must be paid by the intermediary on these borrowed funds. As indicated in Table 12-1, evidence of this asset held by households, businesses, or government can be a savings account passbook, a mutual fund share, or a stock. These liabilities represent costs to the intermediary and, as is the case with any business, the intermediary's profit is the difference between its receipts (receipts on primary securities) and its costs (interest payment on its secondary securities).

All types of securities are designed to reduce the transactions costs associated with direct consumption of financial instruments, such as the problem of indivisibilities and information. But financial intermediaries *specialize* in the types of securities they buy and sell. We now turn to the recent development of these financial institutions, their relative importance, and the nature of their financial "speciality."

THE INDUSTRY OF FINANCIAL INTERMEDIARIES

The growth of assets of various types of financial institutions in the post-World War II era has been phenomenal by any standard. As Figure 12-2 shows, credit expansion at all *nonbank* financial intermediaries has grown at a much faster rate than credit at commercial banks. Primary securities, which are assets to the intermediary and liabilities to households and businesses, are generally held in the form of bonds, business loans, mortgages, and stocks. Home mortgages and consumer installment loans are liabilities to households, but they are primary securities or assets to intermediaries as emphasized above.

Financial intermediaries must sell secondary securities (liabilities), which are claims against the intermediary, in order to finance their activities. The primary and secondary securities that intermediaries buy and sell are specialized

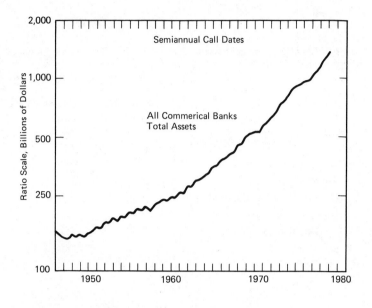

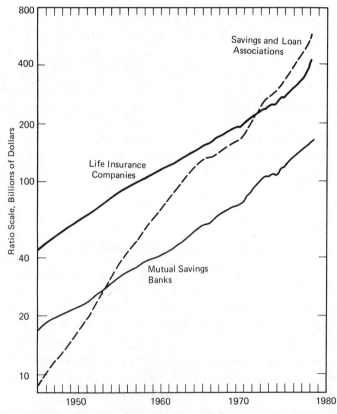

*Figure 12-2. Growth of Assets at major financial intermediaries (1945–1979) (*Source: Historical Chart Book, *Board of Governors of the Federal Reserve System).*

and everyone is familiar with some of these instruments. For example, the primary security most often bought by savings and loan associations (S&L) is the long-term home mortgage whereas the S&L sells savings shares. Commercial banks participate to some extent in the mortgage market (usually of shorter terms than S&Ls), but they also purchase primary securities in the form of commercial, industrial, and consumer installment loans. The sources of funds for commercial banks are obtained by the *sale* of three principal secondary securities—demand deposits, savings accounts, and certificates of deposit (longer-term savings deposits, sometimes called CDs).

Intermediaries of all types and specialities sell tailored secondary securities to meet the needs and demands of consumers of financial products. Total assets of commercial banks in February 1980, for instance, was about 1.5 trillion dollars, while S&L held approximately 520 billion in assets, mutual savings banks less than 160 billion, and life insurance companies about 380 billion. Yet, a growing amount of the public's savings (especially in the second half of the 1970s) was being converted into economic investment in nonbank institutions partly in response to the growth of interest-bearing "checkable" deposits in these "depository institutions." In the following section the "money and credit markets" will be discussed as a whole. Because of their relative importance, in terms of assets and structure, the balance sheet of commercial banks and their institutional characterization as intermediaries will be investigated. Nonbank intermediaries—private, public, and quasipublic—will also be considered.

CREDIT AND LIQUIDITY

Financial intermediaries deal in financial markets of all types and these markets are often conveniently distinguished as "money markets" and "capital markets." "Money markets" are, in this context, not to be understood as "a market for currency or demand deposits"; rather the term refers to those markets in which short-term debt (less than a year) is traded. These items, such as 90-day treasury bills, banker's acceptances, or negotiable certificates of deposit (CDs), are generally very liquid—readily convertible into cash with a minimum of risk of capital loss. (Negotiable certificates of deposit are subject to an 8% reserve requirement.)

"Capital markets," on the other hand, are those in which longer-term (longer than a year) financial instruments are traded. We have already encountered some of these items. Long-term treasury or corporate bonds (of many risk classes), and mortgages of all types fit into this category. These assets are lower on the scale of liquidity. There is, in other words, a clear "liquidity risk" to holding longer term securities, and that risk is comprised of the risk of capital loss if the bond or security should have to be sold before it reaches maturity.

This distinction is important since it would be possible (roughly) to rank financial intermediaries by the liquidity of the major liabilities—financial instruments—they sell or hold. Commercial banks and other "depository institutions" selling checkable deposits would rank first in this characterization since they "sell" demand deposits and demand deposits are money, the most liquid of all assets. Further down the scale, savings and loan associations hold long-term mortgages (the borrower's liability) as assets but sell more liquid savings deposits as well as interest-bearing checkable deposits. Still lower on the scale, the Federal Land Bank System buys assets—mortgages on land—of an exceptionally long-term maturity. The liquidity risk involved in these types of investment is very high.

Such a ranking of intermediaries by the liquidity of the liabilities they sell or by the assets they buy would not be terribly meaningful, however, for most financial intermediaries have a variety of liabilities and assets in their portfolios. How assets and liabilities are structured in order to keep the intermediary itself liquid is a far more important item in a discussion of the process of intermediation. We must not only investigate the kinds of financial instruments that intermediaries hold but inquire why specific intermediaries tend to hold a certain portfolio structure of assets and liabilities.

The central problem of financial management should be very familiar since every economic unit, including the individual, faces it continuously. Simply stated, it is a problem of (1) maintaining and earning profit returns, (2) maintaining liquidity, and (3) maintaining solvency. The individual, as all other economic units, must constantly juggle return on investments with the ability to pay off current obligations (or *liquidity*), making sure that the total value of assets when converted into cash will be equivalent to the total amount of his liabilities (or *solvency*). An individual may be liquid but not solvent or solvent but not liquid. In the former case bankruptcy will be declared if creditors foreclose. In the latter case, assets may have to be sold—possibly at a loss—in order to obtain cash to meet current cash liabilities. The structure of the individual's portfolio will determine the length of time it will take to become liquid once more. If an individual holds land or specialized real estate assets, it may take a good deal of time to become liquid. Risk of loss on these items would be greater, moreover. If the individual holds savings accounts, on the other hand, liquidity may be restored simply by a trip to mutual savings, commercial bank, or S&L, or if the individual uses a ATS Account, funds may be *shifted* into demand deposit accounts by automatic transfer.

The problem of financial management or portfolio management in different financial intermediaries is different in degree and complexity but not in kind. Each intermediary operates in a different environment—different government and self-imposed regulations, different types of specialized assets and liabilities held, different functions performed, and other constraints. But the general problems in portfolio management are the same as those described for the individual or any economic unit. Before undertaking a discussion of the institutional structure of the various financial intermediaries, let us consider some of the complexities of financial management by these institutions. The principles governing the management of regulated financial institutions are applicable to all. Therefore, owing to their primary importance in money creation and intermediation, we will concern ourselves with commercial banks as an example of "how financial intermediaries work."

COMMERCIAL BANKS AS FINANCIAL INTERMEDIARIES

Although a number of aspects of the commercial banking system have been examined elsewhere in this book, bank operations have not been described. A brief examination of the balance sheet of a commercial bank provides many useful insights into the manner in which financial intermediaries handle assets and liabilities. Specifically, a knowledge of the rudiments of commercial bank operations will tell us how a financial institution controls the problems that face individuals (described above) and indeed all economic units. Remember that the portfolios of any of the financial intermediaries discussed later in this chapter may be subjected to the same examination. The underlying principles are the same although some institutional constraints and details differ.

Let us approach the asset-liability problems of commercial banks by looking at a consolidated balance sheet of some 15,000 commercial banks at the end of February 1980. Table 12–2 shows the major assets and liabilities of the entire banking system. Some of these items are obvious and some require an explanation. The item "cash" includes all vault and till cash plus items in the process of collection and deposits in other banks including required deposits in Federal Reserve banks. Investments of security and loan accounts include a large number of items from US government, state and municipal obligations to all types of secured and unsecured loans—home improvement and vacation loans included. (We will return to this item in more detail soon.) Other assets specifically not listed in Table 12–2 include accrued interest on notes and securities, Fed Bank stock, real estate (bank premises, furnitues, and fixtures), and long-term real estate mortgages; these are fairly self-explanatory. Real estate loans are only 26 percent of total loan assets, and the reason for the small percentage of commercial bank assets in long-term mortgage loans on buildings and land will become obvious shortly.

In order to hold assets financial intermediaries sell liabilities. Chief of these liabilities for commercial banks are demand and time accounts, both government and private, which totaled over 70% of all commercial bank liabilities and capital in February 1980 (see Table 12–2). These liabilities include

Table 12-2   Consolidated Commercial Bank Balance Sheet (All Commercial Banks)
(February 1980, in Billions of Dollars)

Assets		*Liabilities and Capital Accounts*	
Cash Assets	$168.8	*Deposits*	
Loans	941.0		
Securities		Demand Deposits	$ 376.8
US Treasury	95.5	Time Deposits	200.3
Other	194.4	Interbank Deposits	492.9
Other Asset Items	86.8	Borrowings	182.9
		Other Liability Items	128.4
		Total Capital Assets	105.2
TOTAL ASSETS	$1,486.5	TOTAL LIABILITIES AND CAPITAL ASSETS	$1,486.5

Source: *Federal Reserve Bulletin.*

interbank deposits that, for the individual bank, are demand deposits held by other banks, often for check-clearing purposes. "Total capital accounts" comprised the capitalization of the bank in common stock (which must be sold at par or above), the bank's surplus, individual profits, and contingency reserves against possible losses on loans and securities.

HOW BANKS MANAGE THE PORTFOLIO: BALANCING CONFLICTING INTERESTS

The essential problems facing the management of the bank or any other privately owned and publicly regulated intermediary are very similar to those with which all economic units must deal.

They are (1) to please stockholders by earning profit returns on their investment and (2) to keep the bank liquid and solvent. Depositors are interested in high liquidity with interest payments on their savings deposits, and both depositors and stockholders are concerned about solvency. Borrowers naturally wish readily available loans at the lowest interest rate possible. The regulatory agencies—Federal Reserve System, Comptroller of the Currency, State Banking Commissions, and the FDIC—are interested in protecting almost everyone concerned, especially the depositor and the soundness of the banking system as a whole.

The difficult task of bank management should be obvious. The banker, in an attempt to earn high returns, may follow a liberal loan policy and/or turn to longer-term and higher risk (but higher yielding) investments. Unfortunately solvency and liquidity can be endangered with such a policy. Cash assets (the most liquid assets) must be available to pay off depositors on demand (honor the instant repurchase clause), and variability in the movement of deposits is not exactly predictable.

Furthermore, the bank (and, in time, other depository institutions) must be able to meet the legal reserve requirement on demand and time deposits of the Federal or state regulatory agencies, as described in Chapter 11. These are called required or legal reserves, and thus all items labeled "cash" in Table 12–1 are not free, lendable-for-profit reserves.[2] Out of total reserves, one must deduct legal or required reserves plus any additional reserves that banks desire to hold before coming to the amount of lendable-for-profit cash reserves of the bank. Thus, in the language and notation developed in Chapter 9 of this text, r^d = required reserve ratio and additonal desired holding of cash, and r = the amount of actual reserves to total deposits.

Bankers ordinarily seek to avoid the embarrassment of being unable to meet their legal requirement against deposits over long periods of time, but over short-term periods banks may rediscount paper at the Fed or borrow in the Federal Funds Market to make up realized differences. Holding extreme quantities of cash, of course, reduces profitability, since interest is not earned on holdings of cash assets. The question is, how much should be set aside in idle reserves? Clearly, the bank does not want to turn away loans demanded by regular customers either. Thus, the amount of free, lendable-for-profit reserves that a bank will hold is a function of a large number of variables, which include deposit variability and the liquidity of the bank's portfolios, and loan demand, which is itself a function of a number of variables including national and local business conditions, industrial development, and population.[3]

Choice of the degree of liquidity of the bank's portfolio, mentioned above, is also extremely important in bank management. Again, the banker must make choices between holding assets that are readily convertible into cash (without great risk of loss) and more profitable but less marketable debt instruments. Highly marketable earning assets in a bank's portfolio are often called *secondary reserves*. These items include treasury bills and certificates, banker's acceptances, and prime commercial paper with maturities of one year or less (see the following section of this chapter). These items are used to meet potential and unpredictable cash or deposit withdrawals and to fill loan demand requests. Secondary reserves perform a dual function of earning income for the bank while serving as a bulwark against unexpected loan demand and deposit withdrawal contingencies.

FINANCIAL MARKETS AND INSTRUMENTS IN COMMERCIAL BANKING

Commercial banks' demand for reserves is an on-going process. Depending on transactions costs and on the reason and length of time for which additional cash reserves are needed, a commercial bank has a menu of choices: (1) it may call loans or let outstanding loans mature without renewal or relending; (2) it may sell off secondary reserve assets; (3) it may use the discount window at the Fed (a choice often made in the late 1970s) or borrow from a correspondent bank; or (4) it may borrow in the Federal funds market. In addition, banks may attract new deposits, sell stock, borrow in the Eurodollar market, or borrow through bank holding companies. A bank, in its role as a profit maximizer under constraints will make positive decisions as to its investment portfolio, both long- and short-term. In this section some of the instruments most often used by banks in the conduct of portfolios management are described and discussed. They trade, as we shall see, in both the "money markets" and in the "credit markets."

Federal Funds Market. Commercial banks—particularly large commercial banks —often deal as buyers or sellers in the Federal funds market. Federal funds are, in the main, commercial bank excess reserves (other parties also participate in the Federal Funds market) ordinarily held in Federal Reserve Banks, which are borrowed and lent in a very short-term market. Most often these funds are borrowed or lent for periods of 24 hours to several days in blocks of one million dollars or more. Total transactions in the Federal Funds Markets are extremely large averaging 45 to 50 billion dollars per week in early 1980.

The rationale behind commercial banks and other depository institutions trading in this market could not be simpler. Those banks with temporary excess reserves may earn an interest return on excess cash holdings without any appreciable loss in liquidity since their loan will mature in a very short period, often a day or two. Banks that fall short of reserves over the two-week lagged accounting procedure can temporarily meet cash reserve requirements while they rearrange their portfolios (sell off treasury bills or other assets). Since banks must hold required reserves this week on the basis of the deposit liabilities two weeks before, they often find themselves in either excess or deficit positions. (In June 1980, the Fed proposed eliminating the "lagged" reserve accounting procedure and adopting contemporaneous accounting to determine required reserves against deposit liabilities.) This practice explains the large volume of transactions in Federal funds. Mechanically, moreover, it is very easy to enter the Federal funds market. Negotiations can take place either through dealers or through correspondent banks. Through this efficient use of excess reserves, commercial banks can avoid having to use the discount facilities of the Federal Reserve for temporary or emergency borrowing.

Treasury Bills (T-Bills). Far and away the most important short-term money market item is treasury bills. Treasury bills are issued weekly either at auction (in the primary market) or resold through securities dealers. They mature in

91 or 182 days. These bills are obligations of the US Government, and as such they are virtually free from risk or default. The difference between the face value and the purchase price (the discount) represents the before-tax yield earned by the holder.

Commercial Paper and Bankers Acceptances. Banks also hold other short-term assets such as secondary reserves; these are noncash but highly liquid assets. Commercial paper consists of short-term (up to six months) notes of large corporations. The notes that are issued provide short-term working capital for corporations and other purposes. Finance companies and companies dealing in installment loan credit often utilize this market. Commercial paper may be placed either through dealers or directly in the market.

Related to commercial paper, and by far one of the oldest money market instruments, is the banker's acceptance. Business firms in need of short-term credit may issue promissory notes promising to pay the holder a given amount at maturity. The business may then have the note or bank draft "accepted" by the bank. Acceptance by a bank means that the bank has lent its reputation to the note and has guaranteed to pay the principal to the holder of the note at maturity. At maturity, the bank pays off the note and draws on the corporation's account, charging a fee for its service. Naturally, if the corporation defaults (which seldom happens), the bank is obligated to cover the draft. Technically, the bank is vulnerable up to the full value of its acceptances. Restrictions, consequently, are placed on the total outstanding value of a bank's acceptances (usually up to 50% of the bank's capital stock plus surplus).

Notes and Bonds. Banks also hold a portion of their portfolio in longer-term obligations such as treasury notes (3 to 5 year maturities) and marketable treasury bonds (up to 40 years). These assets bring a much higher return than short-term investments; however, as we will see, the price and yield of these securities will fluctuate violently given changes in the market rate of interest. (Bond price and yield analysis is discussed at length in Chapter 13.) State and municipal obligations are also held by banks, and the latter type of security is particularly attractive since "municipals" are exempt from federal taxes. Such obligations are often used to finance municipal sewage, water, and highway development. There is a greater risk of default with municipals, but by purchasing them a bank may identify with community development and enhance its own long-term profit prospects.

Bank Loans. Lending money at interest is clearly a primary function of the commercial bank and a primary means of earning profits. Few generalizations can be made about bank loans except that they can be of many types. Loans can be (1) short or long term; (2) secured or nonsecured by collateral; (3)

payable in a large variety of ways (for example, in a lump sum, on installment, on installment with a balloon payment at the end); and (4) made to consumers or to commercial or industrial firms.

There are legal and sensible limitations on bank loans. For example, the total amount that may be lent by any bank to a single borrower is a value equal to 10% of the bank's capital and surplus. Banks are also restricted in the amount that can be lent to one of its own officers, and they are prohibited from lending against collateral of their own stock. Historically, maximum interest rates on loans to individuals have been imposed on banks by many states in the form of usury laws,[4] though these regulations have been applied unevenly over various kinds of credit. The whole matter of usury loans is presently in flux—a three year moritorium on state levels was invoked by the "Depository Institutions Regulations and Monetary Control Act of 1980."[5]

Banks are interested in the liquidity aspects of loans. As few loans these days are against inventory or for temporary working capital (that is, self-liquidating), banks must carefully analyze the financial circumstances of individuals and businesses who seek to borrow from them. Cash flow and collateral of the individual or business and term and type of repayment are but a few of the factors influencing loans. Credit worthiness is often a matter of the purpose of the loan plus the business or financial prospects of the borrower. Large commercial banks hire armies of financial analysts to survey the accounts and credit of loan demanders. The composition of various types of loan assets at commercial banks for a representative period is given in Table 12–3.

Liquidity and Solvency. Banks have been wary of overinvestment in certain types of loans, especially long-term home mortgage and real estate loans. The "Great Liquidity Crisis" brought on by the form inelasticity of the money stock in the Great Depression of the 1930s (see Chapter 16) was certainly aggravated by large bank holdings of long-term mortgages. These mortgages proved to be a big loss for the banks, and most commercial banks have drastically reduced investments in them. Long-term securities and bonds are most likely to be found, however, in the portfolios of large banks with large time deposits. A moment's reflection tells us why: Time deposits are far less variable than demand deposits and, except for the recent development of NOW and ATS accounts, depositors may technically be obliged to notify banks in order to withdraw savings. The larger the amount of savings account liabilities, the greater the profit return the bank makes on longer term loans and securities. In general, the opposite is also true. The smaller the bank, the greater the representation of short-term assets on the portfolios.

All this brings us back to the problem of liquidity and portfolio management in the financial intermediary. Commercial banks and *all intermediaries*, regardless of the special constraints imposed upon them, must transform funds

Table 12-3   Composition of Loans of Large Commercial Banks[a] *(March 26, 1980, in Millions of Dollars)*

Federal Funds Sold	$ 19,098
Commercial and Industrial	152,080
Agricultural	4,831
Loans for Purchasing or Carrying Securities	
To Brokers and Dealers	5,080
To Others	2,207
Loans to Nonbank Financial Institutions	
To Personal and Sales-Finance Companies	9,480
To Other Intermediaries	15,815
Real Estate Loans	96,954
To Commercial Banks	
Domestic	3,544
Foreign	6,407
Consumer Installment Loans	64,579
All Other	11,963
Less Loan Loss Reserve and Unearned	
Income on Loans	11,776
	$380,990

[a]Domestic assets of $1 Billion or more on December 31, 1977.
Source: Federal Reserve Bulletin.

from the (saving) excess funds sector (liabilities) into outflowing funds to the (borrowing) deficit funds sector (creating the intermediary's assets). The kind of markets in which any intermediary participates and the degree of participation at any given time are determined by a large number of factors, as shown in the foregoing case study.

Portfolio management in any intermediary is an "iffy" and inexact activity. In the banking example the manager must keep close tabs on loan demand, on savings, on total deposits and their composition, on the future course of interest rates, and on the return on the bank's overall investments. Assessment of these major factors plus hosts of others determines the kinds of financial markets (short-term, long-term, securities, or loans, and so forth) entered and the quantity of specific instruments purchased. If deposits were expected to grow, for example, and interest rates were expected to fall, the manager would opt for profitable long-term investments. Thus financial intermediation is a process by which savings are converted into investment. Instruments acceptable to savers (checking, savings accounts, Federal funds, insurance policies) are sold by the intermediary, and instruments acceptable to investors (mortgages, bonds, securities, Federal funds) are bought by the intermediary. Because of the quasipublic nature of money and financial markets, the intermediary must face liquidity and solvency constraints, just as any other business, plus various kinds of governmental regulatory constraints. We have considered as a case study, how commercial banks handle the portfolio question, and we now turn to the same issue in the context of nonbank intermediaries.

NONBANK FINANCIAL INTERMEDIARIES

Financial intermediation takes place in a variety of institutions in addition to commercial banks. Even "loan sharks" engage in intermediation. Although nonbank intermediaries is the subject of very detailed study and analysis, here we point only to the main features of the major types of nonbank intermediaries and to the role of government participation and regulation in these institutions.[6]

SAVINGS AND LOAN ASSOCIATIONS

Primary among nonbank financial intermediaries in the United States are the more than 5,000 savings and loan associations (S&Ls) with assets of more than 250 billion dollars at the end of 1979. These are deposit-type institutions (along with commercial and mutual savings banks), and their name provides an accurate description of their activities. These for-profit businesses accept savings deposits from the public and make mortgage loans to demanders of long-term credit. For reasons discussed earlier in this chapter, commercial banks have avoided overburdening their portfolios with long-term credit, though, at times, commercial banks may be the second largest mortgage lender. Demand deposit variability plus a liquidity risk on these instruments makes them somewhat less suitable as assets for commercial banks.

S&Ls, which do not accept large quantities of demand deposits, do not face these constraints. Table 12–4 gives the aggregated balance sheet for S&Ls in 1980 and indicates that savings deposits dominate S&L liabilities. Savings deposits are comprised of either the conventional passbook or the "certificate

Table 12-4   *Savings and Loan Associations Consolidated Balance Sheet (February 1980, in Millions of Dollars)*

Assets		Liabilities	
Mortgages	$477,303	Savings Capital	$473,862
Cash and Investment Securities	50,168	Borrowed Money (advances from FHLBB and other borrowing)	55,276
Other Assets	58,214	Loans in process	8,269
		Other Liabilities	15,385
		Net Worth	32,893
Total	$585,685	Total	$585,685

Source: *Federal Home Loan Bank Board* and *Federal Reserve Bulletin.*

of deposit" variety. Interest payments on the latter with maturity to 10 years are higher though funds must be committed for the specified time period. With much lower variability of these deposits S&Ls can better predict withdrawals, and therefore may invest more freely in higher yield, longer-term instruments, principally home mortgages.

Home mortgages bought (and written) by S&Ls are long-term loans to home buyers. Most of these mortgages are of the "conventional" type, but some are FHA (Federal Housing Administration) and VA (Veteran's Administration) insured. The latter type of loans, which provide insurance against default for the S&L, also have disadvantages when compared with the conventional type. Specifically VA and FHA-insured loans restrict interest rates and total value of the mortgage loan in addition to specifying standards of construction. For these reasons—and especially during times of rising interest rates—S&Ls have tended to avoid them.

PORTFOLIO MANAGEMENT IN THE S&L

S&L mortgages, like stocks, negotiable bonds, and certificates of deposit, may be sold in a secondary market. (The government-insured mortgages have an obvious advantage in these markets, of course.) The ability to alter one's holdings of interest earning assets is not unlike that of the commercial bank that may alter its composition of assets. And the problems of asset or liquidity management are similar for all financial institutions, including S&Ls.

Clearly S&Ls earn interest on their portfolio of mortgage assets, but they must pay interest (and the cost of transacting and servicing) on savings. In addition, S&Ls, like all other institutions, must keep an eye on liquidity and solvency. In part, liquidity may be achieved by staggering the maturities of mortgage assets. Solvency and profitability may be difficult to achieve, however, especially when interest rates are rising.

The rate of profit is determined by the difference between the interest or yield earned on loans and the interest paid on savings deposits. During the late 1960s and the late 1970s S&Ls were caught in a two-way bind. First, government regulations have historically placed maximums on interest rates that may be charged to savers, although new legislation will eventually eliminate these maximums (to be considered later in this chapter). This practice placed limits on the amount of funds which S&Ls were able to attract during periods of rising interest rates. These maximum interest rate regulations created a situation called disintermediation, in which among other things, the supply of funds to the S&Ls (on which profits are made) is reduced.[7]

Rising home mortgage rates, on the other hand, result in a reduced turnover of mortgages in the asset portfolio, since holders of low-rate mortgages have positive incentives not to refinance at these times. More importantly, the same liquidity problem facing commercial banks (or any other institution) on long-term investments (bonds, mortgages, and so forth) pertains to S&Ls as well. When market rates on mortgages rise, the market value on previously issued mortgages falls, causing S&Ls to take capital losses if they are forced to sell them in secondary markets. Liquidity, solvency, and profitability of S&Ls may therefore be threatened during periods characterized by these market conditions. In short, asset management in savings and loan institutions, while of a slightly different character than that described for the commercial bank, can be fraught with as many difficulties and uncertainties.

Regulation of S&Ls and Other Intermediaries. The economic and financial catastrophe of the 1930s engendered numerous (some would say too numerous) types of economic reform. In the financial sphere, commercial banks were subjected to new forms of regulation, and other types of financial intermediaries were brought under Federal regulation. Savings and loan associations, insurance companies, and mutual savings banks were placed under a new agency called the Federal Home Loan Bank System (FHLBS), which operates in 12 districts in the United States and is charged with regulating, chartering, and administering credit to some of these institutions. The FHLBS (1) oversees the federal chartering of eligible mortgage lending institutions (many of these institutions do not belong to the FHLBS and are regulated by separate state agencies); (2) has controlled the lending of short- and long-term funds to member institutions whose liquidity is endangered or that experience large local demands for mortgage credit although, as discussed in Chapter 11, the Federal Reserve Board has opened the discounting privilege to all "depository institutions"; (3) controls the Federal Savings and Loan Insurance Corporation, which insures deposits up to $100,000; and (4) has, until recently, had the power to set maximum interest rates that S&Ls can pay on savings deposits. The role of the FHLBS is roughly analogous to the activities of the Fed concerning commercial banks, whereas the insurance corporation performs the function of the FDIC for S&Ls. About 80% of all S&Ls belong to this system, which hold well over 95% of total assets in the system. The nonmember S&Ls are regulated by appropriate state agencies and are eligible, if they meet certain standards, for federal deposit insurance just as state banks may become members of the FDIC. Other changes in the structure of depository institutions such as the S&Ls will be discussed later in this chapter.

MUTUAL SAVINGS BANKS AND CREDIT UNIONS

An early form of depository institution, and a very close functional relative of the S&L, is the mutual savings bank (MSB). MSBs were founded in the northeastern part of the United States in the early nineteenth century in order to provide safe depositories for the funds of small savers. They, along with early commercial banks, provided invaluable services in financial intermediations as well.

Today, 18 states charter MSBs, and they are still predominantly located in the northeast. Over 90% of the same 500 MSBs are located in the states of Massachusetts, New York, Connecticut, Maine, New Hampshire, and New Jersey. Deposits totaled over 146 billion dollars in late 1979, and assets are heavily concentrated in mortgages with 1- to 4-family residential mortgages the principal type.

Only 50 of the 500 or so MSBs have elected to join the Federal Home Loan Bank System, but all are eligible for deposit insurance administered by the FDIC. Consequently, state regulation predominates over these types of savings institutions, and states have implemented their own deposit insurance plans. MSBs are *mutual* institutions, that is, they are owned by depositors (stock institutions are owned by stockholders, and S&Ls may be organized under either organizational principle). MSBs, however, are run by self-perpetuating boards of trustees.

MSBs and S&Ls might appear to be (and actually are) close substitutes from the point of view of the depositor-savers, but there is one "philosophical" difference that makes portfolio management at the MSBs a bit easier than at S&Ls. In fulfilling the historical role of providing maximum protection for the small saver, most states place maximum limits on the total amounts that may be deposited by a single individual. Larger and more unpredictable savings deposits do not present problems of liquidity for MSBs. Furthermore, MSBs have traditionally held fairly sizeable quantities of highly liquid US government and corporate securities in these portfolios.

Credit unions are another familiar deposit-type intermediary. They are organized around some "common bond" such as occupation, association, or residential location. Member funds are "pooled" and the "excess funds" savers are used to finance member demands for consumer loans. While comparatively small in total assets, credit unions offer a number of advantages to member savers and borrowers, including slightly higher (on average) interest payments on savings deposits and slightly lower interest rates on loans, which are principally used to purchase consumer durables.[8] Credit unions may be chartered either by a Federal government agency (established by the Federal Credit Union Act of 1934) or by state agencies. The National Credit Union Administration regulates and provides services to federally chartered unions, including the provison of insurance for depositors (up to $100,000). State-chartered credit unions are eligible (under specified conditions) for this insurance.

LIFE INSURANCE COMPANIES

The vagaries of human life explain the existence of life insurance companies, which are one of the nation's largest financial intermediaries.[9] Insurance companies build up high amounts of funds that they in turn invest as an inter-mediary. Insurance contributions with rates based upon actuarial (mortality) tables constitute the source of funds for the companies. Most of the public's in-surance payments represent savings to the public, and many policies carry a cash value or "surrender value" upon cancellation of coverage. Policy loans may also be made on policies, or holders of policies with a cash value may borrow against them. During periods of high market rates of interest, policy loans become important to the insurance company, as interest rates have traditionally remained low on such loans.

Since the liabilities of insurance companies are predicted with a high de-gree of accuracy, portfolio theory would predict sizeable investments in long-term assets. This is certainly the case. The two largest assets of insurance com-panies are in stocks and bonds of private businesses (196 billion dollars in November 1978) and in mortgages and real estate (over 114 billion dollars in November 1978). Insurance companies are especially important to the econ-omy in this latter function, since a large proportion of mortgages held are those issued by small and medium size firms for business purposes against business property.

In general, insurance companies are regulated by the states in which they engage in operations (most often by state insurance boards). The job of port-folio selection is much easier for these companies than for S&Ls or commercial banks since, for example, there are few "surprise" demands for liquidity.

CHANGES IN INDUSTRY STRUCTURE

This abbreviated introduction to the composition of the industry of financial intermediaries reveals great diversity and specialization in the kind of products they sell. Nor may we regard financial intermediaries as a dead and never-changing industry. Just as savings banks emerged as intermediators in early nineteenth century America, other institutions, such as pension plans, mutual funds, and savings and loan associations, were molded to meet the demands of the saving and investing public. There can be small doubt as to the importance of these forms of financial institutions in providing security for savers and the availability of credit for investment and capital formation. Certainly one may expect new institutions and "products" to evolve to serve these groups with changing regulatory constraints, market conditions, and changing demands. NOW accounts, automatic transfer services, and credit union share drafts are examples of new product development.

In a *transactions cost* approach to the problem we conclude with recent writers on the subject that "changes in technology and in consumer borne transactions costs alter the type of financial commodities produced, the way in which they are packaged, and the institutions that produce and sell them to consumers."[10] As long as these institutions are malleable in the sense of an unfettered ability to react to changes in technology, transactions costs, and consumer tastes and desires, they will be able to provide extremely important services to the checking, saving, and investing public. But a large part of government regulation of the industry has tended to restrict the ability of these institutions to provide and introduce new financial products efficiently. Thus the remainder of this chapter will be devoted to a discussion of some important regulations—old, relatively new, and very recently enacted—affecting the industry of financial intermediaries.

THE REGULATION OF FINANCIAL INTERMEDIARIES

One may view the basic effects of governmental regulation of financial intermediaries as one would view the regulation of any industry—for example, transportation, communication, or energy-related—by the government. Government regulation may be implemented by effecting (1) entry and exit conditions in the industry; (2) legal control over prices, that is, prices paid or prices received for the inputs or products of the industry; or, (3) tax treatment of the industry, including the possibilities of providing negative taxes (subsidies). Examples from other industries readily come to mind. Entry and exit have been strictly controlled, until recently, by the Civil Aeronautics Board in the airline industry. Price controls have been rigidly enforced (most observers think too rigidly) in natural gas pricing, and for years the oil industry enjoyed the depletion allowance, a form of differential subsidy. Many American products, moreover, are protected from foreign competition by tariffs, another form of subsidy. The financial industry, as any of these others, can be viewed within a regulatory framework.

REGULATIONS AFFECTING BANK SAFETY
As indicated elsewhere in this book, the 1930s were a benchmark in the metamorphosis of the financial system. Between 1920 and 1933 massive bank closings (both member and nonmember banks) led to numerous bank reforms in the post-1930 era, including (1) a deposit insurance requirement of member banks and the provision of insurance facilities for nonbank intermediaries; (2) tighter regulation of bank holding companies; (3) maximum interest rates on time and savings deposits by commercial banks, later expanded to savings and loans by the Federal Home Loan Bank in 1966; and (4) an absolute prohibition of the payment of interest rates on demand deposits.

As we will see, many of these regulations and restrictions have imposed costs and burdens on the public and on the institutions concerned which are neither matched nor exceeded by benefits. One such regulation that does appear to receive high marks, however, is the deposit insurance requirements for the industry managed by the Federal Deposit Insurance Corporation (for banks), the Federal Savings and Loan Insurance Corporation (for savings and loans and mutual savings banks), and the National Credit Union Administration (for credit unions). Almost all nonmember financial institutions have availed themselves of these insurance facilities, and the benefits for the overall system have been enormous. These regulations have seemed to provide a large measure of stability and safety for the system. Other "safety" regulations are far more questionable, however.

REGULATIONS AFFECTING THE PRICE (INTEREST RATES) OF FINANCIAL SERVICES

While all financial institutions are specialized to a degree, there is a great deal of competition among them for saver's funds. This competition is particularly true for commercial banks and S&Ls. Differential regulations imposed by a number of different agencies, both state and federal, concerning maximum interest rate ceilings often distorts the allocation of financial resources between institutions. The regulations themselves can initiate a costly process called "disintermediation." Let us take a closer look at both of these effects.

Regulation Q.[11] Although the maximum interest rate provisions on time and savings deposits (Regulation Q) were imposed on the dubious grounds of "providing for bank safety," they have had the effect, especially in the late 1950s and early 1960s, of shifting saver funds from regulated to nonregulated financial sectors of the economy. When market interest rates on securities (corporate securities for example) were below the maximum set by Regulation Q, commercial banks had no difficulty in attracting funds. But when market rates rose in the late 1950s and early 1960s, saver funds shifted from commercial banks to the then nonregulated savings and loan associations (and to other nonregulated financial segments in the economy). Rather than lift these distorting price regulations on commercial banks, the government, through the FHLB, imposed similar restrictions on S&Ls in 1966. Although the new regulation effectively prevented shifts of saver funds between commercial banks and S&Ls, it encouraged a process known as *disintermediation*.

Disintermediation occurs when the market rate of interest exceeds the maximum allowed at financial intermediaries (commercial banks and savings and loans). Individual saver-investors purchase market securities (for example, corporate), directly by-passing the intermediary. Why does this process have costly economic effects? As indicated at the beginning of this chapter, the information and transaction costs of direct purchase of securities by millions of small savers led to the original development of intermediaries and their specialized instruments. Though small savers might be able to deal directly in securities, they are unable to *spread risk* as the intermediaries are able to do. They will thus demand high compensation (higher interest rates) for higher risk. Add to this the costly problem of gathering information about borrowers, and it is easy to understand why Regulation Q has been regarded by most economists (and commissions studying the problem) as costly and inefficient.

There are yet other reasons why specific groups have opposed these price regulations. First, Regulation Q, far from protecting the financial system from the ravages of "rampant competition," might actually endanger its existence. During periods of high market rates, funds simply flow elsewhere (for example, into higher yielding corporate securities) and sources of funds for these intermediaries are reduced. This pattern often results in reduced profit, solvency and stability, as evidenced by the experience of some S&Ls in the late 1960s and 1970s.

The building trades, moreover, should (and do) loudly complain against maximum interest rates. The saving and loan "profit squeeze" of the late 1960s and late 1970s created a severe constriction of the availability of mortgage funds for new construction. This led to what many regarded as a discriminatory policy against specific capital sectors of the economy.

Although the regulatory agencies (FRS and FHLB) have altered interest controls from time to time and for specific reasons (see Table 12–5), the control is not uniformly applied. As Table 12–5 indicates, deposits over $100,000 are exempt from the provision. The intent of the exemption was to prevent capital flight to countries with no maximum provision, but the result of the entire system of maximum rates has been to discriminate against the small saver.

Price Regulation: Pre-1980. Maximum interest rate provisions have not been the only regulated price control in the industry of financial intermediaries. Part of the revision of financial structure in the 1930s included the absolute prohibition of interest payments on demand deposits by commercial banks. Again safety of the banking system was the underlying reason of the regulation. It was believed that competition for demand deposits as sources of funds would embroil the banks in unsound business practices.

It is difficult to understand, however, how depriving the market of an alternative that would be mutually supported by sellers and buyers of demand deposits could have harmed the soundness of banks or the banking system. Banks might find it profitable to pay interest to attract funds, and the public's cost of holding money would be reduced.

A closely related regulatory ground rule involved, before the 1970s and 1980s, the prohibition of demand deposit sales by S&Ls or other nonbank

Table 12-5 Maximum Interest Rates on Time and Savings Deposits at
Federally Insured Institutions

Type and Maturity of Deposit	Commercial Banks		Savings and Loan Associations and Mutual Savings Banks	
	In Effect April 30, 1980 (Percent)	Previous Maximum (Percent)	In Effect April 30, 1980	Previous Maximum
Savings	5¼	5	5½	5¼
NOW (negotiable order of withdrawal accounts)[a]	5	—	5	—
Time accounts		4½ multiple maturity		
30–90 days	5¼	5 single maturity	—	—
90 days–1 year	5¾	5½	6	5¾
1–2 years[b]	6	5½	6½	5¾
2–2½ years[b]	6	5¾	6¾	6
2½–4 years[b]	6½	5¾	7½	6
4–6 years[c]	7¼	—	7¾	—
6–8 years[c]	7½	7¼	8	7½
8 years or more[c]	7¾	—	8	—
governmental units	8	7¾	8	7¾
$100,000 or more[d]	—	—	—	—

[a] For authorized states only. Federally insured commercial banks, savings and loan association, cooperative banks, and mutual savings banks were first permitted to offer NOW accounts on January 1, 1974.
[b] A minimum deposit of $1,000 is required for savings and loan associations.
[c] A minimum deposit of $1,000 is required.
[d] Maximum rates of $100,000 or more were suspended in mid 1973.
Source: Adapted from the *Federal Reserve Bulletin*, various issues.

intermediaries. Here regulation attempted to establish a sharp line of demarcation between demand and savings deposits in what amounts to a rigid separation of functions between banks and nonbanks.

As with all legal price controls, it is doubtful if all of these regulations of the financial system have had the desired effects. Fortunately, the market has the ability to circumvent much price regulation. When disintermediation begins to take place, drying up sources of investment funds for the intermediaries, the intermediaries turn to alternative, nondeposit sources of funds. Federal Reserve and other bank borrowing increases over these periods as does participation in the Federal Funds market. Financial transactions by American intermediaries with foreign subsidiaries or correspondents are not subject to maximum rate provisions increases. However, even though the market process has managed to soften or redirect the process of disintermediation, it has done so only at much higher costs to the public. Maximum interest rate provisions, therefore, even if totally ineffective during periods of high market rates, increase transactions costs and are not economically neutral.

The market, along with more advanced technology, has also been able to circumvent (to some extent) the prohibition of interest payments on demand deposits. Everyone is familiar with banks that advertise for minimum or no checking account charges, travel discounts, or free dishes with minimum deposits. These schemes to attract deposits are an implicit "interest payment." The commerical banking system, moreover, has not appeared any less sound since these practices began.

Deregulation of Price Controls—1980. Regulatory changes to reflect market circumventions of legal price controls began to appear in the late 1970s and, most significantly, in early 1980. Some of these changes were discussed in Chapter 11. For example, banks have been authorized to provide ATS services, and the Depository Institutions Deregulation Act of March 1980 also extends the authority of all depository institutions to offer NOW accounts as of December 31, 1980. As pointed out in Chapter 11, such deregulation acknowledges (and even fosters) the blurring between savings and demand deposits, between banks and nonbanks, and between "members" and "nonmembers" of the Federal Reserve System.

Of much more significance for the future and for the profitability of the financial system is the (ultimate) deregulation of interest rates at *all* depository institutions. Charging that such regulations have (a) discriminated against small savers, (b) discouraged saving, (c) impeded depository institutions from competing for funds, and (d) failed to provide an even flow of funds for home mortgage lending, the "Depository Institutions Deregulation Act of 1980" provides for a return to free market conditions as soon as economically feasible.

Orderly "phase-out" of interest rate controls will take place over a six-year period under the guidance of a "Depository Institutions Deregulation Committee." As of March 1980 all statutory powers to set interest payments contained in the Federal Reserve Act, the FDIC Act and the Federal Home Loan Bank Act were transferred to a five-member voting board: the Secretary of the Treasury, the Chairman of the Fed Board of Governors, the Chairman of the Board of Governors of the FDIC, the Chairman of the Federal Home Loan Bank Board, and the Chairman of the National Credit Union Administration Board. (The Comptroller of the Currency is a nonvoting member of the Committee.) The Act also provides targets to assist the Committee and requires separate annual reports from individual committee members concerning the viability and progress of the deregulation.

These developments reflect the widespread acknowledgment that interest rate regulation has failed in preserving the soundness of the banking system and in protecting thrift institutions from unregulated money market innovators that paid market rates to savers. As with the emergence of interest-paying checkable deposits, the ultimate effect upon the financial structure of interest rate deregulation is difficult to predict. It seems clear, however, that such regulations to circumvent the market mechanism have been achieved at much higher costs of financial mediation to society. Whatever else may be said about them, interest rate controls have been an odd way of protecting the public's interest.

REGULATIONS AFFECTING ENTRY

Perhaps the most common form of regulation is entry control. Through licensing, franchising, or charter restrictions, freedom of entry into many areas of the economy (medicine, transportation, communication, and hair cutting) is effectively curtailed. The industry of financial intermediaries is no exception. Although we mentioned some banking restrictions such as branch banking in Chapter 10, we now emphasize them as entry control regulation.

Just as any new airline must obtain a C and N (certificate of public convenience and necessity) from the Civil Aeronautics Board, prospective banks—at either the state or the Federal level—must show why a new bank in any locale is needed. Furthermore, it must show financial and managerial capability not only to the chartering body such as the State Banking Board or the Comptroller of the Currency, but also to the Federal Deposit Insurance Corporation. Similar provisions relate to the foundation of savings and loans and other financial intermediaries including insurance companies. In banking, as in many other areas of the economy, the judgment of a board of investigators replaces that of investors (who are risking their money) in determining whether a new bank or a new S&L is desirable.

Opportunities for fraud appear in such a system. First, there is the clear advantage that existing (and chartered) banks have in any given geographic area. But the charter itself (like airline certification, a taxi medallion, or an FM radio station license) has a money value. Sub rosa dealings, especially at the state level, are quite common. But the important point is that these entry restrictions reduce competition and very likely increase the costs of banking to the public. (Remember that depositors are secure from bank failure through FDIC insurance.) The returns to stockholder-investors in banks are protected, however. The number of commercial bank charters applied for far exceeds, by many times, the number of charters granted. Chartering authorities have been very reluctant to increase the number of banks, which has remained fairly constant since 1935.

Other regulatory and institutional characteristics of banks can affect the degree of competition. Branch banking, or the lack thereof, can have some impact on the degree of competition. Mergers and the one- or multibank holding companies have been brought under the umbrella of tighter regulation by the Bank Merger Act (1960) and by the Bank Holding Company Act (1956, amended 1970). Economists, however, are still uncertain of the effects of branching, mergers, and bank holding companies on the conditions of competition in the industry. There is no way to be certain that the decisions of the Federal Reserve, the Comptroller of the Currency, or the FDIC respecting mergers or bank holding companies will increase or decrease competitiveness in banking. Anticompetitive mergers may be approved if, in the judgment of the regulators, better services are provided.

Multiple bank and nonbank intermediary examinations are also wasteful and increase the transaction costs of financial intermediation to the public. Almost 5,000 banks, for instance, are supervised and inspected by the Comptroller of the Currency, the Federal Reserve System, and the FDIC and by State banking regulators. Although some coordination of inspections takes place, multiple (and largely unnecessary) examinations increase the costs of intermediary services through time lost and the additional personnel required.

CONCLUSION

Chapter 12 has been primarily concerned with the major institutional characteristics of commercial banks and with those of other depository institutions and financial intermediaries. Principally, these institutions can be differentiated by the kind of products in which they specialize. Recent regulatory (and legislative) changes, however, have altered the overall design of regulation (or lack of it in the case of interest rate ceilings) and have been instituted with the idea that financial intermediaries, especially thrift institutions, differ in degree but not in kind from commercial banks.

All evidence points to the significant benefits to come from a deregulation of interest rate controls and prohibitions. Monetary control is at the base of new financial system regulation, however, as is the explicit recognition that the concentration of regulatory authority over financial system reserves is prerequisite to effective implementation of monetary policy. The legislative goal of equal treatment respecting reserve requirements within financial intermediaries will be accomplished over the 1980s as will the institution of competitive conditions in attracting deposit funds. These features underline the similarities and importance of all financial institutions in the transmission of monetary policy. Financial markets through which these monetary controls are affected are the subject of Chapter 13.

FOOTNOTES

[1] This discussion derives from the interesting work by George J. Benston and Clifford W. Smith, Jr., "A Transactions Cost Approach to the Theory of Financial Intermediation," *Journal of Finance* (May 1976), pp. 215–31.

[2] Member commercial banks are required to maintain reserve balances over average deposits of the previous two weeks, not at every instant in time.

[3] Individual commercial banks, particularly large banks, engage in ongoing research on deposit variability (composition and structure of deposits) and loan demand, and on general business conditions.

[4] All states except Massachusetts and New Hampshire have imposed some sort of usury law. These maximums range from 6% in Pennsylvania to 21% in Rhode Island, but there are many exceptions. When these laws are actually effective (and enforced), unusual shifting in the allocation of mortgage funds may occur when contiguous states impose different maximums allowable interest rates. See the interesting paper by Norman N. Bowsher, "Usury Laws: Harmful When Effective," of the *Review*. *Federal Reserve Bank of St. Louis* (August 1974), pp. 16–23.

[5] Under Title V of the Act, state loans and constitutional provisions regulating maximum amounts of interest are preempted with respect to loans, mortgages and credit sales after March 31, 1980, that are secured by first lien on residential real property, or with other designated collateral. A state may reinstate many limitations before April 1, 1983, by adopting a law or by certifying by popular ballot that voters of the state wish to preempt the federal usury override.

[6] Readers wishing an extended treatment of financial intermediaries might profitably peruse the introduction by Benton E. Gup, *Financial Intermediaries* (Boston: Houghton Mifflin Company, 1976).

[7] The process of disintermediation has other implications as well. For example, over periods of rising interest rates, people do not go to intermediaries with their savings but go directly to purchase higher interest bearing corporate bonds. The building and construction industry, in particular, suffers from a drying up of mortgage funds at the S&Ls which is a direct result of the maximum interest rate provisions of regulatory agencies.

[8] Credit unions have not been subject to maximum interest rates on deposits as are commercial banks, S&Ls, and MSBs.

[9] We limit our discussion here to life insurance, but there are other types of insurance such as property and casualty companies.

[10] See Benston and Smith, "A Transactions Cost Approach to the Theory of Financial Intermediation," *The Journal of Finance* (May 1976), p. 229.

[11] For an interesting historical account of Regulation Q see Scott Winningham and Donald G. Hagan, "Regulation Q: An Historical Perspective," *Economic Review, Federal Reserve Bank of Kansas City* (April 1980), pp. 3–17.

KEY CONCEPTS

financial intermediary

transaction accounts

intermediation

transactions costs

information costs

liquidity

risk

time to maturity

secondary reserves

Federal funds market

Treasury bills (T-bills)

savings and loan Associations (S&Ls)

disintermediation

Federal Home Loan Bank System (FHLBS)

mutual savings bank

National Credit Union Administration

QUESTIONS FOR DISCUSSION

1. Why is disintermediation harmful?

2. Will the opening of competition (inter-industry), such as that established in new financial system legislation, cause an unstable banking atmosphere (due perhaps to cutthroat tactics)?

3. Most people move through various financial stages that are characterized either by "excess funds" or "short of funds." At what times in their lives are people likely to have excess funds? When are they likely to be short of funds?

4. What conditions would encourage a bank to increase its liquidity? What about an individual?

5. Why do you think municipal bonds are tax-free?

6. What should the policy be on usury laws in your opinion? Why?

7. What are the principal differences between S&Ls and Mutual Savings banks?

8. Describe briefly in your own words the distinguishing characteristics of the other financial intermediaries mentioned in the text, not in the previous question.

9. Why have credit cards and store credit plans become so popular in recent years?

10. Could the functions of the FDIC, FSLIC, and the NCUA be undertaken by private firms?

11. Until recent times, explicit interest payments on demand deposits were prohibited. What are some specific ways banks avoided this regulation?

12. How could investors decide whether or not a new bank is needed? Is this method more or less costly than a board of investigators?

CHAPTER 13

FINANCIAL MARKETS, INTEREST RATES, AND ECONOMIC POLICY

In Chapter 12 the nature and the role of financial intermediaries and of the financial instruments that they generate were discussed. The features of the markets where those instruments are bought and sold, and the place of those markets in the overall economy are discussed in Chapter 13. There are literally thousands of financial instruments having one important feature in common: they are promises to make payments in the future. There are also many markets where financial instruments are exchanged. One of these is the so-called "money market," where short-term instruments (with up to a one-year maturity) are bought and sold. Another is the "capital market," specializing in long-term debt.

In Chapter 13 we concern ourselves with the common features of all these financial instruments and the manner in which these markets are interconnected. We will see how the connection among the various markets permits an analysis of the *financial market*, which is nothing else than the market for loanable funds that was introduced in Chapter 5 (and elaborated upon in the Appendix to that Chapter). At the end of the present Chapter we will visit the financial or loanable funds market, reproduce some of the policy changes analyzed in previous chapters (notably in Chapter 8), and observe in some detail how this market is affected by those changes.

THE ANATOMY OF BOND YIELDS AND PRICES

As indicated before, there are thousands of financial instruments, but all of them are promises to make payments in the future, either as a lump sum or as a series of payments. Here, the representative financial instrument is called a *bond*. Certain standard features of a bond should be analyzed in order to facilitate the economic interpretation of what is going on in financial markets. All financial instruments are particular variations of such a typical bond.

The typical bond is a promise to pay at some time in the future (the *redemption date*) a certain sum specified on the bond (the nominal value of the bond, also called *face* or *par* value), as well as an interest on the nominal value at every period until the redemption date, according to an interest rate specified in the bond (the *coupon rate*). The magnitudes that characterize this typical bond are (1) the nominal value of the bond; (2) the *maturity* or life span of the bond (or, when we refer to a bond issued in the past, the time left until the redemption date); and (3) the coupon rate, according to which the interest on the nominal value is to be paid at every period until redemption.

An example is helpful. Suppose that company XYZ wishes to borrow 1,000 dollars, and that to do so it issues a bond (in this case, called a corporate bond) with a nominal or face value of 1,000 dollars, a maturity of two years, and a coupon rate of 10 percent per year. Thus operation involved is that the company XYZ commits itself to pay an interest of 10 percent over 1,000 dollars (that is, 100 dollars) at the end of the first and the second years, and to "redeem" or buy back the bond at the end of the second year at its nominal value of 1,000 dollars. In other words, future payments include a *flow* of equal interest payments and a *final* lump sum.

This is a typical and generic example encompassing many particular cases. First, the maturity of the bond could have been shorter (perhaps one month, or one week) or longer (5, 10, or 20 years). In fact, there can be no maturity date at all. This last case is indeed an important one, as it happens every time a *perpetuity*— or *consol* as they are called in Great Britain—is issued. Here, the only obligation of the bond issuer is to pay the interest on the bond, so that only the face value of the bond, together with the coupon rate, is necessary to calculate the interest payment at every period. In addition, there may not be any payment of interest until a redemption date; in other words, there may be no flow of payments, but only a final lump sum. This is frequently the case with short-lived bonds, such as Treasury bills or Barbara's two-week loan to Tom. As a third alternative, payments over time can be a mix of interest and repayment of the principal, as in the important case of mortgages (a "bond" issued by the home purchaser and "bought" by a lending institution).

Let us return to the typical XYZ company bond. Since such a bond is transferable and actively negotiated in the financial market, an important issue concerns the *price of such a bond in the market.* Or "How much would one be willing to pay for such a bond?" To answer this question—as well as many others—we must understand the simple but important concept of *present value.*

THE CONCEPT AND USES OF PRESENT VALUE

The concept of present value is an important one, playing a crucial role in practically any economic analysis involving time. The concept itself is only a calculation through which equivalence may be found between payments at different dates or between a flow of payments and a lump-sum payment utilizing a market interest rate or vice versa. In order to understand present value, we should first analyze *future value.*

Suppose the market rate of interest is 10 percent per year and that Tom borrows 500 dollars for one year from Barbara, to be repaid together with interest at the end of that year. Thus Tom will receive 500 dollars today and pay back the principal (500 dollars) plus the interest agreed to in the contract $((500) \cdot (0.10) = 50)$, or a total of 550 dollars, a year from now. If we call V_0 the amount borrowed by Tom, and V_1 the amount of his debt at the end of the year, then

$$V_1 = V_0 + V_0 \cdot i = V_0 \cdot (1 + i)$$

where i is the rate of interest on the loan.

If Tom wishes to borrow the 500 dollars not for one, but for two years, and to return his debt and interest as a final, lump-sum payment at the end of the two years, his debt at the end of the first year would be as computed ($V_1 = V_0 \cdot (1 + i)$, or 550 dollars). At the end of the second year, however, he must pay back such debt (V_1), plus the interest on that debt for the second year ($V_1 \cdot i$, the debt times the rate of interest), or

$$V_2 = V_1 + V_1 \cdot i = V_1 \cdot (1 + i)$$
$$= V_0 \cdot (1 + i) \cdot (1 + i) = V_0 \cdot (1 + i)^2$$

or, in our example,

$$V_2 = (500) \cdot (1.10)^2 = (500) \cdot (1.21) = 605$$

The calculation is an important expression for *compounded interest.* If we wish to generalize it for any number of years, and we call the number of years "n," then we have

$$V_n = V_0 \cdot (1 + i)^n \qquad [13.1]$$

where V_n is called the *future value, n* years from now, if the amount V_0, at the interest rate i. By using this expression, we can answer an important question, namely: "What is the value, today, of an amount V_n to be delivered n periods from now, at the rate of interest i per period?" The answer to the question is immediate from expression [13.1], because such a value is precisely V_0, or

$$V_0 = V_n / (1 + i)^n \qquad [13.2]$$

The term V_0 is the present value (today) of an amount V_n to be delivered n periods from now when the interest rate is i per period, and interest is compounded at every period.

The concept of present value is important because it is full of economic content. If the market interest rate is i, the equilibrium market value, today, of the right to receive the sum V_n n periods from now will be precisely such present value. This is so because no one would be willing to buy such a right for more than its present value: individuals could do better by lending their money at the going interest rate and receiving at the end an amount larger than what they would have received if they had bought such a right. Also, no one would be willing to sell such a right at a price lower than its present value; if an individual owns such a right and needs cash today, he or she can always borrow at the going rate of interest. At the time of receiving payment the proceeds of the payment could be used for paying off the loan, with money left over.

Take, for example, the case of Tom's two-year loan. If numbers ($V_0 = 500$, $i = 0.10$) are inserted into expression [13.2], we can see that the present value of 605 dollars, two years from now, when the interest rate is 10 percent per year, is precisely equal to 500 dollars. No one would be willing to pay any more than 500 dollars (for example, 520 dollars) for the right to receive 605 dollars two years from now if the interest rate is 10 percent per year. The individual could do a lot better by lending the 520 dollars at the going interest rate of 10 percent, instead, and receiving at the end of the two years a total of $(520) \cdot (1 + 0.10)^2 = 629.20$ dollars, rather than 605 dollars. To ask anyone to purchase such a right for more than 500 dollars is the same as asking for a loan at an interest rate *lower* than the going market rate of 10 percent per year (if the price were 520 dollars, a rate of 7.86 percent per year).

Likewise, anyone would be willing to purchase the right to receive 605 dollars two years from now, when the interest rate is 10 percent per year, at a price of less than 500 dollars, say 480 dollars. One could borrow the 480 dollars at 10 percent per year, accumulate a debt at the end of the two years equal to $(480) \cdot (1.10)^2 = 580.80$ dollars, and at that time make a profit of $605 - 580.80 = 24.20$ dollars. In other words, such an offer would provide the possibility of lending at an interest rate higher than the market rate (in this example a rate of exactly 12.27 percent per year).

The *equilibrium market price* for the right to receive a certain amount in the future must equal the present value of this same amount. If it were smaller, everybody would wish to buy that right, and no one to sell it, and its price would go up; if it were larger, no one would want to purchase it, and everybody to sell it, and its price would go down.

An additional step is necessary before we return to the XYZ company's bond and to an analysis of its yield and price. There are already analogies between the case in which Tom borrows 500 dollars for two years from Barbara and the XYZ company issues its two year bond: Tom is the *bond issuer*, and Barbara is the *bond purchaser*. There is, however, something too specific about Tom's example as compared with the typical bond case—there was no stream or flow of interest to be paid during the time until repayment of the debt—only a final, total lump-sum payment for principal and interest. In order to reach a more general formulation, we must calculate the present value of a *stream* of payments, rather than a single payment. And this is an easy task since *the present value of a stream of payments is simply equal to the sum of the present values of each of the payments.*

Let us take, for simplicity, the case of a stream of n annual equal payments and call Z the amount of each of these payments. If the market interest rate is i, the present value, today, of the first payment Z forthcoming a year from now is $Z/(1 + i)$; the present value of the second payment (coming up two years from now) is $Z/(1 + i)^2$; and so on until the last payment, forthcoming n years from now, has a present value of $Z/(1 + i)^n$. That is,

$$PV = Z \cdot (1/(1 + i) + 1/(1 + i)^2 + \cdots + 1/(1 + i)^n) \qquad [13.3]$$

The term in parenthesis on the right-hand side of expression [13.3] is a *discounting factor* that is easily found in financial tables (or from a financial hand calculator).

A special case of expression [13.3] occurs when payments last forever (the case of perpetuities). In this case, and if interest is compounded continuously, expression [13.3] reduces to

$$PV = Z/i \qquad [13.4]$$

From either expressions [13.3] or [13.4] it is evident that, for a certain value Z of the payments, the higher the rate of interest, the lower the present value of the payments stream, and vice versa. This result has important consequences for the economics of bond yields and prices.

As in the case of a single future payment, the equilibrium market price of a future stream of payments is also its present value, for exactly the same reasons. Let us consider the case of an infinite stream of payments (a perpetuity) with continuous interest compounding, and suppose that payments are made at the rate of 50 dollars per year and that the market rate of interest is, again, 10 percent per year. The present value of such infinite stream of payments is 50/(0.10) = 500 dollars. This will also be the market price of the bond or financial instrument giving to its holder the right to receive such a stream. If it were higher than the present value of 500 dollars (say, 520 dollars), owners of such instruments would be better off selling them and depositing the 520 dollars at the going interest rate of 10 percent, thereby receiving 52 dollars per year, rather than 50. If the price of the instrument were lower (say, 450 dollars), everybody would want to buy it; they could borrow 450 dollars, purchase the financial instrument, and at every period receive 50 dollars and pay the interest on the loan (45 dollars)—a gain of 5 dollars per year, forever.

YIELDS AND PRICES
Recall the particular numbers in our XYZ corporation bond example: a face or nominal value of 1,000 dollars, a coupon rate of 10 percent per year, and a maturity of two years. The future payments promised to the bond buyer were,

then, a stream of payments of 100 per year, for two years (as interest) and a final payment of 1,000 dollars (as redemption of the bond at its face value). In order to know the equilibrium price of such bond in the market its present value must be calculated, based on the *market* interest rate, *i* (which may or may not be the same as the *coupon* rate), as

$$PV = 100/(1 + i) + 100/(1 + i)^2 + 1,000/(1 + i)^2$$

The first two terms on the right-hand side of the expression amount to the present value of the stream of interest payments, and the last term to the present value of the final redemption payment of 1,000 dollars.

From this calculation, we can immediately verify that, if the market interest rate is equal to the coupon rate, the present value of the bond will equal its face value (1,000 dollars), and therefore its *market price* will equal the face value. The XYZ company will then be able to issue and sell its bond at the "face value," or "at par." What if the market interest rate is not 10 percent but, say, 12 percent per year, and the company issues and sells exactly the same bond? If the value of 0.12 (12 percent per year) is inserted into the expression above, we can verify that the present value, and therefore the market price of the bond, is no longer 1,000, but only 966.20 dollars. If XYZ corporation wishes to sell such a bond at the time it is issued, the bond will command only such a price: it will sell "below par."

The below par price is a natural result because the future payments implied in the bond conditions (a stream of 100 dollars per year, for two years, plus the lump-sum payment of 1,000 dollars at the end of the two years) would pay only for a two-year loan of 966.20 dollars, given the 12 percent market interest rate. If, instead, the interest rate were below the coupon rate (say, 8 percent per year), the present value or equilibrium price of the bond would be above its face value (in our case, exactly 1035.66 dollars) and it will sell above par in the market.

Thus we should see that it does not matter to the prospective buyer of the bond what the "face" or nominal value and the coupon rate are per se. Rather, it is the amount and timing of the future payments promised in the bond, and the rate of interest implied by those payments given the market price of the bond, that are important. This interest rate is called the *yield* on the bond, and it must equal the yield on comparable bonds, or the *market interest rate.*

Consider what would happen if the market rate of interest were 10 percent at the time the bond was issued, the bond were sold at par (1,000 dollars) at the time of issue, and at some point during the life of the bond the market interest rate rises to, say, 12 percent. As soon as the market rate of interest rises, the price of the bond will fall so that its yield (which was 10 percent) equals the market interest rate. The size of the price reductions depends on the time left until redemption, or on the maturity of the bond at the time the interest rate rises. This precept holds because the bond price must fall to its new present value at that moment, and the present value will depend on the timing of payments during the remaining life of the bond. At one extreme, suppose that the interest rate rises to 12 percent just after the bond has been issued and sold to Ms. Unlucky: the price will fall to 966.20 dollars, and Ms. Unlucky would suffer a capital loss of 33.80 dollars if she sold. At the other extreme, suppose the interest rate rises to 12 percent two years later, just as Ms. Unlucky (not so unlucky in this case), having collected her second interest payment at the second floor of XYZ corporate headquarters, is on her way to the third floor where the bond will be redeemed at its face value. In this case nothing happens. These two extreme cases are enough to suggest that *the longer the maturity of the bond, the higher will be the change in the bond market value for the same change in the market interest rate.*

Suppose that the interest rate rises to 12 percent when the bond has a maturity of one year just after the first interest payment has been received. In this case, the present value of the bond (which at the previous 10 percent market interest rate would have been 1,000 dollars) will now drop to $(100)/(1.12) + (1,000)/(1.12) = 982.14$ dollars, a capital loss of 17.85 dollars for Ms. Unlucky—less than the 33.80 capital loss if the change occurred at the beginning, but more than if it were to occur later. The results revert to a capital gain if the interest rate drops.

The principle involved here is simply that whoever purchases a bond lends the amount he or she pays for the bond at the interest rate at the time of the purchase (the yield on the bond). If the interest rate rises later, the individual is "stuck" for some time (the "maturity" of the bond) with a loan made at a lower interest rate than at the current rate. The longer the bondholder is stuck, the higher the loss (or gain, if the interest rate falls). Table 13–1 shows the present value of a bond with face value of 1,000 dollars, a coupon rate of 10 percent (and, therefore, interest payments of 100 dollars a year) and a maturity of 15 years when the market interest rate is 12 percent. Column (1) reflects the years to maturity—or life left; column (2) the present value (and therefore market price of the bond); column (3) the loss to the bond holder who purchased it at face value if the rise of the interest rate occurred at the various years to maturity: and column (4) the percentage fall in price. Figure 13–1 shows the values of column (2) for years left to maturity.

Because bond prices are more sensitive to changes in the market interest rate the longer their time to maturity, one should expect to observe much more pronounced variations in the price of these bonds (such as US government or municipal long-term bonds), following fluctuations in the interest rate, than in the price of short-term instruments (such as Treasury bills, for example). This presumption is confirmed by actual data. Thus there is a higher *risk* involved in holding long-term bonds than short-term ones.

Table 13-1   *Present Value Calculation*

Years to Maturity (1)	Market Value (2)	Capital Loss (3)	Percentage Price Fall (4)
15	863.78	136.22	13.66
14	867.44	132.56	13.25
13	871.53	128.47	12.85
12	876.11	123.89	12.39
11	881.25	118.75	11.87
10	887.00	113.00	11.30
9	893.44	106.56	10.65
8	900.65	99.35	9.94
7	908.72	91.28	9.13
6	917.77	82.23	8.22
5	927.90	72.10	7.21
4	939.25	60.75	6.07
3	951.96	48.04	4.80
2	966.20	33.80	3.38
1	982.14	17.86	1.79
9 months	986.42	13.58	1.36
6 "	990.82	9.18	0.92
3 "	995.34	4.66	0.47

What about the particular case of perpetuities, without a redemption time? Here, changes in the market interest rate will show the largest influence over the market price of the bond, and such a change in price will be the same no matter when it occurs. This stability exists because the present value depends only on the amount of every payment and the market rate of interest, as shown in expression [13.4]. If payments per period are, for example, 50 dollars per year, as in the numerical example, and if the market interest rate rises from 10 to 12 percent per year, the present value of the perpetuity will fall from 500 dollars to $(50)/0.12 = 416.67$ dollars, no matter the date on which the change takes place. In the case of perpetuities it can also be verified that the percentage change in the market value will be the same as (but of opposite sign than) the percentage change in the market interest rate.

These principles are the "mechanics" of present value. But before proceeding we should understand an important clarification. When calculating the present value of the typical bond, and therefore the equilibrium price of such bond, we used the market interest rate. In order to make such a calculation we must know not only today's market interest rate but also the rate that is expected to prevail at every period until the redemption time of the bond in question. In earlier calculations, we assumed that the same market interest

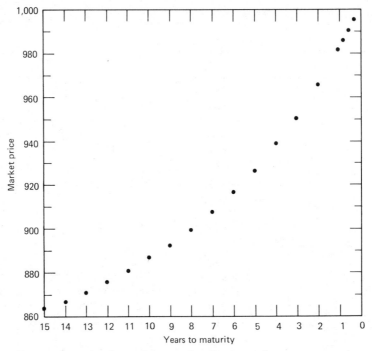

Figure 13-1. A relation between bond price and years to maturity.

rate prevailed during the total life span of the bond. It is possible for the market interest rate to vary in the future, and in such a case the calculation is more complicated. The principles outlined here, however, are accurate guides to a general calculation. In fact, these clarifications are at the center of the important relationship between yields of bonds and their time to maturity.

THE TERM STRUCTURE OF INTEREST RATES

One of the most important characteristics differentiating the large variety of financial instruments is their maturity. Does any relationship exist among the yields of bonds or financial instruments equal in all respects (risk, for example) except maturity? If so, what is this relationship and what is the mechanism by which these yields are interconnected? This topic is usually known as the *term structure of interest rates.*

A term structure or relationship between yield and maturity is represented graphically in the so-called "yield curves," as the ones shown in Figure 13-2, panels (a), (b) and (c). In all three panels, the term to maturity (remaining years left until redemption time) is shown on the horizontal axis, and the yield on the vertical axis. Three possible types of yield curves are shown (but there

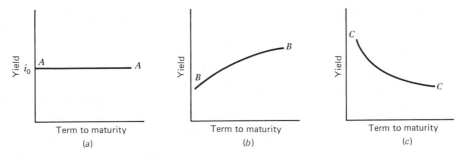

Figure 13-2. The term structure of interest rates: possible yield curves.

are others): curve *AA*, a horizontal line showing a yield i_0 for all maturities; curve *BB*, a positively sloped line showing higher yields for longer terms to maturity; and curve *CC*, showing the opposite—a downward sloping line indicating lower yields for longer maturities. These various shapes (and others) have been observed on occasions and some theories have been suggested to explain them. Of all these, positively sloped type *BB* is perhaps the one most frequently encountered.

Explanations for any given term structure of interest rates are a function of whether there is any difference between interest rates for *short-term loans* (such as the loan taken by the Federal government when it issues a Treasury bill, or the three-month loan for the purchase of a bicycle by Tom) and the rates for *long-term loans* (the loan taken by the Federal government when it sells a 30-year bond, or the *consumer loan* taken by the purchaser of a house to be financed with a 30-year mortgage). The basic theories attempt to explain why these rates might differ when risks are similar.

There are two main theories, sometimes seen as alternative, sometimes as complementing each other: the *expectations theory*, and the *market segmentation* or *hedging theory*. Of the two, the most widely accepted is a modified version of the expectations theory.

THE EXPECTATIONS THEORY OF INTEREST RATE
TERM STRUCTURE

The expectations theory asserts that differences in the yield of bonds of different terms to maturity are explained in terms of market expectations concerning the future course of the interest rate. In other words, the difference, today, between the yield on a longer term bond (say, of five-year term to maturity) and the yield on, say, a three-month Treasury bill, can be explained in terms of what the market expects to happen to yields on three-month bills, and other shorter-than-five year instruments, during the next five years.

We can understand the rationale behind such a proposition by a simple example. Suppose that today market conditions are such that the yield on a one-year bond (or, similarly, the market interest rate for a one-year loan) is 10 percent per year. Suppose, further, that the generalized expectation in the market is that those conditions will not change next year; that is, a year from now same interest rate for a one-year loan (or the yield on a one-year bond) will also be 10 percent. For the sake of simplicity, suppose that both one- and two-year bonds or loans involve only a final payment of interest and principal. Under these conditions, a lender who wishes to lend 1,000 dollars for two years should be indifferent to the two alternatives. The first alternative is to buy a one-year bond for 1,000 dollars (lend 1,000 dollars), receive 1,100 dollars at the end of the first year as interest and principal, and then lend 1,100 dollars at 10 percent for another year (or, purchase a bond with a market price of 1,100 dollars and a 10 percent yield), so as to receive 1,210 dollars at the end of two years. The second alternative is to lend directly today for two years at the interest rate of 10 percent per year (that is, to buy a two-year term bond with a 10 percent per year yield), and at the end of the second year receive $(1,000) \cdot (1 + 0.10)^2 = (1,000) \cdot (1.21) = 1,210$ dollars. The yield curve in this case would be a flat, horizontal line like the one on panel (a) in Figure 13–2; the yield is the same for term to maturity for either one year or two years.

But what if the market expects the interest rate to rise, after one year, from 10 percent to, say, 14 percent per year? In this case, the first alternative would bring the bond purchaser (lender) an expected final amount higher than if the yield on the two-year bond is 10 percent for the duration of the two years. If an individual buys a one-year bond today with a 10 percent yield, he or she will receive, as before, a total of 1,100 dollars at the end of the first year; but now, if for the second year the interest rate for one-year loans (or yield for one year bonds) has risen to 14 percent, he can lend the 1,100 dollars at the 14 percent rate for the second year (that is, buy a one-year bond of market value of 1,100 dollars and receive a yield of 14 percent) and at the end of the second year reap $(1,100) \cdot (1 + 0.14) = 1,254$ dollars.

For an individual to be indifferent to accepting the first alternative or the second one, of lending directly for two years (or, of buying today a two-year term bond), the interest rate for the two-year loan (the yield on the two-year bond) would need to be the one that would bring about a total of 1,254 dollars at the end of the two years—in this example, an interest rate of 11.98 percent per year, because $(1,000) \cdot (1 + 0.1198)^2 = 1,254$ dollars. If the yield on the two-year bond is lower than that, and if the expectation about the rise in the interest rate is generalized, no one would want to buy or hold two-year bonds, while everybody would want to sell such bonds. This situation will lower the market price of these bonds (that is, increase their yield) until the 11.98 percent yield is reached, a point at which once again borrowers and lenders (sellers and buyers of two-year bonds) are indifferent to the two alternatives. The yield curve would look very much like the one in panel (b), in Figure 13-2, with a 10 percent yield on one-year bonds, and a 11.98 percent yield on two-year bonds.

What if, given the same example, expectations for the second year are that the interest rate will fall to, say, 7 percent? The consequences of such a change can be worked out; the final result is a fall in the two-year term yield from 10 to approximately 8.5 percent. In this case, the yield curve would be similar to the curve in panel (c) in Figure 13-2.

Expectations about future short-term interest rates influence today's long-term rates. If short-term rates are expected to rise in the future, no one would wish to be "locked in" with long-term bonds of a lower yield when the time of the rise is expected to come, and whoever lends "long" would require a higher yield. If future short-term rates are expected to fall every lender would wish to be protected by long-term lending at the time such fall is expected to come, and would accept a yield lower than that he or she would obtain by lending short.

In the example we analyze this influence by looking at the simple case of only two bonds (of one- and two-year maturity), but the connection works among bonds of all maturities. The one-year rate, for example, will be influenced by expectations concerning still shorter term rates (say, the yield on three-month Treasury bills), and the expectations about the future course of the yield on two-year bonds will in turn influence today's yield on five- or ten-year bonds, and so on. The analysis not only shows the reasons why expectations about future short-term yields influence today's long-term yields, but also suggests the *arbitrage mechanism* connecting all these rates. The arbitrage mechanism is essentially the same as the mechanism by which, at a given point in time, prices of the same commodities tend to be the same in different interconnected markets.

An implicit assumption in the above discussion is that the "commodities" are strictly the same. Are lenders and borrowers (buyers and sellers of bonds) strictly indifferent about the maturity of their portfolio or their debt as long as yields on the different maturities conform to their expectations about future interest rates? This is the implicit assumption in our example. There is a possibility that lenders and borrowers are not indifferent, a situation that gives rise, on the one hand, to a modification of the pure expectations theory just described and, on the other hand, to a second suggested explanation of term structure—the market segmentation or hedging theory. Consider the possible modifications.

The simple expectations theory can explain *any* shape of the yield curve. Many different shapes of these curves have been observed, but an upward sloping shape (as in panel (c) of Figure 13-2), indicating higher yields for longer terms to maturity, is the most frequently observed shape. According to the simple expectations theory this would mean that, in general (perhaps in the long-run equlibrium), expectations are that interest rates will rise. This "bias" is difficult to explain, for there must be some *long-run equilibrium* at which interest rates are expected to remain the same. Even if the economy frequently departs from that long-run equilibrium, one should expect to observe, on average, a *flat yield curve*, as in panel (a) of Figure 13–2. It is in trying to explain this most frequently observed, upward shape of the yield curve that the assumption of "indifference" among securities with different terms to maturity comes under scrutiny.

Suppose that people on the average expect future interest rates to remain at the same level as they are today. But even if people *expect* something to happen, they can never be completely sure that it will. If there is a change in interest rates in the future, the losses (or gains) will be larger for those who are "locked" into long-run debt (or credit) than for those commited to shorter term contracts. If people on the average dislike risk (that is, if they are "risk averters"), they will require higher yields to hold bonds of longer maturities (or, similarly, to lend for longer periods). This practice results in the so-called *liquidity premium* for longer term bonds, which is an adequate term if one understands "liquidity" to be the flexibility of not being "locked" into long-term financial instruments. The existence of a "liquidity premium" would then make the expectations theory compatible with the upward sloping shape of yield curves to frequently observed.

THE MARKET SEGMENTATION OR HEDGING THEORY OF THE TERM STRUCTURE

The market segmentation approach emphasizes the fact that the financial market is made up of particular markets for particular types of bonds with different maturities, and that lenders and borrowers "specialize" in the particular maturities that best suit their financing needs. For example, commercial banks whose liabilities are mostly short-term demand deposits (Chapter 12) would be involved principally in the short-term financial market (Federal funds, Treasury bills, et cetera). On the other hand, institutions such as insurance companies, savings and loans and farm loans associations, whose major liabilities are long term would tend to match these liabilities with long-term assets such as long-term bonds and mortgages. (Of course adjustments may be made with growing competition and differentiation of instruments sold at all financial institutions.)

How does the market segmentation theory explain yield curves as those in Figure 13–2 (in particular, those in panels (b) and (c))? Commercial banks, at times of "tight money" or of a relatively contractionary monetary policy, will need to borrow in the short-term market, thereby increasing short-term rates (panel (c)). At times of "easy money" or of a relatively expansionary monetary policy, commercial banks will have no difficulty meeting their reserve requirements, and short-term rates will tend to be *lower* than long-term rates (panel (b)). However, if during times of a relatively expansionary monetary policy the public expects inflation—and therefore nominal interest rates— to rise in the future, (and vice versa for the case of contractionary policy), an identical result would be predicted by the expectations theory.

Most economists appear to prefer the expectations theory, perhaps with the addition of the liquidity premium to take account of the extra risk involved in longer term contracts. The market segmentation or hedging theory, besides a theory, is also a recognition of the fact that bonds of different maturities are different things, and that borrowers and lenders cannot be totally indifferent concerning their maturity, even after adjusting for future changes expected to occur in the level of interest rates. It is a position shared by some practitioners in financial markets, who often see the market for every type of instrument in isolation from all the others, and ignore the arbitrage that takes place among them.[1] Perhaps we should regard the two theories as complementing each other, rather than as alternative or competing approaches.

FINANCIAL MARKETS IN THE ECONOMY: THE LOANABLE FUNDS MARKET

We have analyzed the particular features of financial markets and we can now concern ourselves with the manner in which the aggregate market fits into the economic system. The central question concerns the forces behind the supply and demand for financial instruments which were discussed when the *market for loanable funds* was introduced in Chapter 5. The demand for financial instruments ("bonds," to use a generic name for the whole variety of those instruments) is precisely the supply of loanable funds, or lending; and the supply of bonds is the demand for loanable funds, or borrowing. The "flow of funds" accounts showing the components of demand and supply for loanable funds are, essentially, the simple relations described at the beginning of Chapter 5.[2] In the framework of Chapter 5, private lending originated in the household sector, and it was equal to the difference between the household's sector income (y) and what households would decide to use for consumption (c) and the accumulation of cash balances, or hoarding (h), that is,

$$\ell = y - c - h \qquad [13.5]$$

Total borrowing was made up of borrowing by business firms, ℓ, for investment purposes (I) plus government borrowing (gb), or

$$\ell + (gb) = I + (gb)$$

In the analysis of Chapters 5 and 6 (except, of course, the Appendix to Chapter 5) the market for loanable funds was always assumed to be in equilibrium and was thus bypassed. The effects of changes in monetary and fiscal policies on magnitudes such as real income (y) and prices (P) could then be highlighted. Now we will return to the loanable funds market and see how it is affected by policy changes. Remember also that in the framework of Chapters 5 and 6 we considered the case where, in equilibrium, the monetary authority would keep the *level of the nominal money stock* (M) constant. Therefore, in the equilibrium for the nongrowing economy the price level would also be constant over time and the inflation rate would be zero, so that there is no great loss in ignoring the transitional effects of inflationary expectations and the rate of inflation on the cost of holding money. In that framework, a policy change was a once-and-for-all change in the level of the money stock, and the analysis was geared to evaluating how real income (y) and the *level of prices* (P) would respond, once and for all.

Inflation was discussed at length in Chapters 7 and 8, but the effects of changes in the rate of monetary expansion on financial markets were not considered. In Chapters 7 and 8 the monetary authority was seen as continuously changing the level of the money stock (M) at a constant proportional rate—the rate of monetary expansion, $\hat{M}$. A policy change was a change from one rate of monetary expansion to another, and here we will look at the effect of these changes in the financial market.

When the monetary authority is increasing the money stock at a certain rate, it does so not by distributing the new money as gifts, but by open market operations, that is, through lending. This flow of real lending must then be added to expression [13.5], so that it now reads

$$\ell = (gl) + y - c - h \qquad [13.6]$$

where (gl) stands for lending by the Federal Reserve (more precisely, the real value of the nominal additions of new money through lending). The second change regards the expression for desired hoarding on the part of the public, h. The flow of desired hoarding was taken to depend on the monetary disequilibrium of households, that is, on the difference between the desired and the actual money stocks, or

$$h = b \cdot (L(y, r) - m) \qquad [13.7]$$

Expression [13.7] simply states that the flow of desired hoarding in real terms (h) will equal some fixed coefficient (b) multiplied by the difference between the public's desired real money stock, $L(y, r)$ (or m^d), and the stock they are holding, the actual money stock (m). But, if situations of a *continuous* increase in the money stock are to be considered, where in long-run equilibrium the inflation rate will not be zero, the effects of inflation (or, more precisely, of expected inflation) on the hoarding schedule must be incorporated into expression [13.7]. First, the expected inflation rate must be inserted in the demand for money function, so that the desired real money stock is given by $L(y, r + E)$. Second, another term must be added to the expression for hoarding. Remember that "h" stands for the real value of nominal desired hoarding, and that when prices are expected to be rising moneyholders must continuously accumulate nominal cash balances if they wish to maintain the real level of their balances constant. The *real value* of this flow of nominal balances that moneyholders need to accumulate is equal to $m \cdot \hat{P}$, or the level of real balances times the inflation rate.[3] Thus desired hoarding should also include a term equal to $m \cdot E$, since E is the inflation rate expected to take place during the next period. The other term will be the same as before, so that now expression [13.7] becomes

$$h = m \cdot E + b \cdot (L(y, r + E) - m) \qquad [13.8]$$

where the first term, $m \cdot E$, is the real value of the nominal cash balances that the public plans to accumulate to compensate for the expected "depreciation" of real cash balances, and the second term is the desired accumulation necessary to eliminate, over time, any difference that might exist between the desired and the actual levels of the real money stock. In inflationary equilibrium, the second term disappears.

In order to understand better expression [13.8], it is useful to think of the analogy between this expression for real money holdings and the "holding" of real capital, such as machines. We know that the gradual adjustment over time by moneyholders to their long-run desired money stock is similar to the adjustment over time to a desired stock of, say, machines on the part of machine holders. What if machines depreciate at some constant rate δ, while machine owners want to adjust their number of machines (call this number K) over time toward the stock they wish to hold in the long run (K^d)? Then, at every period, the number of machines purchased would be made up of two components. First, buyers would purchase a number of machines $K \cdot \delta$, so as to compensate for the flow of machines that "disappear" at every period due to physical depreciation. A second component would be a term like $a \cdot (K^d - K)$, the number of machines purchased in order to increase the stock when there are fewer machines than desired in the long run. (Of course, this term would be negative if there are more machines than desired in the long run.) The total number of machines purchased per period would equal

$$K \cdot \delta + a \cdot (K^d - K)$$

When the purchaser holds exactly the number of machines he wishes to hold in the long run, $K = K^d$ and the second term becomes zero. Purchases at every period are just enough to keep the number of machines constant. Exactly the same is true with respect to desired hoarding. The expected inflation rate is the expected "depreciation" rate of real cash balances, and even when money-holders are in long-run equilibrium $(m = m^d)$, they will need to accumulate nominal cash balances at every period with a real value $m \cdot E$ in order to offset the "depreciation" due to inflation.

Before the effects of monetary policies on the financial or loanable funds market are analyzed, a purely formal simplification should be introduced. "Savings" (s) is the difference between income and consumption, $(y - c)$, so that

$$s(y) = y - c(y)$$

Since consumption depends only on income in this simple framework, the difference between income and consumption will also depend only on income. As this is not a new concept but only a different notation, it is necessary to write only one magnitude instead of two. This notation could have been introduced much earlier, but it was avoided because the word "savings" is used in many connotations other than its strict definition.

The system can now be summarized. Substituting hoarding by its explicit form [13.8], the total lending and borrowing schedules are

$$\ell = (gl) + s(y) + b \cdot (m - L(y, r + E)) - m \cdot E \qquad [13.9]$$

$$\ell + (gb) = I(r) + (gb) \qquad [13.10]$$

It is important to understand that the lending schedule [13.9] is a short-run schedule. In the long run, moneyholders will be in equilibrium, so that the term $b \cdot (m - L(y, r + E))$ disappears, and the expected rate of inflation is equal to the actual rate and to the rate of monetary expansion. Since (gl) is equal to the real value of the flow of newly printed money, $m \cdot \hat{M}$, then $m \cdot E = m \cdot \hat{M}$, and the long-run lending schedule would become a vertical line in Figure 13–3

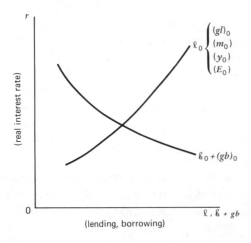

Figure 13-3. Short-run bond market: borrowing and lending.

(rather than the upward-sloping schedule actually depicted), since lending reduces to $\ell^* = s(y)$ (the asterisk indicates that this is the real flow of lending in the long run). As drawn, Figure 13–3 shows the total lending and borrowing schedules at a *point in time*, for a given level of government borrowing and lending ($(gb)_0$ and $(gl)_0$), the real money stock (m_0), real income (y_0), and the expected inflation rate (E_0). The total borrowing function is designated $\ell_0 + (gb)_0$.

EFFECTS OF MONETARY AND FISCAL POLICIES IN THE FINANCIAL MARKET

Three policy changes and the results of these changes on the financial market will be considered: (1) a "pure" monetary policy (that is, an increase in the rate of monetary expansion); (2) an increase in the level of government expenditures, financed exclusively through borrowing, with no change in the rate of monetary expansion (a "pure" fiscal policy); and (3) the same increase in government expenditures financed by borrowing, but with a simultaneous increase, by the same amount, in lending of newly printed money by the Fed (a mix of monetary and fiscal policies).

At this point the relationship between the two government agencies in charge of borrowing and spending on one side, and controlling the money stock on the other, must be made more explicit. We have often referred to "the monetary authority," or to "the Fed," or simply to "government" as interchangeable terms, as in "government expenditures" and "government borrowing." Indeed, it is essentially correct to think of one unit called "government" that spends, borrows and owns the right to print money. But in the case at hand, more information is required.

"Government," who decides how much to borrow and spend[4] (we call this "the Treasury"), must be distinguished from the "monetary authority," who decides and implements changes in the nominal money stock (of course, the Federal Reserve Board of Governors). In Chapter 5, the "government" budget constraint was discussed. A government budget constraint means that if there are no conventional taxes, government expenditures must be financed by borrowing, or

$$g = (gb) \qquad [13.11]$$

The Fed also has a "constraint" since changes in the nominal money stock come about not through gifts but through open market operations.[5] Such a "constraint" is simply the expression

$$(gl) = m \cdot \hat{M} \qquad [13.12]$$

which we introduced in the previous section.

Expressions [13.11] and [13.12] are useful in putting into perspective the three policy changes that we wish to analyze. We will see, when we do so, that we could go a step further and visualize the Treasury and the Fed as being consolidated into a single agency ("government"), thereby writing the two constraints together, as

$$(gb) + m \cdot \hat{M} = (gl) + g \qquad [13.13]$$

where the left-hand side is the "receipts" of the single agency (what it receives from borrowing and from printing money) and the right-hand side the "uses" of those receipts (what it used for lending, or purchase of financial assets, and what it uses to spend for the purchase of goods and services).

EFFECTS OF A PURE MONETARY POLICY CHANGE: AN INCREASE IN THE RATE OF MONETARY EXPANSION

Suppose the economy is in equilibrium, with a rate of monetary expansion $\hat{M}_0$ (say, 2 percent per year, to continue the numerical example of Chapters 7 and 8), equal to the actual and expected inflation rates, and a real interest rate of 4 percent per year. This initial equilibrium is described in Figure 13-4, where the short-run supply of loanable funds is drawn for given levels of the expected inflation rate (2 percent), the real money stock (m_0), real income at its full employment level (y^f), and a given level of government lending (by the Fed) equal to $m_0 \cdot \hat{M}_0$, or $(gl)_0 = m_0 \cdot \hat{M}_0$. Suppose now that the Fed decides to increase the rate of monetary expansion from 2 to 7 percent per year. This increase is accomplished, of course, through a sudden increase in the flow of lending by the Fed (gl), which shifts the supply of loanable funds curve to the

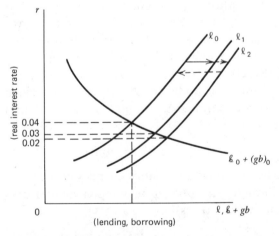

Figure 13-4. A change in the rate of monetary expansion.

right (say, to ℓ_1) thereby bringing the interest rate down to a lower level (say, 3 percent per year). After the initial impact the amount of real lending will go on increasing, because the real money stock starts to rise. The increase in the level of the real money stock over time will in turn prompt the public to lend more (in order to "get rid" of those excess cash balances), and contribute to the further gradual shift to the right of the schedule to ℓ_2, and therefore to further lowering the real rate of interest. This gradual shift is indicated in Figure 13-4 by broken arrows.

As detailed in Chapter 7, the real money stock will, in due time, stop growing (as the inflation rate catches up with the new rate of monetary expansion) and will start falling, while inflationary expectations also begin to catch up with the higher inflation rate. All of these events, plus the fact that real income (output) will also stop rising after a while, produce a reversal of the shifts to the right of the supply of loanable funds schedule. After the point at which this schedule determines the lowest level of the real interest rate (say, 2 percent, for the schedule positioned at ℓ_2), a gradual shift to the left starts. In the new equilibrium, perhaps after some "overshooting," the new supply schedule will return to the same position that it was in the initial equilibrium. In the new steady state, as in the old one, the flow of real lending by the Fed (gl) will once again be equal to the real value of the nominal flow of money the public needs to accumulate in order to keep their real cash balances constant, or $m_1 \cdot E_1$ (where m_1 is the new, lower level of real money, and $E_1 = 7$ percent).

The path of the *real* rate of interest over time is shown in Figure 13-5, as a solid line. The *nominal* rate of interest, which is the sum of the real rate plus the expected rate of inflation, is also depicted in Figure 13-5. If we recall the analysis of Chapter 8 and the likely behavior of the expected inflation rate during the adjustment, we can conclude that the nominal interest rate will adjust in a manner as indicated by the dashed line in Figure 13-5. In the new

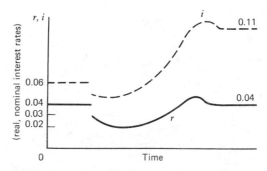

Figure 13-5. Interest rate changes: monetary expansion.

equilibrium, with an actual and expected inflation rate of 7 percent per year, the nominal interest rate will be 11 percent.

PURE FISCAL POLICY CHANGE: AN INCREASE IN GOVERNMENT EXPENDITURES WITH NO CHANGE IN MONETARY EXPANSION

Let us consider the effects of a change in the level of government expenditures financed solely through borrowing by the Treasury, with no change in the rate of monetary expansion. This is exactly the case analyzed in Chapter 6, except that now the *rate* of monetary expansion is 2 percent per year, rather than zero.

Figure 13-6 shows the same initial equilibrium position as in Figure 13-5 and the effects of the change. The increase in the level of government borrowing (say, from $(gb)_0$ to $(gb)_1$) is visualized as a shift to the right of the total borrowing schedule, and an immediate rise in the interest rate from 4 percent to, say, 5 percent per year. Although the immediate reaction of the lending schedule is somewhat ambiguous, the schedule will have to shift sooner or later to the left (to a new position at ℓ_1) because in the new global equilibrium the flow of private lending will simply be equal to savings (income minus consumption), which in turn depend only on income, which will be the same in the new long-run equilibrium. At this new equilibrium, the *real* rate of interest will be higher (say, for example, 6 percent per year). The rate of monetary expansion has remained at its original 2 percent level, and in the new equilibrium the inflation rate will also be 2 percent per year, as it was before the change.

Figure 13-7 shows the results of these changes on the behavior of the real and the nominal interest rates. Since inflation is the same before and after the change, the final equilibrium rise of the nominal interest rate (8 percent per year) is totally due to the increase in the real rate.

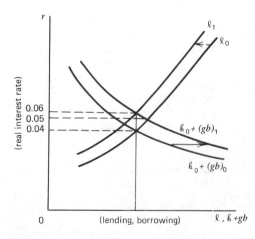

Figure 13-6. Pure fiscal policy.

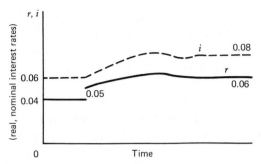

Figure 13-7. Pure fiscal policy: interest rate effects.

A MIX OF FISCAL AND MONETARY POLICIES: "ACCOMMODATING" POLICIES BY THE FED

The last policy change is a combination of the two policies discussed above. Suppose that (starting from the same equilibrium position as before) there is the same increase in the flow of real government expenditures and borrowing by the Treasury (from $(gb)_0$ to $(gb)_1$), but that such an increase is exactly matched by an equal rise in the level of lending of newly printed money by the Fed. As we will see in Chapter 14, this is a common happening, with the Fed "accommodating" additional borrowing by the Treasury in an effort to prevent the interest rate from rising and private investment from being *crowded out*. The change then, amounts to a simultaneous and equal increase in all four terms of expression [13.13].

Figure 13-8 shows the initial position (with the borrowing and lending schedules $\ell_0 + (gb)_0$ and ℓ_0 and a 4 percent real interest rate) in all respects

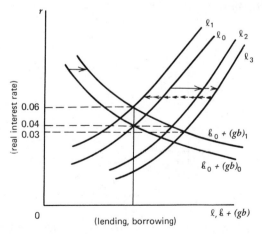

Figure 13-8. Fed "accommodation" to fiscal policy.

equal to the initial equilibrium position in the two previous cases. The increase in the level of borrowing by the Treasury, from $(gb)_0$ to $(gb)_1$, is visualized as a once-and-for-all shift of the total borrowing schedule, as in the case of pure fiscal policy. But, if borrowing by the Treasury is exactly matched by additional lending by the Fed, the total lending schedule also shifts to the right by the same amount, to ℓ_2, and that there is no initial effect on the real interest rate.

The story does not end there, however, for now the higher level of lending by the Fed (as in the first case analyzed, of pure monetary policy) results in a higher rate of monetary expansion, and that initially real cash balances will be rising, so that there is a further gradual movement of the lending schedule beyond its position ℓ_2, and for exactly the same reasons as those in the second-round changes of the schedule in the pure monetary policy case. Thus the real rate of interest rate will start to fall. After some time, and again for the same reasons as in the pure monetary policy change, the lending schedule will reach a "maximum" position to the right (such as ℓ_3) with the lowest level of the interest rate (say, 3 percent per year); it will gradually revert back to its original position and still further to the left, until ℓ_1, as in the case of pure fiscal policy, with a new equilibrium real interest rate of 6 percent per year. But, unlike the case of pure fiscal policy, in this final position the inflation rate would now be higher and equal to the new rate of monetary expansion. Which rate of monetary expansion? It depends on which rate makes the lending of newly printed money by the Fed, in real terms $(m \cdot \hat{M})$, equal to whatever is the increase of real borrowing by the Treasury. In the numerical case, assume such a rate to be, say, 5 percent per year. In the new equilibrium, the inflation rate will also be 5 percent per year, and the *nominal* interest rate (with the new *real* rate at the 6 percent level) equal to 11 percent. Figure 13–9 shows the behavior of both real (full line) and nominal (broken line) interest rates during the adjustment and at the new equilibrium.

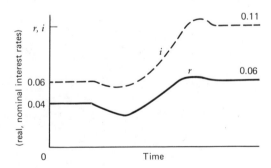

Figure 13-9. *Interest rate changes with Fed accommodation.*

CONCLUSION

The determination of the principles of interest rate through supply and demand has been the major area of concern in Chapter 13. While we have, at times, used the simplification of "one" interest rate, there are thousands of interest rates, and just as many financial instruments sold in financial institutions. The investigation has also brought us to policy discussions of interest rate determination, but these "policy" discussions have been conceptual, not actual, in nature. In Chapters 14 and 16, actual aggregate economic policies, recent and past, will be analyzed in detail. These policies will be seen to affect not only interest rates but also the inflation rate, the unemployment rate, and growth in national income. As indicated elsewhere in this book (Chapter 11, for example), the actual implementation of policy by government controllers—the Fed, the Treasury, and so forth—is a complex and difficult task.

FOOTNOTES

[1] If most market participants are hedging and there are few arbitragers, market prices are made at the margins and the expectations theory dominates.

[2] The loanable funds theory of the determination of total expenditures is discussed at length in the Appendix to Chapter 5. The discussion that follows in Chapter 13 may be studied independently, but the reader's understanding may be enhanced by a review of the full loanable funds analysis in Chapter 5.

[3] This is, of course, the "tax" on real cash balances due to inflation, which we discussed in Chapter 7.

[4] And, of course, how much to tax, a possibility that we have put aside in our analysis.

[5] Naturally, changes in the nominal money stock can also come through changes in commercial banks reserve requirements and in changes in the discount rate. But these are "once-and-for-all" changes in the level of the money stock; only through open market operations and a continuous increase in "high-powered" money can we generate a continuous increase in the nominal money stock.

KEY CONCEPTS

money market	present value	term structures of interest rates
capital market	future value	
bond	compounded interest	expectations theory
face (par) value	bond issuer	market segmentation theory
coupon rate	bond purchaser	liquidity premium
maturity	discounting factor	hoarding
perpetuity (consol)	yield	arbitrage mechanism

QUESTIONS FOR DISCUSSION

1. What is the value five years from now of $10,000 at an interest rate of 8%?

2. What is the present value of a bond with a face value of $5,000 at a coupon rate of 12% per year and a maturity of five years? How much would you be willing to pay for the bond?

3. A bond is being sold in the market for $450. Its coupon rate is 12% and its face value is $500. What is the market rate of interest (two years until maturity)? What would the bond sell for if the market rate equaled the coupon rate?

4. Joe Jock proudly declares that he has signed for 2 million dollars to play football for the Walnut Grove Groundhogs. He is to be paid $400,000 for five years. What is the value of his contract?

5. Company XYZ's ten-year bond is selling below par value. Devise possible explanations using first the expectations theory and then the market segmentation theory.

6. Redraw Figure 13-5 for a monetary contraction and analyze the case in economic terms.

7. Explain the movements in Figure 13-6 for a decrease in the level of government expenditures. What are the analytical differences between a decrease in government expenditures (see Figure 13-7) and the monetary contraction described in question 6?

PART V

APPLICATION OF THEORY AND INSTITUTIONS:
Monetary Policy, the International Economy, and Twentieth–Century Monetary History

CHAPTER 14

THE ROLE OF MONETARY POLICY

The previous five chapters of this book have been concerned with the institutions surrounding money and finance in the United States. Specifically we have analyzed, in Chapters 9, 10, and 11, the commercial and central banking systems and the mechanisms and instruments through which money itself is created and through which money the supply is altered. Chapters 12 and 13 have focused upon financial intermediaries, markets, and interest rate mechanisms. The effects of money supply changes work through these markets and intermediaries, which also serve the function of reducing the costs of transacting between buyers and sellers of loanable funds.

The present chapter returns to the policy concerns raised in the theoretical sections of this book (Chapters 4 through 8). In particular, Chapter 14 evaluates the overall goals of macroeconomic policy and analyzes alternative methods of implementing these goals. Arguments for or against the use of fiscal or monetary policy must, of course, hinge upon the empirical support each receives through empirical testing. Some of this support is discussed in the present chapter, as are the questions of policy lags and targets in real world settings. Recent proposals for the conduct of monetary policy are considered as well. Finally, the record and role of monetary policy in the last twenty years are assessed. (A discussion of the history and role of pre-1960 monetary policy is reserved for Chapter 16.) In sum, the present chapter will provide an in-depth analysis on the contemporary *state of the art* and *state of the debate* on macroeconomic and monetary policy implementation in the United States.

THE BASIC GOALS OF MACROECONOMIC POLICY

There is a strong consensus among economists and the public alike about the four basic goals of macroeconomic policy. These goals are full employment, price stability, sustained growth, and balance of payments equilibrium. Of the four, full employment and price stability are at the top of the list and are well established in and even sanctioned by law. The Employment Act of 1946, for example, states that "... it is the continuing responsibility of the Federal Government to use all practical means ... to promote maximum employment,

329

production and purchasing power." Price stability (implicitly included in the words purchasing power) has always been understood as one of the objectives to be pursued by the Federal Reserve System. Growth and balance of payments equilibrium somehow take a back seat to the goals of full employment and price stability although the former two reappear now and then as important (but almost never overriding) considerations. Economic growth and balance of payments considerations are long-run problems, or at least they are perceived as such. The effects of current policies on the accumulation of capital take some time to make themselves evident in the case of growth.[1] Balance of payments problems are of a long-run nature since the United States, for many years, was producer of the world's reserve currency. That is, dollars served as *reserves* for international transactions, making it possible for substantial deficits in the international accounts to be financed without immediate concern.

The discussion surrounding these goals or objectives of policy is not a statement concerning their desirability; except for a few dissonant voices,[2] there is a consensus that all of these goals are desirable. Instead, the debate centers on how to handle conflicts that arise when some or all of these goals are to be attained simultaneously. At a technical level, it may be possible to follow a combination of policies permitting the policymaker to avoid conflicts so that all economic goals may be satisfied simultaneously. When this possibility does not exist (either because there is an intrinsic incompatibility or because we do not know enough about the economic system to find the "optimum mix"), the conflict is often a source of public controversy and is even a motivation for political reactions and change.

Economists may argue about technicalities concerning tradeoffs among goals, but the fact is that a priority given to some goals over others will, in the short run, harm or benefit different groups unevenly. Take, for example, the case of the short-run tradeoff between employment and price stability. In this case a preference for lowering the inflation rate as opposed to achieving full employment will be more detrimental to a well-defined group of individuals (certain type of workers, teenagers, and members of minority groups) than to others. The long-run benefits of price stability not only will take some time to be realized, but will benefit everybody equally, irrespective of the price paid by each on the stabilization effort.[3] But this is not in the realm of macro- and monetary economics. How can fiscal and monetary policies contribute to the attainment of the four general objectives of macroeconomic policy?

MONETARY POLICY OR FISCAL POLICY?

At a general level, a discussion of macroeconomic stabilization concerns the effectiveness of monetary versus fiscal policy.[4] In this section some of the main arguments for and against each tool will be summarized and some of the evidence will be examined.

THE ARGUMENTS

It is probably in the discussion of monetary and fiscal policies as stabilization devices that the differences between monetarists and neo-Keynesians emerge most clearly. As argued in Chapter 5, the reasons for one sort of policy to be effective were precisely the same reasons that would render the other ineffective.

The extreme monetarist position has been stated succinctly by Milton Friedman:

> In my opinion, the state of the budget by itself has no significant effect on the course of nominal income, on inflation, on deflation, or on cyclical fluctuations.[5]

In this view, pure fiscal policy (understood as either a change in the level of a balanced budget, or a change in government expenditures financed by borrowing) has the effect of changing *the composition* but *not the level* of total expenditures. In the extreme, each dollar increase in government expenditures crowds out exactly one dollar of private expenditures, and vice versa. The reasons for these results (as seen by the Monetarists) were spelled out in Chapter 5. First, if the change (say, an increase) in government expenditures is financed by borrowing, such borrowing will tend to increase the interest rate in the market for loanable funds. The high sensitivity of investment expenditures to changes in the interest rate will reduce private investment expenditures substantially. Second, even to the extent that real income responds to any initial increase in total expenditures, a relatively low elasticity of the demand for money with respect to the interest rate would require a relatively large change in the interest rate. This change in the interest rate would "allocate" existing real cash balances among moneyholders but would bring about further reduction in private investment. In what we have called the *extreme* Monetarist case, the final net result is zero. These are, of course, the same reasons why a change in the money stock would be effective in changing total expenditures: a low elasticity of the demand for money and a high elasticity of investment expenditures, both with respect to the rate of interest. The argument *against* fiscal policy financed by borrowing is, at the same time, an argument *for* monetary policy.

What if additional government expenditures are financed by taxation, say, by an increase in income taxes? For simplicity the case was not introduced in the framework of Chapter 5. In this case, a Monetarist would argue that yet another *crowding out* effect is produced to the extent that government expenditures may be in some degree a substitute for private expenditures. Thus the final net effect of an increase in government spending and taxation may very well be zero.[6]

According to the Monetarist position, changes in the level of government expenditures can have an effect only to the extent that they are financed not by borrowing or by conventional taxes, but through money creation. Thus the effect would be the result not of the fiscal action per se, but of the change in the quantity of money.

The neo-Keynesian camp takes exactly the opposite view: a permanent change in the level of government expenditures, however financed, would by itself be quickly translated into a permanent change in total expenditures, and ultimately into income and price changes. First, the immediate, short-run determinants of the interest rate are the demand and the supply of money so that an additional flow of government borrowing for the financing of an increase in government expenditures will not bring any initial "crowding out." The interest rate does not change, and private expenditures continue to be what they were: a dollar increase in government expenditures financed by borrowing is immediately translated into a dollar change in total expenditures. Second, as income responds to the change in total expenditures, the increase in demand for real cash balances is easily satisfied by modest increases in the rate of interest (because moneyholders are very sensitive to the cost of holding money), and these increases in turn have little effect on the level of investment (because investors are not very sensitive to changes in the interest rate). Once again, the arguments for the effectiveness of fiscal policy are at the same time arguments against the effectiveness of monetary policy.

If the increase in government expenditures is financed through taxation, the extreme Keynesian assumption is that the manner in which the additional tax proceeds are spent will not matter to private spenders, who would reduce their expenditures by less than their tax bill. Government expenditures are not at all a substitute for private expenditures, so that the second sort of "crowding out" discussed by the Monetarists will not take place either.

Keynesians recognize, on the other hand, that if an increase in government expenditures is financed through creation of money the expansionary effect will be larger (to the extent that money matters at all), but not by much. The additional stimulus will be minor compared to the effects of the fiscal action per se.

Has the controversy on fiscal versus monetary policy generated any "cross pollination" over the last twenty years? While the most orthodox Monetarists have taken an uncompromising position (*fiscal policy does not matter*), few neo-Keynesians would say the same about monetary policy. If one were to use the expressions "money does not matter," "money matters little," "money matters much," "money matters most," and "money alone matters"[7] as benchmarks, a sensible judgment would be to say that the Keynesian position has changed from "money matters little" to perhaps "money matters much" (but not "most"), at least in their verbal statements if not in their policy recommendations. In fact, much of the conflict about monetary versus fiscal policies has changed to a debate over (a) a coordination of monetary and fiscal policies, and (b) the conduct of monetary policy. These concerns would apparently indicate that some agreement has been reached. Disagreement in these new areas, however, is just new dress for the same conflict that led to the monetary versus fiscal policy debate in the first place. Let us, however, briefly consider some of the evidence on the effectiveness of monetary and fiscal policies.

THE EVIDENCE

When in need of facts confirming or disproving a hypothesis, economists turn to *econometric models*, that is, a set of relations about a relatively small number of key magnitudes. How large and detailed these models are depends on how complete the theory is, on how well the theory is able to capture the essence of the facts by analyzing only a few relationships.

In the discussion of the relative effectiveness of monetary and fiscal policies, analysis of the empirical evidence has so far failed to bring about any substantial agreement. Keynesians have often obtained results with sophisticated *large-scale models* used for forecasting many variables. The FRB/MIT (Massachusetts Institute of Technology–Federal Reserve System) model, now called the MPS model, the MIT–University of Pennsylvania–Social Science Research study, and the DATA RESOURCES model are some of these constructions. In these models, the effects of monetary policies are traced through changes in a set of interest rates and, from there, to private investment expenditures in various sectors.

Monetarists, in turn, have invariably used the so-called *reduced form models:* very few relationships (sometimes just one) that try to explain directly the global link among the variables under discussion, such as the stock of money, or the level of government expenditures, income, and prices. These reduced forms models bypass any intent to be specific about the precise mechanism through which changes in the policy variables (money or government expenditures) affect the dependent variables (income and prices). Critics of such an approach have coined the expression "the Monetarist black box" to refer to this bypassing of a well-defined transmission mechanism. This has been, indeed, one of the major reasons why such evidence often raises more questions and controversy than it answers.

One such typical reduced form model is the so-called *St. Louis model,* a simple construction first tried out by members of the staff at the research department of the Federal Reserve Bank of St. Louis. (The St. Louis Fed is usually considered the most Monetarist of all districts of the Federal Reserve

System.) First estimated in 1968,[8] the model has been recalculated at various times with new data, and not all results have been consistent. Since this is the single most representative view of the Monetarist approach (both because it is a reduced form model, and because it is the model yielding the kinds of results a Monetarist would expect), it is interesting to contrast some of the results of this model with the ones derived in the more sophisticated neo-Keynesian models. But first the simple nature of the St. Louis model will be described.

Andersen and Jordan, the original authors of the model, attempted to verify whether or not ". . . the response of economic activity to fiscal actions relative to monetary actions is (I) greater, (II) more predictable, and (III) faster." Their conclusion was negative: "The response of economic activity to monetary actions compared with that of fiscal actions is (I') larger, (II') more predictable, and (III') faster." To test their hypothesis, they specified a simple relationship between present and past changes in the level of money (narrowly defined as the sum of currency plus demand deposits) and government expenditures and receipts, as the independent policy variables, and changes in the level of nominal income. Then they conducted a series of statistical analyses (regressions) to determine what set of coefficients would best "fit" the data, that is, to determine what association existed between changes in the monetary and fiscal policy variables and changes in the level of the ultimate goal, nominal income.

The surprising conclusions of the original St. Louis model, estimated with quarterly data from 1953 to 1968, created quite a commotion in the profession. Monetary policy has a *fast and permanent effect*, the totality of which was essentially transmitted to nominal income within a year, while fiscal policy had a transitory effect, most of which was completely eliminated after one year. Table 14–1 shows these effects for the four quarters following the policy change. The first column traces the effects on nominal income of a 100-dollar change in the nominal money stock narrowly defined. By the end of the one year, every initial increase in the money stock has increased quarterly nominal income by almost six times. After that time, nominal income remains at its

Table 14–1 **Effects of 100-Dollar Change in M_1 and in Government Expenditures (per Quarter) in the Original St. Louis Model**

Nominal Income After	Monetary Policy	Fiscal Policy
One quarter	151	36
Two quarters	310	89
Three quarters	457	84
Four quarters	584	6

new higher level. A 100-dollar (per quarter) change in the level of government expenditures, as shown in the second column, generates an increase in quarterly nominal income per quarter that never quite matches the initial expenditures change and that by the end of the fourth quarter has almost disappeared. Monetary policy has a strong permanent effect that is quickly translated into nominal income; fiscal policy has a small and short-lived effect.

The major surprise (even to many Monetarists) was the rapid effect of monetary policy (an effect that was also permanent and strong) and, more important, the weak effect of fiscal policy. To get an idea of the difference between these results and the conclusions of other models, consider the outcome that similar monetary and fiscal policy changes would bring according to the Federal Reserve Board/MIT model.

As mentioned before, the FRB/MIT model[9] is one of a group of more detailed, rather elaborate, econometric constructions where the effects of monetary policy are traced through from open market operations to changes in various interest rates, and later to changes in various components of private expenditures (consumption, residential construction, plant and equipment, state and local construction).[10]

In the FRB/MIT model, fiscal policy has a much stronger and longer-lived effect. For example, a reduction in tax rates equivalent to a decrease in government receipts of 100 dollars would generate an increase in nominal income that reaches 115 dollars at the end of the first year, 118 dollars at the end of the second, a peak of 262 dollars after the end of the third year, and still another 235 dollars after four years. Monetary policy also has an effect. Curiously enough (given the very different structure of the two models) the final effect on nominal income is similar in magnitude to the total effect calculated in the St. Louis model, after correcting for the monetary aggregate that is used to measure "monetary policy."[11] But the similarity ends with the magnitude. In the FRB/MIT model the full impact is reached only after about four years rather than after one year as in the St. Louis model. Fiscal policy is strong and long-lived. Monetary policy, on the other hand, is strong, permanent, but slow in taking effect. Other non-Monetarist models yield similar results, except that monetary policy has a much weaker effect. But the surprise over and the disagreement with the St. Louis results relate to fiscal, not to monetary, policy.

The initial St. Louis results were later brought into question. First, there was the strong argument that a simple and direct relationship between monetary and fiscal variables and nominal income cannot sort out the effects of changes in policy due to changes in income, so that the association of the policy variables with money income cannot be seen as a neat "cause to effect" relationship. Second, some of the initial conclusions of the model concerning the effects of fiscal policy were considerably weakened by later recalculations of the same model with new data. In 1974, Andersen and Carlson[12] reestimated the same model by using data for 1953 to 1973 (the original presentation, recall, covered 1953 to 1968). The estimated effects of monetary policy were about the same as those reported. However, a 100-dollar increase in government expenditures had not a 6-dollar effect, but a much larger effect (54 dollars), at the end of one year.

A second, more recent blow to the initial St. Louis results came through still another reestimation of the model by Benjamin M. Friedman.[13] Again, the results are not substantially different as far as the effects of monetary policy are concerned, but a 100-dollar increase in government expenditures would now bring about an increase of 142 dollars in nominal income by the end of the first year—almost three times the effect reported in the 1974 reestimation by Andersen and Carlson, and almost twenty-five times the results of the original 1968 presentation of the St. Louis model. Furthermore, this new estimation by Benjamin Friedman suggests that the results would indicate a period of influence longer than one year for fiscal policy. With an effect extending over two years, the total effect of 220 dollars (rather than 142) for each 100-dollar increase in government expenditures.

MONETARY POLICY *AND* FISCAL POLICY?

The major existing views over the relative merits of monetary and fiscal policies have been summarized. A natural question, however, is whether much of the discussion is irrelevant. If there are two possible instruments of policy, why not use both? After all, there are at least four global goals of macroeconomic policy, and the more instruments we have at our disposal, the more likely it is that we may eliminate conflict and achieve at least some of them simultaneously. Why then restrict the choice to either monetary or fiscal policy? Why not emphasize coordination of the two policies?

The answer to this question is, unfortunately, that in very few instances would a combination of both policies be able to achieve something that either of the two would not (monetary policy for Monetarists, fiscal policy for neo-Keynesians). The reasons for this general statement is that (when the objective is to influence either real income and employment, or prices) both policies work through changes in total expenditures. They are part of what in general is called *demand management*. And once total expenditures are changed, the effects of this change over income and prices are essentially the same for either of the two policies. As Arthur Okun has expressed it, ". . . the two tools will not serve to implement those two goals (price stability and maximum production) simultaneously. A pen and a pencil are one more tool than is needed to write a letter, but the second tool can't be used to mow the lawn."[14]

There are two possible exceptions. The first arises when the objective is to change total expenditures simultaneously (so as to influence real income and employment, or prices), and at the same time to achieve balance of payments equilibrium. If, for example, an expansionary effect of the domestic economy is desired, both monetary and fiscal policies would increase total expenditures and ultimately income and prices. On this account, both policies tend to worsen the country's balance of payments. The increase in money and prices will bring about an increase in imports and/or a fall in exports in the "trade account." But the side effects of monetary and fiscal policies will be different for another magnitude that is also important for the balance of payments, namely, the interest rate. With an expansionary monetary policy the interest rate will (at least initially) tend to fall; with expansionary fiscal policy it will tend to rise. (The paths of interest rate adjustment are discussed in Chapters 7 and 8.)

Thus the two policies have opposite effects on the other component of the balance of payments, namely the so-called "capital account." A fall in the domestic interest rate will persuade financial instruments holders to hold fewer or these instruments in the country, and more abroad; the capital outflow that would occur would tend to deteriorate the balance of payments. A rise in the domestic interest rate (which would be the side effect of fiscal policy) would instead bring about a "capital inflow," that is, an improvement in the balance of payments. On this account, the sole use of monetary policy (or fiscal policy, for that matter, if the initial situation is one of undesirable surplus in the balance of payments) can be inferior to some combination of the two.[15]

Actual economic events of the early 1960s are sometimes cited as evidence that monetary policy is incapable of achieving dual objectives. In what was called "Operation Twist" the Fed attempted to lower long-term interest rates to encourage domestic growth and investment while, simultaneously, raising short-term Treasury bill rates to prevent capital outflows that were worsening the balance of payments. The term "Twist" refers to the Fed's attempt to alter or twist the term structure of interest rates (discussed in Chapter 13) by purchasing long-term securities while, at the same time, pushing short-term rates up. Whether the Fed ever was able to achieve these results is, unfortunately, inconclusive from the data.

The second exception occurs when there are some other additional goals (other than price stability and full employment) to be attained, and there are reasons to believe that the effects of monetary and fiscal policies would be different for those goals. These are what Okun calls *side effects*,[16] such as the effects on the composition of output and on the rate of growth of the economy. It is argued, for example, that the short-run effects of monetary policy (through the change in the interest rate) introduce an uneven burden on certain sectors, such as building construction (see Chapter 12). Unfortunately, these is no agreement on these effects either. A Monetarist would argue that changes in the level of government expenditures and/or taxes are far from non-discriminatory in character.

Finally, it seems appropriate to point to a circumstance that is often over-looked. As it happens, most Monetarists are strongly opposed to government intervention and regulation. Such a position is by no means as strong among most (but not all) neo-Keynesians, who in general are more optimistic about the changes of success of corrective government action in various sectors of the economy. It seems not to be a coincidence for Monetarists to champion stabilization policies that act through changes in the quantity of money rather than through manipulation of the government budget (either on the side of expenditures or receipts). Budget manipulation requires additional decisions about what taxes to change and what expenditures to increase or diminish.

As mentioned before, the Monetarist position is, in general, that fiscal policy does not matter or matters very little, while neo-Keynesians accept the fact that money can play a role. What is the role of money and monetary policy in the neo-Keynesian view, given that fiscal policy is to carry a large part of stabilization policy? The prevalent view among neo-Keynesians has been expressed by Okun:

> All of this leads up to my first rule for stabilization policy: keep monetary condi-tions close to the middle of the road. Let me explain that . . . the rule must be inter-preted in terms of interest rates and credit conditions, and not in terms of monetary aggregates.[17]

In this *eclectic view*, the role reserved for monetary policy is to keep "orderly conditions" in the money market, which is interpreted as eliminating fluctua-tions in the interest rate. In an extreme form (which few or none of these eclectics would support) the role of monetary policy would be to peg the interest rate to some value for a long time. (As indicated in Chapter 11, the Federal Reserve has announced the elimination of the Federal Funds Rate as a primary target, focusing instead upon monetary aggregates.) Viewed in this form, the role of monetary policy becomes one of "accommodation" to the side effects of fiscal policy. Accommodation policies have important implications for the question of the stability or instability that "pegging" would bring about, and the matter will be discussed in the next section. A separate but related question concerns the more general implications of an eclectic view concerning the role of monetary policy.

THE NATURE OF ACCOMMODATING POLICIES—WHY FISCAL POLICY MAY BE IMPORTANT EVEN FOR A MONETARIST

Let us consider again the effects of reserving the role of preserving stability of interest rates for monetary policy, with fiscal policy in charge of influencing total expenditures. In this case, if expansion is required, the increase in govern-ment expenditures will increase borrowing by government, and will tend to increase the rate of interest. Under its obligation of counteracting changes in the interest rate, the Fed must step in and lend (buy securities) as as to avoid the increase in the rate of interest. If the rate of interest is to be kept at exactly its previous level, the Fed would need to inject at every period an increase in the money stock equal to the additional level of government expenditures in that period. This *even keeling policy* or *monetization of government debt* seems to have been a persistent phenomenon in the past (especially during the pegging of interest rates immediately before the Treasury–Federal Reserve System Accord in 1951, and to a lesser extent during the first half of the 1960s).

Given a tendency of the Fed to pursue such an interest rate objective (at least until late 1979 and possibly later), there is a sense in which fiscal policy is of great consequence even for a Monetarist. If accommodating policies by the Fed are taken for granted, government deficits are in fact financed through money creation, and are inflationary. A look at Figure 14-1 is enough to show the reasons for Monetarist concern about the state of the budget, and to understand that there is not necessarily a contradiction between this concern and the Monetarist belief that fiscal policy does not matter per se.[18] Another matter dividing Monetarists relates to the appropriate target for monetary policy.

WHAT TARGET FOR MONETARY POLICY?

In monetary policy discussion, a recurring topic is whether the interest rate is the magnitude to watch and the target to hit, or whether some monetary aggregate, such as high-powered money, the monetary base, some definition of reserves, or some definition of money is the appropriate target. Here again there is strong difference of opinion. Monetarists invariably advise ignoring interest rates and using a monetary aggregate (preferably the monetary base) as a target and as an indicator of economic conditions. Neo-Keynesians, in-stead, are primarily concerned with the level of some collection of interest rates, and they maintain that monetary policy should be aimed at pursuing a level of rates estimated to be adequate. The eclectic view suggests looking at both, but Monetarists in general reject the compromise.

In some sense, it is easy to see that the discussion relies (on both sides) on much the same arguments as the discussion of the relative effectiveness of fiscal versus monetary policies. In both instances, the eclectic view suggests that both policies are important (monetary policy and fiscal policy, and within monetary policy both interest rates and monetary aggregates to be selected as targets), but in a way that suggests that monetary policy take only an accom-

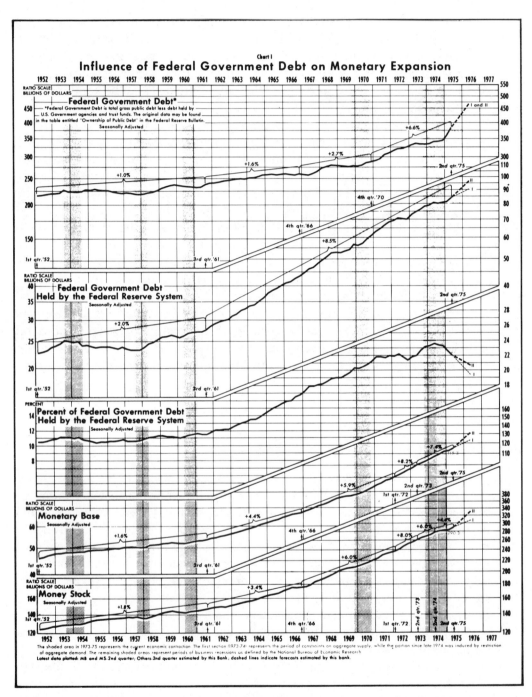

Figure 14-1. *Influence of federal government debt on monetary expansion (Adapted from Susan R. Roesch, "The Monetary-Fiscal Mix Through Mid-1976," Federal Reserve Bank of St. Louis Review (August 1975), p. 3).*

modating role. Thus we can understand the involved argument. So involved, indeed, that Thomas Mayer could say that: "Whether the Federal Reserve should aim at an interest rate target or a money stock target is one of the most important questions in macroeconomic policy."[19] Let us look at the issues, first, in selecting a single policy, and, afterward in selecting and tending both targets.

A MONETARY AGGREGATE, OR THE INTEREST RATE?

In a world of perfect certainty, where the policymaker knows reasonably well the direction and the magnitude of the relationships as well as the lags between changes in policy and changes in the ultimate goals, there is no problem. Once monetary policy is to be used there will be a corresponding level of the money stock and of the interest rate at every desired level of total expenditures. It would make no difference whether the objective to be reached is set in terms of one or the other. The real world of policy is hardly that predictable, however, and the position of the policymaker resembles more the image of physicians as caricaturized by some writers of the eighteenth century: blindfolded men of good will armed with a stick who try to hit the disease and, more frequently than not, hit the patient instead. In the real world we have only an idea about the direction of change and, we hope, some information about the magnitudes and lags involved. Thus there is a need for a certain *target*[20] : a magnitude that can be relatively quickly controlled which would influence the rest of the economic system in a predictable manner and which could also serve as a good barometer of what is going on. Would the interest rate or some monetary aggregate best perform as such a target? For a Monetarist the reliable link (through whatever transmission mechanism, and with whatever lags) is that between money and expenditures, and ultimately income and prices. In the Monetarist scenario, whatever happens to interest rates is a side issue and will depend, even in the very short run, both on real and on monetary considerations. With a fairly stable demand for money, for example, a rise in the interest rate might indicate an increased expansion in the demand for investment which would hardly call' for the *additional* expansion that would be brought about by an increase in the money stock. Interest rates, to a Monetarist, are neither a good variable to attempt to hold constant nor a good indicator of what is going on in the economy.

Extreme Keynesians think differently. The interest rate in the short run is the *sole* outcome of monetary considerations, and the only way in which money can influence private expenditures is by changing the interest rate. Besides, if we observe, say, an increase in the interest rate, this would most likely be the result of an increase in the demand for money, which is very interest elastic and not very stable. The role of monetary policy in this case would be to provide liquidity to moneyholders by increasing the money stock, and so avoid the increase in interest rates that would otherwise be necessary to allocate existing money among moneyholders (and the contractionary effect that an interest rate increase would have on investment expenditures).

Why is it so important to know the reasons behind a change in the interest rate when deciding whether interest rates are a good indicator and a good target of monetary policy? Because if the observed change is the *consequence* of monetary conditions (such as a change in the demand for money), an interest rate target will lead to a change in the money stock in the correct direction; if the observed change is generated in *real* conditions, the interest rate target is misleading and destabilizing.

These results can be visualized in Figures 14–2 and 14–3, which show the conditions in the market for loanable funds. Panels 14–2a and 14–2b show markets that would result from the type of elasticities an extreme Monetarist would expect: a low interest elasticity of the demand for money, and a high interest elasticity of the investment schedule. These figures are mere reproductions of the analysis in Figure 13–3 of Chapter 13 or those constructed in the Appendix of Chapter 5. The first figure (14–2a) shows how an observed increase in the interest rate could be generated by an increase in the desired money stock (with a shift to the left of the supply of loanable funds); the second (Figure 14–2b) shows how a similar increase could be generated, instead, by a change in real conditions (say, a shift to the right of the investment schedule). The second two panels, 14–3a and 14–3b, show similar results for a market for loanable funds with elasticities a neo-Keynesian would believe in: a high interest elasticity of the demand for money, and a relatively low sensitivity of investment expenditures with respect to the interest rate.

Suppose an increase in the interest rate is observed and the Fed follows an interest rate target. If the origin of the observed change is in the monetary

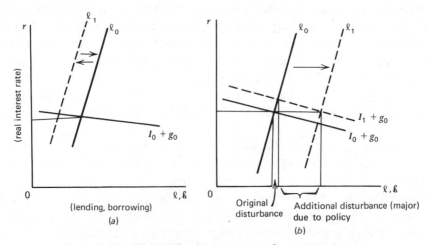

Figure 14-2. Federal funds rate target: the monetarist case.

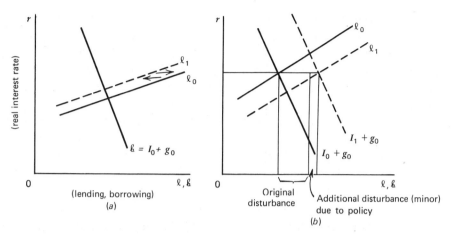

Figure 14-3. *Federal funds rate target: the Keynesian case.*

sector (a change in the demand for money), the rule would indeed yield the correct result. The contractionary effects of an increase in the level of desired real cash balances is counteracted with an increase in the money stock, and the return of the interest rate to its initial level will provide the public with exactly the additional amount of money desired. If, instead, the origin of the observed change in interest rates is the real sector (that is, an increase in the level of investment), the interest rate target would lead to an expansionary monetary policy that would exaggerate, rather than counteract, the initial change in total expenditures. In order to return the interest rate to its initial level, the Fed would have to purchase securities and increase the money stock, adding in this case to the initial unwanted expansion.

These results are correct for both the Monetarist and the Keynesian description of the loanable funds market (in terms of the relevant elasticities involved). Why is it that an extreme neo-Keynesian favors an interest rate target, while a Monetarist opposes it? There are at least two reasons. First, notice that, when the initial shock is originated in the real sector (the case where the interest rate target would lead to the incorrect policy), the observed change in the interest rate is relatively minor in the extreme Keynesian case and substantial in the Monetarist case. If extreme Keynesians are correct about the shapes of these curves, it is most likely for noticeable changes in the interest rates to be of monetary, rather than real, origin.[21] The opposite is true if Monetarists are right. Second, when the interest rate target rule provides the wrong answer (that is, when the change in the interest rate is of real origin), the mistake made in terms of additional unwanted expansion is insignificant in the Keynesian case, but substantial in the Monetarist case—another reason why Keynesians favor the interest rate target and Monetarists reject it. As mentioned before, the way in which Monetarists and Keynesians view the relative sensitivities of the investment schedule and the demand for money with respect to the interest rate (as well as the immediate determinant of the interest rate in the market for loanable funds or directly by the demand and the supply of money) is reason not only for a preference for monetary or fiscal policy, but also for the acceptance of an interest rate target in the conduct of monetary policy.

There is still another, and rather powerful, argument used by Monetarists for opposing an interest rate target as an indicator in the conduct of monetary policy. This argument is based on the difference between the observed nominal interest rate and the real interest rate. The nominal interest rate observed in markets includes the correction for the expected inflation rate,[22] and a high expected inflation rate is normally the result of high past inflation rates due to high rates of monetary expansion. Even if an increase in the rate of monetary expansion may initially, and for some time, lower the nominal market interest rate, sooner or later such an increase will add to inflation and to inflationary expectations, and end up *increasing* the nominal rate. If the money stock is then expanded at a still higher rate, the cycle starts again and the mechanism becomes extremely destabilizing, eventually even explosive. If an interest rate were to be used as a target, it should be the expected *real* rate of interest (that is, the nominal rate minus the expected inflation rate), because this is the rate upon which real expenditures decisions will depend. Certainly, this is a very difficult magnitude to measure, not to mention control.

Finally, an argument advanced by proponents of the strict interest rate target (and by those economists in midstream also) is that to abandon completely such a target would introduce unwanted variability in interest rates over short periods of time, and ultimately cause a disruption in capital markets and in the saving-investment process. The Monetarist response is that these will not necessarily occur if there is arbitrage between short- and long-term rates, and that any short-run changes only anticipate changes that would sooner or later occur anyway.[23] A point to notice (as we will see in Chapter 15) is that the set of arguments concerning such a variability of interest rates if the interest rate target is abandoned is very similar to the arguments heard (from both sides) concerning the effects of free versus fixed foreign exchange rates.

What has the position of the Fed been in recent years concerning the target for the conduct of monetary policy? Before 1970, the objective was to regulate "money market conditions," and this was essentially understood as setting a collection of interest rates as a target. In 1970, the Fed announced that monetary policy would be geared to monetary aggregate targets. Still, it has been convincingly argued that, because of the particular way in which the Fed sets up its targets and the operational procedures used to reach those targets, interest rates (more concretely, the Federal Funds rate) essentially remain the target.[24] Let us consider this argument next, together with other eclectic positions.

A MONETARY AGGREGATE AND THE INTEREST RATE?

As in the case of the two instruments, monetary and fiscal policy, and the possibility of using them both, a similar question arises in the discussion of the appropriate target for monetary policy. Why not watch as indicators, and set up as targets, *both* the interest rate and some monetary aggregate? When some economists urge that attention should not be paid to interest rates in conducting monetary policy, are they not being irrational, "throwing away" information that could give a better idea of what is going on? Indeed, most neo-Keynesians would not argue for an absolute role of pegging interest rates. Arthur Okun, for example, states his "second rule" for the conduct of monetary policy as the following: "Operate fiscal policy to avoid forcing monetary policy off the middle of the road."[25] Professor Walter Heller, a former Chairman of the Council of Economic Advisers under President Kennedy, and one of the architects of the fiscalist policies of the 1960s, clearly argues for looking at both "price" (interest rates) and "quantities" (the quantity of money) in the money market.[26] The policy of "looking at everything" would seem to be more plausible and more informed. In fact, a general view in the profession is that the Fed "should look at everything, in a particular way which yields the maximum useful information and should avoid relying on a particular intermediate target variable."[27]

But most Monetarists seem to be as intransigent in the face of compromise and eclectic positions regarding targets as they are with respect to the use of fiscal policy. In their view, any attention paid by the Fed to interest rates is likely to send monetary policy off its correct course. For example, Milton Friedman criticized the Fed's behavior even after 1970, when a monetary aggregate rather than interest rates was announced as the declared target of monetary policy.

The way the Fed operated so as to hit monetary aggregate targets, until October 1979 at least, was as follows. First, the monetary aggregate targets themselves were set for a certain period. Second, the interest rate (the Federal Funds rate, at which commercial banks lend to eath other) that would be consistent with the monetary aggregate targets was forecasted. From then on, the New York desk operated so as to keep the Federal Funds rate at the pre-established levels. The result, for some time, was very much the same as if monetary policy would have been conducted by using interest rates as a target. If the rate compatible with the desired growth in the monetary aggregate were over- or underestimated and the Fed were to persist in maintaining such a rate, the error would be self-reinforcing. Too low a rate, for example, would encourage commercial banks to add to their borrowed reserves; the excessive monetary growth would add to inflationary expectations and then to a further desire to borrow, still higher monetary growth, and so on. The right operating procedure, according to Friedman, is to translate the desired growth in money into the necessary change in the monetary base ("high powered money"). Even though the money multiplier relating the two is not perfectly stable, such a procedure at least eliminates the *reinforcement* of errors.

The monetarist position of intransigence has had some justification. It is true that additional information should help, and that "looking at everything" seems to be a better strategy than looking at just one thing. But in the Monetarist view, no one can know enough about the economy to be able to always "fit" this information into a complete framework and evaluate it properly. From the operational viewpoint it is not enough to say that both interest rates and a monetary aggregate need to be examined if there is no precise way in which we can interpret the joint signals of these two magnitudes. For a Monetarist, who insists that there is a more predictable relationship between money and income, it is operationally better to avoid the confusion, forget about the interest rate, and stick to a monetary aggregate.

As indicated in Chapter 11 on the instruments of Fed control, the Federal Reserve announced in October 1979 a *reemphasis* upon targeting monetary aggregates through closer day-to-day control over bank reserves and the monetary base. With the change announced in procedures the Federal Funds rate would no longer be narrowly targeted, but narrowly targeted changes in bank reserves would be used to control the monetary aggregates. Thus there may be a growing acceptance at the Fed of a more monetarist position on the matter of the object variable of monetary control. Evidence concerning the conduct of monetary policy over 1980 does not bear this out, at least in Friedman's view.[28]

THE LAG IN THE EFFECTS OF MONETARY POLICY

There is obvious and sometimes considerable delay between the time the need arises for a policy to be enacted and the time at which it is implemented and, finally, the point at which it starts to influence the ultimate goals. It is customary in the literature to assume that two kinds of lags are responsible for such a delay: the *inside lag* and the *outside lag*. The former can, in turn, be reduced to a *recognition lag* (the elapsed time between a policy and the recognition that the policy is necessary) and an *administrative lag* (the time between the recognition and the actual implementation of the appropriate policy). The outside lag is the delay between the implemented policy and its influence over the ultimate magnitudes the policymaker wishes to modify.

There are lags in almost all policy implementation. In the case of fiscal policy, changes in government expenditures and/or receipts can involve a long administrative delay. When in 1963 President Kennedy recommended a tax cut, it took the Congress over one year to approve it. But, in the case of monetary policy, the discussion over "the lag" has been the subject of much controversy. The first impetus occurred around 1960, when Milton Friedman suggested that the lags in the effects of monetary policy were too long and too variable for an active, discretionary monetary policy of stabilization to be used to good effect. The lack of any precise knowledge of the variability of the lag, together with a propensity by the monetary authority to overreact, would make the powerful tool of monetary policy too dangerous a weapon to use.

If this were the case, the natural step was to suggest (and Friedman did) that an attempt to "fine tune" the economy was misdirected. Rather, a policy of maintaining a constant, predetermined rate of growth of the money stock was better: a *rule rather than discretion.* Friedman's prescription has far-reaching and almost philosophical implications. But, because the presence of the long and variable lag turns out to be a major, although not the only, element in the discussion of rules versus discretion, discussion of it is postponed until the next section. For the present a brief comment about the evidence and the controversy over the presence of the lag itself must be made.

The original point expressed by Friedman in 1960 was based on work done jointly with Anna Schwartz. Some of the conclusions have been summarized by Friedman:

> We have found that, on the average of 18 cycles, peaks in the rate of change in the stock of money tend to precede peaks in general business by about 16 months and troughs in the rate of change in the stock of money precede troughs in general business by about 12 months. . . . For individual cycles, the recorded lead has varied between 6 and 29 months at peaks and between 4 and 22 months at troughs.[29]

The estimated lag was indeed very long and very variable.

Friedman's work brought about immediate debate concerning the methods used to derive these results. The essential criticism was that the measure of association between money and income did not take into account what would have happened to income in the absence of the behavior observed in the money stock.[30] Furthermore, the results were later contradicted by the St. Louis model and in 1971 by the (very Monetarist) Laffer–Ranson model,[31] according to which every effect of changes in money takes place in the same quarter in which the changes occur. As a reviewer of the literature pointed out, ". . . it is the monetarists who have taken the view that the lag in the effect of monetary policy is relatively short and the nonmonetarists who seem to be claiming longer lags."[32] The same reviewer concludes that there is indeed a lag, but that ". . . estimates of the lag differ considerably," the most important reason for such a difference apparently being the different variables used in the studies to characterize a change in monetary policy (changes in the money stock, in the monetary base, or in unborrowed reserves of commercial banks). In a recent paper, Tanner reports "significant and substantial differences in the lag in the effect of monetary policy over long periods of time, over different monetary policies and over the business cycle."[33]

The evidence in this matter has failed to bring much agreement. In a more general context, one could say that, independent of many of the technicalities involved in the discussion, the main merit in the contribution originally made by Friedman and Schwartz is to have provided the point of departure for the general debate over rules versus discretion.

RULES VERSUS DISCRETION: THE RATIONAL EXPECTATIONS IDEA

Twenty years ago, as a direct outcome of some of his studies on the lag in the effect of monetary policy, Milton Friedman renewed a rather sweeping proposal. His argument: monetary policy should be conducted merely by following the simple rule of increasing the nominal money stock at some fixed, predetermined rate, "without any variations . . . to meet cyclical needs." The rate of increase, according to the proposal, should be chosen "so that in the average it could be expected to correspond with a roughly stable long-run level of final product prices."[34]

The proposal, which was reiterated in later works by the same author, was justified on the following grounds. First, we do not know enough about the economic system and, in particular, about the nature of the "long and variable lag" in the effects of monetary policy:

> We seldom in fact know which way the economic wind is blowing until several months after the event, yet to be effective, we need to know which way the wind is going to be blowing when the measures we take now will be effective, itself a variable date that may be a half year or a year or two years from now. Leaning today against next year's wind is hardly an easy task in the present state of meteorology.[35]

Second, as a consequence, we are at a stage not only where fiscal policy has been "oversold," but also where monetary policy has promised a "fine tuning" that it cannot deliver:

> By setting itself a steady coarse and keeping to it, the monetary authority could make a major contribution to promoting economic stability. . . . Other forces would still affect the economy, require change and adjustment, and disturb the even tenor of our ways. But steady monetary growth would provide a monetary climate favorable to the effective operation of those basic forces of enterprise, ingenuity, hard work and thrift that are the true springs of economic growth. That is the most that we can ask from monetary policy at our present stage of knowledge. But that much—and it is a great deal—is clearly within our reach.[36]

Friedman's proposal has been supported by some and strongly opposed by many in a debate that goes from the very technicalities of trying to measure the lag to almost philosophical questions. In analyzing the discussion we must realize that the rule is not only an automatic operational device, but one that in some sense reflects the admission that very little can be done to counteract actively shocks originating in the private sector. Furthermore, fluctuations in income and prices observed in the past have occurred because of active monetary policy and not in spite of it. The position of the Monetarists supporting the rule reflects a quite different general attitude concerning the real world than the neo-Keynesians, according to the interpretation of Harry G. Johnson:

> This . . . is . . . the crux of the issue prevailing between Keynesians and Monetarists: the Keynesian position is that the real economy is highly unstable . . . ; the Monetarist position, on the contrary, is that the real economy is inherently fairly stable, but can be destabilized by monetary developments. . . ."[37]

From the purely logical point of view the strongest attack against the rule is the argument that it does not make a lot of sense to separate rules from discretion, since the establishment of the rule is in itself a supreme act of discretion. The attack could be answered, however, by arguing that while it is true that the rule in itself implies discretion, the inverse is also true: "discretion" in the management of monetary policy—unless policy is completely random, and nobody advocates that—implies a strategy or set of rules for the policymaker to follow. Semantics aside, the question boils down to the decision between a simple strategy—the constant growth of the money stock rule—or a more complicated one.

Thus, at the operational level, the important question is whether a more stable path of income and prices is to be the result of a simple rule or of an actively conducted countercyclical monetary policy of the type that we can *realistically expect* in the future, given our limited knowledge about the way in which the economic system works. We will analyze in later sections of this chapter expectations about discretionary monetary management in the future based on experiences of the recent past. The ongoing discussion in this chapter concerning the level of our knowledge and of the possibilities for predicting the delay, the intensity, and the direction of the effects of monetary policy makes it clear that there is not much agreement on the results. But, independent of whether a total agreement on these matters is ever reached, such discussion has the merit of bringing about a much more cautious attitude toward the use of monetary policy not only among academicians but also among policymakers.

On the one hand, the switch (in October 1979) from interest rates to monetary aggregates as a target for Federal Reserve policy indicates, if anything, that a smoother behavior of monetary aggregates might be forthcoming. Of course, this is not the "rule," because the targets still could be frequently changed at the discretion of the Fed, but, once the targets are set, the new policy should assure a less "jerky" behavior of monetary aggregates in the short run. On the other hand, since 1975 the Congress requires the Fed to publicly state its objectives for growth in the monetary aggregates for one year in advance. The resolution neither constrains the Fed to any "rule," nor precludes the Fed from changing the "publicly stated" objectives, but the resolution is an indication of a certain tendency toward less discretionary action.[38]

There is still a further development, perhaps not the direct outcome of the discussion on rules versus discretionary authority, but related to it. For several years a group of economists at various institutions have been working on a *rational expectations hypothesis.* Their work is having an important impact within the profession, and in many respects it represents a radical departure from the way in which economic policy (and especially monetary policy) has traditionally been appraised and analyzed. In fact, the impact is already spilling over into public opinion.[39]

In spite of many intricacies, the nature of the work on rational expectations and its consequences for policy can be intuitively described as follows. According to this view, individuals are "rational," make use of all available information, and, after some time, do have a good idea (perhaps as good as the policymaker) of how the economic system works. Because individuals know the basic structure of the economic "model" (the real world), their anticipations will coincide with the most likely outcome. Of course, in a world of uncertainty, where many outcomes depend on random elements, individuals will not *always* be correct in their anticipations. But they will be correct on the average.

Since much of the rationale for, say, monetary policy, is to induce people to do what they did not intend to do in the first place, the scenario becomes one of both economic agents and policymakers engaging in a game of out-guessing each other, with no guarantee that success will be on the side of the policymakers. The policymakers have the surprise element in their favor: the public may know how the economy reacts, for example, to a change in monetary expansion, but it may have no way of knowing when the change will occur. But if the policymakers show any systematic pattern of behavior (for example, if they increase the rate of monetary growth when unemployment rises), sooner or later the public will figure out such a pattern, anticipate it correctly, and *counteract* the policy change. To have any "teeth," monetary policy would have to be capricious and random—not a very good way to be conducted. Otherwise, it will (after a while) become grossly ineffective.

This is indeed a radical, sweeping conclusion. Of course, everyone does not know exactly and at all times how "the model" works, and this is not a requirement for the general principle to work eventually. On the other hand, this extremely unrealistic view about how alert people are is no less extreme and unrealistic than the opposite, conventional view that people continuously "throw away" information, that individuals do not take information into account in forming their anticipations about the future, and that individuals can be fooled forever. For one thing, the conventional view is not a bad point of departure; starting from that extreme, we can then analyze, for example, the costs of acquiring and handling information and the reasons why, from a viewpoint of individual's benefits and costs, it may be more "efficient" not to use all available information.

One of the areas where we can see the shortcoming of the conventional view in its most crude form is the theory of how people form inflationary expectations. In Chapter 8 we discussed the importance of these expectations. and presented the *adaptive expectations hypothesis*, according to which individuals form their expectations about future inflation by taking account of past inflation rates. Individuals completely ignore other things that are happening at the present (for example, the current rate of monetary expansion) and clearly *do* have an influence on what the inflation rate will be in the future. Anyone who reads current periodicals knows how curious the business community is about the plans of the Fed, and how well the Fed keeps these plans a secret.

If all of this is true, there is little room for policy, and a simple rule would be far more efficient in the short run than a complicated one. The proponents of the rational expectations hypothesis leave no room for doubt concerning their own views:

> The Administration and Congress should stop thrashing around pretending to know better than the economy how much can be produced. And the Federal Reserve should move as quickly as possible to a 4 percent monetary growth.[40]

THE ROLE OF MONETARY POLICY DURING THE LAST TWENTY YEARS

Chapter 16 gives an account of US monetary history until 1960. In concluding Chapter 14, we will examine monetary policy over the last twenty years. These twenty years are filled with change and should illuminate present (and future) monetary policy and provide a ground work that illustrates the principles we have learned throughout this book.

First a short, descriptive, overview of the main events of the period will be given, as well as a conventional interpretation of some of them. In this description four periods are considered.[41] Inevitably, reference to some political events must be made because many political activities—for good or for evil— have helped to shape policy. Table 14–2 and Figures 14–4 through 14–9 condense the most relevant information for these years and much of the description and the analysis can best be seen by continuous reference to these figures. (In several of the figures a trend line has been incorporated.) After an initial description, an interpretation of the role and the effects of monetary policy during these years will be provided and the data will illustrate some of

Table 14-2   Economic Aggregates (Rates and Rates of Change)

	M-1	CPI	GNP Nominal	GNP (1972 Dollars)	Prime Rate	Unemployment
1960	-0.1	1.6	4.0	2.3	4.82	5.5
1961	2.1	1.0	3.4	2.5	4.50	6.7
1962	2.2	1.1	7.7	5.8	4.50	5.5
1963	2.9	1.2	5.5	4.0	4.50	5.7
1964	4.0	1.3	6.9	5.3	4.50	5.2
1965	4.2	1.7	8.2	5.9	4.54	4.5
1966	4.7	2.9	9.4	6.0	5.63	3.8
1967	3.9	2.9	5.8	2.7	5.61	3.8
1968	7.2	4.2	9.1	4.4	6.30	3.6
1969	6.1	5.4	7.7	2.6	7.96	3.5
1970	3.8	5.9	5.0	-0.3	7.91	4.9
1971	6.7	4.3	8.2	3.0	5.72	5.9
1972	7.1	3.3	10.1	5.7	5.25	5.6
1973	7.5	6.2	11.6	5.5	8.03	4.9
1974	5.5	11.0	8.1	-1.4	10.81	5.6
1975	4.4	9.1	8.2	-1.3	7.86	8.5
1976	5.3	5.8	11.2	5.7	6.84	7.7
1977	7.3	6.5	11.0	4.9	6.83	7.0
1978	7.8	7.7	11.7	4.0	9.06	6.0
1979	7.9	13.3	12.0	13.2	12.67	5.8

Source: Economic Report of the President.

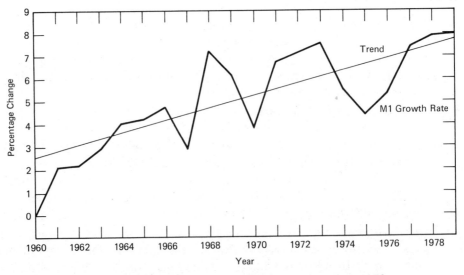

Figure 14-4. Money stock growth rate (M1), 1960-1979.

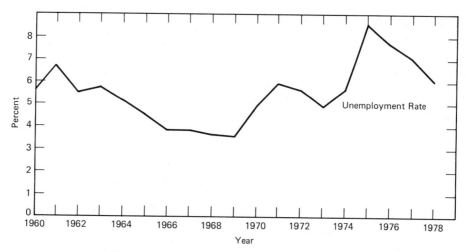

Figure 14-5. Unemployment rate, 1960-1979.

the principles discussed throughout this book, particularly in the present chapter.

AN OVERVIEW

1961–1969: The Rise and Fall of the "New Economics." In January 1961, when President John F. Kennedy was inaugurated, he faced an inherited unemployment rate of 5.5 percent for 1960, just down from a high of almost 7 percent in 1959. With the new Democratic Administration a new team of

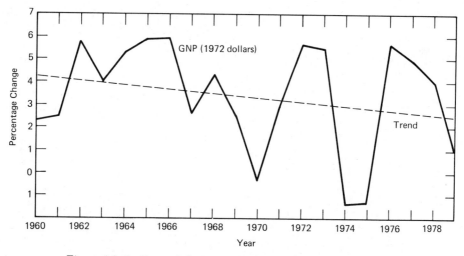

Figure 14-6. Rate of change in GNP (1972 Dollars), 1960-1979.

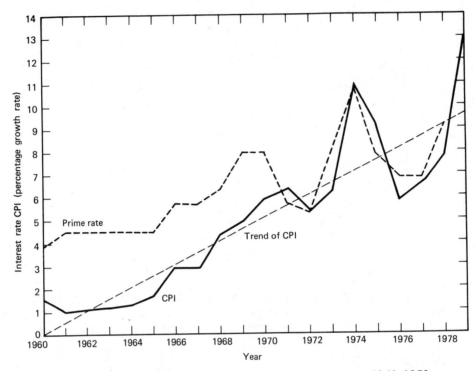

Figure 14-7. Consumer price index and prime interest rate, 1960–1979.

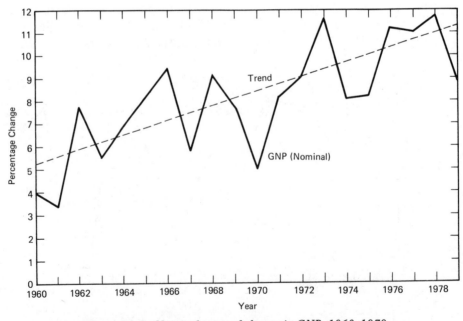

Figure 14-8. Nominal rates of change in GNP, 1960–1979.

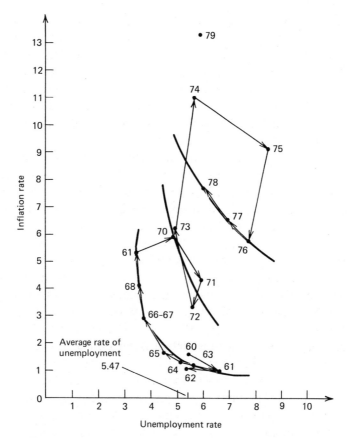

Figure 14-9. Unemployment and inflation, 1960–1979.

experts moved into the Council of Economic Advisers. The mission: to assure a high and continuous rate of employment and economic activity. The team consisted of a highly qualified, homogenous group of individuals with impressive academic credentials. All of them, to one degree or another, were of a definite "neo-Keynesian" bent—the "New Economics," as it was then called by the media.[42] These were not men who believed that "money doesn't matter," but certainly the dominant view among them was that fiscal policy was quicker, more reliable, and more powerful for the management of aggregate demand. After the unsuccessful "Operation Twist" of 1961–1963 (discussed earlier in this chapter), monetary policy was to accommodate the results of fiscal policy by keeping "orderly conditions" in the financial markets.

It took some time for the new view to be translated into concrete policy. In 1962 an investment tax credit was instituted, and in 1963 the administration submitted a package to Congress calling for a substantial and permanent tax cut. The proposal was approved over a year later as the Revenue Act of

1964, which instituted a reduction in income tax rates for individuals (from 20/91 to 14/70 marginal tax rates) and for corporations (from 52 to 48 percent rates). The cut amounted to about a 3 billion dollar drop in tax revenues.

The investment tax credit and the 1964 tax cut (which, through anticipations, probably started taking effect even before they were passed by the Congress) seemed to produce the desired results over the following years. By 1965 the unemployment rate had fallen to 4.5 percent and inflation, although higher than in 1960, was a tolerable level of 1.6 percent, the same as in 1960. Monetary policy, in its "accommodating" role to the big fiscal move, was represented by rates of monetary expansion that went from 2.0 percent in 1961 to 4.2 percent in 1965. By 1966 unemployment was reduced still further, to a rate of 3.8 percent, and inflation was slightly higher (almost 3 percent). The economy was starting to "overheat," and by the second half of 1966 monetary policy became tight, with a "credit crunch" from August to October 1966. After a year, 1967, of relatively low growth of the money stock (3 percent), monetary expansion proceeded, in 1968, at a very high rate of over 7 percent. The Vietnam War acted, throughout the later 1960s, as a strong pressure for an expansionist fiscal policy. While the inflation rate kept creeping up, and unemployment still fell slightly, the expansionary monetary policy of 1968 was counteracted with a more restrictive fiscal policy in the form of a temporary tax surcharge. But (perhaps because the surcharge was explicitly temporary) inflation kept rising, this time to a very high (for those days) 5.4 percent in 1969, while unemployment was at an unprecedented low of 3.5 percent.

It was by then all too obvious that the low 1969 unemployment rates were not sustainable, and that trying to maintain them would require actions that would, at the same time, bring about increasing rates of inflation. The unemployment problem had been solved, but inflation was intolerable. The New Economics, hailed by the media a few years before, had become a disappointment. In January 1969 President Nixon was inaugurated.

1969–1971: "Gradualism." With the Republican administration a new economic team took over, this time perhaps less homogeneous and less committed to a particular line of policy, but definitely of a Monetarist inclination. The enemy was inflation, and the name of the game was gradualism, a policy of trying to bring inflation down in a gradual, smooth maner. The policy lasted two years, and the conventional view is that it proved the failure of monetarism. In 1969 the rate of monetary expansion fell to 6.1 percent from 7.2 in the previous year), but inflation did not fall: it rose from 4.2 to 5.4 percent per year. Unemployment went down to a low 3.5 percent. The gradualist policy reacted in 1970 by cutting monetary growth abruptly, to a rate of less than 4 percent per year. Inflation in that year still rose to almost 6 percent (the highest rate since 1965), and unemployment jumped to almost 5 percent. The "gradualist" policy resulted in no progress in the fight against inflation and the start of a recession. By mid-1971, although inflation was showing signs of softening, the unemployment situation looked bad; in fact, the year was going to end with a unemployment rate of almost 6 percent. Gradualism was dead.

1971–1975: Direct Controls, Expansionary Policy, and the Aftermath. The policy response to the "failure of gradualism" was not so much a change of personnel, but a radical switch to a policy of wage and price controls. In August 1971, the "New Economic Policy" (NEP) was announced, with an initial, ninety-day freeze on wages and prices. Later were to come the so-called Phases II, III, and IV, the first from November 1971 to January 1973, the second from January 1973 to June 1973, and the last one until August 1974, when all controls were to be eliminated. However, most controls were substantially relaxed or lifted by mid-1973.

The apparent result of the controls was an immediate success. By the end of 1971 inflation was down to a little over 4 percent, and during 1972 it fell still more, to a respectable level of 3.3 percent per year. Monetary growth, meanwhile, was high, in a quest for a fall in the unemployment rate that, in 1971 (reflecting the decline in the rate of growth of real output of 1970), rose from almost 5 percent to almost 6 percent. The apparent rationale was that while direct controls would keep inflation low, monetary expansion would take care of unemployment. During 1972 the unemployment picture had improved some, but the rate of 5.6 percent still prompted an expansionary monetary policy.

By mid-1973 most controls were substantially relaxed, and by the end of the year inflation had climbed to the uncomfortable rate of 6.2 percent. Whatever consolation there was that year from the improvement in the employment picture, it was short-lived. In 1974 inflation skyrocketed to an unprecedented 11 percent per year, and the panic prompted the monetary authority to lower the rate of monetary growth by two full percentage points (from 7.5 to 5.5 percent per year). Unemployment was on the rise again. During 1975 the tight money policy persisted, but inflation was still very high (over 9 percent) and unemployment hit an amazing 8.5 percent: it was the trough of the worse recession since the Great Depression of the thirties.

1976–1979: Recovery and the Quest for Monetary Stability. The recovery from the 1974–1975 recession opened a period that has not yet ended. The aftermath of the recession brought a substantially lower inflation rate in 1976 and some improvement in unemployment (lagging behind a very high rate of growth of real output) that kept progressing through 1978. But as soon as the unemployment rate began to fall, inflation started to rise again; a new tradeoff was under way. By 1978 inflation had crept up to 7.7 percent, and it exploded in 1979 with a staggering 13.3 percent, the highest in the post-World War II period.

On the political front, President Carter was inaugurated in January 1977, and the new Democratic Administration, which won the 1976 election supporting the view that the fight against unemployment takes precedent over the fight against inflation, seemed to be more concerned with the latter. After a large increase in 1977 (from 5.3 to 7.3 percent per year) the rate of monetary growth was kept at the stable range between 7 and 8 percent during 1978 and 1979. Seven to eight percent was a high rate but far from the exaggerated overshooting above the trend that characterized the upsurges after 1967 and 1970. The years 1978 and 1979 are still too close to the present to show a definite tendency, but there are indications, some of them announced, that the Fed does intend to provide a more stable monetary growth, without the violent fluctuations in the rate of monetary expansion typical of most previous years. In July 1979, Paul Volcker (until then President of the New York Federal Reserve Bank) was appointed Chairman of the Federal Reserve Board and, since then, several statements have been addressed to the need for a tighter monetary policy. In October 1979 the Fed announced that it will pay less attention to the level of interest rates and more to monetary aggregates as a target of policy, as we have indicated. In addition, a somewhat radical reordering of legal controls over the entire financial system (see Chapters 11 and 12) may improve the Federal Reserve's ability to manage monetary aggregates. There are, in short, reasons to believe that future monetary policy may be not only less expansionary, but also more stable.

In reviewing these last three years we should also note that in October 1978 President Carter announced "voluntary guide lines" for wage and price increases. By mid-1979 it was all too obvious that the guidelines were ineffective. Alfred Kahn, a prestigious former professor of economics at Cornell University, was assigned the job of "inflation fighter" in 1978 after a successful tenure as chairman of the Civil Aeronautics Board, and his own words seem to indicate that such a vew was shared even by the enforcers of the controls: "I can't figure out why the President doesn't fire me. Actually, I do know. Nobody would be foolish enough to take this job."

AN INTERPRETATION OF THE PERIOD

The previous discussion focused simply on a description of the most important policy decisions and upon the behavior of the relevant variables such as inflation and unemployment. In this section we seek to use some of our theory to interpret the relationship between policy decisions and the response of those macroeconomic variables. There are several lessons to be learned.

The Role and Importance of Lags. We should notice from an analysis of the data for the last twenty years is that there is a lag between the implementation of monetary policy (a change in the rate of monetary expansion) and its results on output, unemployment, and the inflation rate. First, the data provide support for the view that the initial effect of a monetary change is a change in real output, and that the effect takes place quickly. To observe this, consider Figures 14-4 and 14-6 and see how (in particular between 1966 and 1976) the rate of change of real GNP very closely follows changes in the rate of change of the money stock.

Second, there is another lag between changes in the growth rate of real output and the resulting rate of unemployment. Such a lag is usually explained in terms of the business firm's costs of hiring and firing personnel, and in terms of the possibility of increasing output in the very short run and for a limited time by means other than adding employees to the payroll. This lag is about one year in duration and we can see it by comparing Figures 14-5 and 14-6, in particular after 1967.

Finally, there is a third lag between the effects of monetary policy on unemployment and the ultimate effects on the inflation rate—a lag of about 6 to 8 months. If we refer to the "dynamic" Phillips curve (Chapter 8), the observed response of the inflation rate to changes in unemployment—and still more, for the response to changes in real output—is not immediate and should include another lag.

All in all, there is a time lag of at least 18 months between changes in the rate of monetary expansion and changes in the inflation rate. Compare the data with Friedman's statement: "A change in monetary growth has a rapid effect on credit markets, but it generally takes some six to nine months before it affects total spending, and then the effect is mainly on physical output. In the United States, it has generally taken some two years before a change in monetary growth has its main effects on prices."[43]

Recognition of such lags helps to explain the behavior of output and prices over the last twenty years and it also sheds some light on why a disregard for such lags generated the behavior on the part of monetary policymakers which we have observed during those years. Consider at closer range the rates of inflation and unemployment, given the operation of these lags.

Inflation, Unemployment, and the Shifting Phillips Curve. Figure 14-9 plots the rate of unemployment and the rate of inflation over the last twenty years. There are at least three (perhaps four, if we consider the two years of 1974 and 1975) short-run "Phillips curves" showing a tradeoff between inflation and unemployment. If we keep in mind the presence of the lags in the effects of monetary policy, the graph provides useful information.

Most of the first period, from 1961 to 1969, corresponds to the experiment with the expansionary fiscal and monetary policies of the "New Economics." We will say more about this period later, but for the moment we should observe the almost ideal textbook case of a short-run Phillips curve up to 1969. Notice, at the same time, the increase in the rate of monetary expansion during the period, with the exception of 1967. Between 1961 and 1965 most of the effect of expansionary policies concerned output and employment, but as the years passed there was a larger and larger effect on the inflation rate.

The time between 1969 and 1970 is the benchmark for a movement from the first short-run Phillips curve to the second one, with higher inflation rates for each rate of unemployment. Between these two years inflation rose by very little, but unemployment increased by almost 1.5 percentage points. What happened? Casual empiricism would tend to suggest that, while inflation (reacting with a long lag) did not show any change, unemployment was already reacting to the abruptly tight monetary policy begun in 1969.[44] The following year, 1971, still shows the effects of the tight policy started in 1969 (that two years later clearly affected the rate of inflation) and of the continuation of such policy in 1970, which one year later affected the unemployment rate.

In 1971 the rate of monetary expansion was up again, starting a three-year period of rapid expansion that lasted through 1973. In 1972 inflation fell once more (as a result of the low monetary growth of 1970) and unemployment started to fall (as a result of the expansion started in 1971). In 1973 unemployment fell a bit more and inflation jumped to 6.2 percent.

The year 1974 was the beginning of a period of monetary growth that was low after having been very high, as occurred in 1969. And, again as in 1969, we can see another (higher) short-run Phillips curve. There was an initial reaction of unemployment (which rose slightly over one percentage point), but the inflation rate exploded to 11 percent as a result of the fast expansion in the money stock during 1972 and 1973. By 1975 the economy was in the worst recession since World War II and inflation (although still high) started softening after the low monetary growth of 1975 (which actually started in the second quarter of 1973).

Between 1975 and 1976 there was again a transition to a fourth short-run "Phillips curve," this time a lower one, which in turn corresponded to a transition from a low to a high rate of monetary expansion. As the result of the increase in the rate of monetary growth that started in 1975, the years 1976, 1977, and 1978 showed a movement toward lower rates of unemployment and higher rates of inflation (in very much the same manner as in the years, say, between 1964 and 1968). But we should notice the year 1979, in which the rate of unemployment did not change with respect to 1978, but during which inflation skyrocketed to over 13 percent. Inflation was reacting to the strong monetary expansion of 1977, but in a more violent manner than in other previous episodes, perhaps showing that inflationary expectations are adjusting a lot faster now than they did in the past.

Let us conclude, with one more question and a tentative answer. Does the evidence from these years give any support to the "natural rate," "shifting Phillips curve" hypothesis described in Chapter 8? The answer seems to be affirmative. Consider the following. For all of these years, the average rate of unemployment has been around 5.5 percent (exactly 5.47 percent). The rate of unemployment usually taken to describe full employment (the "natural rate" of unemployment) was at the level of 4 percent until 1977, a year in which the report by the Council of Economic Advisers suggested that it should be 5 percent. Indeed, several economists have argued that such a natural rate should still be higher than 5 percent, that is, not very different from the average of 5.5 percent for these past twenty years. Cynically, it might be argued that since 1960–1961 all we have done is to trade a one or one and one half percent unemployment rate for a 13 percent inflation rate, moving back and forth around a natural unemployment rate of 5.5 percent.

The Federal Reserve System Overreacts. The natural question to be asked after an analysis of the effect of monetary policy on inflation, output, and unemployment during the last twenty years is "Why does the Fed follow such a jerky, stop–go sort of policy?" This is a difficult and complex question to answer completely. A part of the answer may lie in the observation that Fed monetary policies would have worked quite well if they had had a quicker effect on inflation and unemployment. Indeed, the standard criticism about the Fed is that it waits too long and then tends to overreact.[45] The numbers we have just analyzed show that every important change in inflation and unemployment has been the delayed result of abrupt changes in the rate of monetary expansion. But did the intelligent people at the Fed not realize this? The answer to this second question is that the people at the Fed are not fools. It is very easy to detect mistakes and to talk about what the right policy should have been after the fact. Policy decisions are made in a world of uncertainty; since at some crucial times there is nothing more than a rough indication of whether the economy is slackening or overheating, it may be extremely difficult to engineer a more stable policy. Besides, in the preceding analysis, we have been particularly vague about the precise length of each lag, which has been roughly between one year for unemployment and 18 months or two years for inflation, but not exact at every episode. These answers explain why an important sector of economists supports a rule rather than discretion in the management of monetary policy, as mentioned earlier in this chapter.

Did the "New Economics" of the 1960s Succeed? The Role of "Accommodating Policies." The response of employment to the expansionary fiscal policies of the 1960s has in general been considered a clear cut demonstration of how fiscal policy may work, and not too many economists would argue that the investment tax credit of 1962 and the tax cut of 1964 had no effect. But, just as an iconoclastic intellectual exercise, let us consider the arguments of those who think otherwise.

The declared role of monetary policy in the 1960s was to accommodate the side effects of fiscal policy by maintaining orderly conditions in the financial markets—that is, by avoiding a rise in the rate of interest. That monetary policy did act in such a way during at least some of those years is clear from looking at Figure 14-7, which shows the behavior of the prime interest rate, the rate charged on least-risk short-term business loans by commercial banks. The prime rate did not change at all until 1965, when inflation really started to rise. We should notice that the rate of change of the money stock practically doubled between 1962 and 1964. The question raised by some Monetarists is: did the expansion take place because of the tax cut, or because of a faster rate of money creation? The answer is not conclusive on either side, and it never will be, but we might try our hand at finding such an answer.

Did "Gradualism" Succeed? Another conventional view is that the gradualism of 1969 and 1971 was a failure.[46] Certainly, this was the view within the Administration and also among many Monetarists. True, the inflation rate in 1970 did not fall as a response to the mild decrease in monetary expansion in 1969, while unemployment rose, exactly as we would have expected after taking account of the lags. From the viewpoint of immediate results, the so-called gradualism did fail. From the viewpoint of a wider prospective, and given the lags, the policy was not gradual nor did it fail. The rise in unemployment in 1970 and 1971, and the strong response of the inflation rate in 1971, fit the typical pattern sketched by the Monetarists, who allegedly were in charge. The question is: was the drop in the inflation rate in 1972 a lagged effect of the slow monetary growth two years earlier, or was it due entirely to the controls imposed by the New Economic Policy in August of that year? Obviously, if prices are not allowed to change by legal mandate (and with effective enforcement), they will *not* change. But the read question is: would not prices have grown at a lower rate anyway?

As elements of an answer, we might consider the following. First, an interpretation emphasizing the long lags in the effects of monetary growth works quite well for the period, without taking account of the controls. Second, the initial ninety-day freeze on all prices and wages may well have lowered inflationary expectations. Third, the years of controlled prices did not bring about severe shortages, and this result is an indication that markets were in fact clearing at the prevailing, controlled prices. If prices had been forced well below their market clearing levels by the controls, shortages would have developed. Fourth, the upsurge in the inflation rate in 1973, often attributed to the relaxation of controls, can be explained as well by looking at the jump in the rate of monetary expansion in 1971.

Another Look at Inflation and Interest Rates. Let us close this section by looking at the data for the last twenty years and concentrating on one more piece of information. Figure 14–7 shows, together with the rate of inflation, the level of the prime rate as somehow representative of interest rates in general. Several times in this book, and especially in Chapters 7 and 8, we have seen the difference between the nominal and the real interest rates, and have noted how an increase in the rate of inflation will, after a while, show up in an increase in the nominal rate of interest. Such a nominal rate will include a "correction" term to take account of the rate of inflation expected in the future.

The evidence from Figure 14–7 is clear. Up to 1965 the prime rate was kept at a constant level of 4.5 percent, in spite of the creeping increases of inflation via the accommodating policies of the Fed. Between 1965 and 1969 the nominal rate corresponds very well to the changes in the inflation rate, keeping the *real* ex post rate of interest (the difference between the nominal rate and the rate of inflation) about 3 percent. After 1971 there is again a close relationship between inflation and the nominal rate. The curious thing is, however, that since 1971 (and except for 1973, when the ex post real rate was about 2 percent), the ex post, real rate of interest has been either negative or extremely low. This result indicates a very slow response of the public's expected inflation rate vis-à-vis the actual inflation rate. The indignation about high mortgage rates of 11 to 13 percent in 1979 (a year when the inflation rate was 13.3 percent) seems also to reflect the slow adaptation of inflationary adaptations.

CONCLUSION: A LOOK TO THE FUTURE

The future of monetary policy, as with many other economic events, is difficult to predict with a high degree of accuracy. There are some important indications, however, of the course of monetary policy for the 1980s. We should consider several important bits of information.

In the first place, we may expect commercial banks to continue to react to inflationary pressures in the economy by alterations in interest rates. By mid-February 1980, for example, it was reported that the inflation rate for the month of January was 1.4 percent, which is about 17 percent on a continually compounded yearly basis. The predictable happened as commercial banks raised their prime interest rate to $17\frac{1}{4}$ percent by late February and up to over $19\frac{1}{2}$ percent by April 1980 (see Table 11–10 and the related discussion in Chapter 11).

This period of inflation and high interest rates has provoked Congressional action at the behest of the Fed. The "Depository Institutions Deregulation and Monetary Control Act" passed in March 1980 (detailed in Chapters 11 and 12) provides for the gradual reorganization of Federal Reserve control over member and nonmember banks as well as over other financial institutions. Discriminatory interest ceiling controls, collectively called "Regulation Q," will be eliminated by 1986 and reserve requirements on similar types of deposits will be applied equally to all depository institutions. The probable effects of this regulatory change will be to enhance the ability of the Fed to control system reserves and monetary aggregates.

A second and concluding point is also well worth noting. In early 1980 a Report of the Joint Economic Committee of the US Congress supported the general aim (expressed in late 1979) to restrain the rate of growth in money and credit but warned that the Board may be taking actions *too abruptly. The Wall Street Journal* commented that such a report seems to be a result of a "growing feeling in Congress that policy making . . . has become too much like a 'roller coaster,' full of 'fits and starts.' 'In our estimation,' the report says, 'there is a need for a shift in the focus of monetary and fiscal policies away from short-run crisis management toward steady long-term economic growth.'"[47]

Thus, the future of monetary policy in the 1980s will depend upon considerations such as these. The Congress will undoubtedly have a large input on the "proper" conduct of monetary policy, as will be attitudes of the Federal Reserve Board (and its Chairman) itself. Will the Fed be able to resist the destabilizing accommodation to fiscal policies that it was unable (or unwilling) to resist in the past? As we know from Chapters 7 and 8, most economists agree on the nature of the causes of inflation. Society's ability to control these causes, however, crucially depends upon human institutions and, unfortunately, humans and human institutions are notoriously unpredictable.

FOOTNOTES

[1] Notice, for example, the current concern among some economists (especially Martin S. Feldstein, of the National Bureau of Economic Research) about the implications of the present tax structure for the rate of capital accumulation, and how little attention such concern receives in the media as compared with the headlines made by the last monthly inflation or unemployment figures.

[2] Conservationists' groups, for example, doubt that the objective of a high rate of growth may be feasible, while environmentalists directly oppose it.

[3] One could hypothesize, for example,

that this is the reason why there is an unemployment insurance paid by government, while there is no insurance against the "inflation tax" caused by price increases.

[4] At a still more fundamental level, however, the question is whether there should be any active policy at all. This controversy is discussed later in this chapter.

[5] In Milton Friedman and Walter H. Heller, *Monetary Versus Fiscal Policy—A Dialogue* (New York: W. W. Norton & Company, 1969), p. 51.

[6] Suppose every day you buy a certain lunch that costs 4 dollars, and that suddenly a tax of 4 dollars per day is imposed on you, the proceeds of the tax being used to buy and distribute the same lunch for free. Government action would have no effect on the level of total expenditures (yours plus the government's). This is obviously an extreme and highly unrealistic case, but perhaps not more so than the case usually discussed in the elementary Keynesian model, where individuals are assumed to behave as if government's provision of goods and services did not matter at all (that is, as if goods purchased by government were thrown into the ocean).

[7] Paul A. Samuelson, "The Role of Money in National Economic Policy," in *Controlling Monetary Aggregates*, Federal Reserve Bank of Boston, 1969, p. 7.

[8] Leonall C. Andersen and Jerry L. Jordan, "Monetary and Fiscal Actions: A Test of Their Relative Importance in Economic Stabilization," *Federal Reserve Bank of St. Louis Review*, November 1968, pp. 11–24.

[9] Sometimes known, in different versions, as the MPS Model (for MIT–University of Pennsylvania–Social Research Council).

[10] For a very clear description, see Frank de Leeuw and Edward M. Gramlich, "The Channels of Monetary Policy: A Further Report on the Federal Reserve–MIT Model," *Journal of Finance*, 24 (May 1969), pp. 265–290. Reprinted in Thomas M. Havrilesky and John T. Boorman, Editors, *Current Issues in Monetary Theory and Policy* (Chicago: AHM Publishing Corporation, 1976).

[11] In the FRB–MIT model, the aggregate is unborrowed reserves of commercial banks; in the St. Louis model, money is narrowly defined as currency plus demand deposits.

[12] Leonall C. Andersen and Keith M. Carlson, "St. Louis Model Revisited," *International Economic Review*, Vol. 15 (June 1974), pp. 305–327. Reprinted in Thomas M. Havrilesky and John T. Boorman, *op. cit.*

[13] Benjamin M. Friedman, "Even the St. Louis Model Now Believes in Fiscal Policy," *Journal of Money, Credit and Banking*, 9 (May 1977), pp. 365–367. But see Carlson's rebuttal in "Does the St. Louis Equation Now Believe in Fiscal Policy?" *Federal Reserve Bank of St. Louis Review* (February 1978), pp. 13–19. After discussing a statistical problem of estimation, the author proceeds to estimate the model once more, with a result that confirms the earlier findings.

[14] Arthur M. Okun, "Rules and Roles for Fiscal and Monetary Policy," in James S. Diamond, ed., *Issues in Fiscal and Monetary Policy: The Eclectic Economist Views the Controversy* (Chicago: De Paul University, 1971). Reprinted in Thomas M. Havrilesky and John T. Boorman, *op. cit.*

The exception to this view is stated in an imaginative work by Robert A. Mundell "The Dollar and the Policy Mix: 1971," Princeton University *Essays in International Finance*, #85, May 1971. The point made by Mundell is that monetary policy, which controls nominal variables (the money stock), should be directed to attain price stability (another nominal variable), and that fiscal policy, which influences real variables, should be reserved to influence the level of employment.

[15] A variation of a coordination of fiscal and monetary policies, consisting of using monetary policy for expansionary purposes while trying to avoid a worsening of the balance of payments deficit, was tried in the early 1960s through the unsuccessful "Operation Twist," by which the Fed tried to keep long-run interest rates low (so as to not introduce deflationary pressures at home) while maintaining short-term interest rates high (so as to eliminate capital outflows).

[16] Arthur M. Okun, *op. cit.*, p. 572.

[17] Arthur M. Okun, *op. cit.*, p. 576.

[18] For some views on this concern, see Darryl R. Francis, "How and Why Fiscal Actions Matter to a Monetarist," *Federal Reserve Bank of St. Louis Review*, May 1974, p. 2, and Susan R. Roesch, "The Monetary-Fiscal Mix Through Mid-1976," *Federal Reserve Bank of St. Louis Review* (August 1975), p. 2.

[19] Thomas Mayer, "A Money Stock Target," in *Monetary Policy Oversight*, Hearings Before the Committee on Banking, Housing and Urban Affairs, US Senate, 94th Congress, First Session (1975). Reprinted in Thomas M. Havrilesky and John T. Boorman, *op. cit.*, p. 548.

[20] A target, or an "intermediate target" (to distinguish it from the ultimate targets or goals to be achieved), can in principle be distinguished from what is called "an indicator." The first is something to set and keep at a certain value; the second, something to watch so as to judge the effect the policy is having on the more remote targets or goals. Some authors have argued that the same magnitude should not be used as an indicator and a target; see Thomas R. Saving, "Monetary-Policy Targets and Indicators," *Journal of Political Economy* 75 (August 1967), pp. 446–456. Others even deny that the need for an indicator exists; see Thomas J. Sargent, "Discussion," *American Economic Review* 60 (May 1970), pp. 57–58.

[21] A loanable funds approach is used here to describe the immediate determination of the interest rate. If the Keynesian case had been described in terms of liquidity preference approach, as in Chapter 5, all observed changes in interest rates have their immediate origin in monetary considerations (the demand for and the supply of money), a natural circumstance for Keynesians to advocate the interest rate target rule.

[22] This was analyzed in Chapter 3, and again in Chapters 7 and 8.

[23] For an examination of some of these points, see R. Lombra and F. Struble, "Monetary Aggregates Targets and the Volatility of Interest Rates," *Journal of Money, Credit and Banking*, August 1979, pp. 284–300.

[24] See, for example, Milton Friedman, "Statement on the Conduct of Monetary Policy," from Second Meeting on the Conduct of Monetary Policy, Hearings Before the Committee on Banking, Housing and Urban Affairs, US Senate, Ninety-fourth Congress, First Session, November 4 and 6, 1975. Reprinted in Havrilesky and J. Boorman, *op. cit.*

[25] Arthur M. Okun, *op. cit.*, p. 577.

[26] Walter W. Heller and Milton Friedman, *op. cit.*, especially p. 21.

[27] Benjamin M. Friedman, "Targets, Instruments and Indicators of Monetary Policy," *Journal of Monetary Economics* 1 (October 1975), p. 470.

[28] See Friedman's comments on the conduct of monetary policy by the Fed in 1980 under the reemphasized "aggregate guidelines": "A Memorandum to the Fed," *The Wall Street Journal*, January 30, 1981, p. 20.

[29] Milton Friedman, *A Program for Monetary Stability* (New York: Fordham University Press, 1960), p. 87.

[30] This is the objection of Kareken and Solow (in A. Ando, E. C. Brown, R. Solow, and J. Kareken, "Lags in Fiscal and Monetary Policy." Commission on Money and Credit, *Stabilization Policies* (Englewood Cliffs, N.J.: Prentice-Hall, Inc., 1963), pp. 1–163). See also Thomas Mayer, "The Lag in Effect of Monetary Policy: Some Criticisms," *Western Economic Journal*, September 1967, pp. 324–342.

[31] Arthur B. Laffer and R. D. Ranson, "A Formal Model of the Economy," *Journal of Business*, July 1971, pp. 247–270.

[32] Michael J. Hamburger, "The Lag in the Effect of Monetary Policy: A Survey of Recent Literature," Federal Reserve Bank of New York, *Monetary Aggregates and Monetary Policy* (1974), pp. 104–113.

[33] J. Ernest Tanner, "Are the Lags in the Effects of Monetary Policy Variable?" *Journal of Monetary Economics*, January 1979, pp 105–121.

[34] Milton Friedman, *A Program for Monetary Stability op. cit.*, p. 91. Essentially the same proposal was made over forty years ago by Henry Simons in "Rules versus Authority in Monetary Policy," *Journal of Political Economy*, February 1936, pp. 1–30. Actually, the level of the rate of monetary growth is not as

important as the constancy of it. The reader is reminded that in a growing economy the rate of price changes will, in equilibrium, be equal to the rate of monetary expansion minus the rate of growth. See Chapter 7.

[35] Milton Friedman, *A Program for Monetary Stability*, p. 93.

[36] Milton Friedman, "The Role of Monetary Policy," Presidential Address delivered at the Eightieth Annual Meeting of the American Economic Association, Washington, D.C., December 29, 1968. Reprinted in *The Optimum Quantity of Money and Other Essays* (Chicago: Aldine Publishing Company), 1969, p. 110.

[37] Harry G. Johnson, *Inflation and the Monetarist Controversy* (Amsterdam: North-Holland), 1972, p. 6.

[38] For an interesting analysis of whether the 1975 Congressional resolution really puts any constraints on the Fed, see Edward J. Kane, "How Much Do New Congressional Restraints Lessen Federal Reserve Independence?" *Challenge* 18: (November/December 1975), reprinted in Havrilevsky and Boorman, *op. cit.*

[39] See, for example, "The New Economists," *Newsweek*, June 26, 1978; "The New Down-to-Earth Economics," *Fortune*, December 1978; and "The Rational Expectations Model," *The Wall Street Journal*, April 2, 1979.

[40] Robert Lucas, quoted in *Newsweek*, *op. cit.*, June 26, 1978, p. 60.

[41] The particular grouping of some years within a period makes sense to us, but in some cases a question of interpretation can be raised as to whether a different set of groupings could have been chosen.

[42] Among the most well-known members of this group were Walter Heller (Chairman of the Council), James Tobin of Yale University, and others who joined later: Otto Eckstein, Arthur Okun, and James Duesenberry.

[43] Milton Friedman, *Statement on the Effect of Monetary Policy*, *op. cit.*

[44] Consider a quotation from Milton Friedman once again: "The Federal Reserve System has done it again. Once more it is overreacting as it has so often done in the past" (*Newsweek*, August 1969).

[45] For a different view, see Arthur M. Okun, "Rules and Roles for Fiscal and Monetary Policies," *op. cit.*, especially the section entitled "A propensity to overreact?"

[46] Why the monetary policy of those years was ever called "gradualism" is a mystery. A view of Figure 14–4 shows that, except for a relatively mild decrease in the rate of monetary expansion between 1968 and 1969, only the wild change in monetary growth between 1967 and 1968 exceeds the pronounced year-to-year changes in that rate between 1969 and 1971.

[47] "Joint Congress Panel Urges Moderation in Economic Policy, Promotion of Growth," *The Wall Street Journal*, February 29, 1980.

KEY CONCEPTS

goals of macroeconomic policy
  full employment
  price stability
  sustained growth
  balance of payments
    equilibrium

fiscal policy

monetary policy

econometric models

St. Louis model

demand management

capital account

"accommodating policy"
(even-keeling, monetization)

target

indicator

monetary policy lags

rules vs. discretion

rational expectations

"New Economics"
(1961–1969)

gradualism (1969–1971)

direct controls and expansion
(1971–1975)

recovery and quest for
stability (1976–1979)

QUESTIONS FOR DISCUSSION

1. What common factor has made stabilization programs of the past notoriously unsuccessful?

2. Do you think the "New Economics" of the 1960s was successful? Why or why not?

3. Wage and price controls have proved effective in fighting inflation during the enforcement period, as under the Nixon Administration. What is the problem with this approach in fighting inflation? Is this an effective long-run solution?

4. Explain in your own words the basic tenets that lead to the differences between Neo-Keynesian and Monetarist theory. Be as concise as possible. How may these differences be used as arguments for or against monetary or fiscal policy?

5. What is the difference between an "indicator" and a "target"? Is the interest rate a good target? Evaluate from both points of view.

6. If Milton Friedman's rule is adopted, under what circumstances might we still experience inflation?

CHAPTER 15

THE INTERNATIONAL SCENE:
Trade and Finance

Up to this point the importance of money under the implicit assumption that the economy is closed has been considered. A closed economy does not engage in trade or financial transactions with the rest of the world. We now remove this assumption and account for particular questions and problems brought about by an open economy. International economic arrangements are more important for some countries than for others, since some are more open than others. The question is of increasing importance for economic policy in a world where interdependence and exchange become more pronounced. Foreign trade and finance also constitute a fascinating extension of the basic economic analysis developed earlier in this book.

There are three basic parts to this chapter. In the first section an initial idea of an open economy is developed, with discussion centering around the concept of a balance of payments and the market for foreign exchange. The second part is the main body of the chapter, where the open economy is added to the analytical framework already developed in the book. The third and final section is a compact account of some historical and present international monetary institutions and arrangements.

THE BALANCE OF PAYMENTS, NATIONAL MONIES, AND THE MARKET FOR FOREIGN EXCHANGE

The *balance of payments* is at the center of the analysis of an open economy, so much so that the study of the monetary connections between an open economy and the rest of the world is often called balance of payments theory. The balance of payments is an account of monetary transactions between the residents of a country and the rest of the world during a certain period of time. In principle, the balance of payments is the application, to residents of a country, of a general accounting concept that could be applied to any group of individuals or even to a single individual. Payments are debits, receipts are credits, and the difference between the two during a certain period is reflected in changes in the stock of money held by the individuals or groups in question. Even if accounts refer to a whole country, with a national currency different from the currency in the rest of the world, balance of payments accounts can be designed for a certain group of individuals within a country, using the same currency as the "rest of the world" (the rest of the country, in this case) or, similarly, to a country using the same money as other countries.

A SIMPLE VIEW OF THE BALANCE OF PAYMENTS

There are certain accounting complications brought about by the diversity of reasons behind each payment and receipt, and some of these complications will be introduced later. At this point the structure of the balance of payments will be discussed in order to establish some general principles.

Two main groups of transactions are the counterpart of monetary payments and receipts; these are the sales (*exports*) and purchases (*imports*) of commodities, and the sales (*capital inflows*) and purchases (*capital outflows*) of financial instruments. All transactions in the long list of any nation's balance of payments, with the exception of unilateral transfers (grants and gifts), enter into these two categories. The difference between receipts and payments due to transactions in commodities is called the *trade balance* or the *trade account*, and the difference due to transactions in financial instruments, the *capital account*. The sum of the two is the balance of payments.

Thus the hypothetical balance of payments for country A can take the form shown in Table 15-1. In this example, residents in country A have sold commodities to the rest of the world for 20, and purchased commodities for a value of 35; the country has a deficit in the balance of trade of 15. Or, similarly, there is an excess of monetary payments over receipts, in the trade account, of 15. During the same period, residents of the country have sold financial assets

Table 15-1   Hypothetical Balance of Payments (Above the Line)

	Credits (+)	Debits (−)	Net
Trade Account			
Exports	+20		
Imports		−35	
Balance of Trade			−15
Capital Account			
Capital inflows	+18		
Capital outflows		−10	
Balance in Capital Account (Net capital inflows)			+8
Balance of Payments			−7

abroad (and received payment) for a value of 18 and have purchased financial assets (and paid) for a value of 10. The excess of receipts over payments in the capital account is 8, and this is the surplus in the capital account. The net difference between the two accounts (minus 7) is the total excess of receipts over payments, in this case negative. Thus country A has an overall deficit in its balance of payments of 7.

Formal presentations of the balance of payments do not end here, however. Other items *below the line* make explicit the monetary counterpart of the items *above the line.* To be completely general, suppose that these monetary payments can be made in either country A's currency or in "foreign" currency. Then payments by residents of country A can be made through either a fall in domestic holdings of foreign currency (either private, or those of the Central bank), if payments are made in foreign currency, or through an increase in foreign holdings of country A's currency, or a combination of the two. Receipts accruing to country A's residents, in turn, will result in either an increase in domestic holdings (private, or those of the Central Bank) of foreign currency, or a fall in foreign holdings of country A's currency, or a combination of the two. Suppose, in our simplified example, that all of these possibilities have been used. Then, the part below the line in our hypothetical balance of payments for country A could appear as in Table 15–2. The balance of payments, when the items below the line are also taken into account, always balances, in the same manner as commercial firms' income statements.

The listing of all the items below the line in this example is exhaustive and general. As we will see later, there are particular cases where, either because of international monetary arrangements or because of moneyholder's behavior, some of those items may not exist. Suppose, for example, that there is no official intervention in the market for foreign exchange by either the country in question or the rest of the world; in this case, changes in foreign holdings of country A's money or in domestic holdings of foreign money would take the form of changes only in private holdings.

Table 15-2 Hypothetical Balance of Payments (Below the Line)

	Credits (+)	Debits (−)	Net
Financed by:			
Increase in Foreign Holdings of Country A's Money			
Private	+8		
Foreign central banks	+4		+12
Decrease in Domestic Holdings of Foreign Money			
Private		−1	
Country A's central bank		−4	+7

ALTERNATIVE MONETARY ARRANGEMENTS, AND THE MARKET FOR FOREIGN EXCHANGE

As mentioned before, balance of payments accounts are applicable to any group of economic units whether they are residents of one country or only some individuals within a country. More important, those economic units may be using the same or a different money (as is mostly the case when they are the residents of a country) from the rest of the world.

Let us consider first the case of a country using the same money for hand-to-hand currency as the rest of the world. This case is, for purposes of monetary arrangements, the same as that for a region within a country (say, the State of Rhode Island within the United States). The distinction between "domestic" and "foreign" money vanishes, as does the significance of the local Central Bank (Rhose Island, or any country using some other country's money as hand-to-hand currency, does not have a Central Bank). In this case the items of the balance of payments below the line reduces to changes in money holdings by residents—an increase, if the balance of payments is positive, or a fall, if it is negative.

In a sense, the situation just described is the same as that for the *gold standard*, where different national currencies are all convertible into gold by each country's Central Bank. In this case, however, domestic residents purchasing and selling abroad (either commodities or financial assets) must "convert" the national currency into foreign currency, and vice versa. That is, there is a market for foreign exchange. Importers pay for their purchases abroad in foreign currency, and they are the demanders of foreign exchange in the market; exporters wish to transform their foreign exchange receipts into domestic currency and they are the suppliers of foreign exchange in the market. In the case of the gold standard all monies are the same in the sense that their relative price (the exchange rate among them) is given by the fixed price of each of them in terms of gold. Arbitrage will assure that, except for small variations within the limits given by the cost of transporting gold, exchange rates will remain *fixed*.

Suppose, for example, that France has fixed the price of one ounce of gold at 4 francs per ounce, and in England, the price of one ounce of gold is 2 pounds per ounce. Furthermore, assume that French and English Central Banks buy and sell all the gold necessary to maintain such parity. If at some point in time there is a balance of payments deficit in France, and the supply of francs therefore exceeds its demand, the presence of the gold standard will preclude any rise in the price of pounds in terms of francs (which, as the reader probably already figured out, is 2 francs per pound); rather than pay more than 2 francs per pound, it would be preferable to purchase half a pound of gold at France's Central Bank, take it to the Bank of England, and sell it for one pound. In the case of the gold standard, if residents of each country hold only their national currency, deficits and surpluses in the balance of payments will be financed *exclusively* through changes in gold reserves of the respective Central Banks.

The system of fixed exchange rates used in the Western world from the end of World War II up to the early 1970s (and still used by some countries) is fundamentally only a variation of the gold standard. In this case, a particular country (the "fixer") decides to fix the domestic price of the money of some other country (the "reserve" country), with its Central Bank committed to buying or selling whatever foreign exchange is necessary in order to maintain the fixed rate. If we look at the "fixer" country's balance of payments, the main item below the line will be variations in the country's Central Bank holdings of the foreign reserve currency, and perhaps also private domestic holdings of such currency. From the viewpoint of the reserve country (the position of the United States for several years), the bulk of balance of payments deficits or surpluses corresponds to changes in official (and also private) reserves of the "fixer." As we will see shortly, the manner in which equilibrium is achieved under all these fixed exchange rates systems is essentially the same.

At the other end of the spectrum is the possibility of *no* official intervention in the market for foreign exchange, the exchange rate being determined simply by its private demand and supply. In this case there are no Central Bank holdings of foreign reserves. Deficits and surpluses in the balance of payments can still exist in the short run, but only to the extent that private holders of foreign exchange are willing to change those holdings. Otherwise, the exchange rate will need to adjust in order to equilibrate, at every period, the *flow supply* (given by exports and capital inflows) and the *flow demand* (given by imports and capital outflows) of foreign exchange, so that the balance of payments is equal to zero at all times. In the remainder of this chapter we will analyze more fully several of these points. Before proceeding, let us consider in more detail some of the more specific items of the balance of payments.

A DETAILED VIEW AND ALTERNATIVE DEFINITIONS OF THE BALANCE OF PAYMENTS

Anyone venturing into the dozens of items and figures of any actual balance of payments statistics would certainly have a hard time relating those items to the simplified version presented in preceding sections. The task can be simplified and, at the same time, alternative definitions of a balance of payments surplus or deficit can be expressed. To that purpose let us analyze a hypothetical balance of payments (Table 15–3); here not only are the numbers hypothetical, but also many of the items themselves have also been simplified. Thus Table 15–3 is a construction somewhere between the simple versions of Tables 15–1 and 15–2 and the actual complicated detail of the actual statistics.

Table 15-3   A Detailed Hypothetical Balance of Payments

		Net Balance	Cumulative Net Balance
A.	Merchandise Trade		
	Exports	+30	
	Imports	−25	+5	
	MERCHANDISE TRADE BALANCE		+5
B.	Services		
	Travel and Transportation (net)	−2	
	Military Transactions (net)	−3	
	Investment Income (net)	+6	+1
	GOODS AND SERVICES BALANCE		+6
C.	Transfer Payments		
	Government Grants	−2	
	Remittances and Pensions	−1	−3
	CURRENT ACCOUNT BALANCE		+3
D.	Long-Term Capital Movements		
	Direct and Portfolio Investment (net)	−1	
	Government Loans (net)	−2	−3
	BASIC BALANCE		0
E.	Short-Term Private Capital Movements (net)	−1	−1
F.	Miscellaneous		
	SDRs Allocations	+1	
	Errors and Omissions	+1	+2
	NET LIQUIDITY BALANCE		+1
G.	Liquid Private Capital Movements		
	Liabilities to Foreigners	+6	
	Claims on Foreigners	−1	+5
	OFFICIAL SETTLEMENTS BALANCE		+6
Financed by Changes in:			
	Liabilities to Foreign Official Holders		
	Liquid	−3	
	Nonliquid	0	+3
	Official Reserve Assets		
	Gold	+1	
	SDRs	−8	
	Convertible Currencies	+1	
	IMF Gold Tranche	0	+1	−6

Let us first discuss the specific items. As always, a sign (+) indicates a credit (a payment received by residents, from abroad) and a sign (−) a debit (payments made abroad by residents). Section A is "Merchandise Trade," and is made up of Exports and Imports. The difference between these two items (Exports minus Imports) is the Merchandise Balance of Trade, which is self-explanatory and coincides with the measure of the trade account discussed in the simplified version of Table 15–1.

Section B is Services. The first item (Travel and Transportation) could as well be included in Merchandise Trade: there is conceptually no difference between the purchase in New York, by an American, of a Swiss watch, and the purchase of the same watch by an American on vacation in Zürich. Military Transactions, the next item, are expenditures related to the country's military involvement abroad. The last item in Section B is Investment Income: this is interest and dividends received by residents from their ownership of foreign assets (securities, equity, direct investment, and so forth). In the example of Table 15-3, receipts for those concepts have exceeded payments to foreigners by 6 units. The net result of adding the Merchandise Balance and Services yields the Goods and Services Balance.

Section C of Table 15-3 is Transfer Payments, made up of two items that are self-explanatory, and the addition of this section to the Goods and Services Balance yields the Current Account Balance. In a sense, this is equivalent to what was called the *trade balance* in Table 15-1; in that simplification we implicitly assumed that investment income was of secondary magnitude and that transfer payments did not exist.

Sections D and E both refer to the sales and purchases of financial instruments (what in our simplified presentation we called the capital account). Here, the difference between the two is that those items included in Section D are private and official long-term capital movements, not expected to be soon reversed. Addition of Section D to the Current Account Balance yields the *Basic Balance*, the first important indicator, for some purposes, of balance of payments tendencies.

Section F constitutes miscellaneous items: errors and omissions (because in the case of many transactions only one side of the transaction is reported, and the other needs to be estimated) and Allocations of SDRs. SDRs (Special Drawing Rights) are a creation of the International Monetary Fund, instituted around 1969 in order to help solve the problem of international liquidity. They are rights, allocated to member countries of the Fund, to use other countries' reserves in case of need, in proportion to their quota. The addition of Part E (short-term private capital movements) and miscellaneous items to the Basic Balance yields the Net Liquidity Balance, which is the concept we have used as a definition of the Balance of Payments (and the one we will be using soon, in our theory).

Next, Part G, called Liquid Private Capital Movements, are essentially changes in residents stocks of foreign money, an item that in Tables 15-1 and 15-2 we placed below the line. The result of adding Section G is called the *Official Settlements Balance.*

Below the Official Settlements Balance are the items that "finance" this balance: Liabilities to Foreign Official Holders (changes in reserves of domestic money at foreign Central Banks) and Changes in Domestic Reserves. The latter, we observe, are made up of changes in gold and other currencies, the counterpart of SDR's allocations, and the IMF Gold Tranche, a facility given by the International Monetary Fund for borrowing, automatically, up to 25 percent of the country's quota.

These descriptions make clear that there are several balances, and the question is which of them is a good measurement of "the" balance of payments with which to analyze "equilibrium" or "disequilibrium"; that is, whether the Basic Balance, the Net Liquidity Balance, or the Official Settlements Balance should be used. The Basic Balance gives a good idea of the long run, underlying forces within the international economy. The Net Liquidity Balance, which is the counterpart of what we have called "the" balance of payments in our simplified version and will go on using in the theory, is the actual account of the difference between monetary payments and receipts, based on the assumption that there is no difference whether the changes in money holdings (of domestic and foreign currency) take place among private individuals abroad, or among foreign Central Banks. The Net Liquidity Balance gives an account of the *actual* demand and supply for foreign exchange (the Basic Balance accounts for the *potential* forces of supply and demand) including short-term capital movements (Section E) which may be reversed soon. Thus, a variety of balance of payments concepts are available for alternative purposes. (As noted above, the Net Liquidity Balance is employed in the following theoretical discussion.)

EQUILIBRIUM AND ADJUSTMENT IN THE OPEN ECONOMY UNDER FIXED OR FLEXIBLE EXCHANGE RATES

The macroeconomic adjustment of the open economy is of prime importance in understanding the relation of the international to the domestic economy. Long-run equilibrium and the process by which such an equilibrium is reached are the principal concepts to be learned. For this purpose an extremely simple framework is used—a natural extension of the theory discussed in previous chapters. Even though the model is simplified, the conclusions are essentially the same as those obtained in a more complicated manner. (More "realistic" complications are discussed briefly, however.)

BASIC RELATIONSHIPS IN THE OPEN ECONOMY

In order to account for the "openness" of the economy, both concerning the exchange of goods and services and the exchange of financial assets, basic macroeconomic relationships for the closed economy must be modified. Let us first consider the market for commodities. In the case of the closed economy, equilibrium in the commodity market resulted whenever total production or output (y) was equal to total expenditures, the latter being the sum of consumption, investment, and government expenditures. In the case of the open economy, two items must be added. First, the supply side would be made up not only of domestic production (y) but also of imported goods (imports); second, the demand side components will include not only expenditures on all kinds of goods by domestic residents and government (consumption, plus investment, plus government expenditures) but also foreign expenditures on the country's commodities (exports). Thus equilibrium in the market for commodities will obtain when

$$y + \text{Imports} = c(y) + I(r) + g + \text{Exports}$$

where consumption depends on the level of income, and investment expenditures depend on the level of the interest rate. Since Exports minus Imports is equal to the balance of trade, the equilibrium condition may be written as

$$y = c(y) + I(r) + g + t \qquad [15.1]$$

where t = (Exports minus Imports) is the balance of trade.

The second modification of the closed economy relationships is the addition of an equilibrium condition in the balance of payments. Since the balance of payments is equal to the surplus in the trade account (the balance of trade, t) plus the surplus in the capital account (net capital inflows), it is also equal to the balance of trade minus net capital outflows. For the balance of payments to be zero, the balance of trade must be equal to net capital outflows, or

$$t = nco \qquad [15.2]$$

where nco is net capital outflows.

The third condition for equilibrium, as in the case of the closed economy, is given by the equality of the actual money stock in real terms, m, and the desired real money stock, $L(y, r)$, or

$$m = L(y, r) \qquad [15.3]$$

THE LONG-RUN EQUILIBRIUM

Expressions [15.1], [15.2], and [15.3] contain five unknowns or variables to be determined: real income (y), the interest rate (r), the balance of trade (t), net capital outflows (nco), and the real money stock (m). As we have more variables than relationships, we need further specifications to solve the system.

The first simplification, which we will remove later in the Section, is to assume away the presence of capital flows, so that the trade balance becomes the balance of payments. Expression [15.2] becomes

$$t = 0 \qquad [15.2']$$

The second simplification is to assume that the level of real income or output (y) remains constant, presumably at some full employment level. This is a sweeping assumption, of course, imposing some restrictions on the conclusions, but still fulfilling the main purpose—a basic idea of the mechanism for balance of payments equilibrium and adjustment. Given these simplifications, we are left to determine only three magnitudes: the balance of trade (t), the interest rate (r), and the real money stock (m).

Observe, first, that the long-run equilibrium of these variables is the same as that in the closed economy with a fixed level of real income. There will be only one interest rate such that, with $t = 0$, expression [15.1] is satisfied, and only one real money stock such that, given that interest rate, expression [15.3] will be satisfied.

Long-run equilibrium can be depicted by means of a simple geometrical representation that will also be useful later when we consider the adjustment process. The left panel of Figure 15–1 shows the demand for money and the real money stock equilibrium (m_0) (see expression [15.3]). The right-hand panel is the representation of expression [15.1], for a given level of real income (y_0) and of real government expenditures (g_0). The vertical axis measures the interest rate, as in the left panel, and the horizontal axis measures the balance of trade (which naturally may be positive—a surplus—or negative—a deficit). The line t - t shows the balance of trade that will correspond to each level of the interest rate, and this line is positively sloped for the following reason. An increase in the interest rate decreases expenditures on investment goods, and hence total expenditures (government expenditures are fixed, and consumption expenditures depend on real income, which is also fixed); to eliminate the excess supply of commodities, exports must rise and/or imports must decrease, that is, the balance of trade must increase. There will be only one interest rate (r_0 in Figure 15–1) at which domestic output (y) is equal to total expenditures by residents and for which the balance of trade will therefore be zero.

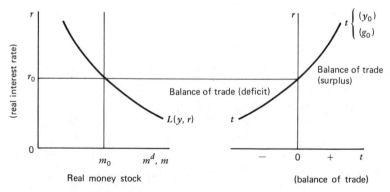

Figure 15-1. Balance of trade equilibrium.

For the system to be in complete equilibrium, the real money stock must be m_0, because this is the only stock that, at the interest rate r_0, moneyholders will be willing to hold.

There is an alternative but equally simple graphical representation, which is shown in Figure 15–2 and which will be particularly handy for the analysis of the adjustment process. If the interest rate varies so as to equate actual and desired real cash balances, a higher level of these balances will correspond to a lower interest rate and a lower balance of trade will be necessary to eliminate the disequilibrium in the market for commodities. Thus there is an *inverse* relationship between the real money stock and the balance of trade, and only one real money stock will be compatible with a balance of trade equal to zero. Figure 15–2 shows the combination of levels of the real money stock and of the balance of trade for which the market for commodities is in equilibrium.

Reference has not been made, with respect to the long-run equilibrium of the variables, to whether the country in question has a system of either fixed or freely floating exchange rates. To elaborate further on this point in a simple manner, we need two further assumptions. First, suppose that we are analyzing the case of a country where *all* commodities are traded internationally. The existence of some goods and services that cannot be traded abroad (haircuts, buildings, and so on) is assumed away. Second, assume that we are considering the case of a "small" economy, where small simply means that the *world price of commodities is given to the country in competitive fashion*, and that it does not depend on the quantity of commodities imported or exported. Notice that such a characterization as "small" does not necessarily refer to the geographic size of the country or to its population, but only to the size of its foreign trade as a proportion of total world trade. Switzerland, for example, is a small country in geography and population, but it is not a small country in the world market for high-quality watches.

With these two additional assumptions, it must be true that the domestic equilibrium price of each commodity (expressed in terms of domestic money) is equal to the world price (expressed in terms of foreign money) multiplied by the exchange rate. Since this will be true for each commodity and its price,

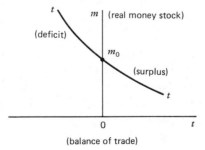

Figure 15–2. Trade equilibrium and real money balances: an alternative view.

it will also be true for the index of general prices, or

$$P = P^*\mathbf{E} \qquad\qquad [15.4]$$

where P is the domestic price level, P^* is the world price level, and $\mathbf{E}$ is the exchange rate. If we assume the country to be Mexico, for example, with a local money called *peso*, and consider the domestic price of automobiles, expression [15.4] indicates that if the world price of an automobile (P^*) is 12,000 dollars per automobile, and if the exchange rate ($\mathbf{E}$) is 25 pesos per dollar, the domestic price of the automobile will be $P = (12,000) \cdot (25) = 300,000$ pesos per automobile. Of course, transportation costs and taxes are included in the foreign price of the automobile. Expression [15.4] is not an identity, but an equilibrium condition. In the short run it is possible for the domestic price to be higher than the world price times the exchange rate. If this is so, it would pay to buy automobiles abroad and bring them into Mexico in order to earn the price differential. For as long as the difference exists, more and more automobiles will be brought in until the domestic price falls to the level indicated by expression [15.4]. In the present analysis we will assume that expression [15.4] holds at all times, even during the adjustment process.

The world price level (P^*) is an index number. As long as it remains at the same value, we can arbitrarily make it equal to one, so that the domestic price level becomes nothing other than the exchange rate, or

$$P = \mathbf{E} \qquad\qquad [15.4']$$

Now fixed and flexible exchange rates in the long-run equilibrium can be analyzed. Since the real money stock is the nominal money stock divided by the price level, expression [15.3] can be written as

$$(M/\mathbf{E}) = L(y, r) \qquad\qquad [15.5]$$

In the final equilibrium the level of the real money stock $[m = (M/\mathbf{E})]$ will be the same irrespective of the exchange rate system. But, if expression [15.5] is used instead of [15.3], the system will contain three expressions, as before, but also four unknowns: the balance of trade (t), the interest rate (r), the nominal money stock (M), and the exchange rate ($\mathbf{E}$).

Let us consider what the election of either a fixed or a flexible exchange rate system implies. In the system of fixed exchange rates the monetary authority fixes the exchange rate ($\mathbf{E}$), and in this case the nominal money stock (M) will have to be determined by the economic system; that is, it will be an *endogenous* variable. In a system of freely floating exchange rates the monetary authority permits the exchange rate to be determined by the economy and fixes the nominal money stock. The specific manner in which this occurs should be fully understood in the analysis of the adjustment process that follows.

THE ADJUSTMENT PROCESS

The adjustment process in the open economy may now be considered for both the cases of fixed and flexible exchange rates. To facilitate the exposition, suppose we are referring to the country called "Mexico," with a domestic money called "peso," trading with the rest of the world where the monetary units are dollars. Thus dollars are the foreign money, and pesos the domestic money.

The Case of Fixed Exchange Rates, Monetary Expansion, Devaluation, and Sterilization. Consider, first, a system of fixed exchange rates under which the monetary authority (the Central Bank) sets an exchange rate and is prepared to buy or sell whatever foreign exchange is necessary in order to keep such a rate at the fixed level. For quick reference, we call these operations of purchases and sales of foreign exchange as being performed at the *foreign exchange window* of the Central Bank.

Suppose, for example, that at some point there is a surplus in the balance of payments (equal to the balance of trade, in our simplified example of no capital movements). A balance of payments surplus implies that exporters' flow supply of foreign exchange is larger than importers' flow demand. In this case the Central Bank, through its foreign exchange window, would be purchasing dollars (foreign exchange) by an amount equal to the excess supply (the balance of trade) in exchange for newly printed domestic money (pesos). If there is a deficit in the balance of payments, the Central Bank will be supplying a flow of foreign exchange equal to the excess demand, thereby *retiring* domestic money from the system. If we assume that no other operations are performed by the Central Bank (that is, that there are no other windows, such as the discount window discussed in Chapter 11), then the change in the nominal (and real, since the price level is given by the fixed exchange rate) money stock due to operations in the foreign exchange window (equal to the balance of trade) is equal to the total change in the money stock, or

$$\Delta m = t \qquad [15.6]$$

where Δm, as always, means the change in the money stock per whatever unit of time is appropriate. If there is a surplus in the balance of trade (t is positive), Δm is positive, and the real money stock will be rising because of the injections of new domestic money as the Central Bank acquires foreign exchange. If there is a deficit (t is negative), Δm is negative and the real money stock will be falling because of the retirement of domestic money as the Central Bank sells foreign exchange. *These resulting changes in the stock of money due to the operations at the foreign exchange window are, precisely, the essential mechanism by which equilibrium is restored in an open economy under a fixed ex-*

change rate system. To analyze why this is so, we can perform some experiments, always starting from situations of full equilibrium.

Assume first that the economy is in equilibrium, with a balance of payments (trade) equal to zero, an interest rate r_0, and real cash balances equal to $m_0 = (M_0/E_0)$, where E_0 is the fixed exchange rate. Such an initial equilibrium situation is shown in Figures 15-3 and 15-4, discussed earlier. As the initial "experiment," assume that overnight there is a sudden increase in the level of the nominal money stock, from M_0 to M_1. The immediate result is a rise in the level of the real money stock from m_0 to $m_1 = (M_1/E_0)$, as shown in the two graphs, and a fall in the rate of interest from r_0 to r_1. The lower interest rate will correspond to a lower level of the balance of trade (minus t_1, a deficit); since the interest rate is lower, investment expenditures are higher and the increase in total expenditures will be satisfied through more imports and/or less exports—that is, by a deficit in the balance of trade. In Figure 15-4, all of this is indicated by an initial jump of the real money stock from m_0 to m_1 (that is, from point A to point B), and another "jump" from $t = 0$ to $t =$ minus t_1 (from point B to point C).

The economy is now in disequilibrium. But, according to expression [15.6], the economy will not remain in disequilibrium. That is, since there is a deficit in the balance of trade, the real money stock will start to fall through the retirement of money at the foreign exchange window of the Central Bank. As the real money stock falls, the interest rate rises, causing expenditures (in investment goods) to fall, and with them the deficit in the balance of payments. For as long as the balance of trade is negative the real money stock goes on falling, the interest rate continues rising, and the balance of trade increasing. This adjustment is shown in Figures 15-3 and 15-4 along the path shown by the arrows, which are self-explanatory. The final result yields the same equilibrium level of the variables as before the change, including the nominal money stock.

This simple experiment is of paramount importance in explaining the

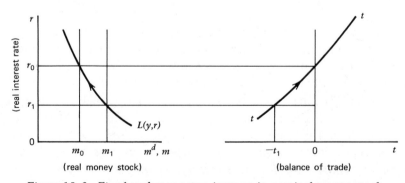

Figure 15-3. Fixed exchange rates: increase in nominal money stock.

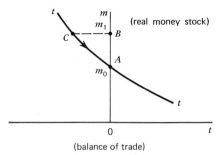

Figure 15-4. Fixed exchange rates: real money balance adjustment.

basic adjustment mechanism under fixed exchange rates, a mechanism much the same in real world situations far more complicated than those in our naïve, simplified model. In fact, this "intellectual experiment" is the same one described by the British philosopher and economist David Hume two hundred years ago. Hume explained the manner in which the stock of money (when gold was the common currency among countries) would adjust to the level desired by moneyholders. Of course, in such a system there was no Central Bank transforming foreign exchange into domestic money and vice versa, and changes in the domestic money stock proceeded directly through remittances of common money to and from abroad. Hume thought of a sudden fall in the stock of money, and called it *annihilation*.

As an additional point of interest, notice what has happened in this first experiment to the level of foreign exchange reserves held by the Central Bank. By the end of the adjustment process, the Central Bank has lost an amount of reserves exactly equal to the initial increase in the money stock. This result implies the existence of a transfer of wealth from the Central Bank to the country's residents, who for some period of time were able to invest at a rate higher than their long-run equilibrium level and still consume at the same rate as before.[1] A sudden initial fall of the money stock (á la Hume) would, of course, result in the same adjustment process working in the opposite direction.

As a second experiment, and always starting from an initial equilibrium position, consider the consequences of a once-and-for-all change in the level of the exchange rate, say, a fall from E_0 to E_1. Such a change is called a *devaluation*. Initially, for example, the price of one unit of foreign money (one dollar, in our example) was 20 per dollar. If the monetary authority increases it to 30 pesos per dollar, a devaluation has occurred. The opposite change—that is, a fall in the exchange rate say, from 20 to 15 pesos per dollar—is called *revaluation*.

The initial, impact effect of the devaluation, as shown in Figures 15-5 and 15-6, is to decrease the value of the real money stock, from $m_0 = (M_0/E_0)$ to $m_1 = (M_0/E_1)$. The immediate consequence is a rise in the rate of interest, from r_0 to r_1, a fall in the level of investment expenditures and a rise in the balance of trade, from zero to t_0. In terms of Figure 15-6, the system goes from

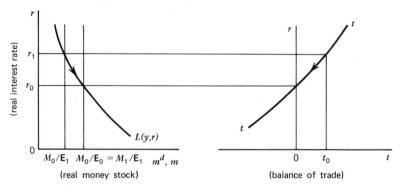

Figure 15-5. Effects of a devaluation.

point A to point B to point C. From then on, changes in the nominal money stock through the foreign exchange window of the Central Bank acts as the force that returns the system to equilibrium. Because the balance of trade is positive, the nominal (and real) money stock starts to rise, the interest rate to fall, and investment expenditures to rise, so that the balance of trade surplus becomes smaller and smaller until it reaches its equilibrium value of zero. At that point the increase in the nominal money stock (from M_0 to M_1) has been just enough to bring the real stock to the same level as before the devaluation, given the new exchange rate, so that $m = (M_0/E_0) = (M_1/E_1)$.

Notice the effects on the level of the Central Bank foreign exchange reserves over the adjustment period. In the process of acquiring foreign exchange and expanding the domestic money stock, the Central Bank has increased the level of its reserves by exactly the same amount of the increase in the money stock. The devaluation has been the equivalent of a transfer to the Central Bank from moneyholders, who for some time have spent less than their level of income, in order to rebuild their real cash balances.

One more important observation concerns these two experiments. A devaluation, as far as the real magnitudes are concerned, is in this simple model exactly equal to a sudden fall in the nominal money stock. The only difference is that the initial fall in the real money stock is brought about, in the case of

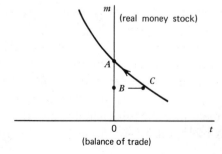

Figure 15-6. Devaluation: real money stock and balance of trade adjustment.

the devaluation, as a rise in the denominator (the exchange rate), and in the case of money annihilation, as a fall in the numerator (the nominal money stock).

Finally, before we assess the general conclusions derived from these two experiments, let us perform a third and final one. When expression [15.6] was written, we assumed that the only monetary actions taken by the Central Bank were those through the foreign exchange window, so that changes in the domestic money stock were only those brought about by the purchases and sales of foreign exchange necessary to keep the exchange rate at its fixed level. Suppose now that the Central Bank operates at the same time through another window—for example, one at which it performs open-market operations, that is, buys and sells securities. Total changes in the money stock per unit of time, then, will have two components: those changes brought about at the foreign exchange window, and those arising from operations at the open market window. The results of performing open market operations will depend on the magnitude and timing of them.

Of all possible policies, consider one special but revealing case. *Suppose that the operator at the open market operations window is instructed to buy and sell securities* (that is, to increase or decrease the money stock) *in such a way as to completely offset changes in the money stock through the other, foreign exchange window.* Thus changes in the nominal (and real) money stock will be equal to zero. If there is a deficit in the balance of trade, the foreign exchange window is selling foreign exchange and retiring domestic money, this same money is passed on to the open market operations operator, who simultaneously introduces it back into the system ("recycling" it, one could say) in exchange for securities. If there is a surplus in the balance of trade, the foreign exchange window is purchasing foreign exchange and introducing domestic money into the system, but simultaneously this new domestic money is absorbed back by the open market operations window through the sale of securities. This policy of neutralizing the changes in the domestic money stock originated at the foreign exchange window through open market operations is called *sterilization.*

Consider what happens if, for example, the nominal money stock is suddenly increased from M_0 to M_1, as in the first experiment, but that a strict sterilization policy is in effect. Figures 15–7 and 15–8 tell the story graphically: as before, the increase in the nominal money stock is also a change in the real money stock, from m_0 to m_1, with the immediate effect of a fall in the rate of interest (from r_0 to r_1), a rise in investment expenditures, and a deficit in the balance of trade of t_1. The system moves from point A to point B to point C in Figure 15–8. Under a passive policy of no open market operations, the adjustment (as we saw it in our first experiment) would proceed through changes in the domestic money stock brought about by the foreign exchange window—in this case, a fall. But under a policy of complete sterilization the money stock

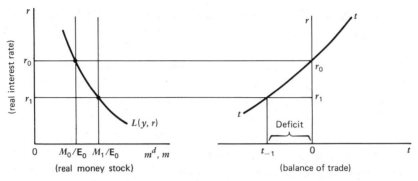

Figure 15-7. The effects of sterilization policies.

will not be changing: whatever fall occurs because of the sale of foreign exchange will be immediately offset by an equivalent purchase of securities and a corresponding increase, so that the net change is zero. The result is that the system will continue to remain at point C, with a *permanent deficit* in the balance of payments (equal to t_1, in the example), a level m_1 of the real money stock, and a level r_1 of the interest rate, while the Central Bank is continuously losing foreign exchange reserves at the rate of t_1 per period. This state has aptly been called a "quasiequilibrium," and it can remain as such *only for as long as foreign exchange reserves last.*

In spite of the simplicity of our model, it is capable of describing the essence of most balance of payments problems faced by many countries. The "problem" is due to the simple fact that the *automatic mechanism of correction to balance of payments deficits or surpluses is not allowed to work.* The late Harry G. Johnson, a world-reknown balance of payments theorist, once expressed this idea superbly noting that "A balance of payments problem presupposes the presence of a Central Bank."

These three conceptual experiments underline some important propositions:

1. There is an automatic mechanism for the correction of balance of payments deficits or surpluses, and this mechanism operates through

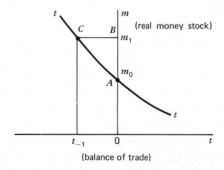

Figure 15-8. Sterilization of real money balances.

changes in the nominal money stock induced by operations at the foreign exchange window of the country's Central Bank.

2. Under a system of fixed exchange rates, for the adjustment mechanism to work properly the monetary authority must give up any intent of controlling the quantity of money, that is, of using monetary policy. Of course, there may be policies to accelerate the working of the automatic mechanism (for example, to reduce the money stock beyond those reductions brought about by actions at the foreign exchange window in response to a deficit), but in the last instance the Central Bank cannot keep the domestic money stock at an arbitrary level. Once it has decided to control the exchange rate, the nominal money stock becomes "endogenous." Notice that in principle there is no such thing as a "right" level at which the exchange rate ought to be fixed: in the long run, the nominal money stock will in any case adjust so as to bring about equilibrium.

3. Only Central Bank policies directed to counteract (sterilize) changes in the domestic money stock induced through the foreign exchange window will result in a persistent balance of payments "problem";

4. In the context of a simple framework, changes in the money stock other than those through the foreign exchange window have the same impact, and result in the same type of adjustment process, as changes in the exchange rate. In both cases the effect is transitory if the adjustment mechanism is allowed to work.

The framework presented here is a simple one; while it captures the essential mechanism of adjustment, there are some additional effects that only a more complicated model can reveal. We will review some of these complications later. For the moment, let us tackle one more question. Why do Central Banks so often try to offset monetary adjustments brought through operations at the foreign exchange window? The answer concerns one circumstance that a simple framework cannot describe, that is, possible fluctuations in the level of employment and output (y), which we have assumed fixed at the full employment level. If one expects slower reactions of the balance of trade to disequilibrium in the market for commodities, and if part of whatever excess demand exists tends to stimulate production and output, it might seem desirable to manipulate the nominal money stock so as to influence this excess demand, and hence real output, in the short run.

The Case of Flexible Exchange Rates. In a world of national currencies another extreme alternative is the monetary arrangement by which the Central Bank does not intervene at all in the market for foreign exchange (that is, it does not have a "foreign exchange window") and lets the exchange rate be determined as any other price, that is, by the forces of demand and supply. After the collapse of the fixed exchange rates system of Bretton Woods ten years ago, the world is, to a large extent, one of flexible or "floating" exchange rates.

When the exchange rate is left to be determined by the demand and supply of foreign exchange, the Central Bank recovers its independence in setting the level of nominal money stock. In terms of expression [15.5], the variable controlled by the Central Bank is M, the nominal money stock, as in the case of the closed economy.

We can perform an experiment similar to the first one discussed for the case of fixed exchange rates—that is, a sudden increase in the level of the nominal money stock, from M_0 to M_1, starting from an initial situation of full equilibrium. The impact is, as before, an increase of the real money stock from $m_0 = (M_0/E_0)$ to $m_1 = (M_1/E_0)$, and a fall of the interest rate from r_0 to r_1 as described in Figures 15–9 and 15–10. The latter brings about an increase in investment expenditures which could be satisfied, as before, by a fall in the balance of trade (an increase in imports and/or a fall in exports). If we continue to assume that private individuals do not hold any foreign money, this state is not possible because nobody will be willing to supply the extra flow of foreign exchange needed for these trade movements, so that the exchange rate must rise.[2] By how much should the exchange rate rise? By whatever amount is necessary to eliminate the excess demand for foreign exchange, that is, the trade deficit. For this to take place the interest rate must return to its previous level, r_0. But this level of the interest rate requires the real money stock to be m_0, the same as before. Thus the result of the increase in the money supply is *a rise in the exchange rate by exactly the same proportion*, so that the real money stock remains exactly as before.

Notice that under a system of freely floating exchange rates, the form of

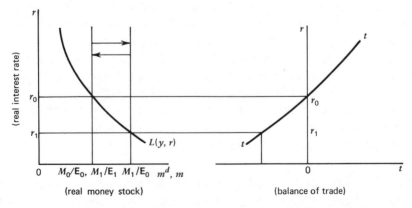

Figure 15-9. Flexible exchange rates: an increase in the nominal money stock.

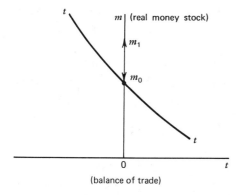

Figure 15-10. Flexible exchange rates: adjustment of real money balances.

adjustment and the response of the general price level to changes in the quantity of money are the same as in the closed economy. The Central Bank cannot control the *real* money stock in the long run, but it preserves its independence with respect to setting the level of the *nominal* money stock.

SOME EXTENSIONS AND COMPLICATIONS

Even though our framework provides a general idea of the basic nature of the processes involved, its simplicity ignores some effects that in many cases are important. In this section some of the effects are reviewed, as are some possible extensions of the simple model.

Allowing for Capital Mobility. The analysis has assumed away, until now, the presence of capital movements, that is, the purchase or sale of financial instruments abroad. Let us consider here the changes needed in order to incorporate the possibility of such movements.

Capital movements among nations are governed by levels of the interest rate in those nations. If, for example, at some point in time the interest rate in Mexico is higher than in the United States, residents in the US will find it attractive to lend their funds in Mexico (that is, to purchase securities there) while Mexicans will in turn have an incentive to borrow (that is, to sell securities) in the United States. This process, of course, will tend to lower the rate of interest in Mexico, and it would also have the effect of raising the rate in the United States, if Mexico were not a "small country" in the financial market.

Transactions costs, uncertainty about future policies in other countries, and lack of market transparency, all make it possible for some interest rate differentials to persist even in long-run equilibrium. For purposes of our analysis let us consider the extreme case of *perfect* capital mobility, where for the small country under consideration (Mexico), capital movements take place so as to equate the domestic interest rate (r) with the rate in the rest of the world (r^*).

We will assume not only that in the long run the domestic interest rate will be equal to the world rate, but also that capital movements act so fast as to assure such an equality at all times.

Under these circumstances, consider once again the economic system described by expressions [15.1], [15.2], and [15.3]. With a fixed level of real income, and the domestic interest rate being at all times equal to the world rate r^*, the system of three expressions now has three unknowns: the balance of trade (t), net capital outflows (nco), and the real money stock (m). The solution is described in the two panels of Figure 15–11. Given the level r_0^* of the world interest rate, the real money stock satisfying expression [15.3] will be m_0. In turn, such an interest rate will correspond to a balance of trade t_0 (a surplus in the example) and, for the system to be in long-run equilibrium, there must be a *permanent* net outflow of capital (nco) of nco_0 equal to the balance of trade t_0. Notice that in this case the horizontal axis of the right-hand side panel measures both the trade balance (t) and net capital outflows (nco).

Consider the process of adjustment (starting from an initial equilibrium position) for both fixed and flexible exchange rates. Two cases are considered: (a) a change in the nominal money stock; and (b) a change in the world interest rate. First, look at the adjustment effects of a change in the nominal money stock. The two panels of Figure 15–12 show an initial equilibrium with the levels r^*, $m_0 = (M_0/E_0)$ and $t_0 = nco_0$ for the different variables. Of course, the initial equilibrium could have been one with a deficit in the balance of trade and a surplus in the capital account, or one where both are equal to zero. Suppose now that at some moment in time there is a sudden increase in the level of the nominal money stock, from M_0 to M_1. The first effect, as always, is an increase in the real money stock to $m_1 = (M_1/E_0)$.

The response of a system with fixed exchange to a nominal money stock increase is seen in Figure 15–12. If we continue to assume that moneyholders

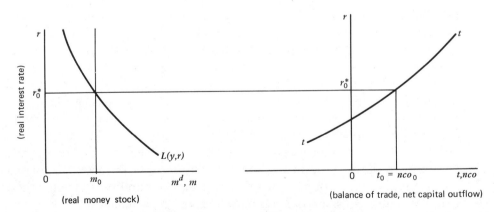

Figure 15-11. The case of capital mobility.

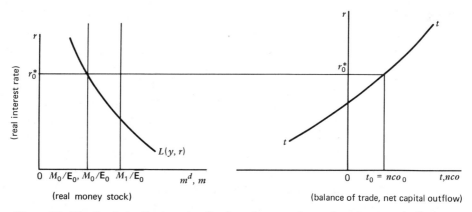

Figure 15–12. *Capital adjustments: fixed exchange rates and an increase in the nominal money stock.*

seek to adjust their holdings instantaneously, they will, at once, transform their initial excess stock of money ($m_1 = m_0$) into securities, in this case through a purchase of securities abroad. Thus there is a *once-and-for-all decrease in their nominal money stock:* to pay for those securities in foreign exchange, the Central Bank must supply the foreign exchange and, in the process, absorb the excess of money. The adjustment occurs at once. The sudden purchase of securities abroad has the dimensions of a stock and not of a flow, and the flow of capital movements, nco_0, continues at the same pace as before.

Consider now the effects of a once-and-for-all change in the world interest rate, say, a rise from r_0^* to r_1^*, under a system of *fixed* exchange rates. As shown in the two panels of Figure 15–13, at the new world rate r_1^* it becomes attractive to lend abroad; moneyholders do so right away, "getting rid" of their nominal (and real) money stock in excess of what they wish to hold at that new

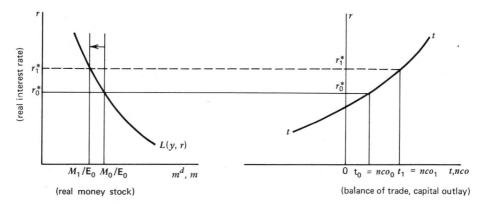

Figure 15–13. *Fixed exchange rates: an increase in the world interest rate.*

rate by purchasing securities abroad. There is a once-and-for-all stock adjustment, in which the nominal money stock falls from M_0 to M_1 and, in this case,
also a permanent change in the continuous outflow of capital, which must increase so as to compensate for the higher resulting balance of trade, which increases from t_0 to t_1.

What will happen under a system of freely floating exchange rates? Again
assume a sudden increase in the stock of nominal money. As shown in Figure
15-14, the real money stock (at the old exchange rate, E_0), rises from (M_0/E_0)
to (M_1/E_0); moneyholders intend to adjust by getting rid of additional money
stocks, but in this case no one is supplying the foreign exchange needed to acquire securities abroad. The exchange rate must rise, up to the point where the
real money stock is at the same level as before [in Figure 15-14, to the level
E_1, such that $(M_1/E_1) = (M_0/E_0)$]. As with the case of fixed exchange rates,
the long-run equilibrium of capital outflows continues at its old level $nco_0 = t_0$.

What if there is a change in the level of the world interest rate, as we analyzed for the case of fixed exchange rates? Figure 15-15 shows that, at the new
higher interest rate r_1^*, there is an excess stock of money; as moneyholders try
to exchange that excess for securities abroad, the exchange rate must rise up to
the level at which moneyholders hold the lower real stock compatible with the
new world interest rate r_1^*, that is, from E_0 to E_1, so that (M_0/E_1) is the new,
lower real stock. An important feature of the "experiment" of a change in the
world interest rate is worth noting. With capital mobility, it does not make any
difference, for the level of the real interest rate, whether the country is under a
fixed or under a flexible exchange rates system: under *both* systems the domestic rate will *equal* the world rate.

The Presence of "Nontraded" Goods. In realistic models, the presence of
"nontraded," or "domestic" goods (those that for technological reasons cannot be exchanged among countries) create additional effects that, even if they

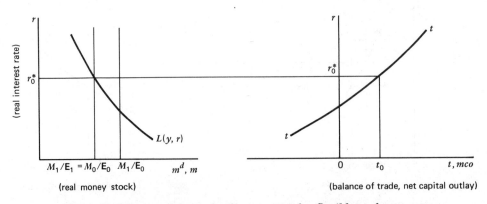

Figure 15-14. A money stock adjustment under flexible exchange rates.

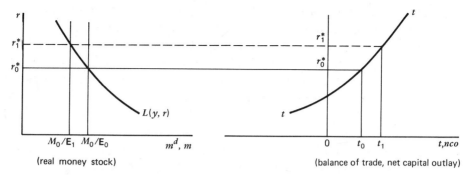

Figure 15-15. Flexible exchange rates: an increase in the world interest rate.

do not invalidate the above conclusions, may nevertheless be important, especially in the short run.

A general index of all domestic prices will, with nontraded goods, be made up of two components. One component will correspond to the group of internationally traded goods, as before, and a second one corresponds to domestic goods whose price is determined by their internal supply and demand conditions and only indirectly by the world price level. If this is so, then the level of imports and exports (that is, the balance of trade) will not be solely a passive magnitude responding to the excess demand or supply for goods in general, but will depend also on the relative price of traded and nontraded goods. If the domestic prices of internationally traded goods (importables and exportables) react very quickly to changes in the exchange rate, while those of nontraded goods do not, changes in the exchange rate will bring about changes in those relative prices, thereby causing "substitution effects" on the balance of trade. In particular, a rise in the exchange rate will increase the domestic price of both importables and exportables relative to non-traded goods. Domestic *production* of both will tend to rise, but domestic *expenditures* on both will tend to fall, so that on both accounts the balance of trade will tend to increase. Indeed, for many years economists believed that this was the main (if not the only) channel through which devaluation would tend to improve the balance of trade. Today, such substitution effects are recognized as important, but only in addition to the "wealth" effects of changes of the exchange rate on the real money stock, which we discussed in our simple framework.

The presence of an important nontraded goods sector results in a certain isolation of the economy in the short run, allowing certain effects of monetary policies over employment and output that would not exist if all goods were traded internationally and if the balance of trade responds quickly and automatically to the presence of excess demand or supply for commodities. Consider, for example, an increase in the quantity of money under these circumstances. The initial effect is a fall in the interest rate and a rise in expenditures;

part of this increase in expenditures is resolved through more imports and less exports (that is, through a fall in the balance of trade), but part in demand pressure on domestic goods production. Only as the process of adjustment in the balance of trade proceeds (through a fall in the real money stock, due to a reduction in the nominal stock, under fixed exchange rates, or a rise in the exchange rate, under flexible rates) will this excess demand for domestic commodities decline.

Thus intentions of increasing or maintaining a high level of domestic activity (often beyond the level of employment corresponding to the natural rate) find the process of balance of payments adjustment (under either of the two systems) to be working at cross purposes. The problem, if it is a problem, is compounded in the case of capital movements, simply because the adjustments are much faster through the capital account, and because the impotence of the Central Bank in controlling the interest rate becomes very clear.

The Inflationary Equilibrium. Until now, the discussion has referred to situations where the monetary authority fixes either the level of the exchange rate (E) or the level of the nominal money stock (M). At this point we should consider the extension of the basic framework to cases of long-run inflationary equilibrium.

In understanding this inflationary equilibrium, we might recall several expressions discussed before. If domestic prices are given at all times by foreign prices times the exchange rate, or $P = P^*E$ (expression [15.4]), it will also be true that the domestic inflation rate ($\hat{P}$) equals the world inflation rate ($\hat{P}^*$) times the proportional rate of change, per unit of time, of the exchange rate ($\hat{E}$), which we can call *the rate of devaluation*, that is

$$\hat{P} = \hat{P}^* + \hat{E} \qquad [15.7]$$

If in addition there is perfect capital mobility, the domestic nominal interest rate (i) will be equal to the world nominal rate (i^*), plus the rate of devaluation ($\hat{E}$), or

$$i = i^* + \hat{E} \qquad [15.8]$$

Why is this so? Because for an American lender, who, for example, considers lending in Mexico, to be indifferent between lending dollars in the rest of the world at the rate i^* and lending in pesos in Mexico at the rate i, this rate needs to incorporate a premium reflecting the rate of devaluation expected to occur during the period of the loan. Thus we can interpret this devaluation rate as *the expected rate of inflation of the price of a dollar in terms of pesos.*

Finally, if we are referring to long-run equilibrium situations in a nongrowing economy, it will be necessary for the rate of domestic monetary expansion ($\hat{M}$) to be equal to the domestic inflation rate ($\hat{P}$), in order for real cash balances to remain constant, that is

$$\hat{P} = \hat{M} \qquad [15.9]$$

By using expressions [15.7] and [15.9], we conclude that the rate of devaluation must equal, in the long run, the rate of domestic monetary expansion minus the rate of world inflation, or

$$\hat{E} = \hat{M} - \hat{P}* \qquad [15.10]$$

Consider, first, what happens under a system of flexible exchange rates, where the Central Bank chooses any rate of monetary expansion and lets the exchange rate be determined by the market. Expression [15.10] indicates that, once $\hat{M}$ has been chosen, the resulting rate of devaluation will depend directly on the rate of inflation in the rest of the world. If inflation abroad rises from 5 to 8 percent per year, the rate of devaluation $\hat{E}$ will rise by three percentage points. A second conclusion, from expression [15.9], is that the domestic inflation rate depends entirely, as in the closed economy, on the domestic rate of monetary expansion.

We can also analyze interest rates within this system. By using expressions [15.7], [15.8], and [15.10], we should easily see that in the long run the domestic real interest rate (r) is equal to the world interest rate ($r*$) under either of the two exchange rates systems. The domestic real interest rate is $r = i - \hat{P}$; using [15.8] and [15.7], we write

$$r = i - \hat{P} = i* + \hat{E} - P* - \hat{E} = i* - \hat{P}* = r* \qquad [15.11]$$

which is the real interest rate in the rest of the world. In the case of the floating exchange rates system, the nominal interest rate will depend only on the world real rate and the rate of monetary expansion, since the domestic inflation rate is given solely by the rate of monetary expansion. If both world inflation and the level of the world nominal interest rate change by the same amount (as they should in the long run), the domestic nominal rate will not be influenced.

What would happen if the domestic Central Bank, instead of fixing the rate of monetary expansion, fixes $\hat{E}$, the rate of devaluation? Such a policy is nothing but the generalization of the usual fixed exchange rate system, except that in this case, instead of announcing and intervening so as to assure a constant future level of the exchange rate, it announces and intervenes to assure a given path of that rate, along which the rate rises continuously at the proportional rate $\hat{E}$. Fixing the rate of devaluation is nothing other than the counterpart of the floating exchange rate system in which the Central Bank, instead of setting a level of the nominal money stock (M), sets a rate of monetary expansion ($\hat{M}$). Systems of this sort have been recently implemented in several Latin American countries (Argentina and Chile, for example).

If the Central Bank fixes $\hat{E}$, we can conclude, from expression [15.10], that the rate of monetary expansion, $\hat{M}$, which is now out of the hands of the monetary authority, will adjust to the level of world inflation; for a given $\hat{E}$, a rise in the rate of world inflation will result in a rise of the domestic rate of monetary expansion. From expression [15.7] we can observe the consequence of such a policy more directly: *the domestic inflation rate will depend, once a rate of devaluation has been chosen, solely on the rate of world inflation.* If the rest of the world decides to pursue inflationary policies, the country in question will "import" inflation from abroad.[3]

Fixed, Floating, or Others? A system of fixed exchange rates (whether the level of the rate or the rate of devaluation is fixed) implies a direct interdependence among world economies: expansions and contractions, as well as stability, tend to be transmitted. We can see such dependence either as a problem or as a blessing. A problem, to the extent that there is a loss of independence in pursuing national monetary policies for domestic stabilization. A blessing, to the extent that monetary authorities need to obey what has been called "the discipline" of fixed exchange rates: the sin of expanding the money stock excessively would be punished with a loss in reserves. In practice, however, such discipline has been eluded more often that not. A common pattern (notable in some less developed countries) has been an excess of monetary expansion, loss of reserves, abrupt devaluation and accumulation of reserves for some time, new excessive monetary expansion, and so on. At the same time, undesirable exchange and trade controls of all sorts are periodically enacted when the level of reserves reaches a dangerously low level. The net result, in these cases, is that from time to time, as the level of reserves falls and the monetary expansion continues, devaluation begins to be expected. Instead of the market guessing about the future exchange rate that would be necessary in the case of freely floating rates, the guess concerns the political decision of when and by how much to devalue. In these situations the problem is that devaluation can easily be forced upon the monetary authority. If the public expects a devaluation, everybody wishes to exchange domestic for reserve money, and this situation tends to drain reserves beyond the drainage that would occur with the same monetary expansion but with confidence in the announced path of the exchange rate. The fall in the level of reserves, of course, increases the expectation of devaluation still further, and so on. Finance ministers rush to declare that there will be no devaluation, capital flows out very rapidly, interest rates rise, even the Central Bank tries to keep interest rates low by injecting more domestic money into the system, and the crisis soon forces the devaluation (among assurances that it is the *last* one).

A system of flexible exchange rates, on the contrary, permits monetary policy to be independent in the specific sense that the monetary authority can set the rate of monetary expansion (or the level of the nominal money stock) wherever it wishes. Fluctuations in the exchange rate will take care of the external or balance of payments balance. Flexible rates, sponsored almost thirty years ago by Milton Friedman, and later by an increasing number of economists, have been in use since the abandonment of the Bretton Woods fixed exchange rates system around 1973. Freely floating rates have been (and still are) opposed on the grounds that the fluctuations in the rates would be too abrupt and too large and this instability would prove to be a highly disruptive factor for trade. In this view, speculators in foreign exchange are a destabilizing factor. Such arguments may be largely dismissed on conceptual grounds, and only in part by the facts. From one point of view, speculation and the existence of futures markets tend to smooth out unjustified fluctuations, rather than the opposite. From another vantage point, the flexible exchange rate system in use since 1973 has resulted in some pronounced fluctuations in exchange rates, but those fluctuations have not been wild, nor have they shown to be a disruptive factor in international trade. If there is any disappointment with floating exchange rates, it is on the part of those who believed in a long-run association between the inflation rate and the level of output and employment (the "Phillips curve," discussed in Chapter 8). A system of floating exchange rates, in allowing the domestic rate of monetary expansion to set the pace of the domestic inflation rate, would assure—in the hopes of Phillips curves practitioners— the possibility of a permanent high level of employment. Experience has everywhere shown that this is not the case, but the problem was not with flexible exchange rates but with the basic premise of a permanent inflation-unemployment tradeoff.

Between the two extremes of free floating and completely fixed exchange rates there is a variety of possibilities. In fact, the adoption of a system of floating exchange rates has almost invariably brought about some intervention by the Central Bank geared to influencing the market exchange rate. This policy is usually called *dirty float*, a general term describing a system by which exchange rates are fundamentally determined by the market, but in which the monetary authority intervenes at its discretion. Dirty floating can be appraised only with information about the intervention rule that the monetary authority sets for itself. In general, however, one could say that if there is any value in a policy of "rules" rather than "discretion" (in the sense in which we defined these terms in Chapter 14), most dirty floating policies are undesirable.

Another possible arrangement has been called the *crawling peg* or *sliding parities.* Under such a system the Central Bank sets a parity and a band around that parity, letting the exchange rate fluctuate within the band, but buying or selling whenever necessary to prevent the rate from falling outside of the band. The novelty is that the parity itself is being continuously adjusted with respect to the tendency shown by the rate in the immediate past. In more technical terms, the parity is periodically set as a "moving average" of past actual exchange rates. Such an arrangement assures that violent fluctuations will not take place, and at the same time allows the monetary authority to adjust the parity over time in an orderly fashion.

THE "REDUNDANCY PROBLEM" IN THE FIXED EXCHANGE RATES SYSTEM, AND THE QUESTION OF SEIGNIORAGE

Before entering the next and final part of this chapter, which relates to the organization of the world monetary system, we should concern ourselves with an additional issue. This issue provides a valuable clue to understanding many world monetary events of the past four decades.

Suppose a certain group of countries (say, the United States, France, and Germany) decide to establish a system of fixed exchange rates among each other. Thus there are three countries and three national monies (dollars, francs, and marks). Since exchange rates are relative prices among monies there will be only two relative prices to be determined independently—since if we fix, for example, the price of dollars in terms of both francs and marks, the price of marks in terms of francs, or vice versa, will automatically be determined. If we decide on a parity of three francs per dollar and two marks per dollar, the exchange rate or relative price between francs and marks will have to be (3 francs per dollar)/(2 marks per dollar) = 1.5 francs per mark. If it were not so, foreign exchange operators would jump at the chance to make a million, and the parity franc-mark would be promptly restored.

This simple observation has an important economic consequence. Of the three countries, only two would need to intervene in the market for foreign exchange in order to assure the parity; the third would need to do nothing, and therefore would not need to hold *any* foreign exchange reserves. In a sense, that country would become the "world central bank," and its national money would be the reserve currency held by other Central Banks for purposes of intervention. To the extent that those reserves are held by other Central Banks, the monetary authority of the reserve country will be collecting seigniorage in exactly the same manner as the local Central Bank in a closed economy collects the revenue from the creation of money or the inflation tax on the real cash balances held by local moneyholders. For acquiring reserves, the other countries would need to run balance of payments surpluses, and the reserve country will be running deficits, that is, acquiring commodities and financial assets in exchange for newly printed money that costs zero to produce. This was the position of the United States during several years after the Bretton Woods agreement.

THE INTERNATIONAL MONETARY SYSTEM AND ITS RECENT EVOLUTION

The history of world money and monetary arrangements and crises is a fascinating one, but in this book we must limit ourselves to a brief account of some of the main events. We take up our account at the beginning of the present century.

THE COLLAPSE OF THE GOLD STANDARD, WORLD WAR II, AND THE BRETTON WOODS SYSTEM

For forty years the gold standard system worked so well that, until the beginning of World War I in 1914, this time has often been called the period of the *classical gold standard*. The pound sterling and the stability of the British economy dominated the international scene, and the pound was "as good as gold." The British pound was an excellent substitute for gold as a world money and was practically the reserve currency for the world. World War I not only disrupted the system, but marked the beginning of the end of the British Empire, and with it, the supremacy of the pound. The first years in the aftermath of the "Great War" were a period of transition, with no definite system in world monetary affairs, signaled later by the problem imposed by the huge German reparations and the virulent hyperinflation on the Continent during the 1920s. Slowly, the system returned to its previous form under the gold standard; the United States reverted to gold in 1919, Great Britain in 1925, and the rest of the European countries followed around that time.

Soon it was evident that many of the national currencies—in particular the pound, for which the pre-war parity to gold had been restored—were incorrectly valued, and persistent balance of payments problems developed. The problem, in the case of England, was that the permanent gold drain and the accompanying fall in the money stock necessary for external equilibrium under the gold standard put a continuous *downward* pressure on prices and employment. In 1931, under unbearable pressure, the Bank of England suspended convertibility of the pound into gold, and in the Spring of 1933, under a similar attack, the United States followed suit. During the 1930s there was the formation of the sterling area, with members of the British Empire and Scandinavian countries pegging their currencies to the pound, and using pounds as their reserve currency. Germany maintained the former parity to gold, and the increasing number of exchange and trade controls (tariffs and quotas)—designed to avoid the drain in its gold reserves—soon made the official parity a very unrealistic value. France, Italy, and other European countries formed the "gold block" until France was forced to devalue in 1936.

The beginning of hostilities in 1939 brought about another waiting period, and in 1944 the Western nations met in Bretton Woods, New Hampshire, to establish the basis for a new international monetary order and to set up the International Monetary Fund (IMF). The basic structure of the Bretton Woods agreement was as follows. All nations pegged their national monies to the US dollar, and the United States was committed to preserve the 35 dollars an ounce parity with gold. This was the manner in which the "redundancy problem" was solved: Central Banks of all nations would act to keep the parity of their monies vis-à-vis the dollar, and the United States would do the same vis-à-vis gold.[4]

In the first years of the system, and especially in the post-1958 period, a *dollar shortage* emerged. American influence in world business was already overwhelming, and the dollar, a very stable currency, provided a satisfactory reserve currency for the rest of the Western world. Central Banks, under their agreed commitment to keep the parity of their currencies, needed to build their reserves, and the United States became the Central Bank of the world. For several years, the United States was able to run permanent balance of payments deficits without compromising its reserve position in gold; that is, it was collecting the seigniorage or "inflation tax" since the rest of the world was willing to accumulate and hold those dollars. The IMF, watchdog for the system, allowed occasional devaluations in order to take account of "fundamental disequilibria" in the case of some currencies.

THE EVOLUTION AND COLLAPSE OF THE
BRETTON WOODS SYSTEM

For a country under a fixed exchange rate system, variations in the level of its international reserves are a fundamental indication of whether policy is being "too expansionary" or "too tight": a fall in reserves is an indication of expansionary policies through the open market operations window and vice versa. In the Bretton Woods system, such a set of signals was supposed to operate not only for each of the countries with national currencies pegged to the dollar, but also for the United States itself, through variations in its gold reserves. If American policy were being too expansionary with respect to the desired accumulation of US dollars by the rest of the world, then the rest of the world would either allow their domestic money stocks to increase at a faster rate, or to start converting dollars into gold. Fundamentally, the history of the Bretton Woods system is the history of the *persistent American excessive monetary expansion* and the efforts by the United States (for some time with the help of Western European countries) to avoid the drain in the US gold reserves.

As mentioned earlier, the US was able to run substantial balance of payments deficits (in its capital account, in particular) as the rest of the world was willing to build up their reserves of dollars. After some time, notably by the end of the 1960s, the situation started to reverse itself, and instead of the previous dollar shortage, a *dollar glut* appeared. World reserves of US dollars were plenty enough and desired real holdings of dollars became less and less attractive as inflation in dollar prices (the "inflation tax") started to settle in. Persistent expansionary monetary policy by the Fed and the reluctance of the Western European nations (in particular Germany, under the bitter memory of the devastating hyperinflation of the 1920s) to accompany these expansionary policies resulted in more and more frequent crises and minicrises, with the final collapse of the system in 1973.

The American and European positions on this issue, and their interpretation of the problem and the solution, were at odds. In the Americna view, adjustment should have come through a revaluation of other currencies with respect to the dollar. But this action was resisted by other countries as too deflationary a move that would not have solved the problem anyway as long as excessive US monetary expansion continued. In the European view, the only way to resolve the issue was by a less expansionary monetary policy in the United States. Thus the United States tended to see the problem as the problem of European surpluses; the Europeans, as the problem of American deficits. Let us consider some of the details of the drama by centering on a few benchmark events.

The Establishment of the Gold Pool (1960–1961). The original dollar–gold parity of 35 dollars an ounce started to show signs of being out of line by the end of 1960, when the price of gold in the private market rose to 40 dollars an ounce. To avoid the logical temptation of Central Banks to acquire gold at 35 dollars an ounce from the US government and to sell it at 40 dollars in the private market, the Gold Pool was established. The agent for the pool was the Bank of England, and the United Kingdom, Italy, France, Germany, Holland, Switzerland, and the United States agreed to supply gold to the pool (with the heaviest burden on the United States) for intervention in the private market in order to maintain the market price at 35 dollars an ounce. This was the first crisis, and the solution worked for some time.

The Closing of the Gold Pool and the Two-Tier System (1967–1968). The next crisis came at the end of 1967 in the midst of heavy injections of dollars abroad and the financing of the Vietnam War. There was a "run" on the dollar and gold purchases of considerable amount. Early in 1968 the Gold Pool was replaced by the *two-tier system*. On the one hand, Central Banks of Western European countries decided to support the 35 dollars an ounce price of gold through sales to only other Central Banks and government agencies; on the other hand, they committed themselves not to buy or to sell gold in the private market. The two-tier system was the first step toward the demonetization of gold by divorcing the private and the official markets. In a few years the price of gold in the private market increased over three times.

The End of Convertibility. The years of 1970 and 1971 marked the beginning of the end for the Bretton Woods system. During 1970, large short-term capital movements worsened the US balance of payments still further, and in early 1971 there was heavy unloading of dollars, and Eurodollars,[5] in exchange for German marks and Swiss francs, with an enormous increase in the levels of these countries' dollar reserves. After some time, Germany and Holland finally gave up purchasing so many dollars and floated their currencies, followed by other European countries. In August 1971, President Nixon announced that convertibility of gold into dollars had ended. According to many, this event should be taken as the date the Bretton Woods system ended.

An intended revival of the system took place in December 1971 with the Smithsonian Agreement, under which all parities were modified, and the "margin" above and below parities was increased from one to two and one half percent. Under this agreement most currencies were revalued against the US dollar and (less so) against gold, which amounted to the first devaluation of the dollar vis-à-vis gold, from 35 to 38 dollars per ounce. The "patching up" of the system through different parities, without removal of the real source of the problem—American expansionary policies—would not last long.

The Final Collapse of the System, and Its Official Ratification. In early 1973 nervousness over the dollar took over once more, with heavy dollar sales in exchange for Swiss francs. The Swiss Central Bank closed its foreign exchange window, refused to prevent the exchange rate from falling, and floated. A few weeks later the United States devalued for the second time, from 38 to 42.22 dollars per ounce, but the devaluation produced no results. Within a month, in the Brussels Agreement, the Western European nations decided to let their currencies float against the dollar. From the viewpoint of seigniorage, the United States had killed the goose with golden eggs. Only three years later, in January 1976, at the IMF meetings in Jamaica, it was decided officially to sanction the freedom to adopt floating exchange rates. The International Monetary Fund became an advisory and discussion agency, and whatever relationship left between gold and the monetary system officially ended.

THE WORLD AFTER BRETTON WOODS

After 1973, the world became characterized by dirty floating, with the exception that a number of less developed countries pegged to some major currency (mostly the dollar, to a lesser extent the pound) and agreements took place among Western European countries. The United States has permitted the dollar to float.

After the collapse of the Bretton Woods system, some Western European nations associated in a rather loose arrangement in order to preserve some parity among their currencies, while letting all of them float against the dollar. The initial agreement evolved into the institution of the European Monetary System (EMS) in the first half of 1978. According to the EMS arrangements, each of the currencies involved was pegged (within different bands for different currencies) to the European Currency Unit (ECU), a "basket" of currencies similar to SDRs. This is the so-called "snake" of currencies moving around each other. In turn, the snake was to be contained in terms of the ECU (the "tunnel"), within a wider bank of lower and upper limits for values of the US dollar.

In principle, the ECU was expected to be not only a unit of account but also a true intervention and reserve currency, but it has not performed that function. In fact, the German mark has become the intervention currency, a "blessing" not welcomed by the Germans, who fear to pay, in the future, the same price finally paid by the US, in the latter part of the years of Bretton Woods, for its role as the world's Central Bank. In other words, the Germans live with the potential instability—a sort of time bomb—implied by their having a huge number of marks in the hands of foreign individuals and Central Banks.

The European Monetary System has neither lived long enough, nor faced critical situations that would allow a prognosis about its future. An important ingredient for its failure or success would be the existence of enough similarity among the degrees of monetary expansion in which each of the countries involved will wish to engage.

CONCLUSION

The international monetary system is in constant flux and further evolution can be expected as nations of the world pursue individual economic policies. The present chapter has elaborated a simple, but suggestive and relatively complete, menu of choices that each might follow. Some of the thorniest problems will involve interrelations and choices between international and domestic stabilization policies.

FOOTNOTES

[1] This results only if the initial monetary change was in the form of a "gift" of money from the Central Bank to the public. If money was initially changed by the purchase of securities, it is a substitution of domestic for foreign assets (reserves) in the balance of the Central Bank.

[2] We employ the very restrictive assumption that residents of each country hold only currency of their country. This is an extreme and unrealistic assumption, but economists have only recently begun studying the more realistic (and interesting) case in which Central Banks do not intervene in the foreign exchange

markets but private residents do hold foreign exchange in such a way that variations in their holdings allow transitory deficits or surpluses in the balance of payments. This situation is usually called *currency substitution*. To explore such a possibility would require substantial complication of our simple framework.

[3] When a country fixes the rate of devaluation, the behavior of the nominal domestic interest rate can be predicted. In this event, as is seen directly from expression [15.8], the nominal domestic rate will depend directly upon the world nominal rate, i^*, even if the world real rate remains the same.

[4] From a formal viewpoint all currencies, the dollar included, were set on a parity with respect to gold, but were all committed, except the United States, to keep the resulting parity with the dollar. The system received therefore the name of *gold exchange standard*.

[5] Eurodollars are simply deposits in banks located abroad (mostly in Europe), denominated in US dollars. The genesis of the Eurodollar market was due, to a large extent, to the presence of ceilings on interest rates enacted in the United States. The importance of the Eurodollar market, for purposes of US monetary policy, is the possibility that US banks might circumvent the effects of tight monetary policies on the part of the Fed, by attracting more deposits in their foreign branches and transferring reserves to their American headquarters. In 1969, the Fed imposed reserve requirements on these deposits in order to eliminate this possibility.

KEY CONCEPTS

closed economy

open economy

balance of payments (surplus and deficit)

market for foreign exchange

exports

imports

capital inflows (outflows)

unilateral transfers

trade balance (trade account)

capital account

gold standard

"below the line" payments

fixed exchange rates

merchandise trade balance

goods and goods and services balance

current accounts balance

transfer payments

basic balance

Special Drawing Rights (SDRs)

International Monetary Fund (Bretton Woods System)

net liquidity balance

official settlements balance

IMF gold tranche

freely floating exchange rates

"foreign exchange window"

devaluation

sterilization

revaluation

crawling peg (sliding parties)

dirty float

The gold pool

Two-tier system

Eurodollars

European Monetary System

European currency unit

QUESTIONS FOR DISCUSSION

1. How can a balance of payments deficit be paid? Does a lack of intervention by a country's government limit the methods of payment?

2. Explain the differences between the several types of balances discussed and when each would have an advantage over another in their use.

3. Describe in your own words what provisions must be added to our previous model to incorporate the foreign sector. How do we add these features to our model?

4. Discuss the role of our limiting assumptions in our simple model of long-run equilibrium analysis. How might we change our model if we withdraw these assumptions?

5. Explain how the system of international exchange (freely floating vs. fixed rates) will affect monetary policy decisions (what determines m in the fixed system vs. what determines m in a flexible rate system) in our simple long-run equilibrium model where we assumed no capital movements and all goods are traded.

6. What mechanism restores equilibrium in our simple model in this chapter when there is disequilibrium in the balance of payments under fixed exchange rates? How about under flexible rates? What will happen if a policy for sterilization is in effect?

7. How is equilibrium restored after a revaluation of our currency? Explain using the simple fixed rates analysis of this chapter. What is the difference between this and a change in the nominal money stock in terms of the adjusted process?

8. If a country has a policy of sterilization under fixed rates, how long will a deficit persist?

9. Explain how the difference between a stock and a flow is important in the adjustment process when capital flows are considered in our simple model under fixed exchange rates.

10. What is the adjustment process after a change in the world interest rate in our simple model that considers capital flows with both flexible and fixed exchange rates?

11. How does the presence of nontraded goods allow better results with monetary policy than those that could be attainable without nontraded goods? Will these still take place if capital movements are included? (Consider the speed of adjustments in the capital, foreign sector, and domestic production markets.)

12. Briefly explain how our static model is extended to dynamic analysis (explain how we extend our analysis to cover inflationary economies).

13. Under fixed exchange rates, why would the expectation of a devaluation force a devaluation to indeed occur.

14. What are the benefits and costs associated with both flexible and fixed exchange rates? If you were the dictator of a country, which system would you choose and why?

15. Explain how the United States was able to export dollars for so long under the IMF–Bretton Woods system. Why did this cause a downfall of the system?

CHAPTER 16

A BRIEF MONETARY HISTORY OF THE UNITED STATES: 1897-1960

In the introduction to the institutional details of the Federal Reserve System (Chapter 10), we took a brief look at the early history of the US banking system (up to the passage of the Federal Reserve Act of 1913). An analysis of recent developments in monetary policy (1960 to the present) was a major topic of Chapter 14. It is now time to examine the performance of the US banking system in the twentieth century in relation to changes in income and, in particular, to changes in the level of prices and to fill in the gap in an understanding of the monetary history of the United States.

We should remember two important points at the outset. First, with the exception of a short discussion in Chapter 10, pretwentieth century monetary history will be largely ignored in the present book. This is certainly not to imply that there were not interesting developments over this period. Indeed, aspects of the First and Second Bank of the United States (particularly the Jackson Era), the era of "wildcat banking," and the Greenback and "Free Silver" eras in the nineteenth century form some of the most intriguing topics in US monetary history.[1] These details, while interesting, are beyond the scope of the present text, which seeks to present the essentials of the banking and monetary system.

Secondly, we should note that the account of twentieth century monetary history in the present chapter is itself a much abbreviated treatment.[2] Since many complete books have been written on single phases of twentieth century monetary history (the Great Depression is a favorite topic), we must of necessity confine ourselves to the high points.

Though abbreviated, the discussion in Chapter 16 provides a firm and organized understanding of the role of money in twentieth century economic development. In this chapter we will utilize a simple interpretative device with which we can analyze in an historical setting money stock changes—and therefore changes in income and prices. Fortunately, we should have already mastered this interpretative device by reading Chapters 9 and 11. The simple money supply model developed in Chapter 9 and expanded in Chapter 11 will now be put to work in our analysis of monetary history.

First we clarify, reintroducing our simple model from Chapter 10, a certain underlying weakness in the pre-1914 monetary structure. Next we will look at some of the major monetary problems and policies between 1914 and 1960 focusing our discussions upon definable monetary "episodes" or periods within the longer time span. Throughout we will attempt to integrate the theory developed in the present text with the interpretation of historical facts so as to integrate a conception of monetary theory, history and policy.

THE NATIONAL BANKING ACT

In Chapter 10, certain aspects of the National Banking System, established in 1863, were discussed. There were important implications of that Act for the course of the monetary system until the establishment of the Federal Reserve System in 1914. As we might recall, Lincoln's Treasury Secretary Solmon P. Chase desired and promoted a unified US banking system, while preserving the concept of dual banking. After 1863, banks were chartered at both state and national levels, but with a 10 percent tax per year levied upon state bank note issue. The latter tax was prohibitive, in that state bank notes ceased to be issued or circulated.

In retrospect, an important feature of the National Banking Act was the provisions under which nationally chartered banks could issue bank currency (National Bank notes) and these provisions were stringent indeed. With the approval of the Comptroller of the Currency (an independent officer of the US Treasury) federally chartered banks could issue notes up to nine-tenths of their capitalizations with a total issue limited to 300 million dollars. As "security" (reserves) the issuing banks had to deposit 111 dollars in eligible US banks with the US Treasurer against every 100 dollars in bank notes issued. In addition, big city banks (designated central reserve and reserve bank cities) had to hold cash reserves (that is, silver or gold specie money or government issue money convertible into specie) of 25 percent of their note issues, with 15 percent requirements for other national banks. Through the years the stipulations regarding National Bank note issuance were changed to become more or less strict, (bank note production was effectively eliminated in 1934), but the "security" against these notes was such that the public never lost through bank default.

Other more specific provisions relating to national bank note issue were contributory factors (as we shall see) to the periodic monetary "crises" that led to the Federal Reserve Act. Though originally limited to a total issue of 300 million dollars in 1875 the limit was completely removed. Unfortunately, until 1907 National Bank note issue could not be decreased by more than 3 million dollars per month. Any bank reducing its note issue could not expand it for some months afterward. There was also a time lag on bank note expansion. In order to enlargen this part of the money supply, banks had to buy eligible government securities and to notify the Treasury of their intentions and wait for the notes. Importantly, the banks may have had little incentives to alter the supply of bank money because of the costly nature of these decisions. For instance, given regulations, years would be required to "work off" a big issue of notes put into circulation to stave off a *currency crisis.*

Other aspects of the National Banking Act of 1863 profoundly affected the nature of US banking. Although the dual nature of banking was threatened by Federal chartering (the number of state banks declined drastically in 1863), state banks were allowed to create demand deposit money. The demand deposit component of the money stock, moreover, grew at a dramatic rate—almost tenfold between 1879 and 1914—and state-chartered banking enjoyed a resurgence over this period. The result is not surprising given the lower state reserve requirements on deposit accounts of these banks in contrast to the relatively high reserve requirements imposed on national banks. National banks were required to hold a "cash" reserve up to 25 percent and such holdings either bore no interest or earned so small an interest that the requirement represented a significant cost to National Bank charter. State banks, on the other hand, were and are subjected to lower requirements with generally higher return securities allowed to count as reserve.

MONETARY PERFORMANCE–1897–1914

The period between the end of the Civil War and the opening of World War I was marked by one of the most rapid industrial expansions in modern history. Industrial production, and with it real income, grew at unprecedented rates. The stock of money and the price level, especially in the latter part of the period, also climbed at rapid rates. Figure 16–1 illustrates the trends that certain important variables took over the period 1897–1914. Wholesale prices rose approximately 40 to 50 percent (2.5 percent per year) over this period, which other than the recent 1970s experience, was the most prolonged period of inflation in US history. Also, as is obvious from Figure 16–1, the economy (with the important exception of 1907) experienced significant increases in economic growth.

Though we must of necessity neglect many important and interesting details of this period preceding the establishment of America's central bank, two essential features of monetary performance over the period stand out. First, why did money stock growth and inflation characterize the period and how might they be explained? Second, what were the causes of the so-called financial panic of 1907 and its predecessors of 1884, 1890, and 1893? Fortunately we can bring a concept already developed in this text to bear on both

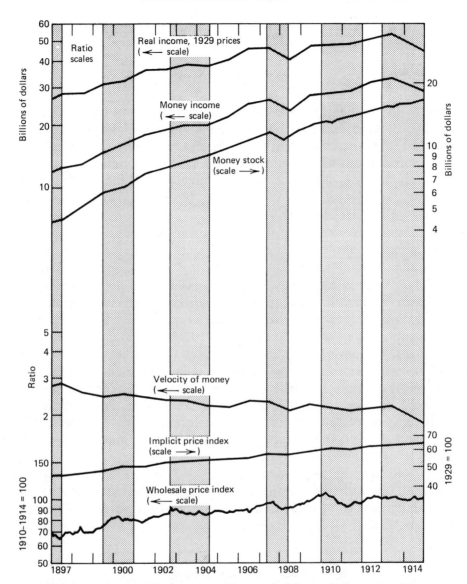

Note: Shaded areas represent business contractions; unshaded areas, business expansions.

(*Source:* Milton Friedman and Anna J. Schwartz, *Monetary History of the United States, 1867-1960* (Princeton, New Jersey: Princeton University Press, 1963), p. 136.)

Figure 16-1. Money stock, income, prices, and velocity, 1897-1914.

these issues—the formulation of the money stock developed in Chapter 9 of this book. A discussion of these two issues using the money expansion equation previously developed provides us with an excellent example of the integration of economic analysis with historical facts. Let us first consider the question of monetary expansion and inflation.

The simple but important money stock equation [9–4] of Chapter 9 will be recognized as expression [16.1].

$$M = H\left(\frac{1+c}{c+r}\right) \qquad [16.1]$$

where M, the money stock equals H, the quantity of high-powered money in existence multiplied by a fraction containing c, the currency–deposit ratio and r, the reserve–deposit ratio. We might also recall that the identity [16.1] may be viewed in functional form so that if $[(1+c)/(c+r)]$ is constant, the quantity of money might be viewed as a "function" of the stock of high-powered money, or $M = kH$, where $k = [(1+c)/(c+r)]$, an expression denoting the money multiplier.

Using this simple model, let us look at the stock of money (roughly) over this period, as shown in Table 16–1. Table 16–1 describes, in millions of dollars, the major components of money *outside the Treasury* between 1899 and 1914. It includes all money held by banks and the public. These components are fairly straightforward, but we should remember that all money at the time (including the growing demand deposit money) was either gold or *convertible* into gold. For example, the holder of 100 dollars in checkable deposits could exchange or convert checkbook money into any other form of money, such as silver certificates. All of these forms of money were, through instant exchange, convertible into gold. When large numbers of currency or deposit holders wanted gold or additional hand-to-hand currency, gold convertibility (from currency or demand deposits into gold) or currency convertibility (from demand deposits into currency) would become impossible, often bringing disaster onto the banking system.

Returning to the information of Table 16–1, let us for the moment adhere to the fiction that the currency-deposit ratio and the reserve deposit ratio are constant—that is, $M = kH$. Clearly, as Table 16–1 reveals, the increase in the size of M, the money stock, can be explained by the *increase* in the quantity of

Table 16–1 Money Outside the Treasury, 1899–1914 (in Millions of Dollars)

	1899	1909	1914
Gold and gold certificates	619	1,419	1,650
Silver and silver certificates	558	554	551
US notes and subsidary silver	397	464	499
National Bank notes	232	650	705
"Deposits"	4,295	8,115	10,306

Source: Board of Governors of the Federal Reserve System, *All-Bank Statistics, 1896–1955*, Washington, 1959, p. 36.

high-powered money. High-powered money, we might recall from Chapter 9, is the raw material from which multiples of demand deposit money is created.

It was in this manner that deposit money was created (take a look at Table 16–1). Demand deposits in 1914 grew by almost 2.5 times their 1899 level, and the explanation for the growth of this component of the money stock is clearly the growth in high-powered money. The sum of silver (and silver certificates) and US notes and minor coin (which included the silver-backed Treasury notes of 1890) hardly grew at all. In fact, the silver component of money declined somewhat. The major increase in high-powered money came in the form of increased quantities of gold and in National Bank note issue (see Table 16–1). To illustrate, the quantity of gold and National bank notes were 44 percent of high-powered money in 1897, but they climbed to 68 percent in 1914. Of course, we do not need to search long for an explanation for the increase in gold supply. The 1890s witnessed the discovery of tremendous quantities of gold in Alaska, Colorado, and South Africa as well as greater efficiency and lower costs in mining.

Thus, as Figure 16–2 shows, the total stock of money rose by about 7.5 percent per annum over the period and the price level by over 2 percent. How might this increase in the money stock and the inflation that accompanied it be explained? Milton Friedman and Anna Schwartz in their pathbreaking *Monetary History of the United States* provide an empirical analysis of the proximate determinants of the money stock over the period (see Figure 16–2) which, with a minor modification, can be integrated into our equation [16.1]. The modification is simply this: Friedman and Schwartz reported *deposit-currency* and *deposit-reserve* ratios in their empirical research, rather than *currency-deposit* and *reserve-deposit* ratios as we have presented in our money supply model summarized as equation [16.1]. In Figure 16–2 (and in Figures 16–5, 16–7, and 16–9 later in this chapter) the reader should simply reverse the movement reported in the deposit-currency and deposit-reserve ratios in order to make the data equivalent to our symbols c and r. For example, a reported increase in the deposit-currency ratio is the same thing as a decline in our symbol c, the currency-deposit ratio. Given this simple alteration, let us now turn to the economic record of the period 1897–1914.

How do we account for the average rise in the money stock of 7.5 percent between 1897 and 1914? A look at Figure 16–2 tells us immediately that the dominant factor in the long-period, 17-year series was the increase in the quantity of high-powered money. Of secondary importance was the long-period fall in the currency–deposit ratio, (rise in the deposit-currency ratio), with changes in the reserve–deposit ratio of relatively minor importance. The meaning of this in terms of equation [16.1] should be fairly clear to us. Increases in M were largely the result of increases in H, high-powered money. But the "power-fulness" of high-powered money also changed. Thus k, which equals $[(1 + c)/$

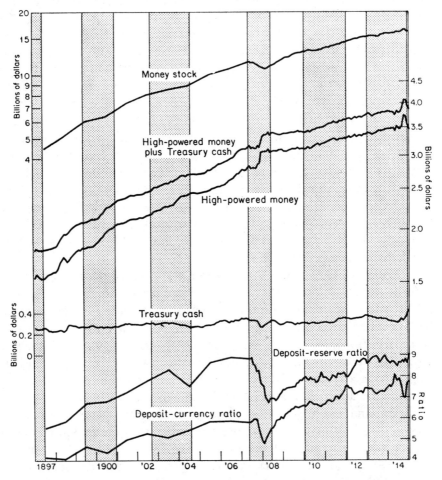

Note: Shaded areas represent business contractions; unshaded areas, business expansions.

(*Source:* Milton Friedman and Anna J. Schwartz, *Monetary History of the United States; 1867-1960* (Princeton, New Jersey: Princeton University Press, 1963), p. 175.)

Figure 16-2. Monetary aggregates, 1897-1914.

(c + r)] increased largely because the public held a lower portion of currency to demand deposits.

Using the analysis that we developed in Chapters 5 through 8, we might proffer an explanation for the absorbtion of the 7.5 percent per year expansion in *M* over the period 1897-1914. As already mentioned with reference to Figure 16-1, the price level increased by greater than 2 percent per year, which "absorbed" that much of the increase in *M*. The rapid growth in real income, *y*, accounted for approximately 3 percent of the money stock rate of increase.

These two variables thus account for about 5 percent of the 7.5 percent increase in M, but Figure 16–1 provides an even fuller explanation. Note that the income velocity of money *declined* over the period by about 2.5 percent. Thus there was a rise in money balances held by the public in relation to income. In other words, in terms of our earlier discussions of the demand for money, the demand for money balances increased, absorbing 2.5 percent of the increase in the money supply. The marked inflation that took place over the period was therefore the result of a too rapid rate of growth in the money supply stimulated by the introduction of large injections of high-powered money (that is, gold) into the system. The economy was unable fully to absorb these injections through increases in real output or through increased holdings of money balances. Inflation was the result.

THE PANIC OF 1907

The foregoing discussion of long-period trends in economic data, along with our framework, provides some understanding of important economic variables of the period. But, while we were able to recognize increases in high-powered money (gold discoveries) as the proximate cause of inflation over the long period, the discussion has masked a very significant short-run aspect of money stock changes—the problem of financial panics. A discussion of panics defined as short but often severe reductions in real output, prices, and the money stock —brings to the fore another variable in the money supply equation. Though alterations in high-powered money were found to play the leading role in economic activity between 1897 and 1914, short-run alteration in the currency-deposit ratio is featured as the joker in one of the most severe business contractions of the pre-Fed era, the Panic of 1907.

THE ANATOMY OF A PANIC

Why do financial panics occur and why were they a continuing feature of nineteenth century economic history? A first answer is that there is "not enough money," that there is no "lender of the last resort." Many observers on monetary history (including the simplified discussion in Chapter 10) have viewed the problem as an *inelasticity* of the total money stock as the *needs of trade* altered during production expansions and contractions. These difficulties, it has been alleged, were the result of an ineffective lender of the last resort. Unfortunately, this is a simplistic view of the matter which fails to take account of the interrelationships between the stock of high-powered money, currency, demand deposits, and the total money stock. Let us now characterize these relationships, which shed much light on the Panic of 1907 and on most financial panics of the past.

Over short-run periods one fact stands out: there was a general inconvertibility between currency and deposits. National bank notes, silver certificates, and US notes comprised most of the hand-to-hand currency in the hands of the public as well as cash reserves for the banking system. Given the limitations on national bank note creation placed upon national banks, it is small wonder that supplies of this type of currency were fairly fixed over short-run periods. The same held for other types of hand-to-hand exchange with the exception of specie. But the quantity of specie (gold) depended greatly upon balance of payments conditions in this era of international specie standards. Thus the supply of government money was fairly inelastic over short periods. But this also meant that high-powered money—the raw-material that banks used as deposit reserves—was also fixed! Additional currency demand on the part of the public caused this raw material to be siphoned from the banks. Since the banking system was a fractional reserve system, one dollar in currency withdrawn from the banks forced loans to be "called" (not renewed) when they came due and thereby reduced the amount of demand deposits outstanding. In other words, after currency withdrawals from banks outstanding liabilities of the banks (demand deposits) had to be contracted by a *multiple* of cash reserve losses. *Thus the public, in changing the currency-deposit ratio (that is, the composition of money holdings) of necessity changed the total money supply.*

We can analyze most financial panics according to the above terms. First, seasonal or unexpected withdrawals of cash from banks (a short-run alteration in the currency-deposit ratio) placed pressure upon *some* banks in the system. (In a 1907 system of 20,000 banks, such withdrawals were destined to have asymmetric effects). When some banks fail (that is, fail to convert demand deposits into currency demanded), a shock effect may be felt through the system causing the desired currency-deposit ratio to further increase. The public concludes that banks are "unsafe." The money stock falls in response to currency withdrawals, loans are called, prices dip, and industrial production and employment decline.

If we look at Figures 16–1 and 16–2 and examine the facts, we can see that something much like that described above happened in the United States between May 1907 and June 1908. Over this period, the wholesale price index fell by 50 percent and net national product fell by 11 percent. The (relatively mild) 2.5 percent initial decline in the money stock between May and September of 1907 can be blamed partially upon a loss of high powered money due to an unfavorable balance of payments and to gold export. But, as Friedman and Schwartz conclude, there ensued a general scramble for liquidity on the part of both banks and the public which had the effect of increasing the currency-deposit and reserve-deposit ratios (see Figure 16–2).

In mid- and late October of 1907, demands for liquidity forced runs on

New York Clearing House banks by correspondent banks and on October 22 the Knickerbocker Trust Company, one of the three largest trust companies in New York, suspended payments (the Knickerbocker was not a Clearing House member). A run ensued with runs developing at other New York banks. At this point, however, suspensions were staved off by Clearing House loans, by government deposits, and by a money pool of 25 million dollars organized by financier J. P. Morgan. But frightened country and interior banks (and their depositers) demanded currency from their New York correspondents which ultimately forced the restriction of payments. Nationwide bank closings and currency payment restrictions followed.

Ultimately the money supply fell by 5 percent, although there was high-powered money injections of 10 percent after the initial decline over the period. We might analyze what happened with the aid of the money supply model developed in Chapter 9. The underlying logic of Figure 16-3 is identical to that of Figure 9-1, but we use it here to show the change in parameters which brought about the Panic of 1907. The onset of this contraction, as we have noted, was probably the initial decline in high-powered money. (Also see Figure 16-1.) Subsequently, however, high-powered money was injected (in significant amounts) into the system. In Figure 16-3 this injection is represented by a shift upward in the intercept of the bank equilibrium function for H_0 to H_1. In the absence of any other changes, such an increase in H would have displaced the $M = H + (1 - r^d)D$ function in parallel fashion upward. The effect would have been to increase the stock of money and demand deposits.

But, alas, an increase was not the result. As we indicated earlier, the *slope* of these functions changed. That is, the scramble for liquidity on the part of the public and the banks increased the currency-deposit and reserve-deposit ratios. Figure 16-2 shows this phenomenon quite clearly. Thus, with reference to Figure 16-3, the public equilibrium function shifts counterclockwise with increases in desired currency-deposit holding from c_0^d to c_1^d. Similarly, the

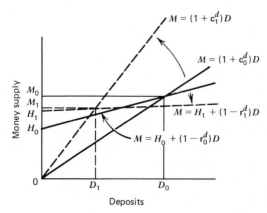

Figure 16-3. Monetary "panic"–graphical analysis.

banks increased demand for cash reserve holdings (from r_0^d to r_1^d) is reflected in the alteration in slope of the bank equilibrium function. The result—in spite of the injection of new high-powered money—was a decline in the money stock (represented here by a reduction from M_0 to M_1). Thus the attempt by the public to change the structure of the money stock coupled with the banks attempt to build up cash reserves (in order to meet the public's demands) led to a reduction in the total quantity of money. As Figure 16–1 reveals, this general contraction resulted in significant but brief declines in real income and in the price level.

THE ALDRICH-VREELAND ACT:
STOP-GAP AND PRELUDE TO THE FED

Fortunately the Panic of 1907 was short-lived and real income and wholesale prices began to turn upward in mid-1908. By 1908 banking reform was in the wind and the Congress passed the Aldrich-Vreeland Act ordering a major study of the US banking system. This study led to the formation of the Fed and provided emergency provisions to help prevent further crises. These latter provisions are interesting in that they validated and sanctioned the private response that banks made to previous crises. During the panic, "money," which was not legal tender, was supplied to the banking system by private banks. Bank clearing house loan certificates were issued either by clearing house banks or by emergency associations of banks in the panics of 1893 and 1907. These "certificates" were issued to individual banks in return for the bank's own obligations. These individual banks in turn issued these certificates to their customers and they circulated as money.[3] In 1907, for instance, these certificates increased the "money supply" by more than 250 million dollars.

The Aldrich-Vreeland Act merely approved officially what private banks were already doing. It allowed ten or more banks to set up an association (called a National Currency Association) to create up to 500 million dollars in emergency currency. In addition, the Secretary of the Treasury could suspend the limit, allowing individual banks to create additional emergency currency.

The National Banking System, so organized, was required to weather only one more storm. When War broke out in Europe in 1914, the US stock market was forced to close because of panicky sales of securities by Europeans. Again the US currency-deposit ratio rose (see the upturn at the beginning of 1914), and a repeat performance of the 1907 crisis threatened. But this time both clearing house notes and Aldrich-Vreeland currency were put into circulation and the threat of inconvertibility was eliminated. The economy made a fast and efficient turn-a-round. The Aldrich-Vreeland Act clearly passed muster.

Meanwhile, in December 1913, the Congress passed the Federal Reserve

Act (which did not begin operations until 1914). In truth, the first part of the Aldrich-Vreeland Act made the second part irrelevant. The "emergency currency" portion was repealed and under the Federal Reserve Act, a Board and 12 Federal Reserve banks had sole authority over the banking system in emergencies and otherwise. But, as we have seen in Chapters 11 and 14 *authority* to control does not necessarily mean *ability* to control. The Treasury-controlled National Banking System passed into history.

THE FORMATIVE YEARS OF THE FED: MONETARY POLICIES AND PROBLEMS, 1914–1929

One might imagine that after 1914 monetary problems in the United States, at least those related to the absence of a true central bank, would vanish or be severely curtailed. The truth is, however, that it took a long time for the Fed to come into its own as a central bank. Many writers date this "formative period" from 1914 to 1929, but others extend the formative phase all the way to the 1940s or 1950s.

What is it, exactly, that a central bank is supposed to do? A commercial bank, as detailed in Chapter 12, is a for-profit business that operates under liquidity, solvency, and regulatory constraints. A true central bank, on the contrary, is not interested in showing a profit. Rather, it should be interested in monetary control as an instrument for the stabilization of such important economic quantities as GNP, prices, and employment. On occasion, when following these policies, a central bank will earn profits, and in general the Fed has historically earned enough to pay for its own operations. But this is a by-product of proper central bank operations and not a major policy objective. The major goal of a central banker is to control the money supply and this implies that the central bank must be able to identify and predict the major determinants of the money supply during periods of both prosperity and depression. The discussion of recent monetary history in Chapter 14 underscores this point.

Unfortunately, it took a long time for the Fed to become willing and able to perform its major function. First, there was a lingering belief on the part of those in the Fed system (with the possible exception of the President of the Fed Bank of NY) that the bank should "pay for itself." This philosophy clearly hampered the Fed's ability to control business and monetary fluctuations. For example, it was thought that the acquisition of a portfolio of bonds and assets through printing and selling currency would place the Fed in the improper role of a profit maximizing bank. But, as we have seen in Chapter 11, open-market operations is a major, if not the major, tool of monetary stabilization policy. Not only must a central bank realize that profits or breaking-even is not a policy to be pursued, but it must be willing to use the instruments of control to enact countercyclical measures during periods of prosperity and depression. During periods of prosperity commercial banks, acting in the interests of stockholders and borrowers, follow liberal lending policies that reinforce consumption and investment. To expect them to do otherwise would violate well-known axioms of economic behavior. But this is precisely the time that a measure of prudence is called for and it is a role of the central bank to impose prudence on the banking system.

When a "panic" arises, such as that of 1907, money supply and economic activity begin to contract. In the general scramble for liquidity on the part of both banks (who "call" loans or let loans mature without renewal) and the public (who desire an increased ratio of currency to deposits), the central bank should have enacted countercyclical measures. These measures would include lending money to commercial banks and in general pumping as much high-powered money (H) into the system as is necessary to thwart the liquidity crisis. It is at this time that the central bank performs its "lender of the last resort function" described earlier.

In sum, the functions of economic stabilization and the provision of a safe and efficient banking system through active countercyclical monetary policy became the sine qua non of the true central bank. Ostensibly the Fed was set up in 1913 to perform these functions, for it was the general lack of the institutionalization of them which precipitated much of the chaos in the pre-1913 US banking systems. Let us look at the record of the Fed in this regard, remembering that old ways of thinking often die slowly and that learning new ways may be a painful, time-consuming process.

THE FED'S RECORD: WORLD WAR I TO 1929

The Federal Reserve System opened its doors at the time of the declaration of War in Europe. All wars are associated with inflationary pressures and World War I is certainly no exception. In general, prices and the money stock in 1920 were double what they were in 1914 as Figure 16–4 (to which we will refer often in this section) reveals. Figure 16–4, from the meticulous research of Friedman and Schwartz, shows a clear and practically uninterrupted rise in the money stock and in the implicit and wholesale price indices (with only modest increases in real income) from the beginning of 1914 through the mid-1920s.

How might this untoward price behavior be explained given that the Fed would more appropriately be following countercyclical monetary policy? The answer is simple and straightforward. The Fed was powerless to reverse the effect of exogenous changes in H, high-powered money, over the period.

In the first place, our European allies, in gearing up for and conducting

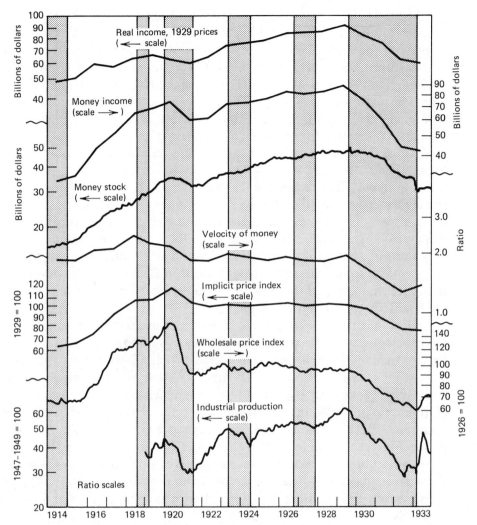

Note: Shaded areas represent business contractions; unshaded areas, business expansions.

(*Source:* Milton Friedman and Anna J. Schwartz, *Monetary History of the United States, 1867–1960* (Princeton, New Jersey: Princeton University Press, 1963), p. 197.)

Figure 16–4. Money stock, income prices, and velocity, 1914–1933.

World War I, exerted a huge demand for exports. Capital exports used to finance the war led to surpluses in the US balance of payments. These surpluses created an inflow of gold in addition to the gold imports resulting from unsettled conditions abroad.

Thus, under a gold standard, balance-of-payment surpluses are a mixed blessing. Suppose that businesses selling goods abroad (the public) are paid in gold. Under a gold standard, the gold received may be presented for redemption at the US Treasury or at a commercial bank that would present it to the Treasury. Either way, the Treasury pays for the gold by writing a check on its account at the Federal Reserve as a means of payment. The Treasury issues a gold certificate or a "warehouse receipt" for the gold which is turned over to the Fed. The Fed then increases its reserve liability by the amount of the certificate which it holds as an asset. The Fed (up until 1968) was bound by law to hold gold certificates up to a certain percentage of its note issue and reserve deposits (25 percent, for example, in 1961).[4]

Thus, in such an operation as described above, the amount of deposits (money) and member bank reserves increased exogenously by the amount of the gold import. The money supply can increase by the amount of new high-powered money multiplied by the factor $[(1 + c)/(c + r)]$. In other words, gold inflows lead to an increase in high-powered money that in turn increased the money stock and prices. These price changes are to be expected under a strict gold standard, but with discretionary control of a central bank such as the Fed they may be *sterilized*, a process explained in Chapter 15. However, evidence shows that for the period 1914–1917 the Federal Reserve acted passively and not countercyclically in the matter.

How might the Fed have sterilized or neutralized the increase in the money stock caused by gold inflows? They can do this, as indicated in Chapter 11, by tightening up Reserve Bank credit, that is, by raising the rediscount rate or by *selling* securities on the open market. The first policy would have been unsuccessful since banks were experiencing large inflows of reserves. More important, open market operations were impossible because the Fed had no bonds to sell! Although the Fed acquired a portfolio from 1917 to 1919, during active US participation in the war, a bit of reflection reveals that an attempt to acquire one would have pumped still more high-powered money into the system. As it was, the Fed actually did acquire some 300 million dollars in assets over the period 1914–1917, all of which increased H and inflationary pressures.

We might interpret money and price behavior of the period in terms of our familiar framework $M = H \ [(1 + c)/(c + r)]$. The money stock grew from 11.5 billion dollars in mid-1914 to 18.3 billion at the end of 1917. A 40 percent increase in H, of which 87 percent came about through gold inflows, is the primary explanation for the rise in M. A slight decline in the c and r ratios (increasing the power of high-powered money) added to the increase in M, but the explanation of the inflation over this period lies squarely with gold inflows and with the increase in H which they engendered.

Over the war years of 1917–1919, an increase in H was once again the source of money stock increases and inflation, but this time the explanation was not gold inflows, which virtually ceased when the United States entered the war. Mobilization of resources for the war effort created large wartime deficits, amounting at the Federal level to 23 billion dollars, a massive deficit at that time. The deficit was financed by borrowing and by printing money, both of which served to increase the stock of high-powered money. Fortunately, the currency-deposit ratio rose over the period or the increase in M would have been even greater. As Figure 16–4 indicates, prices rose, (though at a slower rate over the war years), velocity fell, and real income remained roughly constant. The attempts of the Treasury to finance the war by deficit spending and the Fed's acquiesence to this program—which led to printing money and bond price supports—are clear explanations for the wartime inflation.

Postwar Inflation and the Recession of 1920–1921. The events in the period immediately following World War I are probably a good historical example of the tortuous learning process experienced by the central bank in the United States. A look at Figure 16–4 gives us a good picture of the period. There we observe a sharp increase in prices, both in the implicit price index and in the wholesale index, extending from 1910 through mid-1920. The money stock grew over the earlier part of the period, remained steady over most of 1920, and then went into a decline at the beginning of 1921. Prices, real income, and industrial production all began to fall precipitously.

What is the explanation for this erratic postwar behavior of prices and output? The answer is not difficult to see if we again interpret the behavior of the Fed in terms of our now familiar equation. The postwar inflation may be explained by the decrease in the currency-deposit ratio and by an increase in Federal Reserve Bank credit. The latter increase in H was essentially the product of continuous commercial bank borrowings (discounting) from the Fed and the acquisition of government securities by the Fed. In fact, Fed discount rates were below market rates throughout 1919 and the Fed knew that H and M were being increased thereby and that this increase was causing inflation.

But the Fed refused to take the direct action of increasing the discount rate, preferring to use "moral suasion," or adjurations to commercial bankers, to screen borrowers carefully. Finally, the Fed bumped against its gold reserve requirement and moved to raise the discount rate just to 6 percent and on June 1, 1920, the New York Bank raised the rate to 7 percent, the higherst rate ever enacted by the Fed up to that time. A credit crunch of tight money ensued and sharp declines in industrial production and prices (a contraction) followed. Thus the Fed created erratic alterations in the stock of high-powered money is the prime explanation for the economic events of the postwar period.

One might legitimately ask why the Fed behaved in this fashion? It is not altogether clear whether the members of the Board, as a group, completely understood the power of countercyclical action. Not all of those concerned, however, approved of the policies followed. For instance, Benjamin Strong,

Governor of the New York Fed Bank, urged an increase in discount rates. In opposition to this policy stood most of the members of the Board of Governors in Washington as well as Secretary of the Treasury Carter Glass. Secretary Glass reasoned that over expansion of credit could be forestalled by moral suasion and prudence of commercial bank lending. Clearly, however, it could not, and when the Fed finally decided to put on the brakes loan demand was tapering off. The result, as Strong again predicted, was pro-cyclical action and economic contraction.

A Period of Calm and Prosperity: 1921–1929. In contrast to the early days of the Fed, the period 1921–1929 was one of the general expansion and prosperity, punctuated by only two minor recessions in 1923–1924 and in 1926–1927. Figure 16–4 shows that the pace of economic growth was steady and real output grew at a rate of about 3.5 percent per year. Money stock increases were steady and prices were almost stable, in fact exhibiting somewhat of a decline.

For the Federal Reserve System, it was a period of new freedom and maturation as a central bank. The Fed in its opening years was constrained by the war effort, and in the immediate postwar period the Fed was somewhat confused over its role as a countercyclical agent. But in the 1920s the Fed came into its own as an agency whose conscious effort it was to promote internal stability and balance of payments equilibrium and to mitigate the severity of financial crises.

The 1920s also produced the first blooming of twentieth century American society. Automobiles replaced other forms of transportation, an urbanized culture was replacing agrarian institutions at a rapid rate, and the volume of trading grew and grew on the stock exchange. Along with stock market transacting, the nature of the commercial bank portfolios began to evolve. In addition to traditional "loans and investments" to meet the needs of trade, banks lent money for stock market purchases. Although the Federal Reserve now has the power to determine stock margin requirements (see Chapter 11) or the amount of cash that must be put up by a borrower intending to buy stock, this control did not exist in the 1920s (the Fed did not acquire the power until 1934 with the passage of the Securities and Exchange Act). The result was stock purchases with as much as 90 percent of purchase price as borrowed money. The tide of speculation throughout the 1920s reached a new high in 1928–1929.

A Gathering Storm: Pre-Crash Fed Policy. Banking conditions over this pre-Crash period cast an interesting light on what followed. The traditional "pop history view" is that commercial banks were "unsound" over the period and that the Federal Reserve, especially in 1928–1929, was utterly helpless in the face of the speculative boom. Although we reserve discussion of the former point to a later section, let us consider what was happening at the Fed in late 1928 and 1929.

In the face of speculation and unsound lending by commercial banks, for stock purchases, the Fed might have utilized the discount rate or open market operations to put a brake on reserves and financial expansion. Unfortunately, either of these policies would not necessarily have had much effect. Though the Fed had by this time acquired a working portfolio of securities to trade in the market, their stock of them was at a low level of 228 million dollars at the end of 1928. A massive sale might have made a difference, but such a sale was not in the experience of the Fed and the System would have lost its earning assets. The latter effect should have been inconsequential to a true central bank, of course.

Discount rate increases may have stemmed some of the speculation and in February the New York Federal Reserve Bank in what might have been an effective action again proposed an increase in the rate from 5 percent to 6 percent. The Board in Washington, supported by the new President Herbert Hoover, rejected the idea, however, fearing (as in 1920) that legitimate borrowing would be curtailed and an economic collapse precipitated. Actually, it is not at all certain that small increases in the discount rate would have had much on commercial bank borrowings. Banks were happily discounting commercial paper and bankers acceptances at the Fed for 5 percent and investing stock brokers loans carrying up to 12 percent interest rates. Some movements in this direction might have tightened up the market against high-risk borrowers (speculators), as would have large open market sales of securities.

Throughout the pre-Crash period, however, the Fed took a virtually passive stance. The Fed never asked for control over margin requirements from the Congress,[5] nor did they rigorously denounce the speculative practices of banks aside from gentle admonitions to the banks that they should not use the discount window to borrow for the purpose of making or maintaining speculative loans. The Board of Governors of the Fed seemed to have understood that a serious problem was arising but their passivity to the speculation indicates a desire to disassociate themselves from the impending collapse. The Fed, acting as a commercial bank and not a central bank, simply did not want to "break the bubble." The anatomy of a crisis, such as that of 1907, was at hand.

In September 1929 the market began to fail. In spite of "rolling readjustments" and assurances of soundness by financiers and bankers, the collapse came on Black Thursday, October 24, 1929. On that day, 12,894,650 shares of stock changed hands and prices began to plummet. John Kenneth Galbraith dramatically describes the events of that morning:

> By eleven o'clock the market had degenerated into a wild, mad scramble to sell. In the crowded boardrooms across the country the ticker told of a frightful collapse. But the selected quotations coming in over the bond ticker also showed that current

values were far below the ancient history of the tape. The uncertainty led more and more people to try to sell. Others, no longer able to respond to margin calls, were sold out. By eleven-thirty the market had surrendered to blind, relentless fear. This, indeed, was panic.[6]

Although private attempts were made to shore up the market, much as in the Panic of 1907, they were unsuccessful. There was and still is much debate as to the "cause" of the Great Depression; however, no one denies what economic indicators of the period show—sickening reductions in money and real income, industrial production, and employment between 1929 and 1933. Like 1776 and 1865, but for different reasons, 1929 is a year that America will not soon forget.

FROM THE DEPRESSION TO WORLD WAR II

One might imagine that monetary economists and historians would have a better handle on events relatively close to us in time. Thus, for example, we should have more plausible and powerful explanations for the depression of 1933 than for the Panic of 1907 or the pre-Civil War banking era. Unfortunately, this is not the case for the Depression of the 1930s, and a lively and active debate continues among professional economists on the nature of its causes.[7]

There are two opposing theories or explanations proffered about the Depression. The first, sponsored by Professors Milton Friedman and Anna Schwartz, highlights the early passiveness (and the later mismanagement) of the Fed as the root cause of the length and severity of the Depression. An alternative explanation called the "spending hypothesis"—which has been aired before by economists—has recently been brought forward again by Professor Peter Temin. In this view, the Depression was more the result of a sharp decline in *autonomous* expenditures, particularly consumption expenditures. While Temin believes that the data fit the "spending" explanation more closely than the monetary view, he freely acknowledges that the paucity of data over the inter-War period makes any definitive judgements impossible.[8]

This discussion of the Depression will not attempt to assign blame or to add weight to either view. Rather, it presents a brief detailing of events and leaves the technical debate to specialists in monetary history. It is clear from this debate, however, that any adequate explanations must be based on a large number of complex forces.

WHAT THE FED DID NOT DO: 1929–1933
As noted in an earlier section, a dispute between the Federal Reserve Bank of New York and the Board of Governors in Washington was already under way

before the onset of the Depression. Early in 1929 the New York Fed tried to convince the Board that the speculation (and the untoward expansion it led to) should be halted by increases in the discount rate. Each time, the Board rebuffed these efforts. This conflict extended into the post-1929 era as well, when the New York Fed again attempted to act as a central bank by purchasing large amounts of securities in the face of financial panic. In this case, the Board permitted the New York Fed to lower the discount rate (also proper counter-cyclical policy during depression) in return for cessation of open market purchases of securities!

And so it went. The Fed's Board of Governors over the period 1929–1933 failed to act as a central bank should in the face of financial crises and panic. The Fed failed to do the very thing that it had been explicitly created to do— *to act as a lender of the last resort*. Figure 16–5 gives us a good idea of what was happening to high-powered money, currency-deposit and reserve-deposit ratios and to the money stock over the 1929–1933 period. Friedman and Schwartz summarize the changes:

> From August 1929 to March 1933 as a whole, the change in high-powered money alone would have produced a rise of $17\frac{1}{2}$ percent in the stock of money. The change in the deposit-currency [our currency-deposit ratio] ratio alone would have produced a decline of 37 percent; the change in the deposit-reserve ratio [our reserve-deposit ratio], a decline of 20 percent; interaction between the two ratios, a rise of 10 percent; these three converted the $17\frac{1}{2}$ percent rise that high-powered money would have produced into a 35 percent decline in the stock of money.[9]

While the money stock and the stock of high-powered money remained at fairly stable levels from the stock market crash up to the first banking crises in April 1930, the money stock continued to decline thereafter. Furthermore, we should note the classic effects of bank panics upon the currency-deposit and reserve-deposit ratios. Though the stock of high-powered money grew somewhat over the period, it was not nearly enough to compensate for gold drains and increases in the two ratios (a reduction in the power of high-powered money). The Fed Board did practically nothing to compensate for these adverse effects on the money stock; in fact it voted in early 1933 to reduce the quantity of high-powered money by 125 million dollars.

BANKING FAILURES: ROOSEVELT STEPS IN

It is fashionable among certain historians to blame the Depression on the "unsoundness" and speculative practices of the banking system in the 1920s. The high number of bank failures over the period is often cited as evidence of commercial bank mismanagement. An examination of the facts, however, does not lend great support to these charges. While it is true that a large number of banks suspended operations in 1920s, the overwhelming number were small nonmember banks.

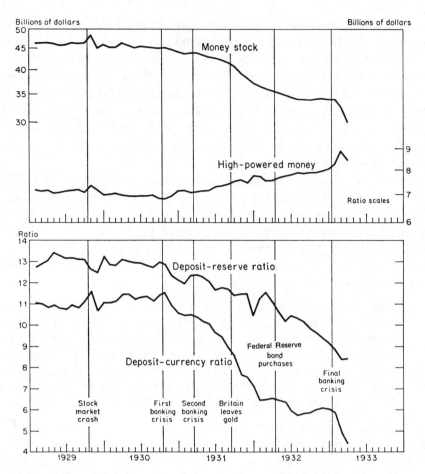

(*Source:* Milton Friedman and Anna J. Schwartz, *Monetary History of the United States, 1867-1960* (Princeton, New Jersey: Princeton University Press, 1963), p. 333.)

Figure 16-5. The stock of money and the reserve-deposit and currency-deposit ratios, 1929–March 1933.

While we expect banks to exhibit a certain amount of caution under any circumstances, they are still for-profit institutions and they are not expected voluntarily to hold large amounts of noninterest-bearing cash reserves on hand to meet any crisis. Prudent investments by commercial banks over the 1920s were the rule and not the exception. But no banking system, even the present one, could withstand the pressures to which the system of the 1920s was subjected. Those pressures, which resulted in a series of banking crises beginning in April of 1930, were:

1. a precipitous decline in the value of the highest quality securities which were used as loan collateral at banks;

2. a panic-induced increase in both currency-deposit and reserve-deposit ratios; and

3. a failure of the Federal Reserve to compensate countercyclically for these losses in the powerfulness of high-powered money.

Thus, the noncompensation in high-powered money, the currency drains, and the failure of the Fed to act as a lender of the last resort accounts for the large number of bank closings in 1930, 1931, and 1932. In spite of these closings, however, evidence shows that the system failed to (ultimately) pay off only a little more than 3 percent of total system deposits. This outcome speaks well of the underlying strength of the banking system.

Nevertheless, a calamitous 20 percent of all banks had closed their doors by early 1933 owing principally to the three difficulties outlined above. But banking reform under the aegis of the Federal Government was at hand. Franklin D. Roosevelt was inaugurated President in March 1933 and, in the two years to follow, engineered emergency banking legislation.

Though various states had declared bank "holidays" to stem panic-inspired currency drains, Roosevelt, on March 6, 1933, ordered closed *all* banks in the country including the Federal Reserve Banks.[10] In a matter of three days the Congress passed the Emergency Banking Act, which provided for reopening of the banks under the Comptroller of the Currency (an official of the US Treasury).

We have already considered in some detail (see Chapter 10 particularly) the banking reform legislation of the period 1933–1935. The establishment of the Federal Deposit Insurance Corporation (FDIC) was of paramount importance to the ailing banking system. Banks were eligible to insure individual deposits (currently up to $100,000) by payment of a small insurance premium. Replacing piecemeal state insurance systems, the FDIC has been a potent force in preventing bank panics and in protecting small depositors from financial ruin.

In addition, reform legislation created a prohibition against the payment of interest on demand deposits. This policy, which was aimed at curbing unrestricted competition of commercial banks for sources of funds, has been of debatable value in maintaining financial "soundness" of banks and is gradually being eliminated under recent laws. However, the rule ended the blurring of savings deposits and demand deposits.[11]

The Banking Act of 1935 further centralized control of the banking system by the Board of Governors in Washington. Although the basic system remained unchanged, the Banking Act of 1935 shifted power over open market operations from the individual banks to an Open Market Committee composed of the (new) seven-member Board of Governors plus five rotating representatives of the twelve banks (see Chapter 10 for the details of this organization). The Board also received the power to fix reserve requirements for member banks within limits set by the Congress. In short, power in the system shifted to the Board in Washington where it remains today.

In early 1934, Congress passed the Gold Reserve Act, which prohibited all private transacting in gold. All gold held by individuals, including banks and financial institutions, was to be sold to the Treasury and the price of gold was raised to 35 dollars per fine troy ounce. After this time, gold no longer could serve as an internal medium of exchange, and the internal price level therefore was disassociated from the quantity of gold in circulation. Authorized individuals, such as dentists and jewelers, were allowed to purchase gold from the Treasury at the legal price of 35 dollars per ounce. And, until 1968, gold was still important in the monetary system to the extent that the Fed was required to hold gold certificates against Fed Reserve notes and deposit liabilities. The Treasury issued the certificate (warehouse receipts) and deposited them at the Fed in return for Treasury deposits. Each time the Fed "bumped against" the legal gold requirement, however, the Congress reduced the percentage of gold "reserves" required against Fed liabilities. Finally, in 1968, the requirement was eliminated entirely and gold was totally disassociated with the US monetary system.[12]

RECOVERY AND FED POLICY: 1934–1941

Recovery in terms of a fairly continuous rise in income and production did not get underway until late 1934. As Figure 16–6 and 16–7 show, the recovery through 1941 was in two phases—between 1934 and mid-1937 and from mid-1938 onward. In the intervening subperiod, between mid-1937 and mid-1938, there was a discernible sharp recession. Let us now consider some of the monetary features of this period.

As we have already seen, the Fed failed, over the period 1929 to 1933, to provide enough high-powered money to the banking system to compensate for the currency drain of the public. Had the Fed done so, it would have enabled the system to forestall the decreases in the money stock which characterized this period.

In interpreting the events of the recovery we must take a close look at business confidence in both financial and nonfinancial institutions. In the case of nonfinancial business, net private capital formation did not become positive until 1936. In 1937, at the peak of the cycle, nondurable purchases (mostly government purchases) was over 20 percent above the 1929 level whereas durables purchases were 6 percent below the 1929 peak. It appears likely that the private business sector was not responding and the reasons for the lack of response are not so intractible. With confidence already low, given the experience of 1929–1933, the federal government's actions reduced private profit expectations even further by a plethora of legal acts. Labor costs rose with the

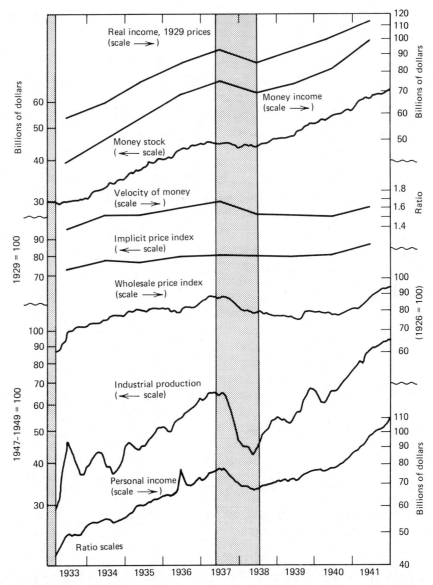

Note: Shaded areas represent business contractions; unshaded areas, business expansions.

(*Source:* Milton Friedman and Anna J. Schwartz, *Monetary History of the United States, 1867-1960* (Princeton, New Jersey: Princeton University Press, 1963), p. 494.)

Figure 16-6. *Money stock, income, prices and velocity, personal income, and industrial production, March 1933–December 1941.*

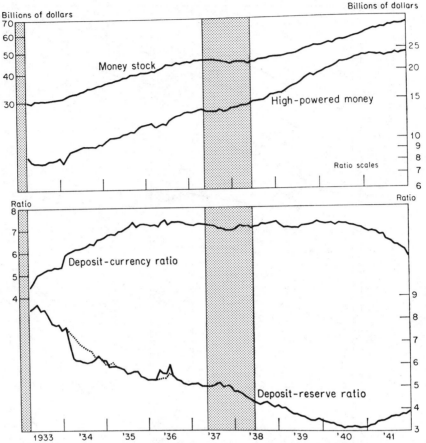

Note: Shaded areas represent business contractions; unshaded areas, business expansions.

(*Source:* Adapted from Milton Friedman and Anna J. Schwartz, *Monetary History of the United States, 1867-1960* (Princeton, New Jersey: Princeton University Press, 1963), p. 500.)

Figure 16-7. The stock of money, high-powered money, and the deposit ratios, March 1933-December 1941.

enactment of the National Industrial Recovery Act (NIRA) (later declared unconstitutional), and the National Labor Relations Act. Social security taxes, unemployment compensation, and undistributed profits tax legislation of the period all took a toll on profit expectations.

The passage of Acts regulating and competing with private business reached an all-time high over this period. The Securities and Exchange Act of 1934, the creation of the Tennessee Valley Authority in 1933, and the Federal Farm Mortgage Corporation in 1934 are all examples of new, experimental federal controls over the private sector. Right or wrong, private businesses were fearful of governmental interferences and they responded by continuous inaction.

The actions of Roosevelt, as well as the memory of the crises of the 1929–33 period, also had important effects upon commercial bankers. Unwilling to lose liquidity again as they had over the painful crisis period, banks sought to build up business (working) cash reserves, and thus held more high-powered money against demand deposits than was required by the Federal Reserve. The deposit-reserve ratio fell steadily between 1929 and 1940 from a value of 13.2 in 1929 to 3.2 in 1940. The consequences of these actions will be understood shortly.

As usual, we can view overall monetary behavior of the period in terms of variables M, H, c, and r. Over the period 1933–1937 M grew by 5.1 percent and H rose by 60 percent. With confidence being restored in the banking system, the currency-deposit ratio fell with what would have produced an even larger rise in M for given changes in H, but bankers' reluctance to lend up excess reserves reduced the effect of high-powered money increases. That is, an increasing reserve-deposit ratio decreased the power of high-powered money and produced a smaller increase in M. Bankers simply decided not to lend out their increased holdings of high-powered money in spite of a falling currency-deposit ratio. (Perhaps there was a lack of loan demand.) We might say that the public's confidence in the ability of commercial banks to convert deposits into currency recovered more quickly than that of bankers.

The Downturn of 1937

As Figures 16–6 and 16–7 indicate, the process of recovery was impeded by brief declines in industrial production and real income from mid-1937 to mid-1938. How might we account for this brief recession in the midst of recovery?

As noted above, the power of high-powered money, given by the expansion coefficient $[(1 + c)/(c + r)]$, was declining between 1934 and 1937 because of a rising r combined with a roughly constant c (see Figure 16–7). Banks, in other words, were holding these excess reserves. One part of bank reserve holdings are certainly required. But the banks, in 1935 and 1936, held reserves in greater percentages than those required by law.

Over this period banks might have been holding excess reserves for one of two reasons: (1) because they were afraid of smaller deposit conversions by the public into currency, or (2) because they could not find credit-worthy borrowers to whom they could lend. In the latter case, as we have seen, the banks would be foregoing interest revenues until such borrowers could be found or until they decided to lend to borrowers of lower credit standing. In the latter event, the existence of these reserves might have had sudden and lowering effects on the money stock and the price level.

In any case, these are what the Fed reasoned when it decided to "mop up" these excess reserves by raising reserve requirements in March and May 1937. But the Fed clearly miscalculated the effects of this action upon the banking system. Required reserves, as we have noted a number of times, cannot be used by banks to meet sudden currency withdrawals by the public. Thus, when the banks were stripped of large quantities of excess reserves by the Fed, they promptly built up additional excess reserves by reducing the quantity of loans to the public and by holding (and not lending) additional quantities of high-powered money. In doing so, they reduced the power of high-powered money and economic expansion was halted.

The Federal Reserve Board had totally misjudged the conservative and cautious nature of commercial bankers over this period. Economic conditions might have justified exactly the opposite cause of action. Fortunately, the Fed reversed its reserve requirement in April 1938 and the recovery proceeded apace.

FROM WORLD WAR II TO 1951

World War II, along with most other wars in history, was not financed at the time by direct taxation. Rather, the US government, through various efforts such as War Bond sales, borrowed substantial quantities of money to finance the effort. The Federal Reserve played a major role in the production of money to finance the war by (1) purchasing bonds from the US Treasury, and (2) by supporting the price of government bonds—that is by open-market purchases. Obviously, the sale of bonds by the Treasury had a tendency to depress their price and increase their yield. With increased yields the Treasury cost of financing the war would rise. In order to prevent this increase, the Fed assumed the role of price supporter for the Treasury issues.

The important point is that the Fed passively financed these bond purchases by creating new high-powered money. Banks also reacted in predictable fashion by expanding loans and the demand deposit component of the money stock. Demand deposits increased from 38 million dollars in 1941 to 76 million in 1945, and currency in the bands of the public increased threefold over the period. Although the public's currency-deposit ratio grew between 1940 and 1945, thereby absorbing a large amount of the increase in H, the reserve-deposit ratio declined over the period as banks regained confidence due to rapid business expansion to support the war effort.

Industrial production soared over the war years and both money and real income grew (money income grew more rapidly). Rapid increases in the money stock accompanied injections of high-powered money, although implicit and wholesale price indices to not indicate a severe inflation problem during these years. Price rises were (somewhat) contained by the institution of general price controls between early 1942 and mid-1946.[13]

Thus, in general, and of necessity, the Fed ceased to act principally as a countercyclical controller to the banking system over the war years. The war had to be financed and the War effort superceeded most other goals of central bank policy. Although the Fed could not prevent massive injections of high-powered money into the system, the Congress responded by the institution of price and wage controls. One might argue that these controls merely postponed the inevitable—the postwar inflation that followed. But, in fairness to the Fed, price stabilization as a goal of society would never take precedence when massive resource reallocations of resources from private to public sectors are necessary for national defense. Thus the Fed performed admirably during the war years and, as we shall see, it deserves praise for its handling of monetary policy in the postwar period before "accord" with the Treasury.

POSTWAR MONETARY DEVELOPMENTS: 1945–1951

After the end of hostilities, price and wage controls were lifted and the implicit price level began to rise dramatically. Undoubtedly, the 20 billion dollar increase in high-powered money during the war accounted for some of the postwar (1945–1948) inflation. Pent-up demands for goods, especially postponed durable consumer goods, were released when price controls were lifted.

Over the period 1945–1948 wholesale prices shot up by almost 50 percent, and pent-up demand generated in the wartime period accounted for a good deal of this rise. But the Fed is often blamed for this postwar inflation. Specifically, Fed policy to support the price of Treasury bonds is given as the root cause of the inflation. Whether the Fed is guilty for the inflation is not entirely clear.

Over the period 1945–1958, M and H increased by only 10 percent. Surely it seems unlikely that a 50-percent increase in wholesale prices could have been caused by a 10 percent increase in M. As we have seen, pent-up demand accounts for much of this price rise. But what of the 10 percent increase in H—is not the Fed's bond support program responsible for the increase? The evidence shows that the Fed acted judiciously and correctly over this period by selling over five billion dollars of bonds, thereby tending to reduce the stock of high-powered money. The actual increase in H of 10 percent was made possible chiefly by a fairly rapid growth in the gold stock over the period. Although the internal monetary system was divorced from that of gold, the Treasury was committed to the buying and selling of gold at 35 dollars an ounce. Furthermore, the Fed still had to hold gold certificates against note and deposit liabilities and was therefore obliged to purchase them, thereby increasing high-powered money. Thus it might have been the gold price support program of the

Treasury and not the Fed bond price support that was the source of post-World War II inflation.

But consider Fed policy over the so-called "recession of 1949" and accompanying deflation. In late 1948, a downturn in business activity occurred which was preceded earlier in the year by a reduction in the money stock. The impetus for this money stock reduction appears to have been the Fed's sale of almost five billion dollars worth of securities (the gold stock actually declined slightly over this period). Here the Fed apparently misread the economic indicators and took falling interest rates (in early 1949) to mean an inflationary signal rather than the indicator of reduced aggregate demand that they were.

THE TREASURY–FEDERAL RESERVE ACCORD

After the brief recession of 1949, interest rates began to rise and the Fed once more had to act as a buyer of bonds in the bond support program. In 1950, the Fed purchased over 2 billion dollars of Treasury securities and generated these increases in H and M. But in June 1951, the United States entered the Korean conflict and the usual deficits were being engendered to finance armed conflict. In order to make the cost of borrowing cheaper and to stop a fall in bond prices, the Fed purchased great quantities of securities. Between June 1950 and March 1951 wholesale prices shot up by over 15 percent. The Fed—now fully understanding its effects on H—moved to reduce the quantity and the power of high-powered money by increasing reserve requirements. But there was a limit to this latter policy and the Fed believed strongly (and correctly) that the bond support program was hampering its charge to control the monetary system countercyclically. Thus in March 1951 the Treasury and the Fed reached an *accord* or understanding that the Fed would no longer be obliged to support the price of Treasury bonds. Henceforth the Fed has been free to pursue a monetary policy designed to meet unemployment, inflation, and growth head on in countercyclical fashion.

POSTACCORD MONETARY POLICY

It is not the purpose of this brief monetary history of the United States to comment on recent, say post-1960, trends in monetary policy. These developments have already become familiar with relatively contemporary development in the discussions of the Federal Reserve System in Chapter 11, and most particularly in the survey of monetary policy from 1960 to the present in Chapter 14. We should, however, note some monetary developments in the postaccord period if only to realize that earlier developments molded an institution that has come to age only in the past 25 years or so.

Figures 16–8 and 16–9 give us a good idea of the Fed's record up to the 1960s, and that record seems to be reasonable on balance. Over this period real income has risen steadily and, over the 1950s (based on a 1947–1949 base) wholesale prices remained virtually stable. Only two brief and relatively unimportant recessions marred the period, one in 1953–1954 and another in 1957–1959 (see Figure 16–8).

The stock of high-powered money remained fairly stable throughout the period but both the reserve-deposit and currency-deposit ratios fell, altering the power of high-powered money. *M* rose steadily, but only 23 percent of the rise in *M* was attributable to the increase in high-powered money, whereas 40 percent was due to a fall in the reserve-deposit ratio and 30 percent to a falling

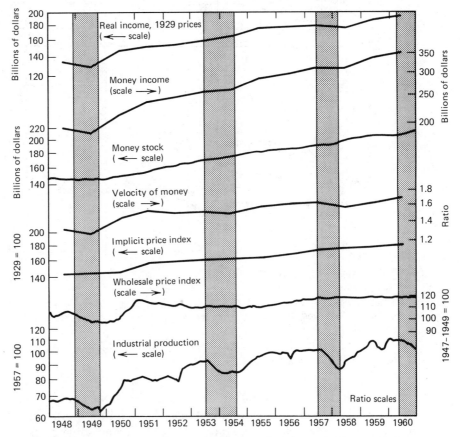

Note: Shaded areas represent business contractions; unshaded areas, business expansions.

(*Source:* Milton Friedman and Anna J. Schwartz, *Monetary History of the United States, 1867–1960* (Princeton, New Jersey: Princeton University Press, 1963), p. 593.)

Figure 16–8. Money stock, income, prices and velocity, and industrial production, 1948–1960.

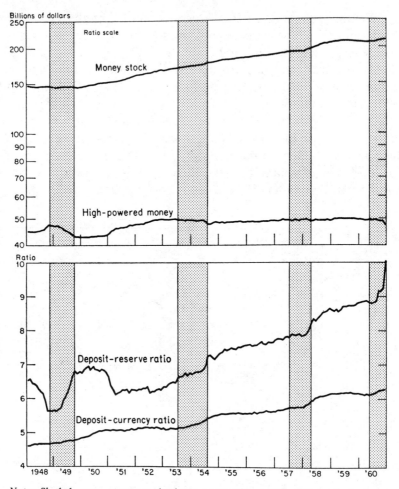

Note: Shaded areas represent business contractions; unshaded areas, business expansions.

(*Source:* Milton Friedman and Anna J. Schwartz, *Monetary History of the United States, 1867–1960* (Princeton, New Jersey: Princeton University Press, 1963), p. 602.)

Figure 16-9. The stock of money and the reserve-deposit and currency-deposit ratios, 1948–1960.

currency-deposit ratio. These latter changes in the money multiplier add emphasis to the discussion of the complexities of predicting the multiplier at the end of Chapter 11. Over the 1950s the Fed itself effected some of these changes such as an alteration in **r** (reserve-deposit ratio) by lowering the reserve requirements for all classes of banks.

The important point is that over the postaccord era, the Fed made a concerted and more knowledgeable effort to control the money stock and interest rates countercyclically. For example, constant alterations in Federal Reserve credit outstanding, margins and reserve requirements, and the discount rate over the 1950s, 1960s, and 1970s reveal a determined Board of Governors in pursuit of appropriate monetary policy. The relative merit of the Federal Reserve System in the contemporary era is a subject steeped in a tremendous amount of controversy and debate. As indicated in Chapter 14, there are lags in policy development and implementation to consider, not to mention the gnawing question of whether discretionary control over the money stock will ever be able to achieve economic stabilization in the face of such factors as (1) short-term and long-term fluctuations in the determinants of the money multiplier, (2) exogenous changes in high-powered money; or (3) sudden changes in both private and public components of expenditures, some of which Fed policy effects.

There are, and have been, political pressures on the Fed.[14] It is, after all, an agency of government, albeit one that is often identified as quasi independent. Although the Fed may correctly perceive an inflation problem, for instance, it may be helpless or politically unwilling to do anything about it. Short-run unemployment and reductions in real income might not be politically acceptable short-run tradeoffs for reduced inflation—until, that is, the inflation rate becomes too great, as it possibly has in the late 1970s and early 1980s. It might also be that, as the Fed has become more knowledgeable and sophisticated, the quality of control expected of it by politicians and academicians has become disproportionately greater.

CONCLUSION

Until the institution of some rule relating to money stock changes (as Milton Friedman has suggested and as is discussed in Chapter 14), discretionary changes in money aggregates by a Board of individual men and women will characterize the US monetary system, thereby providing opportunities for mistakes. In this brief historical review of twentieth century monetary policy, we have seen that institutional change (such as the establishment of the FDIC in 1933) may have been a mighty force in contributing to the stability of our monetary system. Central bankers, moreover, have learned a great deal about the nature of monetary control since 1914. The difficulties of implementing discretionary monetary policy through fine-tuning, however, should not absolve the Federal Reserve System of all responsibility for its economic effects. It may be that, though the Board has "learned much by doing," it can never learn enough to avoid all errors of human judgment. Whatever its shortcomings, however, this brief historical review indicates that the difficulties involved in Fed control of the banking system—short, perhaps, of instituting a money stock growth rule—would not likely be resolved by altering the locus of power to the Congress or to a committee thereof.

FOOTNOTES

[1] The interested reader may consult the following works by Richard Timberlake: "The Resumption Act and the Money Supply," *Journal of Monetary Economics* (July 1975), pp. 343–54; *Money, Banking and Central Banking* (New York: Harper & Row, 1965); *The Origins of Central Banking* (Cambridge, Mass: Harvard University Press, 1978).

[2] See Milton Friedman and Anna J. Schwartz, *A Monetary History of the United States, 1867–1960* (Princeton, N.J.: Princeton University Press, 1964), pp. 158–59. Friedman and Schwartz's work has become a classic reference on monetary history and is highly recommended for further reading. Their approach, by permission, forms the basis for much of the analysis and discussion in the present chapter.

[3] Paychecks of large corporations also remained in "circulation" for long periods of time over this period.

[4] The gold reserve percentage declined over the years and was never an effective constraint on the amount of reserve deposits, liabilities, and Fed currency in circulation. The Congress routinely lowered the requirement at the Fed's request.

[5] Market margin rates were high in 1929 (40 percent–50 percent), but a higher mandatory rate might have considerably lessened the crisis that followed.

[6] John Kenneth Galbraith, *The Great Crash 1929*, 3rd ed. (Boston: Houghton Mifflin, 1972), p. 104.

[7] See Friedman and Schwartz, *Monetary History of the United States*, Chapter 7, and Friedman and Schwartz, *The Great Contrac-* *tion* (Princeton, N.J.: Princeton University Press, 1966). The most readable introduction to the history of the period is J. K. Galbraith's *The Great Crash*.

[8] See Peter Temin, *Did Monetary Forces Cause the Great Depression?* 1st ed. (New York: Norton, 1976).

[9] Friedman and Schwartz, *Monetary History of the United States*, pp. 332–333.

[10] There is an irony in the fact that the bank that was to serve as "lender of the last resort" to commercial banks closed right along with them.

[11] A blurring of these two types of deposits has returned with the recent emergence of NOW accounts, ATS transfers, and credit union draft shares (see Chapters 2, 11 and 12).

[12] But see Chapter 15 for the role of gold in the international monetary system.

[13] This statement does not imply that price and wage controls always work in the intended manner. First, there is evidence that the postcontrol inflation was, in large part, a result of the suppressed monetary accumulation over the control period. Secondly, price increases were concealed. For example, a "used" car, not under the controls, could be sold at higher prices than a new car. It does not take much sophistication to imagine what car dealers could and would do to obtain higher prices.

[14] The relevant and interesting matter of a "political business cycle" (with both the budget and the money stock treated as political tools) is well covered by Edward R. Tufte, *Political Control of the Economy* (Princeton, N.J.: Princeton University Press, 1978).

KEY CONCEPTS

National Banking Act of 1863

money stock equation

"High-powered money"

gold convertability

currency convertability

income velocity of money

financial panic

inelasticity of the money stock

Aldrich-Vreeland Act

National Currency Association

Federal Reserve Act

"lender of the last resort"

stock margin requirements

Federal Deposit Insurance Corporation (FDIC)

Banking Act of 1935

Board of Governors of the Federal Reserve

Gold Reserve Act (1934)

QUESTIONS FOR DISCUSSION

1. During the era of the National Banking Act of 1863, what provisions made it difficult to adjust the supply of National Bank Notes to avoid a currency crisis?

2. Give a brief explanation of the monetary events of the period from 1897–1914 and give reasons for these events in terms of the model developed in this book.

3. What is the income velocity of money? Why is this important in determining the rate of inflation during the period from 1897–1914?

4. Differentiate between the short-run and long-run effects of monetary disturbances.

5. Explain both the long-run and short-run importance of the currency deposit ratio in the pre-1914 era.

6. What factors contributed to the Panic of 1907?

7. What is the difference between control of the money supply through the Treasury System and that through the Federal Reserve System? What is the difference between the Federal Reserve Bank and any other bank?

8. During the 1914–1920 period, why did the Fed not counteract the expansion of the economy?

9. In regard to postwar inflation and recession, was the Fed powerless to act in this case as it was in the 1914–1920 period? What was the cause of the inflation and recession?

10. According to the evidence given here, was the cause of the Great Depression really the unsoundness and speculation of commercial banks? How did the Fed react throughout this era? What steps were taken by Roosevelt to restore the faltering economy?

11. How did the business sector act after the depression in response to Roosevelt's series of acts to rebuild the economy? How did banks react during the recovery period? What effect did the Fed's actions have on the banks?

12. True or false. As evidenced by the lack of inflation during the war period despite excessive money supply growth, it seems that price and wage controls work. Explain.

13. How does the Fed's supporting of the Treasuries bond prices result in inflation? Has the Fed's record of money management been better after the "accord" between the Fed and the Treasury? Why or why not?

INDEX